FINLAND
AT PEACE AND WAR

1918-1993

H. M. TILLOTSON

MICHAEL RUSSELL

© H. M. Tillotson 1993

First published in Great Britain 1993
by Michael Russell (Publishing) Ltd
Wilby Hall, Wilby, Norwich NR16 2JP

Typeset by The Typesetting Bureau
6 Church Street, Wimborne, Dorset
Printed and bound in Great Britain
by Biddles Ltd, Guildford and King's Lynn

Contents

Preface

Many factors affecting European security have altered. In Finland, however, there are certain basic facts that remain unchanged. The size of our territory, the geographic location, the small population and the limited resources of the national economy are enduring and circumscribing factors.

Finland's location between East and West has never been easy. For half a millennium, Finland was fought over and at the beginning of the 1800s the whole country was annexed to Russia. In the turmoil of the Russian Revolution of 1917, Finland declared itself an independent state. A Senate decision to form a national defence force was taken up in 1918, seventy-five years ago.

After the War of Independence the nation had to build up its spirit of coherence but the real criterion was the Second World War. In the Winter War Finland was left quite alone against the Russians. The whole country had to exert all its strength to resist the attacks of the eastern giant. After dramatic vicissitudes and many heroic deeds, Finland preserved its independence and proved to be a united, proud nation.

Every decade after the war has been significant in the development of the Defence Forces. At the end of the 1940s the lines of development were laid down by the Paris Peace Treaty and the Treaty of Friendship, Cooperation and Mutual Assistance. In the 1950s the Law on National Conscription was passed and a large-scale reorganization was carried out. Territorial defence was adopted as the Finnish military doctrine in the 1960s. The 1970s was the decade when the Parliamentary Defence Committees laid down clear lines for the future. The 1980s were called 'The decade of the Army' due to the significant equipment purchases.

The future will see the Finnish Defence Forces in a modernized organization and concentrating on its main tasks. Finland's answer to future security challenges is still a modern, large conscripted army. In the critical economic situation at the beginning of the 1990s, the purchase of the F/A 18 interceptors shows that the national air-space will continue to be under surveillance and Finns are still prepared and willing to defend their national territory.

Finland is ready to commit itself to the obligations of the integrated West European community. Though the reasons for integrating with Europe are more economic and political this does not seem to cause any insuperable defensive problems. The main defensive question in the future is how to reconcile Western integration and the mutual safety interests deriving from being in the neighbourhood of Russia. Finland has its own unique role in Europe and in the international sphere. One example is the contribution to UN peace-keeping operations.

In conclusion I want to express my thanks to the writer of this book, Major-General H. M. Tillotson. As one of the festive publications of the seventy-fifth anniversary of the Finnish Defence Forces, this book has a central role in illustrating the history, the present time and the future of the national defence of Finland for foreigners. In the new Europe it is important that the history is viewed from an objective standpoint by an outside expert and written in English.

Helsinki   JAN KLENBERG
January 1993   Admiral, Commander-in-Chief

Author's Note and Acknowledgements

When asked to say how this book came to be written, I am invariably taken back to a late afternoon in February 1978. After a series of calls in the western Sinai, the helicopter was making its final approach to a circle of whitened stones at Ras Abu Rudeis on the Gulf of Suez. Ahead, over the pilot's shoulder, I could see the small honour guard waiting with two flags: the blue flag of the United Nations and the blue and white flag of Finland. We were forty minutes late and I knew that, as soldiers have been kept waiting since time immemorial, the guard had been there for almost an hour. I had equipped myself for each such stop with a greeting in the language of my hosts, but in this case I already knew it by heart. 'Hyvää päivää – sotilaat' I shouted as soon as the helicopter blades had stopped. 'Hyvää päivää' came back an even louder response. 'He's late but at least he knows the drill,' I read in the soldiers' accompanying grins.

The young colonel commanding the Finnish battalion of the United Nations Emergency Force (UNEF II) introduced his NCOs and men by name. Then we drove off for a briefing on his task of manning the fifty-six-mile-long line of UN observation posts from Ras Sudr in the north to the buffer zone which included the Egyptian oil fields south of Abu Rudeis. We discussed the problems of the United Nations and soldiering until late into the night. As we did so, I knew that this colonel would very soon be a general. Today, Lieutenant-General Gustav Hägglund is Chief of the Defence Staff in Helsinki, reporting directly to the Commander-in-Chief. This book owes much to his encouragement.

The idea that the book should mark the seventy-fifth anniversary of the armed forces of independent Finland came from Lieutenant-General Aimo Pajunen, now the Permanent Under-Secretary of State for Defence. We had first met through the United Nations, some years earlier, but award of the Nobel Peace Prize to the UN peace-keeping forces in 1988 led me to his office in Helsinki and to his suggestion. We sketched out the synopsis for the book together in a matter of minutes. He warned me of possible pitfalls, wished me luck and turned his attention to more immediate matters. I remain steadfastly grateful for his inspiration.

Research in Finland and elsewhere has brought many new friends. For the details of the early life of Marshal Mannerheim, I owe a particular debt of gratitude to Mrs Kerstin Malm, curator of the Mannerheim Museum in Helsinki, and to Mr John Screen, librarian of the School of Slavonic and East European Studies, University of London, for material drawn from his book *Mannerheim – The Years of Preparation* published in 1970. *Finland's War of Independence* by Lieutenant-Colonel Joose Hannula, published in 1939, has proved both an invaluable source in itself and a sound basis against which to check other material from that period. For advice on the evolution of Finland's defence policy from 1945 until the present day, I owe a great deal to Dr Risto Penttilä, Special Adviser for International Security Affairs to Finland's Minister of Defence, whose comments and criticism have been equally enjoyable, and to the forthright remarks of Dr Markku Reimaa, Director-General for Press and Culture, Ministry of Foreign Affairs.

Maisteri Veli-Matti Syrjö, Director of the Military Archives of Finland, and his staff have personified patience in their search for names and details of Finns and others who played a significant part in Finland's four wars between 1918 and 1945 and, especially, of the veterans of 27th Jäger Battalion. Dr Markku Melkko, Director of the Military Museum in Helsinki, most generously allowed his staff to spend many hours guiding my research and seeking out information themselves. In this respect, I owe my special thanks to Miss Aila Helenius, for her information on the Lotta Svärd movement, and to Mr Lauri Honkala for his tireless search for hitherto unpublished photographs from the War of Independence and the Winter War.

The morning spent in the office of Mrs Liisa Knudsen, Keeper of the Archives of the Defence Staff Photographic Centre on Santahamina was a formidable experience. Her subordinates found my every wish entirely reasonable and she traced personally through her computer, from the briefest description, a photograph of two generals meeting in an obscure Russian village in 1943. The full range of photographs that I had requested reached England only a few days after my own return, numbered and listed with meticulous care.

The Defence Staff provided a contact for every aspect of my research: Commander Kimmo Kotilainen amd Lieutenant-Colonel Ossi Kettunen for the Finnish Navy and Coastal Artillery respectively, Major Ari Rautala and Major Reijo Seppänen, for the Army's modern operational concepts and training systems, Major Jukka Sihvo for the Finnish Air Force and Major Risto Häkkinen for the air-defence systems from the Winter War until the present day. All have read and re-read my draft work on their special subjects with the most painstaking attention to correct detail, for which I am most grateful. I am also appreciative of the reception and very detailed brief on the history and work of the War College in Helsinki by the College Chief of Staff, Lieutenant-Colonel Hannu Saarnilahti, at a time when he was especially busy with a revision of the course curriculum.

In the context of research on Finland's extensive United Nations experience, I am indepted to Major Rolf Kullberg of the UN Office at the Ministry of Defence for provision of material and photographs and to Lieutenant-Colonel Bjarne Ahlqvist, Head of the UN Office, and Mr Matti Piispanen of the staff of the Defence Council for their constructive comments of the draft for Chapter 21. I owe, however, the guts of the chapter to that veteran of UN peace-keeping operations, Lieutenant-General Ensio Siilasvuo, whom I first met in Jerusalem in 1978. He has allowed me to draw extensively on his recently published memoirs of UN Middle East service and made valuable additions and corrections to my drafts. I am most appreciative of his authoritative advice and help.

Friendship and encouragement I have had in abundance. My old friend from UN service Major-General Rauli Helminen and his wife Ritva ensured that I made the best of my time in Helsinki. I might well have visited Lieutenant-Colonel Risto Tyrväinen's Air Defence Academy, where Rauli was once a student, without his suggestion but I certainly would not have seen the houses of Jean Sibelius or the Finnish genre artist Pekka Halonen other than by their thoughtful arrangements. I also greatly appreciated their getting together now retired Finnish officers, with whom I had served in the UN Force in Cyprus, and their wives for a summer evening reunion which Sybil and I attended at their home in Tuusula, north of Helsinki.

For counsel on all historic aspects of the book, I am enormously indebted to Lieutenant-Colonel Jarl Kronlund, Research Fellow of the Finnish Commission of Military History, who has led me back to the facts from my flights of fancy more times than I care to remember – and with unfailing courtesy and good humour. I suspect that the grouse we had in my London club during his most recent visit may have seemed a poor reward. Now that the book is done, I shall miss our frequent contacts but wish him every success with his own book on Finnish involvement in the earlier UN peace-keeping operations.

From the beginning to the end of research and writing I have depended mightily on the goodwill and sense of humour of Colonel Kari Kokkonen, until recently the Head of the Information Section of the Defence Staff, and his cheerful and indefatigable assistants, Lieutenant-Colonel Pekka Majuri and Major Pekka Holopainen. Without their advice on whom to approach for information and their careful preparation of the ground for my every inquiry, I would have fallen at the first difficult fence. Whatever their inner feelings may have been, as yet another set of questions snaked out of their fax machine, any dismay was concealed with the equanimity of the true public relations professional. I have a special regard for their resourcefulness and friendship.

Finally, in Finland, I must recognize the advice and administrative support given by the successive Defence Attachés at the British Embassy, Lieutenant-Colonels Miles Thomson and Freddie Clement, both Gunners and so masters of where to go and what to do when one gets there. Amongst a range of helpers in England, my particular thanks are due to Lieutenant-Colonel George Forty, director and curator of the Tank Museum at Bovington, and his assistant Mr Graham Holmes and to Mr Michael Chapman of the Ministry of Defence Library, Whitehall. Their support for my reserch has been both essential and gladly given.

Many places in Finland have two entirely different names, one usually being derived from what is known as the 'Swedish period.' With a view to consistency, I have always tried to use the modern Finnish name. Where a place-name has altered for political reasons, I have used the one current to the period being described. Hence St Petersburg has passed through Petrograd to Leningrad and, perhaps surprisingly, back to St Petersburg within the seventy-five-year span of the book. The names of Finnish lakes and islands often include the suffixes 'järvi' meaning lake or 'saari' meaning island, but not always. To avoid confusing the reader, as there are sometimes towns with the same name, I have invariably prefaced the name with 'Lake' or followed it with 'Island.' I hope that language purists will forgive me. Similar examples are 'niemi' meaning peninsula, 'kylä' meaning village and 'lahti' meaning bay or inlet.

When approaching an historical development or concluding on either its origins or implication, I have frequently allowed my own thoughts to intrude into the text. These ideas remain my own and are not invariably endorsed by the appropriate authority in Finland. I nevertheless consider that they contribute something to the book as a whole. In any event, they are readily identifiable for the reader to put aside if he so wishes. Similarly, I have referred to occurrences remote from Finland when I believe that they might help to put local events onto a broader canvas or to illustrate by comparison.

It has been a privilege and a pleasure to write this book. I am proud that it will be published to mark the seventy-fifth anniversary of the armed forces of a brave and resolute nation. May their celebrations be as successful as they are justified.

Bishop's Waltham,   H.M.T.
Hampshire, England.

Prologue

Finland broke into the world's awareness on 30 November 1939 when she was subjected to a Russian land, air and naval attack. In the following hundred days the Finns fought the invader to a standstill on three separate fronts, thereby writing one of the most memorable chapters in the history of war. This was the 'Winter War' of which every Finn is justly proud and which still weighs significantly in the psyche and philosophy of the nation.

The Winter War and its long aftermath, with the Soviet Union seeming to hang like a menacing cliff over the country, obscured and distorted the outside world's perception of Finland's situation. Except with the peace-keeping forces of the United Nations, one seldom meets Finns outside their home country and, when one does, temptation to remark on their military prowess in the winter of 1939-40 is almost always impossible to resist. Conversely, until recently there was an inclination to shy away from any reference to the relationship between Finland and her eastern neighbour.

These extremes of perception, representing what the majority of foreigners know and do not know about Finland, led to the coining of the epithet 'Finlandization' usually attributed to the German politician Franz-Josef Strauss. It is a term intended to convey what it is thought impolite to describe – an apparent total acquiesence to the views and whims of Moscow in the interest of preserving a precarious co-existence. In fact, nothing could be less in keeping with the Finnish temperament, much as they cherish their national independence.

True independence was a long time coming to a people who can trace their origins to well before the Christian era. Finnish belongs to the Ural-Altiac or Uralic group of languages and has links with Hungarian. This suggests that the majority of the population is descended from a people who migrated from south-eastern Europe in the early part of the first Christian millennium. In Finland they

joined the Lapps who had lived there since, so it is believed, the
second millennium BC. The southern coastal regions were defended
against raiding Scandinavian Vikings and other marauders until the
mid-twelfth century. It was then that the rival expansionism of the
Roman Catholic Church from the west and Greek Orthodox from
the east led to the start of Swedish domination. This was to last for
600 years.

As Sweden grew to be a great power so she extended influence
and control over the whole of southern Finland. Curious though it
may seem today, Sweden was a serious military threat to the then
Novogorod-ruled part of Russia. A halt was called to Swedish expansion by the Treaty of Pähkinäsaari of 1323, which ceded eastern
Karelia to Russia. During the War of the Spanish Succession (1701-
14), while the Swedes were fighting in Europe, the Russians sought to
establish their hold further and occupied all Finland in 1714. What
became known in the Nordic countries as the Great Northern War
continued between Russia and Sweden until 1721 when, under the
Peace of Uusikaupunki, Sweden ceded the whole of south-eastern
Finland.

In the continuing struggle between two eighteenth-century powers,
the Finns found themselves in an unenviable position. Their territory
became the battleground and their menfolk were enlisted into the
army of one adversary to fight against the other. This experience
cannot but have had a significant influence on Finnish attitudes to
war and alliances. Fighting for one's country is one thing but fighting
for someone else's control over it is quite another. The Swedish-
Finnish army was decisively beaten in the war of 1741-43. Finland
was again occupied and the Peace of Turku of 1743 ceded yet more
Finnish territory to the Czars.

As if in atonement for the hardships they had imposed upon
Finland, the Swedes made extensive efforts to fortify their part of the
country in the period up to the onset of the Naploenic Wars. During
the final thirty years of Swedish rule, some effort was made to
broaden the Finnish economy by industrialization and the founding
of new cities. The structure for a modern legal system was laid and a
basis for eventual self-government established. In these several ways,
and in spite of King Gustav III (1771-92) of Sweden seeking to secure
a firmer Swedish hold on the country, Finland was being prepared
for greater autonomy.

Although not directly involved in the Napoleonic Wars, beyond the provision of men to serve in Finnish regiments of the Swedish army, Finland became a pawn in the struggle between the European powers of the day. When Napoleon and Czar Alexander I signed the Treaty of Tilsit on the raft moored on the River Niemen on 25 June 1807, they added a secret protocol. Alexander undertook to try to persuade Sweden to join the Continental blockade against Britain, with a view to dissuading her from continuing the war in Europe. When King Gustav IV Adolf of Sweden declined to join in the blockade, the Czar exercised the second provision of the protocol, which allowed him to seize complete control of Finland from Sweden.

Alexander's objective was different from that of his predecessors in the eighteenth century. He sought not to defeat the Swedes and punish the Finns but to bring the territory and people of Finland into the Imperial fold for the better security of his north-western borders and of his capital of St Petersburg. He therefore took considerable pains to bring about a rapprochement with the people and institutions of Finland. Well-briefed officials followed closely in the wake of the Czar's army to uphold the Finnish administration as the Swedes withdrew. Thus began his carefully planned process of detaching Finland from Sweden once and for all.

Before the Russo-Swedish peace treaty was signed in Frederikshamn on 27 September 1809, Alexander had already called the Finnish Diet together at Porvoo (Borga) on 27 March. There he declared Finland a part of his empire but as an autonomous Grand Duchy with himself and his successors as the Grand Duke. To stress that this was no mere charade, Alexander guaranteed the Finnish senate direct access to him on all key issues of state and also undertook to uphold the Evangelical Lutheran faith of the majority of Finns, their constitutional laws introduced in 1772 and their rights as a nation. Therefore, when evaluating the dramatic switch of Finnish allegiance to Imperial Russia, one needs to bear in mind the degree of autonomy promised by the Czar. This allowed the Finns to continue for a hundred years the liberalizing reforms begun by the Swedes.

As the new Grand Duchy was to be garrisoned by Imperial troops, the Czar saw no need for a separate Finnish army and ordered it to be disbanded in 1809. Napoleon's invasion of Russia changed his attitude and three Jäger regiments of enlisted volunteers were raised during the years 1812-13, equipped and supported by voluntary contributions from the Finnish population. None of these regiments was used against Napoleon but they were sent to St Petersburg to replace units of the Imperial Guard ordered to the front. This service was recognized by award of the title 'Finnish Guard Battalion' to the single unit retained after the Napoleonic Wars. The battalion saw Imperial service in the Polish revolt of 1830-31, during the Hungarian revolt of 1849 and in the Russo-Turkish war of 1877-78, becoming a significant source of pride to the Finnish people of the period.

During the period of autonomy about half the officers who served in Russian units garrisoning Finland were themselves Finnish. Many were graduates of the military cadet school that was founded in Hamina, in south-east Finland, in 1812. These men took their lead from the words of Alexander I spoken at Porvoo, 'Finland is elevated to the ranks of nations'. The whole atmosphere changed, however, with the policy of Russification of Finland, which began under the reign of Czar Nicholas II at the turn of the century. The Finnish Guard Battalion was disbanded in 1905, the Corps of Cadets at Hamina closed down and Finns were required to serve in the Russian Army. These changes were much resented in Finland and the sharply reduced political autonomy of the country led to the growth of animosity towards all things Russian.

Wars and the varying political attitudes first of Sweden and then of Czarist Russia nurtured the spirit of Finnish independence and democratic idealism in the same way as the cold of winter and warmth of spring draws a crop towards maturity. This is perhaps an especially apposite simile for Finland, where the extremes of climate have a significant impact on the character of the population. It is not, of course, just a simple contrast between warmth and cold but also between light and darkness. Except for Iceland, Finland is the world's most northerly country. The climate is moderated by the almost land-locked Baltic Sea, by the 100,000 inland lakes and the warm westerly winds of the Atlantic Gulf Stream. In northern Finland (Lapland) the sun does not set in summer for a period of seventy days and in winter, even in Helsinki in the far south, the days are short, dark and cold. The snow may sometimes begin to settle in October and remains until the end of March.

Map 1: Finland as a Russian Grand Duchy

Retreat of the Continental glacier at the end of the Ice Age scraped Finland almost level, leaving high ground only in the north-western tip of the country. In winter the lakes freeze and are readily passable on foot and by most vehicles. In summer they provide breeding places for myriads of mosquitoes, which reach near-plague proportions in the far north. Vast forests of spruce, fir and pine alternate with a wilderness of sparsely covered and rolling landscape cut with fast-flowing rivers and outcrops of hard deposits left by the retreating ice. Spring and autumn are brief seasons of spectacular beauty. At other times the countryside has an eerie stillness, as if it is waiting for someone bold enough to test its authority.

Environment and experience have moulded the Finns into a realistic and straightforward people. They know that no one will come to their aid in crisis except those who are serving their own best interest. Directness of character is focused by a special clarity of speech. Every syllable of a word is enunciated, with emphasis on the first one. The Finns' characteristic way of speaking English may have contributed to the myth that they lack a sense of humour; but their humour is individual, essentially Finnish. A witticism is seldom received with explosive laughter but enjoyed inwardly, as friends together might enjoy a glass of ice-cold Koskenkorva – Finnish vodka.

PART I
The War of Independence

I
Seeds of Conflict

Finland was able to stand back from the vortex of treaties and guarantees that drew the European powers inexorably into war in August 1914. Even so, as a Grand Duchy of still-Imperial Russia, the country was left neither at peace nor with a population at war. As an integral part of the Russian Empire, the Finns had no armed forces of their own. Their small army had been dissolved by Imperial decree at the turn of the century. The subsequent Military Service Law had been suspended after three abortive attempts to conscript Finns into the Russian Army between 1901 and 1903. There were military garrisons in southern Finland and on the west coast facing the Gulf of Bothnia. All these, together with the naval bases to support the Russian Baltic Fleet, were manned by Russians.

The Russian garrisons were primarily concerned not with suppression of the Finnish population but with defence of the land and sea approaches to St Petersburg. The Gulf of Finland leads directly to the old Russian capital and the south-eastern boundary of the Grand Duchy ran only twenty-five miles from the outskirts of the city. Since the foundation of St Petersburg in 1703, the territory of Finland and the waters of her southern seaboard had been seen by the Czars as the most vulnerable sector of the Empire's system of external defence. This perception was to survive the Empire and bedevil Finno-Soviet relations for half a century beyond.

Until given an opportunity to fight for their independence, the Finns had looked without enthusiasm on the principle of conscription. History had also taught them to be wary of involvement in foreign wars. There is an apocryphal story of the Russians sending recruiting officers to Finland in search of volunteers to join the Imperial army engaged in the Crimean War. After one had explained his mission, a farmer rose from the audience to declare, 'If it is a question of fighting the Russians, men will join up from every one of our homes.'

Finnish military traditions stretch back roots to the Swedish wars in central Europe of the sixteenth, seventeenth and eighteenth centuries, including the Russo-Swedish wars which continued until 1809. Some 950 Finnish officers, trained at the Hamina military cadet school, were serving in the Imperial Russian Army in 1914. Many of these men were with Russian regiments garrisoning Finland. Although some undoubtedly held private aspirations for Finnish independence, the great majority were simply professional soldiers serving their Emperor.

Outside Finland, Finnish volunteers of the Jäger Movement began to receive military training in Germany against the day when their skills would be needed to help wrest their country's independence from Russia. This was a semi-clandestine arrangement, made with the German authorities in December 1914 after a request for similar facilities had been rejected by Sweden. The Jägers were to play an important military role in the War of Independence and subsequently. An outline of the organization of the 27th Jäger Battalion is shown in Appendix 1.

The onset of the First World War found relations between the Finns and their Grand Duke in St Petersburg distinctly strained. While some elements of Finnish political opinion aligned themselves with the Emperor, the majority wished to see his authority in Finland either curtailed or overthrown. An Imperial decree of June 1900 had ordered the gradual introduction of Russian as the principal language of Finnish state administration. This met with opposition from the Finnish authorities and people alike and a national committee of resistance was formed in Helsinki in the following year. The committee was chiefly made up of middle-class liberal intellectuals who advocated passive resistance to unwelcome Russian decrees. While never seriously influential as a political force, the committee encouraged the flouting of the conscription levies of 1901 and 1902, which led in 1903 to the suspension of the Russian Military Service Law after a further failure of the levy.

Long-smouldering unrest in Russia finally exploded on the streets of St Petersburg on 25 October 1905, to be followed by five days of rioting and a general strike. This upheaval incited the Finnish passive resistance committee to convene in Helsinki on 29 October. The meeting proclaimed a general strike from the following day, elected a strike committee and unilaterally rescinded the appointment of all Imperial officials made over the previous five years. These events, which coincided with Czar Nicholas II's manifesto promising citizens of the Empire political reform and improved civil liberties, were to have a profound effect on the Finnish politico-social structure for a generation. By chance, they also provided the nucleus from which Finland's armed forces were eventually reborn.

All Finnish newspapers carried the news of the Emperor's manifesto on 31 October 1905, before they closed down to allow their employees to join the general strike. This swiftly became popularly nationalistic rather than destructive in nature. As the strike spread throughout the country, the Russian gendarmerie were systematically disarmed while the Finnish police force joined the strike. In response to widespread concern for public order in the capital, public-minded volunteers formed the Järjestyskaarti or Orderly Guard vigilante group. These volunteers were soon joined by left-wing activists who supported revolutionary reform. These two diverse elements were not slow to identify themselves and their interests. In consequence, the Järjestyskaarti in Helsinki split into the Soujeluskaarti or 'Protection Guard' and 'Red Guard' factions. Only the ending of the general strike, on 6 November, averted an open clash between them on the streets of the capital. Two separately minded militias had nevertheless been established.

Restoration of public order in Russia, which followed the Emperor's manifesto promising reform, brought an end to the general strike in Finland. Moderates in Helsinki, who sought reform of relationships with Russia by constitutional means, pulled the main strands of government together again. Then, following a series of debates in the national Diet, proposals for wide-ranging change were submitted to St Petersburg. The Emperor subsequently confirmed virtually all the Finnish proposals in a decree of 20 July 1906, which became known as the 'July Decree' and an important source of constitutional reference thereafter.

The July Decree replaced the Finnish Diet, with its archaic separate representation of the aristocracy, clergy, bourgeoisie and the peasantry, with a single assembly of 200 members, to which a governing Senate would be responsible. The 200 representatives to the assembly were to be elected by all Finns over the age of twenty-four through a system of proportional representation. Thus the system of government in Finland leapt from autocracy to universal suffrage ahead of any country in Europe.

Formation of the Suojeluskaarti in Helsinki, during the general strike of October 1905, was matched by the setting up of related organizations in the towns and countryside in the course of the following year. Their affirmed purpose was to stand ready to oppose any attempt to overthrow the newly established political order. They were largely clandestine and many had only a loose organization, sometimes linked with the local fire brigade. It could be argued that the very existence of these unofficial groups stimulated the spread of the rival Red Guard cells, especially in rural districts where the benefits of electoral reform were becoming more slowly apparent.

A serious incident in 1906 demonstrated both the rising strength of the Labour Movement in Finland and the alignment of the Red Guards with acquisition of power through revolutionary tactics. The hitherto small Social Democratic party had received a huge boost in popularity and membership during and immediately after the general strike of 1905. Electoral reforms introduced from 1906 left the majority of the estimated 100,000 Social Democrat members feeling cheated of their more extreme demands, even though they had received the vote. A mutiny by sailors of the Russian Baltic Fleet on the fortress of Sveaborg, overlooking the harbour of Helsinki, provided an excuse for a show of strength.

It remains uncertain whether the Sveaborg mutiny was spontaneous, arising from the sailors' dissatisfaction with their conditions, or whether it was part of a wider conspiracy within the Russian Fleet that broke out prematurely. It had no connection whatever with political interests in Finland but the Red Guard commander in Helsinki, Johan Kock, decided to mobilize and arm his men in support of the mutineers in the fortress. The Social Democratic party leadership prudently dissociated themselves from this reckless action. Undeterred, Kock called for a general strike to frustrate measures designed to contain the mutiny until such time as the Russian authorities were able to deal with it. The strike call led the Senate to mobilize the Suojeluskaarti and an armed clash between them and the Red Guards occurred in Hakaniemi Square in front of the Sähkölaitos building. Fortunately, a detachment of Russian troops sent to suppress the naval mutiny arrived in time to clear the square.

The Sveaborg incident led to a strengthening of moderate political opinion in Finland and emboldened the Senate to proscribe the Red Guards. Although there was no direct link between the Social Democratic party and the Red Guards, membership of the party began to fall away after the Sveaborg affair. This was a short-lived phenomenon, however, as the Social Democrats began to increase their support in the countryside amongst the small farmer communities. This was particularly apparent along what became known as the 'red belt'. This stretched from Satakunta province in the west, across the southern hinterland to Lake Ladoga in the east. When political allegiances polarized immediately before the War of Independence, the front between the opposing forces formed along much of the line of the red belt, chiefly due to Red Guard influence in that region.

As the Social Democrats came to be seen to represent the whole Labour Movement in Finland, so their position improved in the parliamentary body, the Eduskunta. They secured eighty of the two hundred seats in the elections of 1907, although the same year marked the beginning of a period when the authority of the Finnish Parliament was curtailed by the Russians. This change arose through renewed efforts in St Petersburg to bring Finland under closer Imperial control following the appointment of Peter Stolypin as Russian prime minister in 1906. Alarmed by the prospect of a self-governing Finland in control of a strategically vital sector of the Empire's defensive system, civil servants and soldiers in the Russian capital set out to limit the effects on Finland of the liberal reforms instituted by the Emperor during the Russian domestic crisis of 1905.

Stolypin put up no resistance to these pressures and introduced a bill into the Russian Duma in 1908 that virtually suspended the authority of the Finnish Parliament as a legislative body. For the remaining years of its existence, until 1917, the Eduskunta was restricted to legislation on relatively minor matters and confined to putting forward opinion only, on matters of state interest, to St Petersburg. Thus the universal franchise and the representative assembly granted by the Emperor were emasculated by his prime minister three years later.

At first sight it appears strange that the strength of the Social Democratic party should have continued to grow, in both the country and in the national assembly, during a period when the latter had very little power to influence events. The reason for the sustained growth lay in the huge expansion of Finland's Labour Movement and its consequent need to find some outlet for coherent political expression. The aspirations of the great majority of party members had little in common with the middle-class intellectuals who made up most of the party leadership. The latter were content to theorize about Marxist principles while remaining firmly nationalistic in their opposition to Russian rule by decree. This significant difference in outlook was to lead to a lateral split in the party when the prospect of independence finally became a reality.

The attitude of the Labour Movement towards bourgeois nationalism, whether apparent in their own leadership or in that of the bourgeois parties themselves, was unambivalent. The small farmers and factory workers saw the bourgeois struggle against Russian domination as being motivated simply by their wish to preserve, and eventually enhance, the middle-class position in Finnish society. This perception of motives led the Labour Movement to form a lateral affinity with Russian Marxist views. When an opportunity was presented, as in the case of the Sveaborg mutiny, dissent from their own leadership could be expressed by support for a form of imported ideology.

Stolypin systematically filled the Finnish Senate with his own nominees, so that by 1910 the Eduskunta had been reduced to little more than a political debating society. Chiefly due to the consequent political apathy, membership of the Social Democratic party again began to fall. Numbers fell to as low as 50,000, half the strength in 1905, but 30,000 of these formed a hard core of rural workers across the red belt region. Electoral apathy in other parties, due to the total suspension of the Eduskunta for the duration of the war in 1914, led to the Social Democrats achieving an absolute majority of 103 seats in the parliamentary elections of 1916. Meanwhile, although proscribed by the Senate, the Red Guard cells in the cities and rural areas maintained contact with previous and potential new members throughout the country.

Outbreak of war in 1914 had led to a very substantial reinforcement of the Russian garrison in Finland. Some 42,000 men were deployed in the south of the country and on the west coast. These were perceived as the most likely areas for any German offensive launched through Finland. The Russian garrisons in Helsinki and

Map 2: Principal Russian Garrisons in Finland in the summer of 1917

Viipuri were each about 10,000 strong, with a further 8,000 men stationed at Lahti on the southern tip of Lake Päijänne in south central Finland. These garrisons were all under direct command of XLII Army Corps at Viipuri, which controlled the Helsinki-St Petersburg railway line as it passed through the Karelian Isthmus.

In the west, 106th Division had its headquarters at Tampere, where the 422nd Kolpana Regiment was also stationed. Other regiments of the division were the 421st Tsarskoye Selo at Rauma, the 424th Tchudi Regiment with battalions at Riihimäki and Hämeenlinna and the 432nd Luga Regiment at the railway junction of Seinajoki to the south-east of Vassa. Battalions or companies of these regiments were deployed to nearby towns and ports. The most northerly garrison was formed by two companies at Tornio, at the extreme northern point of the Gulf of Bothnia on the Finnish-Swedish frontier. In addition to these Russian army garrisons, there were some 20,000 sailors of the Russian Baltic Fleet based on the port of Helsinki.

Serious mutinies in the Baltic Fleet broke out on 16 March 1917, motivated by political agitation against the war rather than in protest about conditions. Revolutionary committees had been established in most of the Russian naval and military units in Finland early in 1917. Initially they were symptomatic of war weariness but quickly became allied, in their leadership at least, with either Bolshevik or extreme socialist opinion in Russia. They were united in their opposition to the Provisional Government which had taken power on the abdication of Czar Nicholas II, in March 1917, with Alexander Kerensky as Minister for War.

In parallel with the collapse of the Imperial regime, the Finns secured a manifesto from the Provisional Government rescinding the decrees restricting Finnish rights and allowing the Finnish Parliament elected in the 1916 elections to be convened. The same manifesto also dissolved the Finnish Senate that had been packed with Stolypin's nominees. While welcomed by the great majority of the Finnish population, these events started the controversy as to who or what could legally replace the Russian Emperor in Finland's new political structure. Meanwhile, continued advances of the German army in the Russian Baltic provinces of Latvia and Lithuania led to increasing concern in St Petersburg. In anticipation of a possible threat to the Russian capital through Finland, Kerensky reinforced the garrison there so that it had become 100,000 strong by August 1917.

The turbulent summer of 1917 also brought an end of orders to Finnish factories for munitions and stores for support of the Russian Army. Substantial laying off of workers coincided with a halt to the construction of fortifications, which alone had given war work to 100,000 Finns. Clashes broke out between groups of unemployed Finns and the increasingly disaffected and ill-disciplined Russian soldiers in the garrison towns. These disputes had little underlying political motivation, being chiefly fights over local girls and the right of exclusive patronage of drinking houses. In July, however, news of Lenin's first and abortive coup against the Provisional Government in St Petersburg reached Finland within hours. It flashed through the Russian garrisons like wildfire, causing further indiscipline and unrest.

Shortly before these dramatic events, the Finnish Social Democratic party had laid a bill before the newly convened Parliament proposing that discussions should be initiated with the Russian Provisional Government on the future relationship between Finland and Russia. The parliamentary debate became drawn out and, in an effort to increase the political momentum, the Social Democratic party conference of mid-June 1917 drew up a resolution demanding full Finnish independence from Russia. This was presented to the Congress of All-Russia Soviets convened in St Petersburg in early July. While the Finnish Social Democrats' resolution received unqualified support from the Russian Bolshevik minority at the Congress, only the right of Finnish self-determination was conceded by the majority. Hastening back to Helsinki with what they chose to interpret as a go-ahead for independence, the Social Democrats pushed through Parliament, in which they had the controlling majority, what became known as the 'Law of 18 July'.

The Law was based on the Social Democrats' party conference resolution and granted to the Finnish Parliament virtually all the prerogatives previously reserved to the Emperor and, more recently, to the Provisional Government. Unfortunately these would-be constitutional changes coincided with Lenin's first and abortive coup, which was firmly suppressed by the Provisional Government. Lenin himself fled to Finland. Failure of the attempted coup strengthened the hand of Kerensky, who was appointed Russian prime minister. He immediately repudiated the Finns' Law of 18 July and dissolved their Parliament for good measure.

August and September 1917 were marked by feverish political activity in both Finland and Russia. Fresh elections to the Finnish Parliament were arranged for 3/4 October and, as the authority of the Russian Provisional Government continued to falter, the Soviets controlling the Russian garrisons increased their hold. The October elections gave the Finnish non-socialist parties a narrow collective parliamentary majority of eight seats. Then, at the end of the month, Lenin and his Bolsheviks finally overthrew Kerensky's Provisional Government.

Viewing their own electoral defeat with dismay, Finland's Social Democrats looked to the rising success of their Marxist comrades beyond the nearby frontier with Russia. Acting with a new cohesion, the party leadership joined forces with the trades unions to promote the formation of 'workers' guards'. In some cases these were formed round the Red Guard cells that had remained underground since the general strike of 1905. Hardly surprisingly, this activity led to a strengthening of the still only semi-official Suojeluskaarti units in the cities and towns. A Social Democrat initiative in Parliament to implement the Law of 18 July was defeated by the non-socialist majority on 9 November. The non-socialists tabled their own motion calling for the election of a Regency Council under the still extant (Swedish) Gustavian Act of Government of 1772. The motion was passed and the resultant Regency Council acquired the power to exercise temporary supreme authority in the governing of Finland.

The Social Democrats responded with extra-parliamentary action and called a general strike on 13 November. This new threat of anarchy caused a moderation in the non-socialist stance. Some long-overdue reforms on working conditions were introduced. For their part, the more moderate Social Democrats also perceived the dangers of a rapidly worsening situation and withdrew from the revolutionary council of militant workers. Thus a decisive break was finally made between the moderate Social Democrat leadership and the bulk of the workers, leaving a vacuum of power waiting to be filled by the political militants and Red Guards. On 16 November the revolutionary council voted by a narrow majority to attempt a seizure of power. Significantly, the trades union leadership rejected and so frustrated this move, which induced the more extreme elements of the Red Guards to threaten to break from party control to pursue the struggle in their own way.

It was at this point that Pehr Svinhufvud, a lifelong political opponent of Russian rule over Finland, returned from exile. He placed before Parliament a programme of measures to secure Finnish independence in a constitutional manner, which received the support of the non-socialist majority in the assembly. The Social Democrat minority also supported Svinhufvud's measures but argued for further negotiations with Petrograd (as the Russian capital had by then been renamed). At first the non-socialist majority chose to ignore the opposition's advice. When, however, no foreign recognition of the unilateral declaration of independence appeared forthcoming, Svinhufvud set out with a delegation to present a request for independence to Lenin and the new Soviet government in Petrograd.

Svinhufvud must have drawn considerable confidence in his mission from Lenin's order to withdraw 60,000 of the Russian garrison, those of the summer reinforcement, back to Russia. Meanwhile the Red Guards intensified their recruiting drive, attaining a total strength of 30,000 by mid-December 1917. Everywhere they sought to forge links with the Soviets now in total control of the largely officerless Russian regiments and naval units, from whom the Red Guards began to receive substantial quantities of arms and ammunition. Alarmed by these developments, the Suojeluskaarti also began to increase their strength and to gather what arms they could find.

To this dangerous and worsening situation there returned, on 18 December 1917, a fifty-year-old Finn who had served for thirty years in the Imperial Russian Army and achieved the rank of lieutenant-general in command of an army corps in the war with Germany. His name was Mannerheim.

2
Mannerheim

History has a habit of thrusting forward a man or a woman to confront crisis. Some are prepared by character and experience to lead men and to shape events, while the latent qualities of others might have for ever remained untapped. Seldom are they the obvious or constitutional choice. Some succeed but the majority fail. If there is one attribute needed in national crisis, assimilating courage, skill, stamina and wisdom, it must be a clear objectivity of purpose, a purpose without the blemish of personal ambition. The Russian Revolution of October 1917 returned to Finland a man of this breed: Gustaf Mannerheim.

In strict ethnographic terms, Mannerheim was a Finno-Swede, in that his ancestors had come to Finland from Sweden in the seventeenth century. The family was originally Dutch, with the name Marhein, and had gone to Sweden from Germany. The youngest son of Augustin Marhein was ennobled by King Charles XI of Sweden in 1693, when he changed the name of his branch of the family to Mannerheim. Although the name has a seeming German spelling, the correct pronunciation is 'Mannerhaim', reflecting the Dutch ancestry. Two of Augustin's soldier-sons were raised to the rank of baron in Sweden and the younger of these two, Johan Augustin, was father to Carl Erik Mannerheim, who founded the Finnish arm of the family in 1793.

Following the landowning tradition, Carl Erik Mannerheim bought a substantial property at Louhisaari, in south-western Finland, from the family of the Swedish Admiral Klas Fleming. He joined the government of the Grand Duchy of Finland and was raised to the rank of count by Emperor Alexander I of Russia in 1824. Under the custom of the Empire, this title descended only through the elder son, while the younger sons inherited the lesser title of baron. Each generation comprised five or more children, as was then the practice throughout Europe, which established broad and strong family ties including those with the Swedish Mannerheims.

Although the second count, Carl Gustaf, entered Imperial government service, the family as a whole retained its commercial and local connections, thus in no sense becoming aristocrats in the grand sense. In fact Finland had no such strata of society. Government officials, the professional class and the landowners mixed freely and sons undertook the vocational avenue best suited to their talents. Family interests were broad and varied. As an example, Count Carl Gustaf was better known as an entomologist than as President of the Viipuri Court of Appeal.

The third count, Carl Robert Mannerheim, was of a literary and radical disposition, producing poetry and political satire whilst still an undergraduate at the University of Helsinki. This drew him to the attention of the Russian Imperial authorities, as did his support for the European radicals in the 1848 Year of Revolution. Marriage in 1862 to the daughter of the prominent Finnish industrialist Johan Jakob von Julin had a moderating effect and he began to devote himself increasingly to family interests.

Count Carl and his wife Hélène von Julin produced four sons and three daughters. The third child and second son was born in the year of the Finnish famine, 1867, and was christened Carl Gustaf Emil. Gustaf proved unruly and at times rebellious. He did not begin to speak until the age of three but was physically active to a compensating degree. Countess Mannerheim brought much of the influence of Victorian England to the household from contact with English friends of the von Julin family. All the children became fluent in Swedish, English, French, German and Russian, as the languages were spoken in the house in rotation through the schooldays of the week. Finnish was not spoken and Gustaf made no serious effort to master the language until after he returned to his homeland in 1917.

The literary and musical ambiance of the Louhisaari household was in sharp contrast to the Spartan conditions, reflecting Victorian England, under which the children lived. The extensive park and woodland of the estate and the beaches of the nearby sea drew them all into an outdoor life and an appreciation of both nature and adventure. The three girls joined their brothers on expeditions into the countryside. Gustaf and his eldest sister Sophie shared a love of horses and riding which was the basis of a close personal bond that was to last for the whole of their long lives.

When Gustaf was eight years old, he and his eldest brother Carl were sent to the preparatory and main schools respectively of the Private Lyceum in Helsinki. It was not necessary for them to become boarders as the family had an apartment in the capital, where their father lived for much of the time in order to conduct his business affairs. Gustaf took his rebelliousness to the Lyceum and soon established leadership over his contemporaries. During a snowball fight in the nearby Kaisaniemi Park he was knocked over by a horse-drawn sleigh, only to get up, throw a final snowball and utter the prophetic remark to the curious bystanders, 'My name is Mannerheim and I am general of the lower form.' General or not, he was expelled in 1879, when aged twelve, for deliberately breaking windows.

The next two years were to see a dramatic change of circumstance in the Mannerheims' affairs. Count Carl's business interests had always been subordinate to his artistic and literary inclinations and the lure of gambling. Debt obliged him to sell a family estate near Louhisaari in 1879 and he became bankrupt the following year. Leaving his wife and family in the care of his wife's stepmother at Sällvik, he moved to Paris to seek fresh fortune there. Countess Hélène died of a heat attack in January 1881 and the seven children were split up amongst relatives in Finland and Sweden. Count Carl's sister Wilhelmina, who took care of the two younger girls, became the new owner of Louhisaari.

Before her death Countess Hélène had thought that Gustaf might be trained for a military career at the Corps of Cadets at Hamina in south-eastern Finland, where his rebellious spirit might be curbed to some extent by the rigours of military discipline. After failing the entrance examination in 1881, Gustaf entered Hamina in 1882 when, at last, he began to show academic promise approaching his physical prowess. Even so, he was held back in the preparatory class for a second year but moved up after only six months. He began to excel in history, natural history and other science subjects as well as in French and Swedish. He did not enjoy Hamina, however. He missed the artistic atmosphere of his former family home, disliked the enforced intimacy of dormitory living and, unlike most of his fellow cadets, was chronically short of money.

Military training at Hamina was adversely influenced by the small size of the Finnish Army of the period. It comprised one regular battalion of the Finnish Guard, a regiment of dragoon cavalry and a handful of militia infantry units. The military instructors at Hamina were a mixed lot and few had active service experience. Despite these limitations and his distaste for the petty restrictions inseparable from the routine of a military school, Gustaf appears to have resolved to make a career for himself in the Imperial Russian Army. Letters from Hamina to his much-loved sister Sophie, by then living with von Julin relatives in Sweden, show a new maturity of outlook, possibly brought about by the breakup of the family following the financial disasters of 1879-81.

Countess Eva Mannerheim, Gustaf's paternal grandmother, and his uncle Albert von Julin, who had assumed responsibility for his welfare, were gladdened when their rebellious charge began to make plans of his own. Having studied the best route to advancement in the Russian Army, Gustaf proposed that he should leave Hamina to join the Imperial School of Pages in St Petersburg as an essential step towards the General Staff Academy and a commission in a Guards regiment, which would keep him near the capital and more in the official eye.

The von Julin side of the family had reservations about the plan, fearing that Gustaf would become Russified and divorced from his family roots. They were eventually won over, however, and application was made to the Minister-Secretary of State for Finland in St Petersburg for one of the free places kept for Finns in the School of Pages. This was duly referred to the Head of the Corps of Cadets in Hamina who, to the distress of Gustaf and his family, flatly refused to endorse the application on grounds of Gustaf's indifferent record of behaviour. Countess Eva's efforts to overcome this impasse by writing again to the Minister-Secretary were unsuccesful. Deeply disappointed, Gustaf allowed his conduct to deteriorate further and was obliged to leave Hamina after going absent without leave while confined to barracks.

While this serious setback encouraged his devoted Uncle Albert to seek a career in commerce or industry for Gustaf, it only fired the latter's determination to find a way into the Army. He spent the summer of 1886 studying Russian at Kharkov, returned to the Helsinki Lyceum for an intensive year of work and matriculated from there in June 1887. This qualified him for entry to the

University of Helsinki but also, if a place could be found, into a Russian military school instead. After intensive lobbying of a family connection in Russia, Major-General Baron Gösta Aminoff, he secured a place at the Nikolayevskoye Cavalry School in St Petersburg. Cavalry had long been Gustaf's choice of military arm, not only because he loved horses but because he felt he would serve with men such as he had himself become: self-reliant and independent of view, physically hard but cultured in taste – and loyal to the Emperor.

Mannerheim began the two-year course at the Nikolayevskoye Cavalry School in September 1897, just three months after his twentieth birthday. He was impressed but not dazzled by the sophistication of St Petersburg. The historic city offered the distractions of any capital but Mannerheim knew that he would have to work exceptionally hard to win a place in the Guards Cavalry that he had made his goal. Although later in life, when his mother country needed him most, he eschewed all personal opportunity, as a young man he was healthily ambitious. From now on he aimed at nothing less than excellence.

His hard work and fine horsemanship at Nikolayevskoye were rewarded by passing out second in the group of cadets graded first class in 1899. A commission in the Guards Cavalry, however, initially evaded him. The vacancies were granted through a complex procedure of checks and balances but the competition was intense. It seemed that, at this time at least, Mannerheim lacked the connections able to pull the necessary strings. He was commissioned into the 15th Aleksandriyskiy Dragoons, a cavalry regiment of the line, stationed in Russian Poland. He went without complaint but continued to seek a place in the Guards through his family connections in Russia. After seven months his patience was rewarded by transfer to the Chevalier Guards, the premier Guards Cavalry regiment, in St Petersburg.

Mannerheim served with the Chevalier Guards for the next thirteen years. In 1892 he married the rich Anastasia Arapova, daughter of a Russian general, thereby solving his increasingly difficult financial problems. He decided about this time not to try to enter the General Staff Academy, as the new financial security he enjoyed opened the way to advance in the Guards Cavalry. He rode unusually well and took his profession more seriously than was customary in the Russian Army of the period. Becoming responsible for the training of recruits to his regiment, he discovered that he could bring out the best in men who were not particularly energetic or keen to learn by mutual inclination.

In 1897 his skill as a horseman prompted an invitation to become the assistant to the Director of the Court Stables unit, who was himself a general and had commanded the Chevalier Guards. Mannerheim accepted with alacrity; the post carried great prestige, extra pay and fine lodgings. But by 1903 he knew that he should return to regimental duty and pursue the command of a squadron of the Chevalier Guards. Instead, he was appointed to command the demonstration squadron at the Officers' Cavalry School, a position from which it was possible to move direct to command of a regiment.

Mannerheim took up his post at the Cavalry School in St Petersburg in the month of his thirty-sixth birthday. He was promoted to first captain to command the demonstration squadron but, after sixteen years' service, yearned to put his military training into practice in something more serious than annual manoeuvres of the 1st Guards Cavalry Division. His chance came with the start of the Russo-Japanese War in Manchuria in 1904.

Russia had not sought this war; rather she had provoked it by a policy of domination and steady expansion in the Far East. The Chinese were in no position to retaliate to broken border treaties but the Japanese were less patient, especially when Russia declined to give assurance that Korea was a recognized sphere of Japanese interest in 1903. Taking the initiative, and without declaring war, the Japanese fleet attacked Russian warships of their Far East Fleet at Port Arthur (Lüda) in February 1904. Shattered and demoralized, the Russians were unable to prevent the Japanese Army from crossing into Korea and then over the northern frontier at the Yalu River into Russian Manchuria. General Kuropatkin, the Russian local field commander, found himself defending the north-south line of the Harbin to Port Arthur railway against substantial Japanese forces advancing from the Yalu to the east.

Against the advice of his family in Finland and the commandant of the Cavalry School, Mannerheim volunteered to serve in Manchuria. Accepted, he was promoted to lieutenant-colonel as second-in-command of the 52nd Nezhinskiy Dragoons, a line cavalry regiment serving with the 2nd Independent Cavalry Brigade. No doubt he imagined that his years of practising bold cavalry manoeuvres were to be put to the test at last. In fact, his first experience of war was to instil in his mind much more wide-reaching principles. Russia was unprepared to fight a full-scale war in the Far East. The Trans-Siberian railway was a long and tenuous line of communication and the General Staff had made a serious underestimate of the Japanese offensive capability.

Mannerheim found the 52nd Dragoons in not especially good shape, while the performance of the General Staff in planning operations was distinctly worse. Kurapatkin was a hesitant commander and, through lack of reliable intelligence and over-dispersal of his forces, allowed the Japanese to cut the railway at Yin-kou, occupy the port and cut off the whole of the Liaodong Peninsula. Mannerheim took part in a large-scale cavalry raid, under Major-General Mishenko, to cut the railway north of the Japanese and retake Yin-kou. Subsequently he commanded a reconnaissance and raiding force of two squadrons of the 52nd Dragoons in a series of encounters with the Japanese. He received a battlefield promotion to the rank of colonel for coolness and gallantry under fire during the Battle of Mukden. Later he commanded a force of Chinese irregular cavalry on raiding and reconnaissance missions behind the left flank of the Japanese. The war ended in September 1905 with both adversaries exhausted.

The lessons that Mannerheim drew from this indecisive campaign were chiefly concerned with the proper organization and support of an army on active service, the importance of reconnaissance and intelligence of the enemy's capability, and the devastating effect, especially against troops untrained in the best use of ground and cover, of modern artillery and machine-guns. He also learned the significance of maintaining men and horses in sound condition for war and how the least neglect of either is compounded many times over by the tensions and confusion of battle.

His ability to invigorate the 52nd Dragoons, who had taken part in several unsuccesful and dispiriting actions before he had joined them in Manchuria, owed much to his experience in training the young troopers of the Chevalier Guards. He had learned then how to gain the confidence of his men through a genuine concern for their well-being and by personal example, in particular in horsemanship and care of horses. Equally important, he had recognized the necessity of keeping soldiers informed of not only what is expected of them but why the battle has to be fought. This military maxim is as old as war itself and one which every commander professes to understand and practise. Curiously, therefore, it is almost always the first significant lesson to be relearned in the opening stage of each campaign.

Manchuria took its toll of Mannerheim's health. Inflammation of his left ear left him partly deaf for a while, although not permanently on that side as is sometimes asserted, and an old kneee injury sustained from a horse kick while serving with the Court Stable unit became exacerbated by rheumatism. He was still physically hard and strong, however, and promotion to colonel at thirty-eight was a great en- couragement. He was now on the waiting list for appointment to a regimental command and well placed to receive one shortly. After a month-long delay on the Trans-Siberian railway, where he witnessed with dismay the wretched state of morale of the returning conscript soldiers, he went on leave to Finland. He was received with delight by his relations there and represented his branch of the Mannerheims at a Diet of the Four Estates from February to June 1906. This was the last occasion that the Diet was to assemble.

A mid-leave visit to St Petersburg brought an invitation which reflected the high regard with which he was coming to be known in the capital. To his complete surprise, Mannerheim was not offered the regimental command that he sought but an opportunity to conduct a two-year expedition to gather military and political intel- ligence in the Russian border provinces between Tashkent and Peking. The ambitious young colonel's dilemma on receiving this offer, from the Chief of the General Staff in person, is not difficult to imagine. Every dedicated professional soldier is acutely aware of the dangers of being out of the mainstream of military life for long. All too probably he will return to find that he and his mission are both forgotten while contemporaries and even juniors have been promoted over his head. Against such considerations, Mannerheim had to weigh the attractions of establishing a new reputation as an explorer, emulating his uncle Baron Adolf Erik Nordenskiöld, and also being absent from St Petersburg during a period of new authoritarian rule over Finland. He examined the offer carefully and read all the reports of previous, similar, expeditions on which he could lay his hands. Only then did he accept the assignment, albeit in his customary calm and deliberate manner.

The mission of what was later to become known as 'Mannerheim's Asian Ride' was to gather geographic information and military intelligence in the Chinese provinces of Sinkiang, Kansu and in particular about the provinces of Shensi, Honan and Shansi that lie south of the Great Wall. His journey covered more than 8,500 miles, almost all of them on horseback. Initially, the expedition was combined with another led by Professor Paul Pelliot, of the French Ecole d'Extrème Orient in Hanoi, so as to provide some disguise for the true purpose of Mannerheim's journey. The two men did not get on well, however, and their routes diverged after they reached Kashgar 500 miles from their starting point. It was considered essential for the collaboration of the Chinese authorities in the provinces through which Mannerheim would travel that his status as a Russian officer should remain unknown. He therefore travelled on a Finnish passport but the ruse failed to deceive the Chinese. On reaching Kashgar, he was presented with a Chinese laissez-passer made out to 'the Russian subject the Finn Baron Mannerheim'.

The expedition proved a striking success and brought Mannerheim to the personal attention of Czar Nicholas II. In spite of occasional bouts of ill-health inevitable on such a journey at that time, he maintained a meticulous diary of all he encountered. He corrected and in some cases entirely redrew the maps of the regions through which he passed, recording at the same time each area's potential for military operations, including the type of ground surface, the availability of local transport and fodder for horses. He travelled from Kaifeng, the capital of Honan province, by train to Taiyuan and then for an audience with the exiled Dalai Lama at the monastery of Utaishan, to become – it is believed – the first European to be so received.

On his eventual return to St Petersburg in 1908, Mannerheim was sent for by Czar Nicholas who expressed his wish to hear an account of the two-year reconnaissance at first hand. But the new cartography and intelligence were secreted away by the Russian General Staff. It was not until thirty years later, when Mannerheim was commander-in-chief of the Finnish forces engaged in the Winter War, that the diary of the Asian Ride was published in Finland. His contemporary report on the expedition was completed by October 1908 and the new year of 1909 saw Mannerheim's long-awaited appointment to a regimental command. This was of the 13th Vladimir Uhlan (lancer) Regiment of Grand Duke Michael Nikolayevich, a cousin of the Czar.

Although the Asian Ride was aside from the mainstream of his military career, it would be a mistake to underestimate its influence on Mannerheim in the most testing times of his life that still lay ahead. The hardship of the journey and his patient determination to overcome all the obstacles of the route are certainly significant. Perhaps more so was the sense of personal isolation in bleak and dangerous circumstances. No man knows the loneliness of command until he experiences the extreme demands that great responsibility exerts when lives and perhaps the future of a nation are at stake. Whatever the value of the military intelligence gathered on that epic journey, it must have been of only small account in comparison with what Mannerheim himself gained, in preparation for the trials ahead.

The immediate future appeared both stimulating and enjoyable. The 13th Uhlans were stationed some twenty-five miles east of Warsaw, in then Russian Poland. Mannerheim was eager to put into practice the active service experience he had gained in Manchuria. He introduced a completely fresh training schedule for his new regiment with special emphasis on dismounted action and marksmanship. These were military attributes that were not particularly highly prized by the cavalry arm of any nation at that time. Mannerheim's personal dedication to the teaching of these skills and his personal example soon won over the enthusiasm of his new command. This success brought an unexpected reward. In February 1911 he was offered command of His Majesty's Life Guard Uhlan Regiment which, as a regiment of the Guard, carried the rank of major-general. Mannerheim accepted with delight and transferred to the Independent Guards Cavalry Brigade stationed in Warsaw.

The next three years were probably the happiest of Mannerheim's Russian military career. Being a major-general of the Guards Cavalry entitled him to be appointed to the Emperor's suite, which was both prestigious and influential. He applied his training methods to his new regiment and was called to command the brigade on manoeuvres on several occasions. He was offered a cuirassier cavalry brigade in 1913 but turned it down in the hope of being selected for the Guards Cavalry Brigade in which his regiment continued to serve. His patience was rewarded and he received that appointment in January 1914.

One cannot help but wonder as to the thoughts of this now worldly-wise and politically aware but still youthful general during that fateful summer before the descent into world war began. He could look with experience beyond the confines of regimental daily life to the awful perils that were threatened by Great Power rivalry in Europe. On 29 July, just one month after the assassination of Archduke Ferdinand of Austro-Hungary in Sarajevo, Mannerheim was ordered to mobilize his brigade and move it to the frontier with Austrian Galicia. Austro-Hungary declared war on Russia on 6 August 1914. Mannerheim's cavalry brigade was placed under command of Prince Tumanov's cavalry corps, tasked to cover the deployment of the Russian 4th Army advancing against the Austrians.

The early clash of forces in 1914 favoured those that were trained to value the ground, to deploy infantry, cavalry and artillery with skilful cohesion and to appreciate the devastating effect of machine-gun fire. Mannerheim's training for dismounted cavalry action saved him casualties and enhanced his reputation as a competent tactician. He commanded his brigade in the battles against the Austrians at Ivangorod, in October 1914, and reached as far west as Kraków, on the River Vistula, in November. This marked the limit of the Russian advance before the Austro-German Carpathian offensive of January 1915 led to a regrouping of the Russian forces. In the course of these changes Mannerheim was moved to command the 12th Cavalry Division.

Except for three periods as acting commander of the II Cavalry Corps, Mannerheim was to command 12th Cavalry Division until June 1917. The two intervening years saw the hardest fighting against the German and Austrian advance into Poland and Romania, with the Russian Army forced back onto the defensive and under constantly increasing pressure. At first the four regiments of the 12th Cavalry Division compared Mannerheim unfavourably with General Aleksey Kaledin, who had led them with success until wounded. Mannerheim, with his still thick 'Swedish' accent in Russian and closely controlled manner, appeared both aloof and foreign to the largely Ukrainian peasant troopers and battle-experienced officers. It was not until they saw the aloofness manifested into absolute steadiness under fire and his care for the lives of his men and their horses, whatever the pressures of the moment, that he was accepted as a worthy successor to Kaledin.

A divisional command is probably the highest, in any army, in which a general can have an intimate knowledge of every one of his regiments and supporting units, while also having command over fighting elements appropriate to any phase of war. The classic duties of a cavalry division were advance to make contact with the enemy, reconnaissance, protection of an exposed flank and, most important of all, swift and decisive exploitation of an enemy's tactical defeat or perceived weakness in his dispositions. Every one of these tasks places men and horses under severe physical strain due to the constant need to cover ground against time.

12th Cavalry Division formed part of II Cavalry Corps and comprised four cavalry regiments and two batteries of horse-drawn light artillery but no integral infantry unit. It was thus able to move quickly but unable to hold ground for long without infantry support. Twice Mannerheim found himself required to hold a bridgehead south of the River Dniestr, in March and again in April 1915. On each occasion lack of infantry forced him to withdraw his division. Of all the main phases of war, withdrawal while in close contact with the enemy requires the closest control, if casualties are to be kept low and the withdrawal is not to become a rout. Secure withdrawal was achieved on both occasions and, with his division switched to defence of a sector of the Dniestr front, Mannerheim was placed in command of II Cavalry Corps for the first time in the spring of 1915.

That summer ended with a return of rheumatism to the commander of 12th Cavalry Division but also with invaluable battle experience gained. Mannerheim had been in command of II Cavalry Corps as part of the Russian 9th Army in an attempt to bring pressure on the flank of the German offensive against Gorlice. The latter was eventually to break the whole of the Russian front in the region of Galicia taken in the earlier fighting to the west of the Ukrainian frontier. Subsequently, Mannerheim's division covered the withdrawal of the Russian XI (infantry) Corps over the Dniestr and that of XXII Corps over the Gnila Lipa tributary in June. A retaliatory attack by II Cavalry Corps across the Dniestr in July proved incapable of exploitation, chiefly due to the inexperience of the irregular cavalry division that was intended to provide 12th Division with support. Mannerheim commanded the corps during the defensive battles on the Dniestr and Sereth rivers during the autumn and defeated a German infantry force by a totally unexpected cavalry night attack in October.

After leave in Finland in early 1916, Mannerheim returned to command of 12th Cavalry Division in time for a fresh Russian offensive against the Austrians. This met with initial success and 12th Cavalry Division was able to exploit General Brusilov's breakthrough by forced marches through the broken Austrian defence. Although intervention by German divisions halted the Russian advance, much territory was gained and Romania joined the war on the side of the Entente Powers. Mannerheim gained further valuable experience during the second part of this offensive, especially in the confused fighting that followed the German intervention. On several occasions his division was required to guard an exposed flank to permit infantry regrouping or to relieve pressure by flank counter-attacks. The Romanians were ill-prepared for war, however, and Brusilov ordered the 12th Cavalry and another division to march south to their aid in October 1916. Mannerheim was able to observe at first hand the folly of a small nation entering a war on the side of a great power without adequate preparation and resources. Perhaps, of all his war experience until 1917, the sight of a shattered Romanian Army and country had the most far-reaching influence on his future strategic thinking.

The winter of 1916-17 found Mannerheim again on leave in Helsinki. While passing through the Russian capital, he witnessed the onset of the revolution, followed by the collapse of order and morale in the Army. Even so, 12th Cavalry Division were still well-disciplined on his return, probably because they were on foreign territory and far away from the areas of unrest in Russia. Mannerheim was promoted to lieutenant-general in May 1917 and appointed to command of VI Cavalry Corps in June. By this time the all-pervading atmosphere of unrest had reached the Russian troops in Romania. The summer was spent in the line against Austro-German divisions but without any attempt to initiate any offensive.

The widening collapse of military order in Russian units at the front made Mannerheim ask himself whether the time had not arrived for him to end his Russian service and return to his homeland.

As in other key moments in his life, it seems as if Providence took a hand in deciding the course of events. He was exercising a new horse one morning in October 1917 when the horse fell and Mannerheim put his leg out of joint. The headquarters medical officer insisted on a two months' rest. Next day the corps commander said goodbye to his staff and left for Odessa for treatment and recuperation. It was there that he received a telegram from the by then commander-in-chief of the Russian Army, General Nikolai Dukhonin, which relieved him of command of VI Cavalry Corps and placed him on the Army Reserve 'on account of political conflicts'.

There was no further ground for hesitation, no matter what his loyalties to Russia may have been. He left Odessa on 3 December and travelled through a turbulent Petrograd to reach Helsinki on 18 December.

3
The Red Offensives

Turmoil threatened Helsinki in December 1917. The Senate had declared independence from revolutionary Russia on the 6th of the month but recognition was not immediately forthcoming from Petrograd or from anywhere else abroad. The new Finnish government of the veteran politician Pehr Evind Svinhufvud recognized that they had but a tenuous hold over swiftly moving events. The Red Guards had mobilized on 10 November and were receiving arms and support from troops of the Russian garrisons. The soldiers' committees in control of the latter fostered ill-discipline and urged revolution on the Finnish peasant farmers and factory workers.

Concerned by agitation from the Social Democrats only narrowly defeated in the recent parliamentary elections, Svinhufvud led a delegation to Petrograd and secured Lenin's acceptance of Finnish independence. Although this was to take effect promptly, from 31 December 1917, Lenin's acquiescence was almost certainly less benign than it outwardly appeared; the architect of one revolution wished to see another rise in the country which had given him shelter from Kerensky's police the previous summer. In this hope he was ultimately to be disappointed but, in the meantime, moderate Finns still faced the future anxiously. Welcome recognition of independent Finland by Britain and France followed Svinhufvud's announcement of Lenin's assent to the Senate on 7 January 1918. This was not matched, however, by any order from Petrograd for withdrawal of the still 40,000-strong Russian garrison or any relaxation of the tensions induced by Red Guard units across much of the south and south-east of the country.

A military committee of retired or recently returned Finnish officers was set up to prepare measures to expel the increasingly troublesome Russian troops. After attending Svinhufvud's declaration of independence of 7 January, Lieutenant-General Gustaf Mannerheim was invited to join this committee. He had been back in his homeland from Russia for less than three weeks and was deeply concerned by the situation fast developing around him. A decision to form a national army, to restore order and evict those Russians who could not otherwise be persuaded to leave, was taken by the Finnish Parliament on 13 January. Measures continued to be discussed by the military committee but Mannerheim found these deliberations vague and indecisive. He also sensed the acute vulnerability of the capital to revolutionary takeover. Mannerheim's assessment was political as well as military. When returning to the Romanian front through Petrograd in March 1917, he had witnessed the power of the mob to reduce a government to impotence.

General Claës Charpentier, the chairman of the military committee, submitted his resignation on 15 January and the Government immediately invited Mannerheim to replace him. Next day Svinhufvud and Mannerheim met in private in the Senate chamber to discuss how Finland's fragile independence might best be defended. Their discussion concluded with Mannerheim receiving authority to raise a national army based initially on the Suojeluskaarti, the units of which were soon to become known as the White Guards.

Mannerheim's first priority was to establish a rallying point that could become an alternative seat of authority should Helsinki fall to the Reds. He chose with consummate perception; indeed it could be argued that his choice had a decisive influence on the course of the war that followed. Ostrobothnia was then and to some extent remains today a province of staunchly independent opinion. Radical socialism had failed to gain any foothold in the southern, more populated area which lies between the coast of the Gulf of Bothnia and the watershed of the Soumenselkä range of hills. On this coast stands the port of Vaasa, a mere sixty-five miles by sea from Sweden and forty-five from the railway junction of Seinäjoki, which had rail links to the most important communication and population centres of the country. On 18 January Mannerheim confronted the military committee with his own resignation and the remark, 'If you gentlemen can travel north on the overnight train this evening, you should do so.' The overnight train carried him, four members of the military committee and a handful of senators north to Vaasa.

It would be a mistake to imagine that Mannerheim arrived in Ostrobothnia on a wave of popular enthusiasm. Although he carried Svinhufvud's authority to raise a national army, he was completely unknown to the authorities in Vaasa. Even many of the recalled officers who did know him harboured suspicions of this calm and self-confident Finn who had served the Czar for thirty years. Aware that hard work keeps idle speculation in check, Mannerheim set his new subordinates to gather details of White Guard strengths and locations, while summoning other ex-officers to join him at Vaasa. Amongst these came Major-General Ernst Löfström, who had served in Russia and whose competence impressed Mannerheim. Hard and sensibly directed work had the required effect. Murmurings against the 'Russian general' quickly died away when his remaining detractors perceived his dedication and leadership.

On the very day that Mannerheim arrived in Vaasa, a skirmish between Red and White Guards broke out in the port and railway junction of Viipuri, which stands at the head of the Karelian Isthmus and contained the headquarters of XLII Army Corps – supposedly commanding the Russian garrisons. Precipitately, some of the local White Guards attempted to disarm the local Red Guards but failed and were obliged to flee from the city. This left the strategically important gateway from Petrograd under the exclusive control of the Red Guards and their Russian revolutionary supporters.

The next week saw an acceleration in the pace of hostilities. A confrontation between Mannerheim's headquarters and the Russian garrison from 432nd Regiment in Vaasa occurred on 24 January. This was effectively faced down but Mannerheim realized that he would have to move quickly and decisively to secure his base in Ostrobothnia. Events began to play into his hands from that day onwards, politically if not militarily. The extremist wing of the Social Democrat party, frustrated by the hesitancy of their own leadership, established an executive committee on 25 January with authority to 'bring the class war to a successful conclusion'. The committee ordered the Red Guards to initiate local action from midnight on 26 January. The Russian garrison in Viipuri immediately declared their unequivocal support for the Red Guards. Whether this declaration was initiated by or even included headquarters XLII Army Corps is uncertain. The majority of the Senate still in Helsinki reacted decisively to the worsening situation. The Suojeluskaarti were declared Government troops from 25 January and Mannerheim appointed commander-in-chief

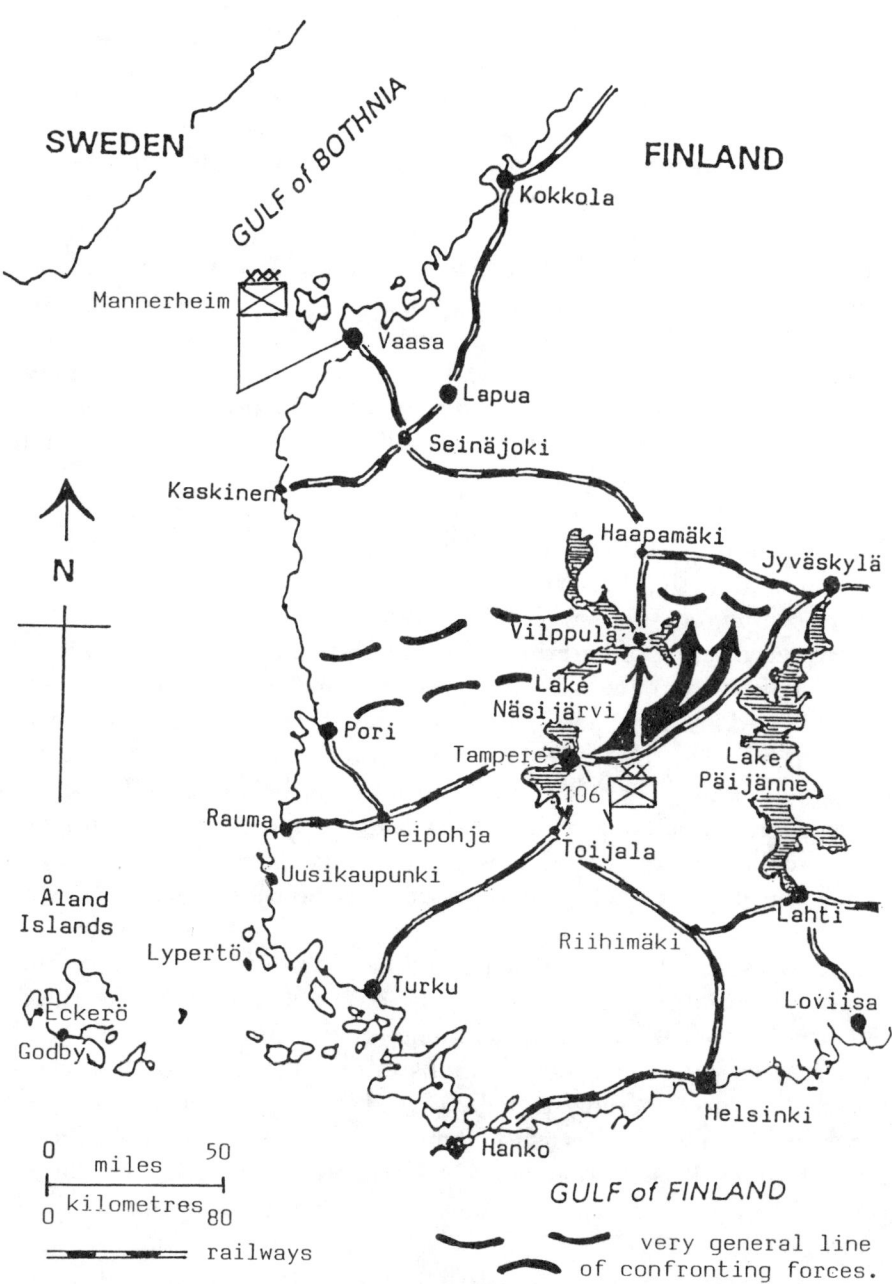

Map 3: Situation in South-Western Finland in January 1918

in northern Finland from the following day. He received the telegram of appointment in Vaasa via Sweden.

These were the two final acts of the Finnish Senate, as it was deposed by the Red Guards in Helsinki on 26 January 1918. Mannerheim's apprehension about the political security of the capital had been justified. Four senators had already joined him in Vaasa and Prime Minister Svinhufvud was later able to escape by sea from Helsinki to Tallinn, capital of Estonia. He and other senators who had escaped with him travelled to Germany to reach Vaasa two months later, on 24 March. In the meantime Mannerheim was left with a virtually free hand to deal with a situation of widespread insurrection. Whereas he had initially regarded the sullen Russian garrisons as his primary problem, the Red Guards in the industrial centres of the south were quick to respond to a call from the newly formed council of people's commissars, which had replaced the Senate, to remove all officials of the legitimate regime. While Mannerheim knew that he had to act quickly, securing his base in Ostrobothnia remained his first priority.

Through a series of carefully planned and calmly executed operations, which began before dawn on 28 January, the Russian garrisons in and around Vaasa were surrounded, disarmed and interned without bloodshed. There could scarcely have been a more encouraging augury for wider success, not least because the Russians surrendered some 8,000 rifles, thirty-four machine-guns and thirty-seven artillery pieces together with large quantities of ammunition. While the move to Vaasa had proved his political insight, it was Mannerheim's resolute refusal to launch larger-scale operations at that early stage that affirmed his military wisdom. His embryonic army comprised dispersed and largely makeshift groups of ill-armed but usually well-led local detachments of the Suojeluskaarti. Communications with these were tenuous in the extreme and, as yet, he had formed no coherent strategic plan. He therefore firmly resisted those of his subordinates who clamoured for immediate operations against other Russian garrisons and the Red Guards. Instead he pointed to the advantages of thorough preparation within a broad strategy.

Mannerheim was able to see that the politico-military situation across southern Finland had begun to evolve into a roughly discernible 'front' between the north and south. This division was a general reflection of the 'red belt' of Social Democrat supporters in the Red Guard-dominated industrial centres and areas of rural crofters that lay between them, which ran south-westwards from Vaasa towards Lake Ladoga. Helsinki remained under the complete control of the Red Guards, backed by disembarked units of the Russian Baltic Fleet. Rumours of Russian troop movements were rife and the railway from Petrograd, along which Russian reinforcements might come, was secure in enemy hands.

Appreciation of his own and the enemy's strengths and dispositions led to the formulation of Mannerheim's strategic plan. He would endeavour to hold the east-west line of the emerging front, while inflicting maximum casualties on such Russian or Red Guard units that chose to attack, and build up his own strength for a decisive offensive when he was ready and the enemy dispirited and weary. It was a strategy that he had some difficulty in persuading some of his hotter-headed subordinates to understand. They could see many opportunities for local tactical gains and consolidation of their own situation. Some local initiatives were taken against Mannerheim's instructions but his strategy and orders were followed in the main.

Map 3 (page 37) shows the line of the front in January 1918 across south-western Finland, between the coast and Lake Päijänne. The attitudes of the Russian garrisons in the region varied from active participation in operations against Finnish Government forces to one of indifference to a conflict that many felt was of little interest to them. A crucial factor in the effectiveness of such operations as were carried out was the degree of revolutionary zeal of the men finding themselves remaining in command or having leadership thrust upon them. The first to show his mettle was Colonel Michail Stepanovitch Svetjnikov, the commander of 106th Division with its headquarters at Tampere.

Svetjnikov was an experienced soldier who had become an ardent convert to Bolshevism during the summer of 1917. He was quick to appreciate the significance of the Finnish railway system in the forthcoming campaign, as it linked the main centres of population while having lateral lines both north and south of the front. Placing himself in command of the Red 'Western Army', consisting primarily of men from his own division but with a leavening of the more fervent local Red Guards, he decided to launch an attack northwards

against the Government forces holding Vilppula. His intention was
to take and then pass through Vilppula to the key railway junction at
Haapamäki. It was at this point that the north-south link from Tampere met the northern lateral railway from Vaasa through Jyväskylä
to Karelia. Control of Haapamäki junction would sever Mannerheim's lateral communications and divide his still-scattered forces
into two separate groups.

It was fortunate for the Government side that Svetjnikov was unable to persuade the greater part of the Tampere garrison to join
in this bold enterprise. Undeterred, he set off with a force roughly
equivalent to two battalions and on 4 February began the assault
with two companies each of 150 men astride the railway, with artillery support of two guns. He was probably correct to move swiftly
with relatively light forces, if only to attempt surprise and gain some
intelligence of the strength and resolve of the defenders of Vilppula.
When this initial foray was repulsed after six or so hours of fighting,
Svetjnikov paused to prepare a deliberate attack. This he launched
against Vilppula on 7 February with a force of 1,300 men, an armoured train, four guns and eight machine-guns, while other units of
his by then enlarged force made a right-flanking move round Lake
Näsijärvi along the road leading to the lateral railway to the east of
Haapamäki.

Svetjnikov's plan was tactically sound and well directed. Strong
frontal pressure on Vilppula was intended to deny the defenders
opportunity for significant redeployment to counter the flanking
force of some 5,300 infantry attempting ever-widening flanking
movements to the east. The White Guards defending Vilppula were
commanded by Colonel Martin Wetzer, a Finn who had served in the
Russian Imperial Army with Mannerheim. He quickly saw through
Svetjnikov's plan and switched enough troops to the flank to prevent
any serious threat to the railway east of Haapamäki. The battle
continued until 14 February, when the Reds called off their offensive
north of Tampere.

At much the same time as Svetjnikov's operations against Vilppula,
two other Red offensives had opened in south central and south-
eastern Finland. Together with the attack on Vilppula, these appear
to have formed elements of an overall strategy to seize control of
both main junctions on the northern lateral railway. This would
have broken up Mannerheim's dispersed forces into three isolated

groups, against which the Reds would have been able to concentrate their combined resources in turn.

It is difficult to be precisely certain who in the Red High Command was responsible for devising this plan. The Red Commander-in-Chief at the time was Eero Haapalainen. This one-time journalist and ardent revolutionary had replaced Ali Aaltonen, a Finn who had served in the Russian Imperial Army with the rank of lieutenant. Haapalainen had no military experience, so it seems probable that Svetjnikov should have the credit. He alone of the Russian senior officers in Finland threw in his lot whole-heartedly with the Finnish revolutionaries. It is also significant that the period of Svetjnikov's field command marked the only phase of the war when the Reds embarked on an apparently coherent strategic initiative. After its failure, the Russian colonel was moved to become adviser to the Red Guard headquarters in Helsinki.

The Red offensive in south central Finland began in earnest on 7 February in the Savo district between Lake Päijänne and the extensive waters of the Lake Saimaa complex to the east. As may be seen from Map 4 (overleaf), the railway ran from Kouvola on the southern lateral line to the junction with the northern lateral line at Pieksämäki. The line continued westwards from there through Jyväskylä to Haapamäki, which was the goal of Svetjnikov's attack in the west. The first thrust of the Savo offensive was made from Kouvola towards Mikkeli, where the local Red Guards had surrended to the local White Guards on 29 January.

There had been inconclusive skirmishes in the same region during the previous two weeks. A tentative advance of Red Guards from Varkaus towards Pieksämäki had been repulsed by White Guards there on 31 January. The Reds had withdrawn into Varkaus from where they continued to threaten the rear of Government troops which had begun to move southwards from Mikkeli. This force succeeded in occupying the railway station at Mäntyharju on 2 February and so blocked the planned Red advance northwards from Kouvola. At this point it appeared that the Government forces had stolen the initiative for control of the railways in the Savo district. The Reds counter-attacked on 7 February, however, with a spearhead of Russian-conscripted Latvians supported by an improvised armoured train. There was a hard fight to retain Mäntyharju but the numerically superior Red forces recaptured the town by nightfall.

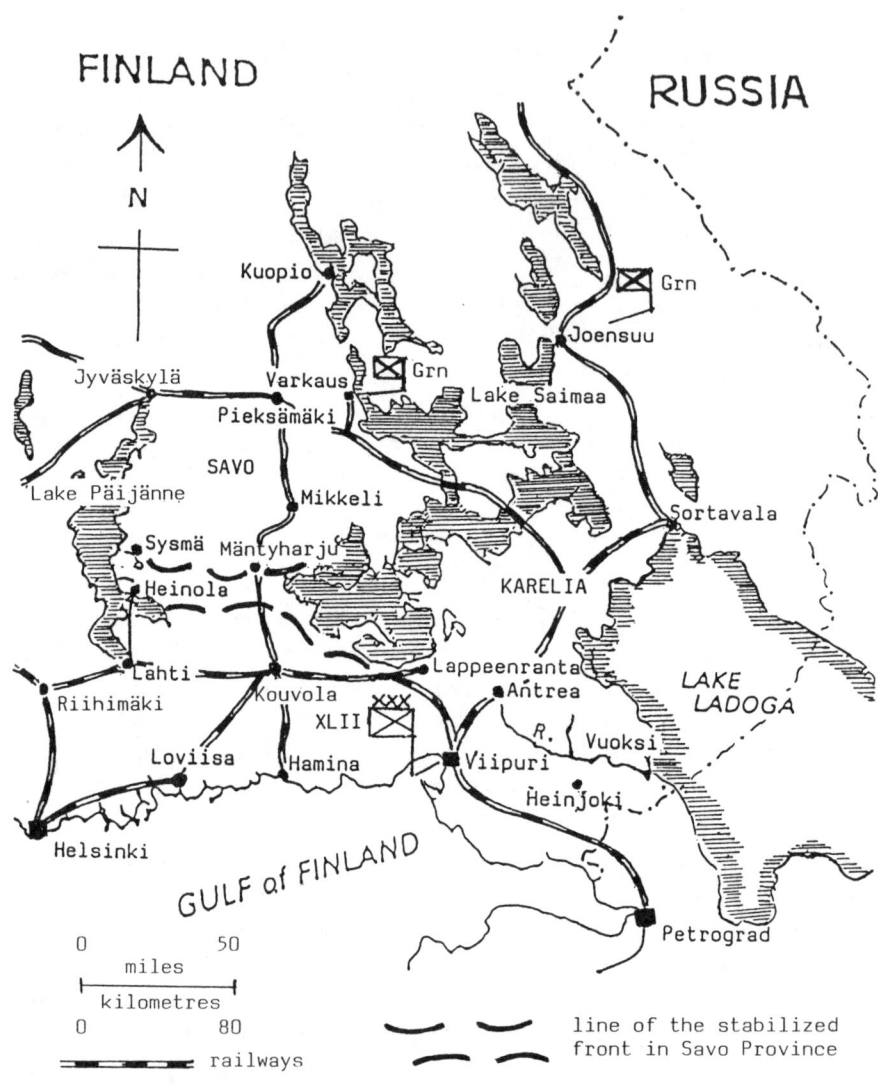

Map 4: Area of fighting in Savo Province and Karelia in Jan-Feb 1918

With the local initiative now regained, Aleksei Osipov, from the Russian Tuckum Regiment, in command of a combined Russian, Red Guard and Latvian force, launched an infantry attack with artillery support northwards from Mäntyharju on 11 February. The Government force had used the intervening three days to good effect preparing well-sited positions in and around Mikkeli. From these they were able to withstand the Red attack. It was at this time that Major-General Ernst Löfström arrived with orders from Mannerheim to take command of the Savo front. Löfström paused only for the arrival of reinforcements from the west before making his own attack. His troops recaptured Mäntyharju on 14 February. The Reds withdrew into Kouvola, leaving the railway to the north in Government hands.

In marked contrast to his opponents, Löfström did not rest after the battle for Mäntyharju but turned his attention northwards towards Varkaus from where the Reds still menaced his eastern flank and connections with Government troops in Karelia. He advanced on the town with a force of six infantry companies suppported by several machine-guns on 20 February. Red resistance was fierce from well-placed positions around the mills in the western outskirts, but Varkaus finally fell to Löfström's men on the evening of 21 February. Conscious that his reinforcements were urgently needed elsewhere, Löfström next reacted quickly to a Red attack on Sysmä, a small town on his western flank close to the shore of Lake Päijänne. He successfully regained control of Sysmä but a subsequent drive southwards towards Lahti on the railway between Kouvola and Riihimäki was halted by stiff Red force resistance at Heinola. Having suffered unexpectedly severe casualties in an attempt to force his way through Heinola and keenly aware of the need to conserve his strength, Löfström called off the Heinola attack. His front then stabilized along a line just to the south of Mäntyharju, spanning the shortest distance between Lakes Päijänne and Saimaa.

The most easterly of the Red offensives aimed to establish complete control over the Karelian Isthmus and so the vital rail link from Petrograd. It was from Viipuri that Lieutenant-General Nadezhny, commanding XLII Army Corps, and his soldiers' committee had declared their support for the Red Guards in January. Nadezhny remained apprehensive of Government forces' intentions and reacted to Mannerheim's pre-dawn moves against Russian garrisons in

Ostrobothnia on 28 January by cautiously ordering Svetjnikov to withdraw his 106th Division to Viipuri. This was with a view to making the rail link to Petrograd secure and avoiding further widespread capitulations of Russian troops with their weapons. As has been explained, Svetjnikov was made of sterner stuff and launched his first offensive against Vilppula instead.

Operations in Karelia in January and early February 1918 were notable as being the first in which the Government troops operated under command of Jäger officers. On 23 January Captain Woldemar Hägglund was appointed to command of all the Suojeluskaarti units in the Viipuri district. It was his attempt to disarm the Red Guards in Viipuri that had actually opened hostilities between the two sides. Following an initial setback he gathered his men together and concentrated them at Antrea, some twenty miles north of the Viipuri-Petrograd railway, by the end of January. Hägglund was joined by Captain Aarne Sihvo on 2 February with instructions from Mannerheim to take command of all Government troops on the Karelian front.

The outposts of the Government force in the Isthmus ran along a line to the south of the River Vuoksi. These were perceived by General Nadezhny and the Red forces in Viipuri as a serious threat to the rail link with Petrograd and also with Varkaus and Joensuu, both of which were still at that time in the hands of the Reds. When Sihvo began to push forward patrols towards Lappeenranta and Viipuri in early February, Nadezhny decided to launch an offensive to drive the Government troops back over the Vuoksi. After some skirmishing on the line of outposts until 10 February, a force of 1,200 Red Guards with 270 Russians and four artillery pieces attacked on 11 February with the aim of capturing the Antrea bridgehead over the river.

This resulted in a particularly hard fight. The Reds had a slight numerical superiority in trained infantry, even if they were not especially highly motivated troops, and artillery support of which Sihvo had virtually none. The balance was turned by the sudden intervention of another improvised armoured train, this time by the Government side, the fire from which threw the attackers into some confusion. It was particularly galling for Nadezhny to discover that Sihvo had captured the train from his own men and then not lost a moment before using it against them. Sihvo followed up this Red reverse by launching a counterattack on 12 February. This gained some ground to the south of Antrea but the Reds renewed their assault the following morning. Sihvo held his ground and took advantage of the Red concentration against Antrea to extend his left flank as far as Heinjoki by nightfall.

Not all the operations initiated by the Government side ended well during this first phase of the war. The White Guard units in the previous capital port city of Turku on the south-west coast had reached a strength of over 600 men by the end of January. They were commanded by Captain Christian Fabritius who, being a man of initiative, prepared plans for the disarming of the Russian garrisons at Lypertö and Rauma. (See Map 3 on page 37.) The force for this intended operation assembled at Uusikaupunki to the north of Turku, at which point it adopted the title 'The Uusikaupunki Corps'. Before this nobly named formation could get to grips with the enemy, Fabritius was replaced by one Colonel V. J. Forssell who quite clearly outranked him.

Forssell judged the proposed expeditions to Lypertö and Rauma too hazardous. He therefore countermanded the orders that Fabritius had issued and ordered the White Guards at Rauma to join him at Uusikaupunki. They came, but once there the whole force was able to achieve very little beyond acting as a vague threat to the rear of Colonel Svetjnikov's self-styled 'Western Army' which was then preparing to launch its attacks against Tampere. Impatient to see the force he had raised playing a useful part in operations, Fabritius, who had remained as Forssell's chief of staff, urged his commander to march over the ice and disarm the Russians in occupation of the Åland Islands.

In spite of a snowstorm that accompanied the corps on its icy march, the Russians at Godby surrendered to them on 15 February. Eight field guns, ninety rifles and a large stock of ammunition were also taken. Due to a shortage of weapons on the mainland, only 300 men of the corps had crossed the ice to the Ålands. This small force found itself in difficulty when the Swedish cruiser *Thor* anchored off the port of Eckerö and her captain informed Fabritius, who was in command of the Ålands expedition, that the *Thor* had come to evacuate all civilians from the islands and prevent fighting between the Finns and the Russian garrison.

The true Swedish intention was to wrest control of the Åland

Islands from Finland during the period of uncertainty. In this they were very nearly successful. After a further encounter with the Russian garrison, the corps captured another 150 rifles and a machine-gun, at which point those of the residents of the islands who had not joined the corps requested both the Russians and the White Guards to leave. In this situation Fabritius was tricked by a telegram, purporting to come from Mannerheim, seeking Swedish assistance in returning the Uusikaupunki corps to Government-controlled Finland via Sweden. He complied in good faith. The weapons of the corps and those they had taken from the Russians he left behind.

Mannerheim had indeed sent a telegram instructing Fabritius and his men to remain on the Åland Islands but the message was never delivered. Fabritius and the survivors of the corps were eventually repatriated to Finland at the end of February, while the Russian garrison was allowed several weeks to pack up and leave. This strange little incident is chiefly of note as an indication of the part played by the Åland Islands in Finno-Swedish relations at this stage and in later years. The incident itself resulted in no change to the status of the islands after the war, although they became demilitarized under terms of the Treaty of Dorpat signed by Finland and the Soviet Union in 1920.

In all three of the failed Red offensives – north of Tampere, in Savo province and in Karelia – Russian troops had taken the leading role during the initial stages. While they had continued for longer in this role in Karelia, the Red Guards soon took over the leadership in the western and central regions. With the sole exception of Svetjnikov's setpiece attack to take or bypass Tampere from 7 to 14 February, the offensives were characterized by hasty preparation by the Reds, lack of real determination in the face of tenacious resistance by Government troops and, probably most important of all, failure to apply their superior strength and firepower.

The consequent reverses caused the Red High Command to pause to review their organization and tactics. They took only one week for this, from 14 to 21 February, but the breathing space also gave Mannerheim the opportunity he sought to strengthen and redeploy the Suojeluskaarti, the experienced officers and men of 27th Jäger Battalion and the new conscripts who came trooping in at the end of February and beginning of March. The Reds had missed their early chance to snatch victory through neglect of one of the main principles of war: concentration of effort and resources. It was a failure that was to cost them the war and many of them their lives.

4
Mixed Fortunes in the Field

That temptress 'the welcome pause' has denied many a commander his strategic goal. The Red Guards and their Russian allies withdrew to lick their wounds amd rethink tactics after sharp reverses in January and early February 1918. The Government forces' commander-in-chief, General Mannerheim, seized this opportunity to gather his emerging army for a decisive offensive. By this point he knew that his primary strategic aim must be to secure control over the Karelian Isthmus in south-east Finland. It was from there, at the port city of Viipuri, that command over Russian troops in Finland was exercised. More importantly, the Isthmus and the Viipuri-Petrograd railway provided a link between the Russian commander of XLII Army Corps, General Nadezhny, and Lenin's Bolshevik government in the now-Soviet capital. The railway line would also be the means of any Russian troop reinforcement.

Two immediate factors limited Mannerheim's ability to launch an advance in the Karelian sector. First, he needed to strengthen his command structure by introducing experienced officers and the German-trained officers and men of the 27th Jäger Battalion. Secondly, the Vaasa-Viipuri railway, on which any Karelian offensive would depend for supply, was still seriously threatened by enemy forces to the immediate south at Tampere. In mid-February Mannerheim was still unaware that his Finnish political colleagues were, with the best of intentions, engineering a third and even more urgent distraction of his attention from Karelia.

From the outset of his involvement in the struggle for Finland's independence, Mannerheim had been convinced that the prize must be won by Finland alone. This was no reflection of any extreme chauvinism or sentimental attachment on his part. He considered that for his country to join the ranks of free and independent nations with self-confidence they must achieve that status by their own efforts. He was especially opposed to any German participation in Finland's battles against either external or internal enemies. He recognized that many of his countrymen, especially of the middle and upper classes, looked towards Germany as their natural ally against the Russians. Having fought against the Germans for three years, Mannerheim also had a hard-headed professional respect for their military capability, but this did not change his view.

From mid-February Mannerheim was preoccupied with preparations for an early March offensive, first to defeat Red Guard and Russian troops threatening the railway running north of Tampere and then to use that rail link to reinforce Karelia. He was therefore very surprised to receive information on 3 March from the German representative to the acting Finnish Government in Vaasa that the German Government had acceded to a request for a German expeditionary force to support him. This news had significant politico-strategic implications, none of which he welcomed. There can be no doubt that the request for German military support had originated from Finnish sources, although its legitimacy and wisdom are more questionable. Prime Minister Svinhufvud, while still in hiding in Helsinki after the overthrow of the Senate, sent a message to the Finnish ambassador in Berlin, Edvard Hjelt, instructing him to seek foreign intervention for the liberation of southern Finland. This message, despatched on 15 February, took some time to reach Berlin and was meanwhile overtaken by events. Hjelt, acting largely on his own initiative but in tune with various sympathies at home, had applied to the German General Staff for help. The day before Svinhufvud's message left Helsinki, Berlin invited Hjelt to submit a formal request for German military assistance. This he duly did and on 21 February his request was approved.

It can be argued that Hjelt fell into a trap that the Germans had made ready for him. Collapse of the Russo-German peace talks at Brest-Litovsk on 18 February was closely followed by a German offensive into the Russian Baltic provinces. Germany needed to threaten Russian interests from a fresh direction in order to bring Lenin to terms. Naively, but with his own country's interests uppermost in his mind, Hjelt provided exactly the opportunity that Germany sought.

On hearing the news of the German intervention Mannerheim made two appreciations, both of which were to prove correct. The

Germans would enter Finland through the Finnish ports on the Gulf of Finland and their initial objectives would be the occupation of Helsinki and Viipuri. If the embryo Finnish Army were to play its proper part in the liberation of the country, there was not a moment to be lost. As a start, a swift victory over the Red Guard and Russian revolutionary volunteers at Tampere was imperative to demonstrate that the Germans were merely a supporting element. The Finnish Senate recognized this point too and insisted, during negotiations with Germany, that a Finn must remain in charge of the war as a whole. This was given emphasis by the promotion of Mannerheim to the rank of general of cavalry, to which only a field-marshal would be superior.

The Russian 106th Division was still based in Tampere and other nearby towns. Mannerheim's intelligence network in western Finland reported a total of 25,000 Red Guards and Russian troops deployed in the area between the coast of the Gulf of Bothnia and Lake Päijänne. Colonel Svetjnikov, who had commanded 106th Division in the first Red offensive, was by now chief of staff to Eero Haapalainen, the elected but militarily inexperienced commander-in-chief of the Red forces in Finland.

Svetjnikov had earlier appreciated the importance of the northern lateral railway through Haapamäki, fifty miles north of Tampere. The Red forces needed to take Haapamäki to deny Mannerheim contact with his troops in the Savo and Karelian sectors, then to bottle up his headquarters and several thousand Government troops in south Ostrobothnia. Rumours of a possible German intervention added urgency to Svetjnikov's intentions, as did news of the despatch of the main body of 27th Jäger Battalion by sea from Germany for Vaasa on 13 February. With the Jägers came two of their German company commanders, Captains Eduard Ausfeld and Ulrich von Coler. These two were to command Finnish battalions with distinction in the fighting that followed. Although only 1,500 strong, the 27th Jäger Battalion combined three characteristics that, in sum, were denied to any other unit on either side. They were trained professional soldiers, battle-hardened and highly motivated. Skilfully handled, they could be used by Mannerheim to reap rewards out of all proportion to their numbers.

In consequence of these new pressures, the Reds attacked for a second time before they were fully prepared or had a properly

LEFT Colonel Michail Stepanovitch Svetjnikov, commander of the Russian 106th Division in 1917-18. An ardent Bolshevik, he led the first Red offensive against the Government force in Vilppula in February 1918. RIGHT Ivar Monthén sending secret coded signals to the White Army in the north from Helsinki, through Estonia, after the Red Guards seized the capital.

Captain Woldemar Hägglund (left), Captain Aarne Sihvo and a third Jäger officer. Both Hägglund and Sihvo became general officers, Sihvo serving twice as commander-in-chief 1926-33 and again in 1946-53.

ABOVE, LEFT. Colonel Martin Wetzer, a Finn formerly of the Imperial Russian Army, who commanded the Häme Group of White Guards in Vilppula during the first Red offensive. He later commanded Army Corps West as a major-general. RIGHT Colonel Ernst Linder, a Swedish officer who commanded the Satakunta group of Government troops between the west coast of Finland and Lake Kyrös-järvi. He later commanded the Savo Group of Government troops as a major-general. BELOW A group of Russian troops and Finnish Red Guards 1918. The banners read, 'Live free, Finnish people. Unite all nations, in a free state of holy work', and 'Salutations to free Finland and Russia'.

The first aircraft of the Finnish Air Force, a Thulin Type D presented by Swedish Count Erik von Rosen in February 1918. The blue swastika marking was von Rosen's personal good luck emblem, with no political significance.

A group of Red Guards at Mäntsälä 1918. All are armed with Russian M1891 Mosin-Nagant rifles and bayonets other than the man fourth from the left, who has the shorter M95 Winchester rifle.

ABOVE, LEFT Colonel Karl Wilkman, a Finn formerly of the Imperial Russian Army who commanded the Jämsä Group during Mannerheim's March 1918 offensive and, as a major-general, a division-sized force in the Karelian Isthmus. RIGHT Hugo Salmela, commander of the Red Guards in the western sector. Although without any military training, he displayed considerable tactical insight as well as personal courage. He died of wounds received while organizing the final defence of Tampere on 28 March 1918. BELOW A squadron of the Uusimaa Dragoons in a school yard in the Töölö district of Helsinki, where they established camp after the capital was retaken.

ABOVE Heikki Kaljunen, the ruthless leader of a group of Red Guards in the Karelian Isthmus who shot a number of White Guard prisoners taken at Terijoki railway station. BELOW, LEFT Warrant Officers Perttula and Uotila of the 1st Jäger Artillery Battalion at Mikkeli in formal pose against a photographer's backdrop, such as was frequently used throughout Europe at the time. RIGHT Colonel Harald Hjalmarson, the Swedish officer in command of the Virrat detachment during Mannerheim's offensive of March 1918.

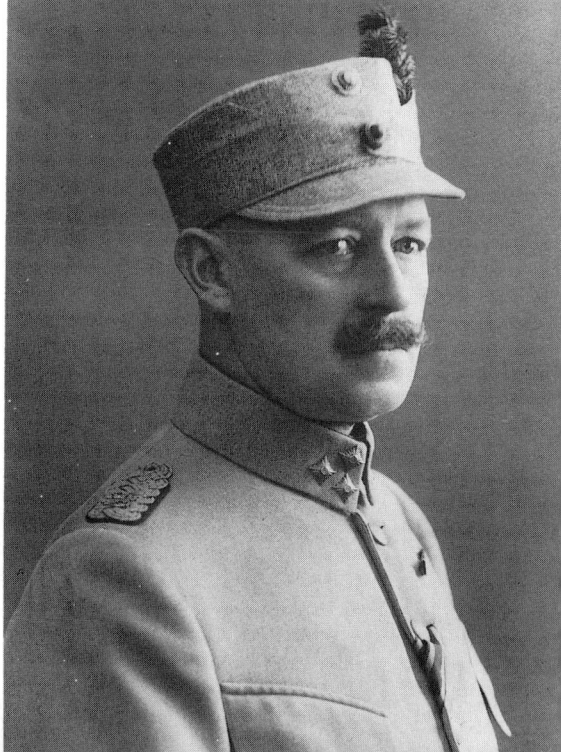

ABOVE Officers of No. 4 Company of the White Guards Mänttä battalion: Verner Kaatiala (company commander, centre), Vilo Vuorikoski (company sergeant-major on his right) and platoon commanders Esa Harju, August Luoma and Kalle Ritokangas. The cylindrical objects on their belts are hand grenades. BELOW Red Guard prisoners and White Guards outside the railway station in Tampere after the surrender of the city on 5 April 1918.

ABOVE, LEFT Major-General Count Rüdiger von der Goltz, commander of the German Ostsee Division, arriving at Mannerheim's headquarters in Mikkeli, May 1918. Mannerheim is accompanied by Major-General Nickolai Mexmontan, the Inspector of Training (in fur hat) and Major-General Ernst Linder (extreme right). RIGHT The Borgström tobacco factory in Helsinki after being shelled by the German cruiser squadron under command of Admiral Hugo Meurer in April 1918. BELOW An armoured train manned by troops of the German Ostsee Division near Hämeenlinna, north of Helsinki.

ABOVE, LEFT Major-General Ernst Löfström, commander of the Army Corps East responsible for the defeat of the Russian troops and Red Guards in the Karelian Isthmus, April 1918. RIGHT Captain Yrjö Elfvengren, commander of 1st Keralia Regiment and architect of the defeat of Russian reinforcements sent to Rautu in early April 1918, accompanied by his adjutant. BELOW Some of the many artillery pieces abandoned by the Red garrison of Viipuri when the fortress fell to Government troops during the night of 28/29 April 1918.

coordinated plan. What may be conveniently termed the second Red offensive began on 21 February, with renewed attacks on two principal axes: the railway running north from Tampere to Vilppula, employing some 3,500 of the estimated 15,000 troops in that immediate sector, and a much larger-scale assault using 5,000 Red Guards and, according to one estimate, some 1,200 Russian troops against Government positions south of the River Vuoksi, in the Karelian sector.

Fighting was hard and prolonged in both sectors and Mannerheim, concerned for the security of his base for intended operations in Karelia, took the first opportunity to visit hard-pressed units there on 23 February. He travelled by train through Haapamäki and Pieksämäki. Then, after seeing the conflict at close quarters for himself, he issued the first of his historic Army Orders at the height of battle : 'Relying on our just and noble cause, relying on our brave men and self-sacrificing women, we will create a powerful and great Finland.' Mannerheim knew how to appreciate courage as well as how to demand it.

Confident that both the Vilppula and Karelia fronts would hold, which they did until the second Red offensive petered out on 11 March, Mannerheim returned by train post haste to Vaasa. There he found much to do. The main body of the 27th Jäger Battalion had reached the port on 25 February, their little convoy of ships, led by the Finnish icebreaker *Sampo* carving its way through the frozen surface of the Gulf of Bothnia. He reviewed the battalion in the main square of Vaasa on 26 February and, speaking in public for the first time in Finnish, the C-in-C greeted them with an address containing a carefully worded announcement: 'Finland's young army of the future sees in you its teachers and leaders to come. There now awaits you a great, glorious task – that of creating, over the whole of Finland, an army that can set Finland free.'

There were many under Mannerheim's command, including the majority of the returned Jägers themselves, who believed that best advantage could be drawn from this highly professional and experienced battalion by using it as a *force de frappe*, to stem an enemy advance or to spearhead an attack. Mannerheim's prudence and experience led him to an entirely different plan: he would use them as individual commanders and instructors in the army he required to defeat all of Finland's current enemies. What was more, the acting

Government had just handed him a legislative instrument to exact his purpose. On 18 February the Conscription Law of 1878 was invoked which gave him authority to call up sufficient men to form twenty-one battalions.

There were difficulties and objections of course, some individuals believing that they knew better than Mannerheim how best to employ the Jägers, but the C-in-C got his way. In the remaining days before the start of his planned offensive in mid-March, Mannerheim and his staff formed from his Russian-trained and Swedish officers, Jägers and civilian volunteers a fighting force of six infantry battalions, each of 600 men formed into three rifle companies and a machine-gun company, one cavalry regiment (the Uusimaa Dragoons), six two-gun batteries of 75 or 76 mm artillery and six demolition engineer companies. The latter were formed almost exclusively from enlisted volunteers.

These units were all in addition to the existing White Guard units which were ordered to form themselves into regiments, each of three battalions. This was easier said than done, not least because those in the Tampere and Vuoksi river sectors were heavily engaged in fighting the Reds. Some adopted the new organization quickly and effectively, for example the North Häme Regiment at Jämsä, which was part of Colonel Karl Wilkman's group of White Guards. Wilkman had returned from service with the Russian Imperial Army, like Löfström, Wetzer and Mannerheim himself. Since the early part of February Mannerheim had been receiving a most welcome addition to his force in the form of volunteers from Sweden. These were provided very largely in consequence of an initiative taken by Baron Johan Mannerheim, the C-in-C's younger brother, who had lived in Sweden for several years before 1914. When the Swedish Government declined to provide help to Finland on an official basis, Johan Mannerheim had formed the Friends of Finland. Swedish public opinion in support of this association had obliged the Swedish authorities to sanction volunteers from both within and outside the Swedish armed forces, to go to Finland to fight for the Government side.

Mannerheim responded with a request for officers and NCOs with special expertise or training. Early volunteers included Colonel Ernst Linder and artillery Captain Adolf Hamilton; the total of Swedish officers had reached twenty-five by mid-February. It was at this point and in view of the many Swedish volunteers clamouring to join him, that Mannerheim requested 200 NCOs as specialist instructors to his newly forming units, plus fifty artillerymen and fifty machine-gunners.

The Friends of Finland also set out to form a Swedish brigade of volunteers. Although records show that a total of 675 Swedes served in this unit during the course of the war, it never exceeded a strength of around 550 on the ground at any one time – the equivalent of a weak battalion. Sweden also provided a volunteer ambulance group. A total of 1,169 Swedes served with the Finnish Government forces during the war, providing not only urgently needed command experience and specialist skills, but also a clear indication of the support of the Swedish people to Finland in their fight for independence.

As his freshly formed and reorganized units trained hard for the forthcoming offensive against the Reds, Mannerheim was able to establish a command structure that would allow him to concentrate on the key strategic aspects of the battle once it was joined. He had officers of ability and recent operational experience at his disposal and he divided the front into six main sectors, each under a commander on whom he felt that he could depend. The northern lateral railway ran across the rear of this front.

The sectors are shown on Map 5 overleaf. Running from west to east, Mannerheim's immediately subordinate commanders were:

Colonel Ernst Linder, a Swedish officer, commanding the Satakunta group covering the sector between the sea and Lake Kyrösjärvi, with under command:
  four infantry groups totalling 2,700 men with nineteen machine-guns;
  an artillery group with five guns.
Colonel Harald Hjalmarson, a Swedish officer, commanding the Virrat detachment of 2,300 men, made up of:
  three infantry battalions, with twelve machine-guns;
  three artillery batteries, with a total of eight guns.
Colonel Martin Wetzer, commanding the Häme group of 2,870 men around Vilppula, comprising:
  four infantry battalions, with a total of thirty-three machine-guns;
  two artillery batteries, with a total of seven guns.
Colonel Karl Wilkman, commanding the Jämsä group of 3,750 men, comprising:
  four infantry battalions, with twenty-two machine-guns;

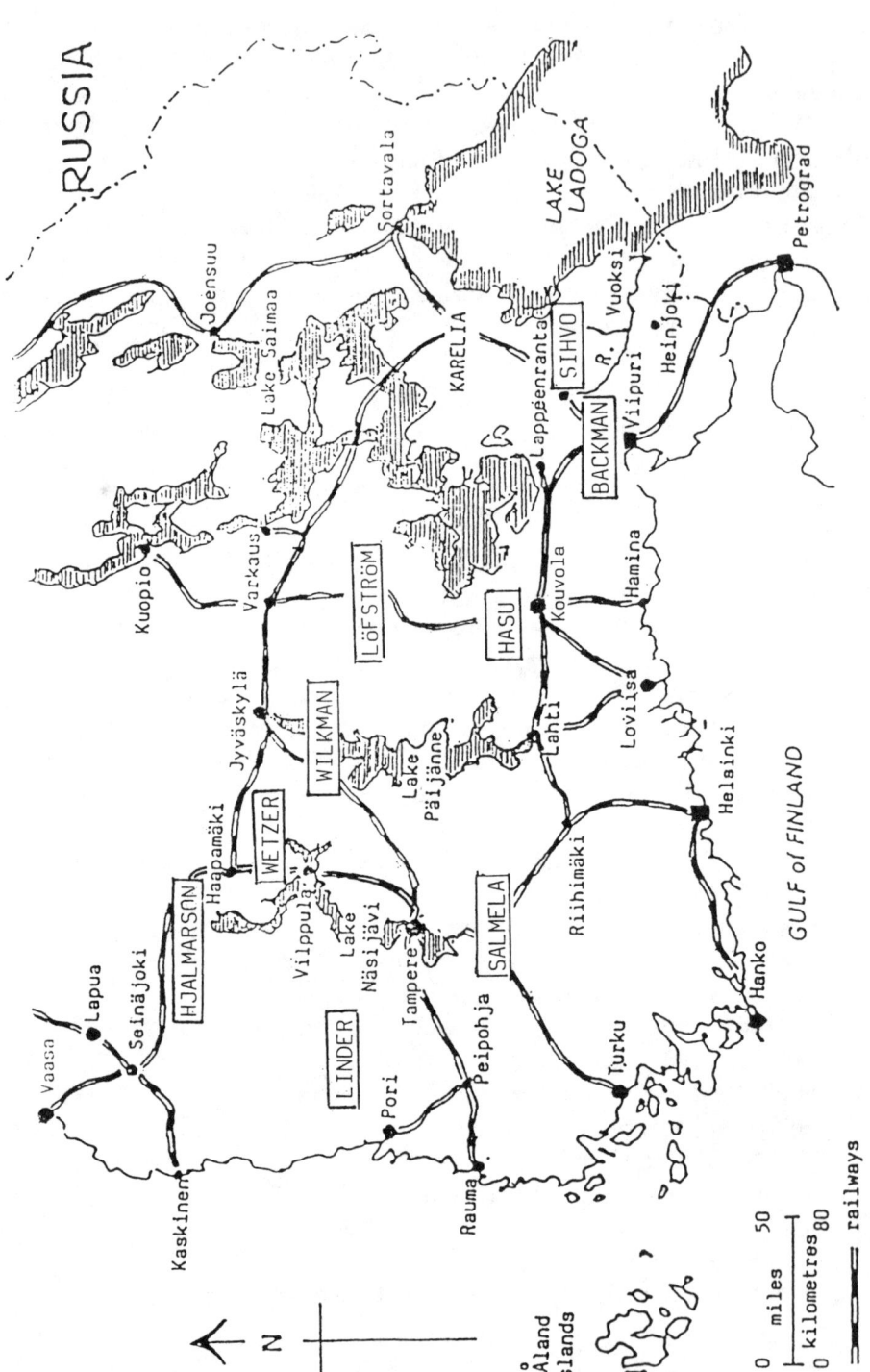

Map 5: The Opposing Fronts on 15 March 1918

three artillery batteries, with a total of nine guns;

the Uusimaa Dragoons of 625 cavalrymen.

Major-General Ernst Löfström, commanding the Savo sector between Lake Päijanne and the Lake Saimaa complex, where, at that stage, it had not been possible to form the White Guard units into regiments and battalions under the new organizational structure;

Lieutenant-Colonel Aarne Sihvo, commanding the Karelian sector along the line of the River Vuoski and the western shore of Lake Ladoga, comprising 1st, 2nd and 3rd Karelian Regiments, totalling some 7,000 men grouped into eleven infantry battalions.

With the resumption of hostilities between Russia and Germany, orders were issued from Petrograd for Russian army units to withdraw from Finland. Only individuals who wished to serve as volunteers with the Red Guards were authorized to remain. This change resulted in the reorganization of the Red Guard command into three main sectors. The western sector, from the sea to Lake Päijänne, was commanded by Hugo Salmela with the Russian Lieutenant-Colonel Bulatsel from the 421st Regiment at Rauma as his chief of staff. The central sector, between Lake Päijänne and Lake Saimaa was commanded by Vihtori Hasu and the eastern sector, from Lake Saimaa to Lake Ladoga, by an individual identified simply as 'A. Backman'. He should not be confused with Major G. A. Bäckman, who commanded a battalion of the Government forces during the battle for Viipuri in April 1918. The Red Guard commander A. Backman had a Russian Captain Vladimiroff as his chief of staff. Eero Haapalainen was appointed commander of all the Red Guards, with Colonel Svetjnikov as his chief of staff.

Although the Reds had excellent lateral communications via the southern railway line from Tampere through Lahti and Kouvola to Viipuri, scant efforts were made to redeploy their forces in response to Government forces' pressure or in preparation for any planned offensive of their own. It is thought that this was largely due to a reluctance of Red Guard units to operate away from their home towns. Administrative support for loosely formed groups sent away from their native localities would certainly have been difficult to sustain without a broadly coordinated logistic plan. Whatever the reason, and absence of experienced military leadership and organizational ability almost certainly lay at the bottom of it, the Red High Command showed a critical lack of enterprise in terms of concentrating their forces for best effect. In consequence, they surrendered the strategic initiative to the Government side.

The first phase of Mannerheim's overall plan was to capture Tampere and so remove the threat to his rail communications from Vaasa to Karelia through the junction at Haapamäki. To ensure that the Reds would be unable to achieve more than minimal reinforcement of the Tampere sector, he instructed Linder and Löfström to initiate pressure all along their fronts in the Satakunta and Savo sectors respectively. This was designed to keep the Reds fixed in their positions and guessing as to where the main attack would come.

Orders for the attack in the Tampere sector were given out by last light on 12 March, with dawn on 15 March set for the start of the first advance. The plan was based on phased operations to be initiated by the Virrat detachment, commanded by Hjalmarson, and Wilkman's group, which had been concentrated at Jämsä. In the first phase Hjalmarson and Wilkman were to get behind the enemy's main force from the west and east while Wetzer's Häme group held them in position by a frontal attack on the line Ruovesi-Vilppula-Mänttä. With the main enemy force surrounded to the north of the town, a second phase should encounter only light opposition in the streets.

Mannerheim's plan was certainly ambitious, bearing in mind that many of his units were only very recently formed and most of his troops faced their first test of battle. He was confident of two key factors that applied to his men but not to the great majority of those who opposed him. His commanders down to regimental, and in many cases to battalion level, were experienced soldiers who had been fully informed of where and how their operational tasks fitted into the overall plan. Secondly, every man under his command knew that he would be fighting for the independence of his homeland.

The C-in-C also knew that time was neither on his side nor on that of the enemy. Whoever struck the first major blow – and won – would achieve the moral ascendency essential for complete victory. He was taking some risks with his plan for the capture of Tampere, but they were carefully calculated risks in which every factor known to him had been weighed and tested. Even so, and as is almost always the case in war, not everyone lived up to his expectations.

A lesser man than Mannerheim might well have been thrown off balance when the Reds attacked on 10 March, during the final stages of preparation for his own offensive. Again it appears that the enemy's objective was the Haapamäki railway junction, to cut the railway to the east of the town. The professional approach of either Svetjnikov or Bulatsel may perhaps be detected behind this initiative. The principal Red attacks were launched in Wetzer's Häme sector, although there was also intensive pressure along the whole of the front from the sea to the western shores of Lake Päijänne. All the Red troops involved were under command of Hugo Salmela who, although without military experience or training, proved to be both brave and competent.

Salmela's Red Guards attacked the Government force positions in and around Eväjärvi and Kuhmoinen to the south-west and south of Jämsä respectively. There was a stiff fight at both places but 1st North Häme Battalion under command of Lieutenant-Colonel Karl Bergström, repulsed the Red attack decisively on 10 March. No ground was given at Eväjärvi, where a second defeat was inflicted on the Reds on 12 March. The successful defence of these two points in the Häme sector were important to the Government side, as their loss would have severely prejudiced the security of Wilkman's force which was still in the process of concentrating at Jämsä.

The Reds also attacked at Vaskivesi, a mere ten miles south of Virrat where Hjalmarson was concentrating his infantry and artillery in preparation for Mannerheim's offensive. The Red intention appears to have been a left-flanking movement round the northern tip of Lake Vaskivesi, so as to bypass Virrat and strike towards Haapamäki, which lay only some twenty miles to the east. Hjalmarson's Virrat detachment gave a good account of themselves, holding the Reds on the day of their attack and then sending them headlong southwards again on 11 March. It seems possible that this two-day action may have taken some of the shine off Hjalmarson and his troops, as they did not perform as well as expected when Mannerheim opened his own offensive on 15 March.

This third Red offensive finally petered out on 15 March after fierce attacks on the line Ruovesi-Vilppula. The Government troops' defence was marked by especially well directed artillery fire and no ground was lost except at Väärinmaja, when a heavy artillery exchange set ablaze most of the buildings in the area of the Government force positions. Fighting in the Häme sector continued throughout 13 and 14 March and such was its intensity Wetzer felt obliged to ask the C-in-C for a brief postponement of the offensive in his sector and for some reinforcement. Mannerheim sent him an infantry battalion from his reserve, held at Haapamäki, but insisted that Wilkman's advance westwards from Jämsä must begin as planned early on 15 March and without a preliminary artillery bombardment, so as to take the enemy by surprise.

In spite of having had his preparations interrupted by the Red attacks, Mannerheim actually drew some advantage from what had occurred. Many of his hitherto unblooded troops had gained battle experience in successful defensive battles, while the enemy in the Häme sector – on which his main attack would be concentrated – had suffered extensive casualties and a series of defeats. His insistence on its beginning on 15 March, as planned, is a measure of his military insight rather than just stubborn determination. He knew that the enemy would be both exhausted and dispirited by their fruitless attacks during the past five days and therefore off balance. The temptress of the welcome pause did not tempt him or, if she did, was thrust firmly aside.

While Wilkman's advance guard moved covertly westwards from Jämsä at dawn on 15 March, sixty miles away to the north-west Hjalmarson's Virrat detachment began their march southwards in two columns astride the road from Vaskivesi to Kuru. As already mentioned, it appears that some of the polish had been taken off Hjalmarson by the fierce fighting round Vaskivesi on 10 and 11 March. During his approach march to Kuru he failed to keep his two four-gun artillery batteries up with the advance of his infantry battalions. In consequence, although he reached the outskirts of Kuru before last light on 15 March, he felt unable to take the town without artillery support. This caused a check on Mannerheim's right flank.

Away to the south-east Wilkman also had to call a halt on the evening of 15 March, so as to regroup his force. The advance restarted early on the following morning and he had achieved all his initial objectives by late evening on 16 March. He had approached the heavily defended village of Länkipohja in three columns, to have one hold the enemy in position while the other two encircled him. Red resistance was determined and well-directed. In consequence, the Reds were able to extract the greater part of their force from the

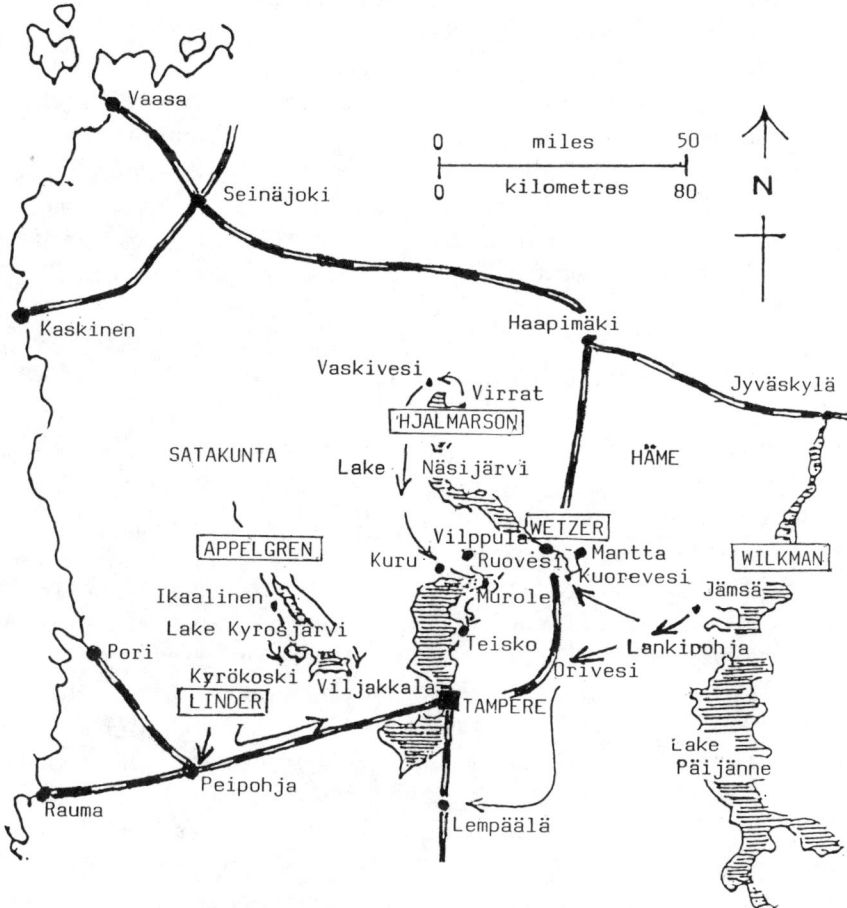

Map 6: Investment of Tampere in the Häme and Satakunta sectors,
March 1918

village before Wilkman's encircling columns could close the noose.
Even so, the road to Orivesi, fifteen miles to the west, was opened up
by capture of the village.

Orivesi stood on the north-south railway halfway between Tampere and Vilppula. Wilkman despatched his engineers with an infantry escort by forced march along the road. This party reached the
railway north of Orivesi on the evening of 16 March and blew the
line behind 5,000 Red troops under Erkki Karjalainen, who were
continuing to attack Wetzer's Häme group to the north. Meanwhile,

one squadron of Wilkman's Uusimaa Dragoons had established contact with Wetzer's left flank at Kuorevesi.

On the Satakunta front between the sea and Lake Kyrosjärvi, Linder had been keeping the Reds under resolute pressure. The principal action in this region was between Lieutenant-Colonel Waldemar Appelgren's battalion, which had advanced west and east of Lake Kyrosjärvi from Ikaalinen, and a force of about 1,700 Red Guards in the region of Kyröskoski at the lake's southern tip. Appelgren's troops west of the lake met determined resistance and were forced to pause.

Reviewing the overall situation on the morning of 17 March, Mannerheim could draw little satisfaction from his group commanders' reports. It was clear that Wilkman in particular had done well, but his continued advance southwards towards Orivesi could lead him into an isolated situation unless either Hjalmarson or Wetzer, preferably both, could join him there. Hjalmarson was still bogged down in Kuru and Wetzer appeared unable to begin his advance, in spite of being further reinforced by the second of the C-in-C's reserve battalions held at Haapamäki. Only Linder's left flank under Appelgren had resumed the advance in the Satakunta sector.

The next three days saw some confused and indecisive fighting. Hjalmarson was finally persuaded to leave Kuru and resume his advance down the east side of Lake Näsijärvi towards Teisko, after having passed through the abandoned village of Murole on 19 March. Wilkman, on the point of making an attack on Orivesi on 18 March, was instead driven into taking up a defensive position to the east of the town by a strong force of Reds under Hugo Salmela. Salmela, who was learning his tactics as he went along, wisely refrained from pressing home his attack on Wilkman's force. He had needed Orivesi simply to use the railway through the place for evacuation of the bulk of the 5,000 Reds under Erkki Karjalainen who were coming under increasing pressure from Wetzer to the north.

Although the progress of his offensive apparently fell far short of what Mannerheim was seeking, its effect on the Reds opposing Wetzer and Wilkman in the Häme sector was far more serious than was evident on the ground. Ironically, the Reds were still under the impression that the fighting was part of their own offensive and the aggressive 'defence' of their adversaries on every front totally demoralized them. A retreat of the Reds back into Tampere was the outcome. Wilkman was able to occupy Orivesi on the morning of 20 March without a shot being fired, as the Reds had left during the previous night. Wetzer joined up with him there that evening and Hjalmason's group, by then under Wetzer's command, reached Teisko some twelve miles to the west. Thus, the first phase of Mannerheim's offensive had secured the intended area of ground but the main enemy force had managed to slip out of his grasp and back into the city that he needed to capture.

The C-in-C was now faced with having to devise a new plan. Tampere was still his most immediate objective, as he could not afford to switch his attention or the bulk of his forces to Karelia until the estimated 12,000 Red troops in the city had been captured or killed. This was not a situation to be welcomed as the ground around Tampere was largely open and so well suited for defence. A prolonged siege was not an operation that he relished, as it would absorb many of the units urgently needed for Karelia. Keeping the enemy off balance was nevertheless essential, so he decided to isolate Tampere with the forces ready to hand.

Fresh orders were issued on 20 March. Wetzer's group was ordered southwards down the railway to put pressure on Tampere from the north. Wilkman, who had demonstrated boldness and initiative in the first phase of the offensive, was despatched with his all-arms force of infantry, cavalry and artillery round the south-east of Tampere to sever the railway at Lempäälä, twelve miles to the south of the city. Finally, Linder who had fought a strenuous holding operation in the Satukunta sector during the first phase, was ordered to move further south to the line of the Pori-Tampere railway, destroy the eastern segment of the line and then advance on Tampere from the west. Hjalmarson was instructed to cooperate with Linder by sending his battalion west of Lake Näsijärvi to attack Viljakkala, where a strong force of Reds were in well-fortified positions holding up Linder's advance.

Having issued his orders, Mannerheim moved his headquarters from Vaasa forward to Vilppula on 21 March. That evening news was received from the now Lieutenant-Colonel Aarne Sihvo commanding the Karelian sector. Sihvo reported Red pressure all along his front south of the River Vuoksi and urgently requested reinforcement together with additional ammunition supplies. Mannerheim granted neither; instead he ordered Major-General

Löfström commanding the Savo sector to attack towards Savitaipale so as to reduce pressure on Sihvo. This action bought a little time in the Karelian sector but Mannerheim knew that he must reinforce Sihvo within the week.

During this phase of redeployment Mannerheim was unaware that Eero Haapalainen had been dismissed as the Red commander-in-chief and replaced by a triumvirate of three hitherto little-known personalities: People's Commissionaries Adolf Taimi and Evert Eloranta and a Red Guard regimental commander named Eino Rahja. Colonel Svetjnikov remained as adviser and chief of staff to the Red High Command but appears to have undergone some eclipse of his influence around this time. Hugo Salmela continued in command of the western sector with the Russian Lieutenant-Colonel Bulatsel still at his side. The latter two were busily preparing the defence of the now virtually surrounded city of Tampere.

As planned, Linder drove the 3,000 Reds out of their positions at the southern tip of Lake Kyrosjärvi on 23 March, thus opening up the approach to Tampere from the west. The next five days brought a series of Red counter-attacks or possibility of counter-attack. The most threatening of these was at Lempäälä on 26 March, where a screen of Government troops under Lieutenant-Colonel Bergström was protecting the left flank of Wilkman's move to cut the railway south of Tampere. A force of several thousand Reds also appeared north of the River Kokemäenjoki near Pori, from where it would be able to attack Linder's group in the rear.

Mannerheim's offensive had gained much ground, bottled up a large Red Guard force in Tampere and made secure the northern lateral railway, but it had not yet given him the strategic freedom he needed to redeploy his main effort to Karelia. A fresh initiative was needed.

5
The Decisive Battles

Hard fighting in western Finland during March 1918 failed to shake the Government side commander-in-chief, General Mannerheim, in his conviction that control over the Karelian Isthmus in south-eastern Finland remained his key strategic objective. Meanwhile the city of Tampere, the railway junction central to the western sector of the front, was still held by Red forces and could not be ignored. Although Mannerheim held the more northerly rail junction of Haapamäki, the Reds would continue to threaten his line of communications to the east so long as they remained in strength in Tampere. Furthermore, Mannerheim needed to move south through Tampere to link up with the German force rumoured to be due into southern Finnish ports during the first week in April.

Government troops under Colonel Karl Wilkman attacking from the south and Colonel Martin Wetzer attacking from the east had all but taken Tampere on 28 March. This day was subsequently to become known as 'bloody Maundy Thursday' because of the losses suffered by both sides. Action had been broken off late to avoid further casualties at precisely the moment when victory was within Wetzer's and Wilkman's grasp. Unknown to both of them, the resolute and competent Red commander of the Red forces in the western sector, Hugo Salmela, had been mortally wounded in the battle after all his local reserves had been committed.

Mannerheim appreciated that he must defeat the Reds in Tampere before he could switch his main effort to Karelia. Moreover, he had to reinforce both Wetzer and Wilkman to enable them to take Tampere. Major-General Ernst Löfström was standing firm along his line on the Savo front, but Lieutenant-Colonel Aarne Sihvo urgently needed reinforcement to hold out in Karelia. This presented the unwelcome prospect of deploying the newly formed Jäger regiments before their preliminary training was properly completed. Characteristically, Mannerheim took the bold decision.

Keeping only 1st Jäger Regiment as his reserve, the C-in-C despatched 2nd Jäger Regiment, less one battalion, with a supporting artillery battery to join Wilkman south of Tampere. The 350-strong Swedish Brigade until then held in reserve joined Wezter to the east of the city. Löfström and Sihvo each received an extra artillery battery of four guns. These may not seem substantial reinforcements but they were to prove critical to the success of their holding operations.

The final battle for Tampere began on 3 April 1918. This was the day that the German Ostsee (Baltic) Division, under command of Major-General Count Rüdiger von der Goltz, began to disembark at the port of Hanko, eighty miles west of Helsinki. News of the arrival of this 9,500-strong force could only have had a disquieting effect on the Reds in Tampere. It also urged on Mannerheim the need to clear the city quickly. Politically, he needed a significant Finnish victory under his belt before the Germans joined the fight against the Reds.

Tampere stands astride the narrow Tammerkoski waterway linking Lake Näsijärvi in the north with the tip of Lake Pyhäjärvi to the south. The defenders thus had natural water obstacles on their northern and southern flanks with a 1,300-yard-wide isthmus to their west. The western approach was strongly defended while that to the east was wider and more open, especially beyond the railway line running up the eastern side of the city.

Wetzer's Häme group, having been reinforced by the Swedish Brigade, was ordered to attack Tampere from the east. Wilkman was told to exert pressure from the south, while Linder was to prevent the Reds from bringing in any reinforcements from Pori on the coast. Wetzer began his preliminary bombardment on 30 March together with an intensive patrol programme designed to locate all Red positions on the eastern approach to the city.

The artillery barrage opened at 0230 hours on 3 April with the infantry attack scheduled to begin half an hour later. As may be seen from Map 7 (opposite), the broad and largely open approach from the east favoured a three-pronged assault. In the north-eastern A Sector Major Lauri Malmberg with four battalions under his command had responsibility for seizing the north-east suburb as far south as Häme Street. In the central B Sector Colonel Eduard Ausfeld, a German officer and formerly a company commander in 27th Jäger Battalion, also had command of four battalions. He was

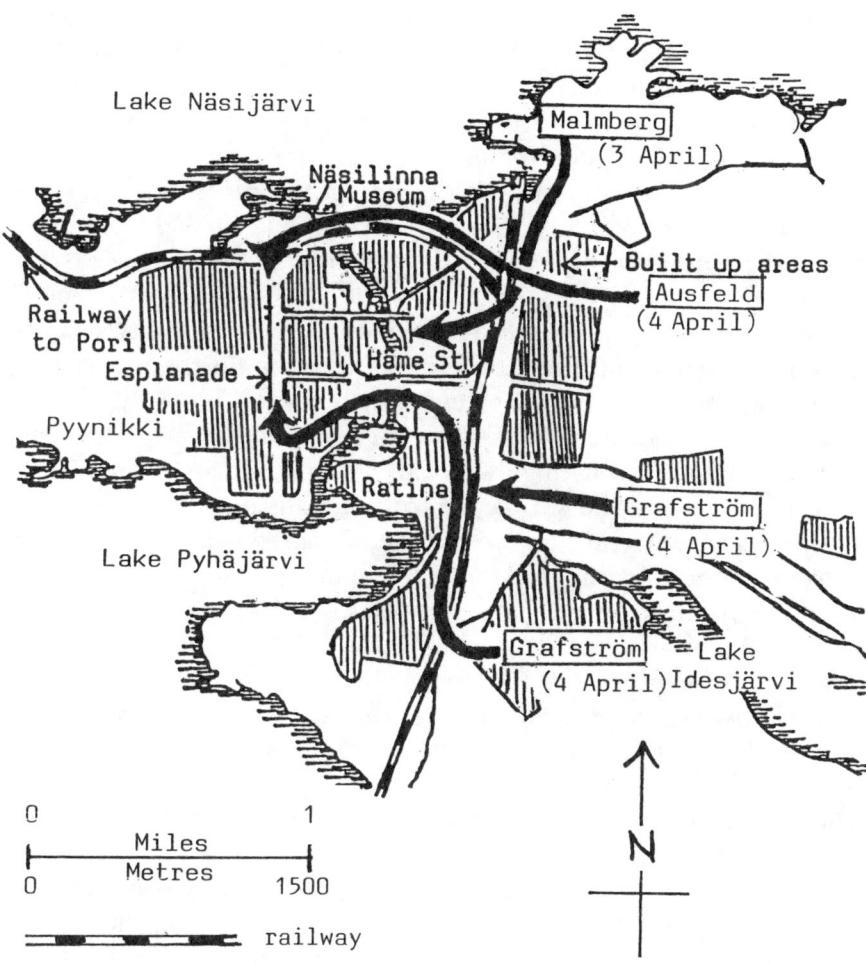

Map 7: Final phases of the battle for Tampere 3 to 6 April 1918

directed to cross the Tammerkoski by the Häme Street bridge and occupy the southern sector. Both these groups were given the Esplanade as their final objective from where they were to repulse any counter-attack made by the Reds defending the western approach to Tampere. Colonel Erik Grafström's group of four battalions was ordered to occupy the suburbs of Ratina and Pyynikki in the south and to the west of the city.

The plan was clear and simple with realistic objectives and easily defined boundaries between attacking battalions. Red resistance, especially in the central and southern part of Tampere, was much stiffer than expected but the Reds' situation was a trap. The Government side must in no circumstances allow the enemy a bolthole through which to escape. Mannerheim not only needed passage through Tampere but also the destruction or capture of the 10,000 to 12,000 enemy troops defending the place. He and his immediate operational staff moved from Vilppula to Vehmainen to observe the course of the battle from the high ground to the east of the city.

All went well in the northern sector during the first day's fighting. Malmberg's group fought their way into the north-east part of the built-up area and began to clear it, block by block. Less fortunately, neither Ausfeld nor Grafström achieved the surprise effect they had sought by attacking in the early hours of the morning. Only one company of Ausfeld's force, Ostrobothnians under command of Captain Gunnar Melin, got across the Tammerkoski and through the town to occupy the Näsilinna Museum at the north-western corner. Their effect on the battle was out of all proportion to their numbers. A company of the Government force breaching the very heart of their defence was extremely unnerving to the Reds. Melin then tied down more of the defenders who laid siege to the Näsilinna Museum. He was eventually able to extract his company although with more than half killed or wounded.

The following day, 4 April, saw bitter fighting in all sectors. The Reds knew that they had no possibility of escape and in many instances fought to the death. The Red units composed of women volunteers proved especially tenacious in defence. Using the north-eastern part of the town, secured by Malmberg on 3 April for his approach, Ausfeld crossed the Tammerkoski by the bridge carrying the railway west towards Pori. Once across, he was able to take control of the Näsilinna district and establish a firm base for operations southwards. Grafström crossed the rapid waterway by a footbridge south of Häme Street and so reached the southern end of the Esplanade. Thereafter, with all four corners of Tampere held by Government troops, only the hard slog of clearing each street and house remained.

A Red party with a flag of truce appeared at 2030 hours on 5 April after a day's fierce fighting in the western suburbs. Surrender terms were not agreed, however, until after the Government force had resumed the conflict next morning. It is difficult to estimate the numbers of Red casualties in the final few days of the battle for Tampere. Figures of 1,800 killed and 11,000 taken prisoner are quoted for the whole phase of the fighting in and around Tampere between 15 March and 5 April. Thirty artillery pieces and seventy machine-guns were also taken. The Government forces lost around 600 men killed and more wounded.

The strategic significance of the fall of Tampere was immense. Not only was the threat to Mannerheim's communications to Karelia removed, but the one competent Red military commander, Hugo Salmela, was dead and a force of many thousands of Red troops – the 'Western Army' – was defeated and largely captured or dispersed. Mannerheim had secured the strategic victory he needed to look von der Goltz in the eye and, even more important, to secure the agreement of the acting Finnish Government that the Germans in Finland should operate under his command.

Disembarkation of the German main force at Hanko during the final battle for Tampere obliged Mannerheim to reconsider his strategy yet again. With the way south through Tampere open, he had the option of joining up with von der Goltz's division advancing towards Helsinki and sweeping up the Red forces to the east. He rejected this temptation for the same reason as he had decided on Karelia as his key strategic objective in the first place. He needed to destroy or capture the Red forces in their entirety so as not to have a frontier or guerrilla-type war on his hands after their defeat. The C-in-C well appreciated that his recently raised army needed some time to rest and reorganize after the exhausting battles of March and early April. Confident that Sihvo would be able to hold out in Karelia after further reinforcement, he set about organizing the Government forces into two Army Corps. Lake Päijänne was designated as the boundary between them.

Martin Wetzer, who had led his group so competently in the battles for Tampere, was promoted to major-general and appointed to command Army Corps West. He was given the task of holding the line between Pori on the coast, through Tampere to Lake Päijänne. Wetzer whose troops had borne the brunt of the fighting until that time, was ordered to rest, reorganize and prepare for his next task. This was to advance south-eastwards following the line of the railway to the junction at Riihimäki. There he was to link up with von der Goltz whose objective was to cut the Red line of withdrawal at this point.

Major-General Ernst Löftström, who had commanded the central Savo front during the earlier battles, was appointed to command Army Corps East. His troops, although involved in some tough defensive battles – especially along the River Vuoksi in Karelia, had suffered less severely than those of Army Corps West. After taking Sihvo's Karelian Regiments under command, Löftström was tasked to prepare his troops for the final operation in Karelia – to prevent the Reds escaping through the Isthmus to possible sanctuary in Russia.

Before examining the operations undertaken by the German forces, it is necessary to review the background to their involvement in Finland's War of Independence. As explained in Chapter 4, the representative of the acting Finnish Government in Berlin, Edvard Hjelt, had been induced to request German assistance – ostensibly to clear his country of the Russians. The German High Command had two reasons for ready acquiesence to this request. Breakdown of the Russo-German peace talks at Brest-Litovsk in February 1918 had necessitated extreme military pressure to be put on Lenin so that he would send his commissar for foreign affairs, Leon Trotsky, back to the negotiating table. The German offensive through Latvia and Estonia was designed for this purpose and it would be complemented by another through southern Finland – with Petrograd as the combined objective.

The second reason was closely linked with the first. Anxious to see Russia out of the Entente Alliance in the Great War, the German High Command was disturbed to hear that the British had disembarked a force of divisional strength through the northern Russian ports of Archangel and Murmansk. Although this Allied contingent was eventually to be seen as supporting White interests in Russia, it had originally been sent there to try to keep Russia in the war against Germany. The threat, however remote, of a new Allied front against Germany had to be quickly countered. These related reasons can be seen to lie behind the German decision to send some of their best troops to Finland.

The German Ostsee Division was made up of the 2nd Guards Cavalry Brigade which had been dismounted to fight as infantry, under command of Colonel Prince Hans von Tschirschky und

Bögendorff, 95th Infantry Brigade commanded by Major-General Konrad Wolf, one battery of mountain artillery and two heavy batteries plus a mounted squadron of 3rd Cuirassiers and supporting engineer and transport units. The division had a total complement of 9,500 men, 18 artillery pieces, 10 heavy mortars and 165 machine-guns. Five cyclist companies were provided for reconnaissance. A battalion of the Finnish White Guard, comprising 400 men who had escaped across the ice from Pellinki to the Estonian coast of the Gulf of Finland in January, was attached.

Separate from this main force, the German 14th Jäger Battalion had been landed on the Åland Islands in collusion with Sweden at the beginning of March. This move was intended to ensure the safety at sea of the Ostsee Division during its voyage to Hanko. A German naval squadron, including two battle cruisers, the *Posen* and the *Westfalen*, under command of Admiral Hugo Meurer, stood off ready to give support. There was still a considerable force of the Russian Baltic Fleet based at Helsinki. In exchange for a guaranteed safe passage of the Russian ships to their base at Kronstadt, the Germans secured an unopposed landing at Hanko. Then, with Admiral Meurer's cruisers protecting his sea flank, von der Goltz began his march on Helsinki. He reached the outskirts by 11 April and would probably have secured a surrender without a shot being fired but for the vainglorious intervention of a People's Commissary named Kiviranta who unwisely urged the 4,000 Red Guards in the capital to fight.

Von der Goltz had been met at the approaches to Helsinki by Captain Sigurd af Ekström, serving with the Swedish consulate in the capital, with an offer of negotiated terms on behalf of the Revolutionary Council. Von der Goltz allowed until 1600 hours the same day for acceptance of his terms. When Ekström telephoned to say that the Reds declined to accept them, von de Goltz ordered the advance to continue. Unknown to either party, some 1,000 White Guards organized into ten companies, were already mobilizing inside the city to support the relieving German division.

Virtually all the main Red defences had been taken by the German troops by 12 April when the White Guard companies made their appearance. Some fighting continued on 13 April, chiefly around buildings that had been fortified by the Reds and in which they were resolved to hold out. All resistance ended soon after dawn on 14

April, whereupon von der Goltz made a formal entry into Helsinki to accept the thanks of the Government supporters and the surrender of the remaining Reds. Admiral Meurer anchored his squadron in the harbour and put ashore a landing party of 400 marines.

The Finnish capital was an important military and political objective for the German forces. Not only had the Red Guards and Russians holding Helsinki been either killed or captured, but the seat of government was restored to the legitimate national authority. Even so, Mannerheim and von der Goltz, who was operating along the broad strategic lines set out by the C-in-C, both perceived that capture of the railway junction at Riihimäki would be a crucial factor in preventing the Reds shifting their defeated troops from the west to reinforce the Karelian front. It will be remembered that the task given by Mannerheim to Wetzer's newly constituted Army Corps West, as soon as it was rested after the battles for Tampere, was to move down the railway to link up with von der Goltz at Riihimäki.

Appreciating that the Reds were in strength at Riihimäki, the German divisional commander decided to ask for an additional brigade which, if landed quickly, could cut the railway east of the junction while he was dealing with the Reds in Helsinki. Accordingly, a third German brigade under command of Colonel Baron Otto von Brandenstein was made ready to sail from the Estonian port of Tallinn. The German plan was for this 2,500-strong force to land at Loviisa fifty miles east of Helsinki, and then advance northwards to the line of the railway between Lahti and Kouvola. By the time his second transport vessel had disembarked troops at Loviisa on 11 April, von Brandenstein assessed that he had enough men in hand to begin the move against Lahti. With only two infantry battalions, two artillery batteries, half a squadron of cavalry and two cyclist companies, he was undoubtedly taking a risk; but he reckoned on speed and surprise as factors in his favour. He left Loviisa defended by the 400 White Guards and marched inland on 12 April.

Pushing Red Guard detachments aside as he advanced, von Brandenstein reached the lateral railway to the east of Lahti by the evening of the following day. Conscious that counter-attack by a stronger force of Red Guards must be inevitable, he ripped up a sizeable section of the track and consolidated his position. Even so, when a large force of Reds supported by two armoured trains appeared from the west on 15 April he felt obliged to withdraw southwards leaving the torn up track abandoned.

Not to be deflected from his purpose, von Brandenstein called forward his freshly disembarked third battalion and remaining half-battery of guns. Establishing wireless contact with von der Goltz in Helsinki, he inquired what support he could expect from the Ostsee Division. Von der Goltz responded by despatching his main force towards Riihimäki junction and a Finnish White Guard battalion with half a German artillery battery to strengthen von Brandenstein's rearguard at Loviisa. Confident that his base was now secure, von Brandenstein decided to attack Lahti with his complete brigade. He took the town after a stiff fight on 19 April. The defenders fled westwards, leaving behind 500 prisoners, twelve artillery pieces and a large quantity of urgently needed railway rolling stock.

True to his undertaking, von der Goltz sent a force of three battalions, three artillery batteries and a cavalry detachment under command of Major-General Wolf to Riihimäki. Wolf's force took the railway junction town on 22 April, defeating determined resistance from the Reds. Thus the Red forces were split into two main groups as the railway system fell increasingly within the control of the Government and German troops.

It would be a mistake to imagine that the Reds had lost the will to fight at this stage of the war. During the period of the advance of the Ostsee Division on Helsinki, culminating in the relief of the capital on 14 April, a large-scale Red offensive was launched south of Tampere. This was under the near-fanatical direction of Eino Rahja, one of the triumvirate in control of all Red forces. Rahja had several experienced Russian officers on his staff and his offensive was supported by a weight of artillery superior to that mustered by the Government force defenders at Lempäälä. Rahja's offensive was held in check but only at the cost of significant casualties on the Government side.

The Reds showed less resolution in the extreme west where intelligence reports suggested that they were preparing to abandon Pori, but not before inflicting serious damage on the port and industrial area. General Linder ordered an attack on the town on 12 April to forestall these intentions and it was taken on 13 April. Although the majority of the Reds in Pori escaped, the Pori-Tampere railway and the branch line to Rauma came under Linder's control.

There were still an estimated 40,000 Red troops operating in south-western Finland but Mannerheim knew he could leave Linder with his Army Corps West and von der Goltz's Ostsee Division to mop them up. At last he was able to turn his full attention to Karelia, where the Reds and such Russian troops as had elected to stay in Finland controlled the rail link from Petrograd. Until this point the Government troops in Karelia under Sihvo had stood on the defensive along the line of the River Vuoksi. Sihvo had performed this task with skill and enterprise. His intensive programme of aggressive patrolling had pinned the Reds down in positions protecting the Viipuri-Petrograd railway. The same patrolling had also provided Sihvo with intelligence of the Reds' strengths and deployment.

Efforts by predominantly Russian units had failed to make any impression on Sihvo's determined defence around Antrea in early March. They consequently devised a more subtle plan utilizing the Petrograd railway running north-north-west to the junction at Hiitola. (See Map 8 opposite). The railway was under Red control from the frontier as far as and including the small town of Rautu. A plan was therefore made to transport between 2,000 and 3,000 Russian reinforcements from Petrograd to Rautu by rail, then turn Sihvo's left flank by crossing the River Vuoksi at Kiviniemi. It was a good plan that might have worked if Captain Yrjö Elfvengren, commanding Sihvo's left between Heinjoki and Lake Ladoga, had not got to hear of it.

Elfvengren's local intelligence matched his initiative. Using his own 500-strong force he cut the railway south of the frontier, blocked any advance of the Russians already arrived at Rautu station and called for reinforcements to help destroy them. He received 8th Jäger Battalion commanded by Captain Lennart Oesch and the outcome was a truly famous victory. Oesch tightened the noose round the Russians at Rautu station while they sat patiently awaiting relief from Petrograd. Finally, an attempt to break out to the south-west of Rautu led the Russians into the Maanselkä valley. Repeated attempts to escape from there against Oesch's well-sited machine-guns cost them 400 dead and 700 prisoners. This adventure ended Russian reinforcement across the frontier.

Mannerheim's intelligence reports in mid-April suggested that the Red forces in the Isthmus were not grouped along a defined front. Rather they were concentrated in centres essential for regional

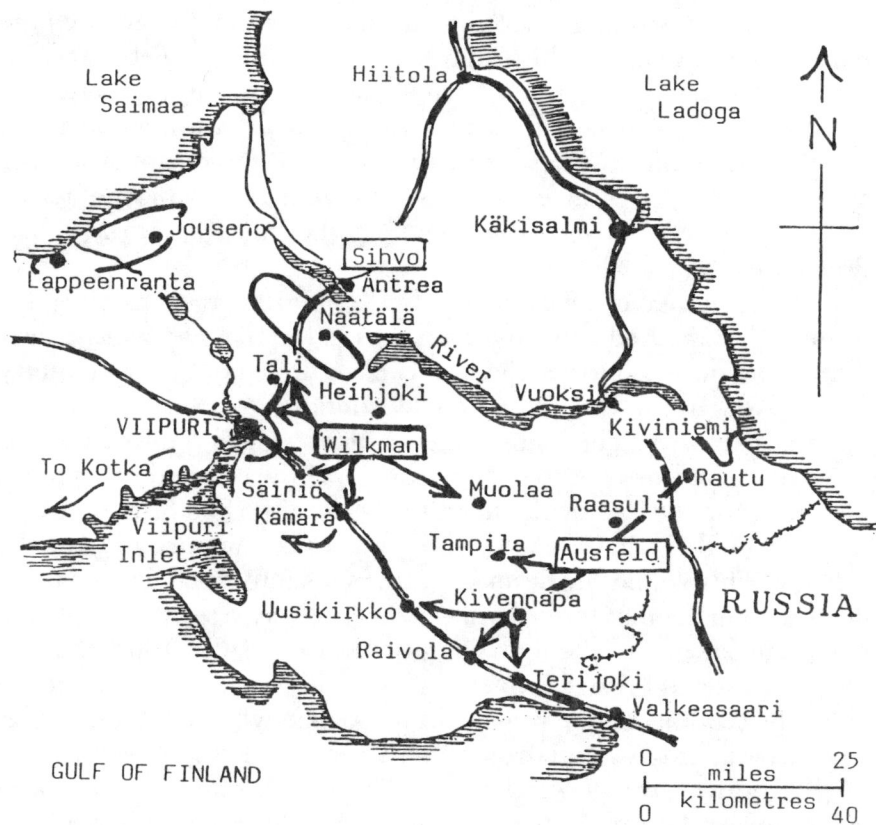

Map 8: Initial moves of the Government forces against the Red 'Eastern Army' 24 to 30 April 1918

control from where they could deploy quickly. This was an appropriate deployment in the Finnish arctic conditions, when one ventured into open country only under the demands of offensive or defensive operations. The total force amounted to almost two divisions, around 18,000 Red Guards and Russian volunteers with more than eighty guns under the command of 'Backman'. His appointed chief of staff, the Russian Captain Vladimiroff, appears to have been eclipsed by the reappearance of Colonel Svetjnikov. He and the rest of the Revolutionary Council had fled from Helsinki before the arrival of von der Goltz and established themselves in the fortress of Viipuri.

The largest force of Red troops, some 3,700 men with twenty-two guns, was grouped facing Antrea, around where there had been the hardest fighting during the Red offensive in Karelia in February. To the north-west, based on Jouseno and Lappeenranta, there was a force of 1,700 men with fifteen guns and a battalion of about 350 men at Säiniö in the south-east. A second large force totalling some 7,000 troops with more than forty guns was deployed across the narrow neck of the Isthmus along the line Kämärä-Muolaa-Raasuli.

Mannerheim gave Löfström's Army Corps East responsibility for dealing with the Red and Russian troops in Karelia. He made it clear that he did not wish to see the Red Guards driven out of the country into Russia from where they could continue to pose a threat to Finland's security. The commander-in-chief wished the Red Guards to be destroyed or captured. Löfström's plan was based on exploiting the gap in the Red deployment between Säiniö and Kämärä, so as to get behind the main enemy force, then take Viipuri and cut the railway. This would break up his opponents into small groups to be dealt with in detail. On 11 April intelligence was received of Russian troop movements to the immediate south-east of the frontier. Mannerheim ordered Löfström to counter this threat without a moment's delay, by sending a large brigade of 6,000 men with eight guns under Colonel Eduard Ausfeld from Rautu through Kivennapa to blow up the railway bridges at Raivola. Once that objective had been achieved, Ausfeld was instructed to face south-eastwards ready to obstruct any Russian force crossing the frontier.

Löfström therefore modified his original plan into one involving an advance on his left flank under Ausfeld and one in the centre under Major-General Wilkman. A third force comprising 4,500 men and fifteen guns, under command of Sihvo, was instructed to hold the main enemy force in their positions facing Antrea and Captain Unio Sarlin's 3rd Karelian Regiment around Jouseno-Lappeenranta by pressure along the whole of that sector. Well aware that Löfström needed substantial forces for this enterprise, Mannerheim placed twelve of his eighteen regiments of infantry under his command together with artillery amounting to more than fifty guns. The reported possibility of Russian interference obliged Löfström to launch his left flank move first. Ausfeld's brigade began their advance on 20 April. Action was quickly joined and a two-battalion group commanded by Captain Edward Kumlin forced the enemy back almost as far as Kivennapa in a three-hour battle. A right flank column under Captain Edvard Hanell overwhelmed the Reds at Tampila on 21 April and Kivennapa fell to Kumlin's force the same day.

Ausfeld concentrated his brigade at Kivennapa before dividing into three columns for completion of the first phase of his task. He directed his right-hand column towards the railway at Uusikirkko, the centre column towards Raivola and the left-hand column towards Terijoki. The advance re-started on 23 April with Ausfeld holding only a single battalion in reserve. The Reds fell back but stiffened their resistance as they neared the railway. An unwelcome thaw had softened the ground so that Ausfeld was unable to bring up his artillery. In spite of this handicap, Ausfeld's columns each achieved their objectives by 24 April, when a twenty-five-mile sector of the railway fell into their hands. The Russians had made no move to interfere.

The attack in the central sector of the Karelia front was entrusted to a force of divisional strength under Major-General Wilkman's command. He divided his force of eleven battalions, two squadrons of the Uusimaa Dragoons and eighteen guns into three columns, each with a clearly defined objective. On the right, a group of five battalions and ten guns, under command of the German ex-27th Jäger Battalion Colonel Ulrich von Coler, was committed to getting behind the enemy around Näätälä, seizing the small town of Tali and then, as a final phase, attacking Viipuri from the north. In the centre, Lieutenant Colonel Erik Jernström's column of four battalions and six guns was ordered to move swiftly to cut the railway at Kämärä and Säiniö before turning to attack Viipuri from the east. On the left a small column of one battalion, one squadron of dragoons and two guns, under command of Major Helge Savonius, was responsible for flank protection, by moving out to prevent any interference from the Reds in and around Muolaa.

The first phase of these operations was successful, especially on the right where von Coler's column surprised and overwhelmed large forces of Reds and, by nightfall on 24 April, cut the north-eastern arm of the railway on both sides of Tali. Jernström cut the railway to the east and Savonius came close to Muolaa. Thereafter the battle became bogged down in a prolonged siege of Viipuri, which was precisely what Mannerheim had sought to avoid. Responsibility for the period of confused fighting and the severe casualties that followed must rest with Löfström and Wilkman, both of whom appeared to be more concerned with the capture of Viipuri than with the destruction of the Red forces in the region.

The fortress finally fell during the night of 28/29 April when a force of about 5,000 Red Guards attempted to break out of the fortress and march westwards towards the coast at Kotka. Escape by large numbers of Red Guards to Russia was prevented by troops under Generals Linder and von der Goltz, both of whom had been ordered eastwards by Mannerheim. Linder took under command the troops remaining in the Savo region and advanced south-eastwards through Kouvola. Von der Goltz moved elements of the Ostsee Division towards Kotka, while Admiral Meurer's squadron stood by to prevent the Reds getting away by sea.

Some 4,000 Red Guards surrendered with their arms at Kotka on 4 May. The total number of prisoners taken by Government and German troops during the fighting in Karelia in April and May amounted to approximately 11,350. This figure included Red Guards and their civilian supporters. Before this final phase of operations in south-east Finland, troops under Linder and von der Goltz had closed around a force of 14,000 Red Guards at the southern tip of Lake Päijänne in the area of Järvela-Koski-Lahti. After several days of fierce fighting, during which the Reds made repeated attempts to break out of the ring around them, most gave up the fight in the first few days of May.

Mannerheim entered Helsinki on 16 May 1918 at the head of the army that he had formed and led. In the four months since his appointment as commander-in-chief, this most capable and resolute soldier had won a decisive victory over the revolutionary Red Guards and their Russian allies. He was greeted with enthusiasm by political leaders and the population alike but, as we shall see, this gratitude proved short-lived.

Judged by its duration and the scale of forces involved, the Finnish War of Independence may seem but a small fragment of history. Yet there are many military lessons to be learned from the manner in which it was planned and fought; these are as relevant today as they were three-quarters of a century ago. Of these lessons perhaps three are of enduring value.

In making any strategic plan for battle, the commander should avoid any emotional attachment to a particular city or place. To fall into this trap can not only distort the true nature of the plan but waste valuable resources of men, material and time. This principle was admirably demonstrated by Mannerheim in his move away from Helsinki as war threatened. The lesson is learned the other way round through the preoccupation of Löfström and Wilkman with the capture of Viipuri. It would have been to their advantage to defeat, or at least isolate, the main Red force nearby. Then the comparatively weak Viipuri garrison would have had no option but to surrender.

The inter-relationship of the ultimate and immediate objectives need to kept in proper balance in the mind of the commander. In this respect Mannerheim kept the strategic significance of his need to have control over Karelia and the threat posed by the enemy in Tampere in correct perspective until the latter were defeated. The temptation to deploy more of his forces to the east in February and early March 1918 must have been enormous. To have succumbed to this lure might well have cost the Government forces the war, in spite of the German intervention.

Finally, no matter how able the commander-in-chief, nothing worthwhile can be achieved in war without skilled and resolute leadership below him. The decisive edge held by the Government troops over the Reds, throughout, was their quality of leadership. The experience of the senior Finnish and Swedish professional soldiers who commanded in the field at divisional and regimental level made a contribution of incalcuable value, as did the German training of the more youthful veterans of the 27th Jäger Battalion. The Reds had motivation enough but they lacked commanders, experience and training.

PART II
Peace and Preparation

6
Laying Foundations

Viewed from a distance of seventy-five years, the strongly pro-German attitude of the Finnish Government during the summer and early autumn of 1918 appears as a collective aberration. A close examination of all the circumstances, however, may lead one to a different conclusion. While the skilful leadership of the Finnish commander-in-chief – General Gustaf Mannerheim – was widely acknowledged, it had been the German Ostsee Division that had freed Helsinki from revolutionaries and a German naval squadron that had sent the vessels of the Russian Baltic Fleet scurrying home to Kronstadt.

There also persisted in the minds of many Finns a conviction that Germany would win the Great War. Field-Marshal Ludendorff's March offensive on the European Western Front had thrown the British 5th Army reeling back between Arras and the River Oise, with 240,000 casualties, and carried the German Army to within forty miles of the Franco-Belgian coast. It was not by then apparent that this was Germany's last offensive of the war. Fresh American and Canadian troops would shortly reinforce the exhausted French and British forces to turn the tide. In addition, the Germans were more guileful in their efforts to draw the newly independent Finns into their camp than were the British, for example. Recognition of independent Finland was being withheld by Britain and France until her status could be determined at the peace conference after the war. In the meantime, the Germans were able to point to the threat ostensibly posed by the small British expeditionary force in northern Russia, despatched by the Western Allies in a desperate attempt to keep Russia in the war against Germany.

This situation led to the curious 'Petsamo incident'. The Arctic port of Petsamo had been promised to Finland by Czar Alexander II in the days of the Grand Duchy and the fluid situation of the summer of 1918 seemed to provide an opportunity for the Finns to take possession. This led the Finnish Government to hand a note to the British ambassador in Stockholm laying claim to the port. Perhaps setting too much store on the peremptory tone of the Finnish note, the British Government chose to interpret the timing of the claim to Petsamo as an attempt by Finland to pick a quarrel with the Allies. The port was already occupied by British troops and a detachment of the so-called 'Murmansk Legion', the latter largely comprised of fugitive Finnish Red Guards. The combined force was positioned to prevent the Germans from taking over Petsamo for use as an an ice-free submarine base. Prior to delivery of the Petsamo note, a small detachment of Finnish Government troops had attempted to occupy the port but had been driven off by fire from Royal Marines and elements of the Murmansk Legion.

Against this general background, it is perhaps not difficult to reach a position of understanding with the Finnish Government's pro-German attitude. It should also be remembered that no opprobrium was attached to Germany such as was later to be associated with the Nazi régime in the Second World War. Even so, the alignment with Germany and her interests in the Baltic region led the Finnish authorities into difficulties that might have been more conveniently avoided. Although Mannerheim had been rapturously received during his triuphant entry into Helsinki in May, General von der Goltz commanding the German forces in Finland had already caught the new Government's ear. Von der Goltz was under no illusions as to his true mission in Finland. Defeat of the Finnish revolutionaries and their Bolshevik allies was but a preliminary to an advance on Petrograd and defeat of the British expeditionary force around Murmansk. Ideally the Germans needed at least the tacit cooperation of the Finns for either enterprise.

The Finnish Government forces were not substantially reduced after the end of hostilities, with only the youngest and oldest of the conscript age groups being demobilized. Moreover, even while planning his final successful offensive in Karelia, Mannerheim had already sketched out a structure for a wartime Finnish Army of twenty-seven regiments formed into nine divisions. This plan was to bear fruit but not initially under his personal direction. The leader of the acting Finnish Government during the War of Independence, Pehr Svinhufvud, had been elected regent – an appointment having its origin in Finland's Swedish history – on 18 May 1918. Svinhufvud was pro-German by long-standing conviction and it will be remembered that he found refuge in Germany when the Red Guards overthrew the Finnish Senate in January 1918.

One of Svinhufvud's first acts as regent was to appoint Wilhelm Thesleff as Minister of War. Thesleff was a Finn who had served as a lieutenant-colonel in the Imperial Russian Army and who had later joined the Germans and accompanied the Finnish Jägers to Vaasa. He had earlier offered himself as commander-in-chief at a time when Mannerheim had raised objections against any German intervention in the War of Independence. Now he was in a strong position to influence the Finnish Senate against what the majority saw as Mannerheim's over-ambitious plans for a Finnish Army independent of German staff and instructors. Thesleff and von der Goltz drew up a design for a Finnish Army with predominantly German instructors and a German general staff working alongside its Finnish counterpart. These proposals were presented by Thesleff to the Senate but he shrewdly made sure that they contained nothing that specifically challenged the position of Mannerheim as commander-in-chief. The proposals did require the resignation of all the Swedish and other foreign officers who had served with the Finnish Government forces during the recent war.

At a detailed discussion with the Senate on 30 May 1918, Mannerheim pointed out the dangers of putting the Finnish Army virtually under German control. He went on to make explicitly clear that he would not be prepared to continue as C-in-C under circumstances that would make him a mere figurehead, with authority vested in a German officer as chief of staff. The Senate heard him out in silence. Mannerheim tendered his resignation at once and left to join his relatives in Sweden three days later.

The final summer of the Great War brought influences to bear which allowed the Finns to extricate themselves from the German involvement. On the European Western Front the third Battle of the Somme in August provided the Allies with a breakthrough that prefaced a complete German collapse. Finland was on the point of famine and shipments of desperately needed grain promised by Britain and the United States were being withheld pending clarification of the country's allegiance. No government could hope to retain authority when their political attitude promised only starvation.

September saw the spectacular victories of the British over the

Turks in Palestine and Syria. Germany's co-belligerent Bulgaria sued for an armistice at the end of that month. At the beginning of October the Finnish Foreign Minister, Otto Stenroth, applying a perception and pragmatism that in no sense diminished his political standing, proposed that Finland should turn to the one figure they had who still commanded respect amongst the Western Allies – Mannerheim. At the invitation of the Senate, the former C-in-C returned to Helsinki from Sweden for discussions in mid-October. He then accepted a mission to travel to Britain and France with a view to securing recognition of an independent Finland, obtaining the earliest possible release of the promised grain shipments and sounding out opinion in London and Paris on the idea of Finland becoming a monarchy. Mannerheim fully appreciated the urgency of the first and second of his commissions but was inclined to keep his own council as to the wisdom of the third.

Finland's new plenipotentiary arrived in London on 12 November, the day after the armistice between Germany and the Western Allies. He had many personal and political friends in the British capital but, although his views were courteously heard, it was made plain that any continued Finnish adherence to German influence would be an obstacle to close relations with Britain. In Paris Mannerheim found the French Government harbouring some doubts as to the democratic credentials and the motives of the members of the Finnish Senate. There was also some strenuous lobbying of the Government by the large White Russian émigré group that had established itself in Paris; they did not perceive an independent Finland as part of their scheme for an attempted restoration of Imperial Russia.

The armistice of 11 November 1918 finally disposed of speculation about who was going to win. The Finnish Cabinet under Prime Minister Juhani Paasikivi acknowledged that new men were needed to handle Finland's affairs and so resigned. Mannerheim was invited to replace Svinhufvud as regent and a coalition administration was formed to grapple with the economic crisis the country faced. With his appointment as regent made public, Mannerheim found himself in a significantly improved position to deal with the authorities in London and Paris. His appointment also carried the additional advantage of brushing aside the distracting question of Finland possibly becoming a monarchy.

Towards the end of his discussions in France, Mannerheim was able to convince the Foreign Minister, his old friend Stéphan Pichon, of the Finnish claims for recognition and *ipso facto* for urgent shipments of food. He returned to London to find a warmer welcome than previously and had little further difficulty in securing release of grain stocks in British ports. The new regent landed at Turku on 22 December at the end of a tumultuous year for his country during which he had played the most consistently conspicuous role. Now he had more on his mind than the future structure of Finland's defence forces but that matter continued to find its place in his overall design.

The arrangements for control of Finland's armed forces put in place during the seven months of Mannerheim's regency provided the basis for evolution during the following twenty years. He reassumed the appointment of commander-in-chief vacated by the outgoing president and appointed three immediate subordinates. These were the Army chief of staff, chief of the general staff and commander of the embryonic Finnish Navy. The still-mobilized Suojeluskaarti was made a responsibility of the Minister of War. It was also about this time that this voluntary organization become more generally known as the Suojeluskunta or Civil Guard.

Mannerheim was persuaded to stand in the Finnish presidential election of July 1919 but was defeated by the President of the Court of Justice, Dr Kaarlo J. Ståhlberg. This was chiefly due to the support that Ståhlberg received from the Agrarian, Progressive and Socialist parties in Parliament. Once again Mannerheim stepped down from affairs of state. The new president became commander-in-chief but with the understanding that he would hand over that responsibility to an experienced soldier in war.

The command arrangements were modified under the Constitution of 1919 so that the President was served by the Minister of War, the newly designated 'Chief of the Armed Forces' and the chief of the general staff. Under this system the ministry dealt with matters of military administration and budget, for which the minister was answerable to Parliament. The Chief of the Armed Forces was responsible for their day-to-day running and training, while the general staff concentrated on planning national defence and advising Parliament on matters of weapon and equipment procurement.

The Army continued to be organized on a peacetime framework of three divisions and one independent mountain brigade. Plans for expansion to a war footing relied on a cadre system under which each regiment would form a second regiment from called-up reservists. This would double the order of battle to a force of six divisions, two brigades and support troops on mobilization. It is easy to be critical of such arrangements, not least because the early stages of any emergency would find the standing army commited to organizing the mobilization process in their peacetime barracks. The latter had all been built during the Russian period and their locations bore no relationship to general staff plans for defence against Soviet attack from the east. In fact, the mobilization plans were better-suited to the second echelon forces of a large or medium-sized power with other fully operational standing forces available to deploy to meet any external threat. In spite of this important shortcoming, the Army's organization and mobilization plan had undeniable appeal to a government struggling to recover from a war that had wrecked the economy, divided the social fabric and resulted in the collapse of the previous administration. The plan was cheap to run, the small standing forces would have a low public profile and could be housed in barracks built by the Russians. Comfortingly, the only threat to national security came from the chaos and political subversion still permeating across the eastern frontier.

Even such a relatively modest military establishment could not exist without conscription. This concept had never caught the enthusiasm of the Finns, who had fiercely resented being taken from their homes to fight for the interests of either the Swedes or the Russians. Nor had conscription worked particularly well in the dire emergency situation of the War of Independence, when some thirty percent of those eligible avoided service. New legislation was clearly required and this was introduced in February 1919, based on the Conscription Law of 1878, which had been imposed by Russia but suspended in the face of resolute Finnish opposition.

The new law of 1919 set the period of conscript service at one and a half years. This was soundly based from the military point of view, as it allowed six months for basic training followed by a year's service with an active regiment. In this way recruit and individual training could be kept separate from the function of providing standing forces at readiness to deploy to meet a national emergency. Unfortunately this plan was at odds with the urgent need for manpower to restore the Finnish economy. The law was consequently amended in July 1920 when the period of conscript service was reduced to one year only. With a perceptive gesture towards the future, the same amendment provided for the call up of reservists for a total of sixty-three days' training during the whole of their period of reserve liability. This was a modest but important beginning.

A second conscription law was passed in November 1922. This maintained the standard period of call up of one year but permitted an extension to fifteen months for men to be trained as specialists such as artillerymen, engineers and those selected for training as reservist officers or NCOs. Although several bills aimed at further reducing the period of service were presented to the Finnish Parliament during the subsequent decade, these arrangements remained in force until a reorganization of the Finnish armed forces called for a third conscription law in 1932.

Training during the War of Independence had been largely in the hands of the experienced Jäger volunteers but the majority of these veterans returned to civil life when peace came. It says much for the determination of the small cadre of professional officers remaining as the nucleus of the new armed forces that a basic structure for training conscript recruits was established. Officer training was started at the Cadet College at Hamina in 1919 and the course brought up to date in light of experience in the Great War of 1914-18. Short courses were also run for officers on the Reserve.

The cohesion of training suffered to some extent through interfactional rivalry between the different groups of officers. These comprised the German-trained Jägers, those trained in Sweden – most of whom were primarily Swedish-speaking Finns – and those who were loosely classified as 'the Russians'. The latter were Finns who had served in the Imperial Russian Army, such as Mannerheim himself and Major-General Karl Wilkman. It is scarcely surprising that different ideas on training evolved, due to the wide variation of the background and experience of the officers in charge. A completely new arm of service was established in the form of coastal artillery. Finland's extensive coastline demanded this and fortunately the greater part of the guns and emplacements installed during the Russian period remained intact when the Russians withdrew in 1918. The coastal artillery is an important integral feature of Finland's defence organization at the present time.

The impetus of founding new armed forces created the need for a national defence philosophy, something which had been absent during the centuries of foreign domination. Mannerheim had foreseen this need while still directing the strategy of the War of Independence but his brief tenure as regent was too busy to allow him to do more than plant a seed in the mind of the general staff. The essence of this emergent philosophy was the need for a practical and speedy mobilization system so as to allow the frontiers to be manned while the nation was geared up for war. Stress on the defensive nature of Finnish military thought was laid with the change of the War Ministry's name to the Ministry of Defence in 1922. This example to other western nations was not adopted for the most part until after the Second World War. More significantly, a Defence Revision Commission was set up in 1923. One of its first recommendations was the formation of a Defence Council to advise the president on defence matters. This proposal was accepted but little was actually achieved until Mannerheim became chairman of a revitalized Defence Council in 1931.

From the point of view of the middle stratum of officers and the general staff, the opening of the War College in Helsinki in 1924 was a significant step towards the development of a more uniform policy on military training. The War College was established to train officers for service on the staff and in specialist and technical appointments. While taking account of the lessons of the recent World War, the strategy and tactics taught were specifically related to the terrain and circumstances of Finland. There appeared little to be gained from abstract studies of military philosophy, as made up much of the staple diet of staff colleges elsewhere in the world. The ground over which battles would be fought was there to be seen and the potential enemy easy to identify. On the other hand, care was taken not to allow Finland's future commanders and senior staff officers to become isolated and so insular in outlook. Selected officers were sent to foreign staff schools, notably in France, Germany and Italy. All of this acquired expertise and wisdom was subsequently passed on through a battle school where officers and NCOs received advanced training. This was initially situated at Viipuri but later moved to Tuusula, north of Helsinki.

Large-scale manoeuvres were not feasible in the early days of the new armed forces. This was in part due to lack of command and administrative experience in handling formations made up of the three main combat arms: cavalry, artillery and infantry. There was also a distinct shortage of financial resources to support the costs of calling up reservists and concentrating large numbers of troops. The first full-scale manoeuvres were carried out in 1928 with all elements of the defence forces involved. Civil Guard units also took part but only within the boundaries of their own military districts. By the close of the first decade of independence Finland had evolved a strategy for defence that took account of the country's position, terrain and climate and also of the reality that only strictly limited national resources could be applied to defence in peacetime. It was clear that the key to defending Finland lay in making an invader fight where and how the Finns chose to fight. This implied battles around the swamps and lakes in summer and in the frozen forests in winter.

In spite of all these positive steps towards the development of a credible defence policy, procurement of modern weapons and equipment progressed at a much slower pace. The army was equipped almost entirely with weapons which German and Russian units had discarded at the end of the War of Independence. Many dated from the last decades of the nineteenth century. Only thirty-two Renault FT 17 tanks, each mounting a 37 mm gun and an 8 mm machine-gun, were bought new from France in 1919. This modest acquisition reflected not so much the difficult tank terrain in Finland, except when the ground was frozen hard in winter, as the acute shortage of funds for new military equipment. The Navy and the newly formed Air Force received rather more generous attention. The Naval Development Law was passed by the Finnish Parliament in 1927. This provided for the national shipbuilding industry to design and construct five submarines based on the German 'Baltic Class' boats and two armoured coastal vessels, the *Ilmarinen* and the *Väinämöinen*. The aircraft left over from the War of Independence and those acquired shortly afterwards soon became outdated, due to the pace of international aircraft design and development.

The attention of Western and Scandinavian countries was reluctantly refocused on the prospects of war by the abrupt revival of aggressive German nationalism in 1933. In the military field there were more than enough examples of the impact of the air arm and armoured forces on modern war: in the Japanese invasion of Manchuria, the Italian invasion of Ethiopia and in the Spanish Civil

War. Finland responded with diversion of some extra resources to defence from the mid-1930s. The Department of War Economy was established in 1936 for the express purpose of coordinating domestic production and the acquisition of weapons and equipment from abroad. The department was headed by Colonel Leonard Grandell, who had earlier directed the work of one of the departments of General Headquarters responsible for the development of defence policy.

The most important single organizational change of this period was the restructuring of the Finnish Army onto a regional basis. This concept had been first proposed during the 1920s but shelved, chiefly because it would demand such a convulsive change in defence and mobilization policy. The principal architects for the new structure were the same Leonard Grandell, during his period of service in General Headquarters, and Lieutenant-Colonel Aksel Airo who was also a head of department there. Both Grandell and Airo were to become general officers in later years. The regional system that they devised together merits close study, as it was the key organizational factor that allowed a rapid deployment to the eastern frontier at the outset of the Winter War in 1939. The system also has possible application for the defence plans of medium-sized and smaller powers today.

It will be remembered that the mobilization system adopted after the War of Independence relied upon existing units doubling in size in their peacetime barracks, using called-up reservists. The central aspect of the new approach was to separate the rapid deployment of the standing forces from the function of mobilizing the reserves. The standing army would thus be available for immediate deployment to the area under the gravest threat. Reservists would no longer have to travel long distances to mobilization centres based on barracks built by the Russians for entirely different purposes but, instead, travel to selected centres conveniently close to where they lived. This new system came into effect on 1 May 1934.

The 1934 mobilization plan divided Finland into nine military regions based on the civil administrative provinces; each province was subdivided into two or three military districts depending on its size and density of population. The manpower required to administer this regional organization was mainly drawn from the Civil Guard units already existing throughout much of the country. Each military district was required to form one infantry regiment of three battalions and a field artillery battalion of twelve guns from the reservists called up from within its boundaries. The more populous military districts were required to provide support troops in addition or, in some cases, additional regiments. The weapons, equipment and vehicles for the mobilized reserve units were stored near the points of concentration under the control of the military district headquarters.

This regional system had a potential to provide Finland with fully mobilized defence forces of 337,000 men, which was equivalent to 8.6 percent of the population. The resultant army structure bore a marked resemblance to the force first conceived by Mannerheim in the closing weeks of the War of Independence. There were to be three army corps with a total of nine divisions (twenty-seven regiments) and supporting troops. Confident that realistic and potentially effective mobilization plans had been made and their implementation prepared, the Finnish general staff turned its attention to the refinement and improvement of operational policy and techniques.

There is much in the Finnish character that supports the theory that attack is the best form of defence. Unfortunately, the harsh economic and political perspectives of the 1930s demanded a more cautious outlook. It had been recognized from the early days of independence that the Soviet Union was the only obvious potential enemy and, particularly in view of the vast manpower and material resources under Moscow's control, the Finns were obliged to adopt an overall defensive policy. There were some advocates of the operational counter-attack to be delivered on such a scale as to halt the aggressor at a selected strategic point on the line of advance that he had chosen. This was in pursuit of the idea of forcing an enemy to fight on the ground that the Finns themselves would choose. Although such a strategy had much appeal it was set aside because of the huge disparity in the numerical strength of the attacking and defending forces. The strategic counter-attack concept would be a gamble on the strength of the enemy's nerve and resolve. If that gamble failed, the heavy expenditure of men and resources in launching the counter-offensive would leave the whole country virtually at the enemy's mercy.

Once a mainly defensive strategy had been decided upon, the

general staff became determined to plan a stubborn defence from the frontiers. Even then, the advantages to be gained from a successful counter-stroke were not forgotten. While operational plans for the defence of the Karelian Isthmus were predominantly defensive in nature, local commanders were ordered to prepare for offensive operations along the whole of the extensive eastern frontier with the Soviet Union from Ladoga-Karelia northwards. As was to be decisively proved when war came, much of this largely desolate region favours the defender, especially if he is bold enough to make deep and aggressive forays around and behind the invader's lines of advance. There is little or no scope for deployment off the few roads and tracks, other than on foot or skis.

Much of the progress towards the evolution of a credible and coherent defence policy was due to the energy and persuasiveness of Mannerheim, who was honoured with the rank of field-marshal in 1933. He utilized his position of chairman of the Defence Council to urge upon successive Finnish Governments the need to spend more money on defence procurement. He frequently drew attention to Finland's requirements for more modern weapons, on one occasion issuing the formal statement to the Government: 'Russia's artillery has a considerably longer range than ours, Russia's aircraft are greatly superior to ours, we are almost entirely lacking in tanks, anti-tank guns and anti-aircraft guns.'

When extra defence appropriations that he had proposed were repeatedly turned down, Mannerheim suggested that the Government should consider raising a defence loan, possibly with the United States, so as to lift the defence debate above the financial controversies of domestic party politics. Nothing was done to pursue this suggestion until May 1938, until when only very modest orders for foreign weapons and military equipment were made.

While Mannerheim achieved relatively little in material terms during the early years of his stewardship of the Defence Council, there was another and substantial side to the balance sheet. A national policy for defence had been devised, together with a complementary mobilization system. An awareness of defence needs amongst the civil population owed a great deal to his public statements and the authority with which he made them. The potential enemy was identified and realistic operational plans were under development, should the need arise. Mannerheim may not have succeeded in convincing the Government of the day of the dangers that lay ahead but he was not alone in Europe in that respect. The man to whom Finland had already twice turned in adversity, patiently but with relentless purpose, continued to pursue his self-imposed objective to prepare his country for the next challenge to independence.

7
Racing the Storm

Identification of a credible threat to national security or survival is essential to any politician or service chief seeking to increase defence expenditure in peace. Protagonists of a strong defence policy face more than the apathy of their opponents and the population; they must overcome, or at least moderate, rival claims for national resources. Seldom can this dilemma have been more aptly demonstrated than when Finnish Prime Minister Aimo K. Cajander reviewed 100,000 Finnish reservists on manoeuvres in August 1939. Many of the older reservists had no uniform and carried only a rifle and bandolier. In his speech to the soldiers the Prime Minister declared, 'We are proud of the fact that we do not have a lot of weapons and rifles rusting away in warehouses or a lot of uniforms mildewing in store. But we do have a high standard of living in Finland and an educational system of which we may be justly proud.' War with the Soviet Union was then just three months away.

At the moment in mid-twentieth century history when Prime Minister Cajander made this speech, the most bellicose German regime that the world had known threatened peace throughout Europe. Finland's Soviet neighbour, concerned for the security of her western provinces and the approaches to Leningrad in particular, was seeking to fortify the coasts and islands of the Gulf of Finland. Covert negotiations with Helsinki for the lease of territory and islands for this purpose had already begun. Cajander had himself been approached by a Soviet emissary but had sent him away.

Earlier in the decade Finland might have been concerned for world peace but not felt threatened herself. Germany had reoccupied the Rhineland, Italy attacked Ethiopia and the Japanese invaded Chinese Manchuria, but these were distant conflicts and of no immediate consequence to the small Baltic state with clearly declared neutrality as the cornerstone of her foreign policy. Finland had no natural resources coveted by a neighbour. The Finns had no internal irredentist problem; they had a language dispute but the small minority of Swedish-speakers were Finns! There was a strong but largely vocal political movement of the extreme right and, although it was one of the best organized in Europe, the Finnish Communist party attracted little popular attention. Yet those in Finland who considered they had nothing to fear had forgotten their history.

When General Gustaf Mannerheim first became chairman of the Defence Council, in March 1931, he enjoyed the full confidence of President Pehr Svinhufvud, who had taken over that office for the second time at the beginning of the month. Svinhufvud inherited a weak economy, however, and defence appropriations were only 13.8 percent of the state budget. Appalled at the low level of defence preparation, but relieved that the previous Social Democrat administration had failed to persuade Parliament to reduce the conscription period below one year, Mannerheim began a process of rebuilding. He met with immediate opposition. Svinhufvud had formed an Economy Committee to tackle the country's financial ills. One powerful member was Risto Ryti, Governor of the Bank of Finland and a future prime minister. When Mannerheim approached him informally to argue for increased defence preparations, Ryti retorted, 'What is the use of spending so much money on the armed services when there won't be any war?'

Mannerheim was above all a realist, a man who knew from training and experience that a systematic and logical approach to seemingly insurmountable difficulties could reap results. Recognizing that the Soviet Union posed the only real threat to Finland, he drew up a list of priorities. Later, in his memoirs, he was to term the period from 1931 to 1939, while he was chairman of the Defence Council, as the years of 'Racing the Storm'.

At the head of his list of priorities Mannerheim placed defence of the Karelian Isthmus. Just as he had perceived this narrow neck of land, between the waters of the Gulf of Finland and those of Lake Ladoga, as the potential escape route for his enemies in the War of Independence, so he now saw it as the prime attack route for the Red Army. This had been established as the fundamental tenet of Finnish defence planning since the early 1920s and Mannerheim saw no reason to challenge or change it.

Although Finnish politicians of the 1930s, as in other democracies, preferred to speak of education, living standards and welfare rather than war, Mannerheim did not fail to take account of history. Finland could provide others with a facility useless to herself – a route to someone else's war. In the eight years of his chairmanship of the Defence Council, Mannerheim brought about a steady increase in defence appropriations until they reached twenty-three percent of state budget in 1938. Even this achievement fell far short of what he knew to be necessary to meet the Soviet threat.

The layout of Finland's internal communications system, and of the railways in particular, favoured defence from the frontier. Not until an invader could penetrate far enough to sever and then utilize the rail network would exploitation by ground forces be fully open to him. Defence from the frontier also suited the Finnish national temperament. Land was near sacred in its importance and nowhere more so than in the minds of the fervently patriotic Karelians. Many lived within artillery range of the frontier.

Mannerheim's professional eye saw in the Karelian Isthmus the potential for a delaying action by a strong covering force close to the frontier. This would buy time for full mobilization and a stubborn defence on ground of the Finns' own choosing. If the main thrust of Red forces could be confined to the Isthmus, they could be made to dissipate their strength trying to fight through a network of strongpoints set amongst lakes, swamps and minefields. If the Finns could hold out long enough, a threat of foreign intervention might force a compromise peace.

Later, when war came, the international press made much of the 'Mannerheim Line', likening it to the vast chain of French fortifications from the Belgian frontier to Switzerland. In fact the concept, as well as the structure, was entirely different. The defensive layout was designed and built in accordance with Finnish tactical philosophy of the time. Mannerheim planned an infantry dominated battle, in which the enemy's armour would lose much of its potency, and where the defender could retain some initiative to redeploy his own forces within the obstacles, mines and wire. Lieutenant-General Oskar Enckell had begun the construction work, while he was Chief of the General Staff in the mid-1920s. This was intensified towards the end of the 1930s at Mannerheim's instigation.

The concept of battle from the frontier suited Finland in other respects. Arguably, the relatively narrow Karelian front was defensible using the country's small standing army, at least in the early days of war. In effect, the standing army would provide the covering force to allow the main defensive positions to be manned. To the north of Lake Ladoga the ground would permit a limited Finnish offensive designed to draw off Soviet forces from the main attack in the Isthmus, thereby weakening it. The central and northern frontier regions had great depth of largely empty countryside, where an invader could be absorbed, isolated and then destroyed. Such tactics would require lightly equipped and highly mobile troops, confident in the difficult terrain. Looking to the international response, Mannerheim judged that determined opposition to invasion from the outset, especially if sustained, would be the best means of drawing in foreign assistance. He had no vainglorious dream of winning unaided against the full power of the Soviet Union.

THE ARMY

Finland's peacetime army of the 1930s had three infantry divisions, each based on three infantry regiments of three battalions, together with supporting arms and services. The 1st Division had two regiments of field artillery, producing a total of six batteries of 4 x French 75 mm guns and three batteries of 4 x 121.9 mm howitzers. The 1st Division was designed to form the backbone of defence across the Karelian Isthmus. It therefore also contained the only Finnish tank company.

The army as a whole was seriously under-equipped with armour. The thirty-two French Renault FT 17/18 tanks, although representing the latest technology when bought in 1919, had become seriously outdated by more modern designs. From 1933 these were gradually replaced by British Vickers-Armstrong Six-ton tanks. Curiously, this excellent light tank was not taken into service by the British Army, although many were sold abroad. Finland ordered thirty-four but without armament, radios or observation devices. This was a short-sighted economy. Instead of the 47 mm quick-firing gun and Duplex mounted 7.62 mm machine-gun, the 37 mm Puteaux guns and 8 mm machine-guns were transferred from the Renault FT 17s and 18s.

The 2nd and 3rd Divisions were without tanks. These formations were designed for manoeuvre rather than defence, and included light infantry battalions and some cyclist units, which became ski troops in winter. In addition, there was one Jäger brigade and a cavalry brigade. The latter comprised two horse cavalry regiments: the

Häme Cavalry and Uusimaa Dragoons, each of four squadrons of 170 mounted men and a machine-gun squadron equipped with 8 x 0.3 inch Maxims of Russian manufacture.

Although the order of battle included an army corps headquarters, there was a distinct shortage of supporting units not under command of the divisions. This was particularly the case with regard to long-range heavy and medium artillery, essential for sustained defensive battle. Without them counter-battery fire against the enemy's artillery and harassing bombardment of his supply routes and support units would be impossible. Although the harassing task could alternatively be undertaken by ground-attack aircraft, the Finns had very few of these and they were totally dependent on clear weather conditions for the identification of targets.

The three peacetime standing army divisions were responsible for training the annual intake of conscripts. Battle readiness consequently largely depended on the stage reached in conscript training when an order to deploy to battle positions was issued. Each year a minimum of 19,000 conscripts were called up. From 1931 recruits were of not less than twenty-one years of age, as it was judged that younger men lacked the physical maturity to benefit fully from military training. Conscripts for the infantry were called up in two batches: one in the spring and the other in autumn. Conscripts for the more specialized arms, such as artillerymen, engineers and aircraft technicians, who were to serve for fifteen months, were called up at quarterly points in the year.

Training was divided into three phases:

Seventeen weeks of basic recruit training, which was common to all arms and services.

A further seventeen weeks of individual training, at the end of which a soldier was considered to be fit for war.

Sixteen weeks training at battalion level, including field training and manoeuvres.

Thus, there would be 9,500 or so men at the end of their training in March and September, with another 9,500 having completed half their training, including two months' training for war. The most vulnerable periods were the second and fourth quarters of the year, when half the conscripts would still be engaged in recruit-level training. The dangers of this predicament were foreseen, and provision made for trained conscripts to be kept in service after completion of their training. This measure could not be implemented except in circumstances of a threatened national emergency and, so it was expected, with Parliamentary approval.

THE SEA FLANKS

Finland has a 1,000 miles of coastline but two-thirds of this look towards neutral and unthreatening Sweden. The vulnerable sector lies along the southern coast facing onto the Gulf of Finland, which has barely fifty miles of open sea at its narrowest point between Helsinki and the Estonian port-capital of Tallinn. Mannerheim remembered the speed with which von Brandenstein's brigade had crossed from Tallinn to Loviisa in 1918. He also appreciated the susceptibility of Estonia to Soviet pressure, together with the two other small Baltic states of Latvia and Lithuania further south.

Contingency plans prepared by the Defence Council to repel any assault on the Finnish south coast depended significantly on guns and emplacements left by the Russians in 1918. This Russian defensive system, designed to block the sea approaches to St Petersburg and named after Peter the Great, covered both the northern and southern coasts of the Gulf of Finland and incorporated several of the islands. During the 1920s a group of British experts, led by Major-General Walter Kirke, had visited Finland to advise on the adaptation and development of the coastal artillery system. Consequently provision was made to use it in two specific defensive roles.

The first was to counter any naval bombardment of the Finnish south coast towns and ports, Helsinki in particular. This was a serious threat as the Soviet Baltic Fleet, by the mid-1930s, had vessels mounting 12-inch guns capable of firing high-explosive shells up to a range of twenty-six miles. These could inflict serious casualties and damage. The second but equally important task was to repel any attempt to land a hostile military force on the south coast. In this role the coastal artillery needed support by infantry units ashore.

In the main, the guns and emplacements left by the Russians were suitable or readily adaptable to the roles that the Finnish Defence Council allocated to them. Inevitably, technological development had advanced since the Russian guns had been installed, especially with regard to armour-piercing capability. This was to some extent offset, as a disadvantage, by the huge stocks of coastal artillery ammunition left behind with the guns. Practice firing was difficult to arrange on a regular basis, as in peacetime the Gulf of Finland is a busy shipping lane.

The coast artillery was organized into five regimental sectors on the Gulf of Finland and the shores of Lake Ladoga. The service had a total complement of 20,700 men, with regimental or battalion emplacements on the Hanko peninsula, at Suomenlinna to protect Helsinki harbour, at Kotka to the east, and around the fortress city of Viipuri. Two remaining defence zones were at Sortavala on Lake Ladoga and on the Pellinki archipelago, running south from Porvoo thirty miles east of Helsinki. The guns of Viipuri and Sortavala were capable of firing both out to sea and landwards, into the Karelian Isthmus. The average range of the coastal artillery batteries was twenty-six miles and therefore a match for the heaviest guns of the Soviet Baltic Fleet.

The Finnish Navy, with a wartime complement of 13,000 men, was equipped to intercept hostile vessels intent on either coastal bombardment or an assualt force landing. The offensive capability of the small fleet was concentrated in five submarines. These boats, designed for the shallow Baltic waters, were all torpedo-firing and of three classes:

500-ton class, with a sea range of 700 miles, two torpedo tubes and mounting a 76 mm gun forward: the *Iku-Turso, Vesihiisi* and *Vetehinen.*

250-ton class, with a sea range of 700 miles, two torpedo tubes and mounting a 20 mm conning-tower gun: the *Vesikko.*

99-ton class, with a sea range of 250 miles, two torpedo tubes and mounting a 13 mm conning-tower gun: the *Saukko.*

In addition to threatening any hostile naval vessel, all five submarines were capable of reconnaissance missions in the Baltic.

Two surface vessels, the armoured ships *Ilmarinen* and *Väinämöinen,* both of 4,000 tons, were primarily designed for the seaward defence of the Åland Islands, which were demilitarized in peacetime. The vessels' main armament were four 10-inch guns mounted in twin turrets. They also mounted four 40 mm quick-firing anti-aircraft cannon and eight 105 mm naval guns. For inshore water operations, the Navy had two 450-ton gunboats, the *Hämeenmaa* and *Uusimaa,* each mounting two four-inch guns and the 370-ton *Karjala* and *Turunmaa* mounting two 75 mm guns, together with ten 25-ton motor torpedo boats. The Finnish Navy and Coastal Defence

Artillery were both commanded by Major-General Väinö Valve, who came under the operational control of the Commander of the Armed Forces (C-in-C).

AIR DEFENCE

Finland was not alone amongst European nations in being woefully under-equipped in the field of air defence in the closing years of peace. In most countries, such anti-aircraft guns and fighter aircraft as were acquired were destined for deployment in defence of ports, cities and industrial plants. This fundamental flaw in strategic and tactical thinking most probably had its origin in the widespread apprehension, in the minds of civilian populations, about the casualties and havoc that air attack on towns and cities could produce. While Mannerheim did not hesitate to stress the danger of air attack on Finnish cities, when arguing for more funds for aircraft for the Air Force, he gave first priority to air support for the Army when war came.

In the main, only the aggressor nations had appreciated that the air arm, greatly developed by Germany, Italy and Japan in the 1930s, could have the most immediately decisive effect in direct support of the land battle. This support took two forms: air attack on troops and other ground targets, as practised by the German Luftwaffe during the Spanish Civil War, and defeat of enemy aircraft attempting to attack one's own ground forces.

The Finnish Army's mobilization order of battle contained two anti-aircraft regiments. The 1st Regiment was garrisoned at Viipuri with wartime responsibility for city and port defence. Nominally, the 2nd Regiment was part of the 2nd Infantry Division but the unit's wartime task was vulnerable point defence, including those in Helsinki. Both regiments were equipped with 40 mm Swedish Bofors and 75 mm anti-aircraft guns, the latter of either Czech or German manufacture.

Acquisition of modern aircraft by the Finnish Air Force in the 1930s was bedevilled by two persistent controversies. The first was the debate, taking place concurrently in other nations, as to whether the fighter or the bomber should have priority for development or purchase. In a country such as Finland, which maintained a steadfastly defensive philosophy, the need for fighters appeared paramount. Nevertheless, the bomber enthusiasts seem to have won the argument, as it was decided to order eighteen fast light bombers to complement the Fokker D XXI fighters bought from Holland or assembled under licence at the Finnish aircraft factory at Tampere.

The second discussion concerned from which country the modern aircraft should be bought. Mannerheim took a close personal interest in this issue, attending air displays and exhibitions in Britain, France and Germany. The final choice lay between the German Junkers 88 and the British Bristol Blenheim bomber. Mannerhein was inclined to favour the German option, as he judged that the German aircraft industry had invested more in research and development and, because of its size, would be more reliable in terms of delivery.

Mannerheim may have been influenced in favour of the bomber by the German Minister for War, Werner von Blomberg, who persistently stressed the value of the bomber in modern war during their conversations. In the end Mannerheim gave way to the choice of the Air Force commander Colonel Jarl Lundqvist, who favoured the Blenheim. In this choice Lundqvist was probably correct as, although dangerously susceptible to catching fire, the Blenheim had distinct performance advantages over the Junkers 88. An altogether different but better balanced choice might have been an equivalent number of either German Messerschmitt ME 109 or British Hawker Hurricane fighters. Either of these outstanding aircraft could have made a valuable contribution to air defence against Soviet aircraft in the Winter War. Towards the close of Mannerheim's race against the storm, the Finnish Air Force had a complement of 118 aircraft rated as operational. The aircraft order of battle for 1939 is shown at Appendix 2.

THE SUOJELUSKUNTA OR CIVIL GUARD

The Civil Guard had its origins in the volunteer vigilante corps, or 'Orderly Guards', set up in the troubled years before the War of Independence. A Finnish Government statute issued in 1919 gave authority for the organization to be incorporated into the national defence forces in time of war. The Civil Guard was structured on a regional basis, similar to that of the Army, but was kept separate in matters of equipment and training. When the Army was established on a regional basis in 1931, local Civil Guard units were given extra responsibility for mobilization arrangements. The Suojeluskunta continued to be voluntary, however, and government financial appropriations had to be supplemented by collections and donations from businesses and wealthy individuals.

In the 1920s and early 1930s the Civil Guard was regarded with suspicion by the working classes. Trades unions, in particular, insisted that none of their members could also be members of the Suojeluskunta and this animosity was to a large extent reciprocated. Many senior officers of the Civil Guard, who combined that function with a business or profession, perceived themselves as protectors of the national liberties that the Suojeluskunta had won in battle in the War of Independence. Members of the Social Democrat party were denied membership of the Civil Guard and it was not until war came in 1939 that the Soujeluskunta, the Democratic Party and the trades unions appreciated the essential need for the closest cooperation between all three.

The Suojeluskunta had 100,000 members in 1938 and a trainee Boys Department of 30,000. The country was subdivided into twenty-two Civil Guard districts, each responsible for training its members and making preparations for the mobilization of Regular Army reserves. There was a cadre of Regular Army officers, reponsible for organization and training. Summer camps of two weeks' duration were arranged each year and there were specialist courses for Civil Guard volunteer officers and NCOs. Training of the rank and file concentrated on marching and shooting. While these are certainly prime infantry skills, little time was available for instruction in even platoon level tactics. Personal weapons were kept at home by the volunteers. This may have contributed to the apprehensive regard in which the Suojeluskunta was held by some elements of the population.

THE LOTTA SVARD WOMEN'S AUXILIARY SERVICE

Tradition of women's service to the Army dates back to the Russo-Swedish War of 1788-90, in which many Finns took part. The organization takes its name from a character in an epic poem by J. L. Runeberg, Finland's national poet, called Lotta Svärd. She accompanied her husband to war and, when he was killed, remained to cook for his comrades, tend their wounds and write their letters home. Her example was followed by other women and 'Lottas', as they became known, served in the War of Independence. Subsequently, their organization developed alongside that of the Civil Guard and became formally titled the 'Lotta Svärd'. As with the Civil Guard, the Lottas were initially viewed with suspicion by the working classes. Apprehension persisted that the women soldiers were part of a conspiracy to keep the workers in their place. It was not until war came that it was generally appreciated that the women volunteers were motivated purely by patriotism.

By 1938 the Lotta Svärd almost matched their male counterparts in numbers by achieving 100,000 members, with a 20,000-strong trainee girls' department known as the 'Little Lottas'. Their organization followed the regional pattern, with responsibilities for signals, clerical, medical work and catering, together with air-observation as part of the country's air-raid warning system. Training was mainly achieved through evening classes but courses for the assistant nurses were full-time and lasted for seven months. The organization had its own Syväranta College at Tuusula, which was used chiefly to train Lotta group and section leaders. There were both active and supporting members; the former subdivided into service and welfare Lottas. Service Lottas undertook to commit themselves full-time in the event of national mobilization and, if required, to serve anywhere in the country.

Credit for expanding the Lotta Svärd from a strength of 50,000 in 1930 to double that number by 1939 rested chiefly with Miss Fanni Luukkonen, who led the organization during the whole of that period. Born in Oulo in 1882, she qualified and worked as a school teacher from 1906 but became closely involved in women's voluntary work. She became secretary of the Sortavala district of the Lotta Svärd in 1921, a member of the organization's Central Governing Board from 1925 and its chairman from 1930 to 1944. She visited every place where the Lottas were working during the war years, including many locations close to the fighting. She was decorated on several occasions during the wars, remaining the head of the organization until it was disbanded in 1944 in accordance with the terms of the armistice agreement.

COASTGUARD AND FRONTIER GUARD

Finnish troops were first assigned to frontier guard duties after the War of Independence. These were transferred to control of the Ministry of the Interior in 1919, on the understanding that they would revert to military command in war. Conscripts could volunteer to carry out their national and reserve service with the Frontier Guard, although conscripts were not used on actual guard duties in peace. By 1939 the Frontier Guard comprised five units along the eastern frontier.

The Coastguard service was a similar organization, comprising regulars supplemented by reservists in war. Their organization followed the geographic pattern, with three Coastguard districts covering the Gulf of Finland, the Gulf of Bothnia and the Åland archipelago.

FINLAND'S DEFENCE INDUSTRY

At the instigation of Mannerheim, in his capacity as chairman of the Defence Council, an armaments factory was set up at Tampere in the early 1930s. Mannerheim had opposed the selection of the site, in the country's largest industrial city, on the grounds that it would be particularly vulnerable to air attack in war. As in other matters, his advice was not taken.

The purpose of the state armaments factory was chiefly to produce artillery, of which Finland had only a mixed and largely outdated complement at the end of the War of Independence, and artillery ammunition. Small arms also became a speciality, in particular the Lahti-Saloranta rifle and the Suomi 9 mm machine-pistol. This had an effective range of 150 metres and was a competent forerunner of a sequence of similar automatic light weapons produced by the adversaries of the Second World War. Design and manufacture of mortars was also undertaken, which has since developed into a Finnish speciality with substantial recognition abroad. Unfortunately, both design and manufacture were handicapped by the strict limitation on defence expenditure during the 1930s.

8

Into the Crucible

The Soviet Union's attack on Finland on 30 November 1939 appeared to the outside world as yet another gross abuse of military power. Germany had absorbed Austria, invaded the Czech lands and overrun Poland. Fascist Italy had been playing a similar hand in Albania, Cyrenaica and Ethiopia, while Japan wrought havoc in an expansionist war against China. To the Western democracies and their dependencies, dismayed by the paralysis of the League of Nations, there seemed to be nothing to deter totalitarian states from subjugating their smaller neighbours.

Yet, in this case, there was a difference though not one that would have been too apparent to the Finns, who found themselves fighting for their lives and independence. Immoral though their actions were, the Soviet leadership actually brought themselves to believe that they had no other choice. Even now, half a century later and after the collapse of the Communist Soviet Union, it is difficult for the world to perceive the Russians as thinking defensively.

There is a deep-seated defensive mechanism in the Russian mentality. It has roots in the wars with Sweden over five centuries. Napoleon's capture of Moscow in 1812 left a lasting scar on the nation, in spite of the ignominious retreat of the invader. These events were almost certainly magnified by the Russians' sense of isolation from the more socially and technically advanced nations of Western Europe and the Americas. The need for a policy of forward defence with buffer states and well-protected sea approaches between Mother Russia and her potential enemies was carried forward from the Czars to the reign of Stalin.

The Soviet Union's invasion of Czechoslovakia in 1968, incredible though it appeared to rational opinion elsewhere, was also motivated by defensive thinking. It is barely conceivable that the worldwide outrage that followed the invasion was not anticipated by the Kremlin. While the consequent defection of the Communist parties of France and Italy from Moscow may not have been anticipated, it is unlikely even that would have been an effective deterrent. Czechoslovakia was seen to be wobbling dangerously in the centre of the Russian military and political arch in central Europe. It had to rammed back into its slot in the overall scheme of things and then cemented into place.

There was no thought in the 1930s that Finland presented either an ideological or military threat to the Soviet Union. Unfortunately, her border stood only twenty miles west of Leningrad and at some points less than fifty from the Murmansk railway and the newly completed Stalin canal, connecting the Baltic to the White Sea. The vulnerability of Lenigrad was real. The British and French fleets had attempted to bombard the Imperial capital during the Crimean War, after an approach through the Gulf of Finland. Now the great city had taken on significant economic importance, following industrialization and construction of the northern railway and canal. A threat to the Soviet Union's prestigious second city came from an increasingly bellicose Nazi Germany.

There must have been a day in the winter of 1936-37 when a staff officer to Admiral Nikolai Kuznetsov, commander of the Soviet Baltic Fleet, unrolled a dusty chart to explain how the Russian Imperial Navy had planned to defend Leningrad, then St Petersburg, before the First World War. As may be seen from the map overleaf, it was not a plan of inventive subtlety or surprise. It was simply a matter of taking advantage of the narrowness of the Gulf of Finland and its more strategically situated islands.

In essence, the Czarist naval plan depended on a forward patrol line by a cruiser squadron, between the Åland Islands and the islands of Dagö and Osel, and three successive lines of minefields, with essential gaps controlled by destroyers and submarines. Approaches to the gaps and the minefields themselves were covered by naval gunfire or coastal batteries, as minefields must be to prevent them being swept and cleared. The greater volume of fire was to come from the heavy and long-range coastal batteries placed along both shores of the Gulf and on the islands of Suursaari and Tytärsaari. The key difference between 1914 and 1936 was that, unlike the former empire, the Soviet Union controlled neither the shores of the Gulf of Finland nor its centrally placed islands. The latter had been ceded to Finland under the 1920 Treaty of Dorpat, which specified

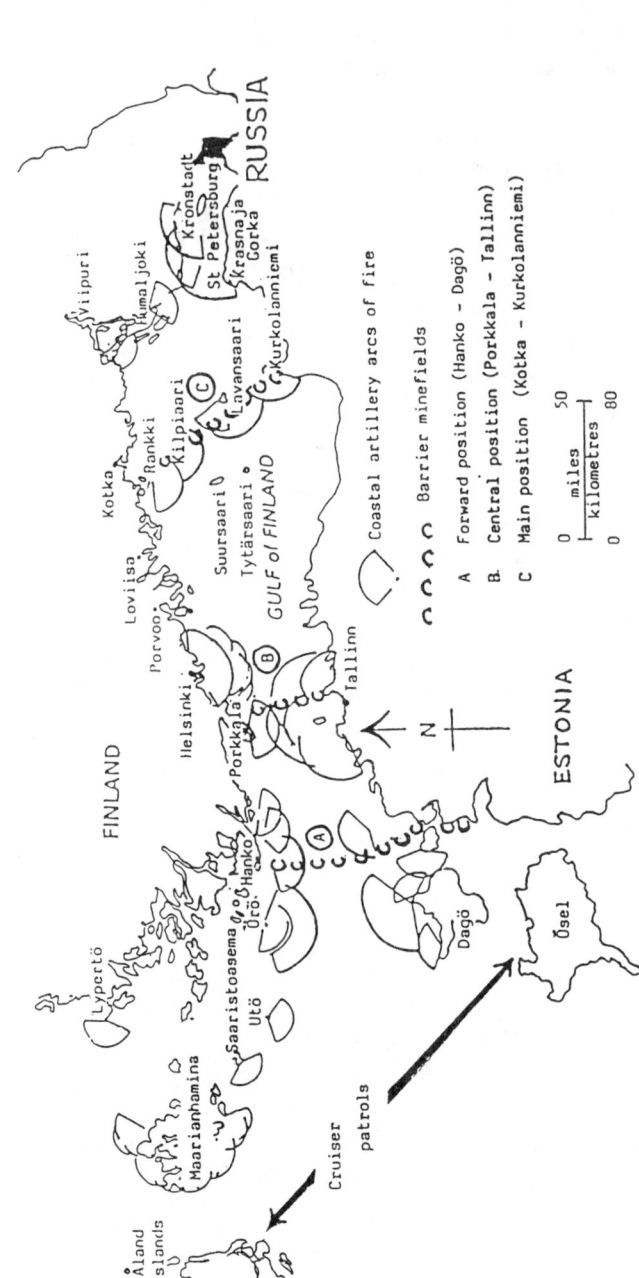

Map 9: Imperial Russia's seaward defence plan for St Petersburg 1914
(With acknowledgement to the research of Lieutenant-Colonel Jarl Kronlund)

that they should not be fortified. The northern shoreline was Finnish and the southern that of Estonia. Finland and the Soviet Union had signed a Non-Aggression Treaty in 1932. This had three articles:

Article 1 confirmed the frontiers agreed under the Treaty of Dorpat and each signatory undertook not to go to war against the other.

Article 2 provided for each signatory to remain neutral if the other were attacked.

Article 3 obliged each signatory not to make treaties with any state hostile to the other.

On the initiative of the Soviet Union in 1934, the Non-Aggression Treaty was extended for ten years until 1944.

Moscow's apprehension as to Finland's ability and resolve to adhere in full to the principles of Articles 2 and 3 of the Non-Aggression Treaty was reflected in a question put to Rudolf Holsti, the Finnish Minister of Foreign Affairs, when he visited Moscow in 1937. 'What would Finland do,' he was asked, 'if some country should threaten the Soviet Union through her territory?' Holsti replied that Finland would not make its territory available to any foreign army, including the enemies of the Soviet Union.

Fresh negotiations were opened in the spring of the following year, but in such a curiously oblique fashion as to dissuade the politicians and officials approached from taking them at face value. Boris Yartsev, a second secretary in the Soviet Embassy in Helsinki and a known officer of the GPU (Soviet Secret Police), approached Foreign Minister Holsti, and several other personalities in Helsinki, on a mission 'to improve relations between the Soviet Union and Finland'. Yartsev explained that Stalin was convinced that Germany had long-term plans to attack the Soviet Union and that the route through Finnish territory towards Leningrad must be safeguarded. If, said Yartsev, Finland were to undertake to oppose any such German move, Soviet economic and military assistance could be made immediately available. A similar approach was made to Finnish General Aarne Sihvo, commander of the Karelian front during much of the War of Independence and a former Commander of the Armed Forces (1926-33). Yartsev also approached Mrs Hella Wuolijoki, a prominent Finnish Communist.

Prime Minister Aimo Cajander also received Yartsev at the latter's request. Here the discussion appears to have followed a slightly different course, with emphasis on Nazi Germany's attitude towards both Finland and the Soviet Union. Discussion of Yartsev's proposition appears to have been only within an inner caucus of the Finnish Cabinet and neither Parliament nor Mannerheim, as chairman of the Defence Council, were consulted. An official Finnish Government response was nevertheless sent. The Finnish note made clear that Finland would not permit any foreign troops on her territory and that she expected, on that guarantee, the Soviet Union would continue to respect the sovereignty of Finnish independence. The note gave no hint that any further negotiations were expected. On the contrary, it was intended to bring the Yartsev conversations to a close, albeit in a polite, positive and friendly manner.

The Finnish response to the Yartsev approaches had precisely the opposite effect from that intended. Moscow chose to interpret the formal written note as a basis for more specific discussions, but the point of contact was changed. On 18 August 1938 Yartsev approached Väinö Tanner, the Finnish Finance Minister and Socialist leader with five specific Soviet proposals:

The Soviet Union would guarantee Finland's integrity and, if needed, would provide armed assistance.

Finland would agree to resist any German attack on her territory and, in return, the Soviet Union would provide (in peace) military assistance to help strengthen Finnish defences.

The Soviet Union would agree to the fortification of the Åland Islands, on condition that Soviet forces could make use of them.

The Soviet Union would fortify Hogland (the island of Suursaari in the eastern part of the Gulf of Finland ceded to Finland under the Treaty of Dorpat).

The Soviet Union offered Finland a trade agreement.

Two items in this agenda for discussion were of particular interest to the Finns. They were keen to see fortification of the Åland Islands, not only for the obvious reason of improving their control over the straits leading into the Gulf of Bothnia but also because it would promote defence relationships with Sweden. It was already known to the Finns that the Swedes would participate in the fortification of the Ålands only if they could be certain of Soviet acquiesence. Secondly, the Soviet request for rights to fortify Hogland (Suursaari) made plain to the Finnish Government that the Soviet Union was intent on re-establishing the Imperial defence plan for the Gulf of Finland. The request to fortify Suursaari could therefore be placed in perspective.

It was but the first of a series of subsequent demands for military facilities on Finnish territory, each of which could be identified in advance by reference to the plan of 1914.

Notwithstanding these useful revelations, the Government in Helsinki found nothing attractive about the Soviet proposals. Even Soviet acceptance of fortification of the Ålands carried with it the penalty of Soviet use of the islands in war. The theme of the Moscow proposals was an inextricable Finnish entanglement in Soviet defence preparations and, therefore, serious compromise of Finland's declared policy of neutrality. For a second time the Soviet overtures were rejected by Finland, again politely and accompanied by carefully reasoned argument about preserving her neutrality.

Sensing the need for rather more subtlety than had been employed so far, Moscow instructed the indefatigable Yartsev to put forward modified suggestions in October 1938. These laid stress on trade talks, on which the Helsinki Cabinet retained an open mind, and suggested that the Finns themselves should fortify Suursaari, ready for it to be taken over by the Soviet Union in war. Hardly surprisingly, the second proposal was rejected by the Finnish Government but agreement was reached to begin trade talks in Moscow in early December. Once in the Soviet capital, the trade mission was not slow to perceive the underlying, and crucial, defence aspects of the discussions. The Finnish mission was adamant in discussing trade matters only.

Nothing happened during the winter months of 1938-39 to reduce Stalin's apprehension of Germany's ultimate intentions towards the Soviet Union. Seldom one to see anyone else's side of an argument, he found Finland's continued refusal to negotiate over joint measures to strengthen defences in the Gulf of Finland incomprehensible. It was decided to give Yartsev one final hand to play, while a more heavyweight character was instructed to return to Helsinki.

Yartsev's last hand comprised four proposals only and two of them, to Soviet minds at least, would seem likely to be welcomed by the Finns. He presented them to the new Finnish Foreign Minister, Eljas Erkko, on 3 March 1939 in Helsinki:

Finland would guarantee to defend her territory against Germany (an undertaking already given by Helsinki).

The Åland Islands were to be fortified against a German landing. (This was a development, in collaboration with Sweden, that Finland sought.)

Suursaari (Hogland) was to be fortified by Finland.

Finland would purchase military equipment, in order to strengthen her defences, from the Soviet Union.

Notwithstanding certain attractions in the first and second proposals, the Finnish response was swift and to the point: Finland would defend her territory against all comers, Suursaari was demilitarized under the Treaty of Dorpat and equipment for the Finnish armed forces was bought on the principle of the best available at the right price. Underlying these objections, the Finnish Cabinet cannot have failed to guess that, once any defence concessions were made to Moscow, other even more difficult demands would quickly follow. The bear was to kept beyond the gate.

It seems probable that Yartsev's proposals were simply a Soviet ploy to get negotiations restarted. The Finnish negative reaction had scarcely reached Moscow by telegraph before the Commissar for Foreign Affairs, Maxim Litvinov, summoned Finnish ambassador Aarno Yrjö-Koskinen to his office and presented him with a fresh set of demands. These were on such a radically different scale from those previously discussed that it seems highly improbable that they had been concocted overnight. While the exchange of notes until that point had concerned matters of largely tactical significance, Litvinov's suggestions moved into the entirely new field of long-term leasing of islands. Then, when the Finns declined to discuss this proposal, Litvinov played his trump card. He suggested that the Soviet Union would consider a transfer of some Soviet territory to Finland. This would be a part of East Karelia occupied by ethnic Finns.

In summary, the Soviet basis for negotiations, as they stood after the early March 1939 exchange of diplomatic notes, were as follows:

Finland was requested to lease the islands of Lavansaari, Seiskari, Suursaari and Tytärsaari, all in the eastern part of the Gulf of Finland and ceded under the Treaty of Dorpat, to the Soviet Union for thirty years.

In return, the Soviet Union would cede to Finland the East Karelian communes of Porajärvi and Repola, which the Finns had requested during the Dorpat negotiations in 1920, to take account of the wishes of the local population.

The Soviet Union would undertake not to fortify the islands to be leased but would agree to Finland fortifying the Åland Islands.

Finland and the Soviet Union would sign a trade agreement.

While these significantly widened proposals were being studied in Helsinki, the Soviet heavyweight who had been selected to support Yartsev arrived in the Finnish capital. Boris Stein was no stranger to the city, as he had been Soviet ambassador to Finland in 1934-35. Now the ambassador in Rome, he came back for a short holiday for his health – a story met with expressions of polite concern by the Finns who were nevertheless not deceived. Stein had been a reasonably well-liked ambassador and he knew virtually all the principal Finnish politicians active at the time. He was also known to Field-Marshal Mannerheim.

It was at this point that discussion of the Soviet proposals was widened to the full Cabinet and Mannerheim's opinion was sought for the first time. Far from adopting a rigid military stance, the Field-Marshal gave an illuminating glimpse of his grasp of *realpolitik*. He pointed out that the islands the Soviet Union wished to lease played no part in the defence of Finland, indeed their protection would be an unwelcome extra liability in war, as they were dimilitarized. He then went further to urge the Cabinet to shift the Finnish border in Karelia some ten kilometres to the north-west, so as remove the threat of Leningrad being subjected to artillery bombardment from Finnish territory.

Prime Minister Cajander's Cabinet remained adamantly opposed to all the Soviet proposals in the face of Mannerheim's conciliatory suggestions. It is difficult to judge what effect on their attitude was brought about by the German Army's entry into the remainder of Czechoslovakia on 15 March. While this brazen act, in defiance of the Munich agreement, must have focused the Finnish min-isters' minds on the helplessness of small states threatened by their larger neighbours, the earlier Czech relinquishment of the Sudetenland border area to Germany almost certainly hardened the Finns' resolve against any territorial concessions to the Soviet Union.

This second stage of negotiations, if the one-sided proposals can be granted that status, extended into early April. Boris Stein was in possession of the Soviet proposals and, once he had re-established his previous contacts in Helsinki, made plain his readiness to act as a conduit for any alternative or modified suggestions. To the last, Mannerheim urged Cajander and the Finnish Cabinet not to allow the ambassador to leave empty-handed, but to no avail. Finally, both Stein and Yartsev were recalled to Moscow.

At that point Prime Minister Cajander had not yet made his 'We are proud of having no rifles rusting in store' speech to the Finnish Army and reservists during manoeuvres. It may be that this one-time professor of forestry at Helsinki University could not bring his academic and logically-trained mind to contemplate a war with the Soviet Union arising out of the latter's desire to control a handful of islands. In the light of subsequent events it is easy to criticize Cajander and his Cabinet colleagues for not reaching a negotiated settlement with Moscow on terms less severe than were eventually to be dictated. This would be a shallow assessment, however. Elsewhere there was widespread evidence that acquiescence in the face of threats was but the first step down the slope to total subjugation. There was to be fearful loss of life, on both sides, but the Finns did not acquiesce. The Finns fought and they were not subjugated.

Those then alive will remember the summer of 1939 as one of glorious weather and a strange sense of suspension from reality. It was as if the awesome train of world events had become too dreadful to contemplate, leaving the mind free to dwell on everyday concerns. The most horrific and extensive war the world had until then seen was only as distant in the past as the Arab-Israeli Yom Kippur of 1973 is in 1993. The grief of the Great War was still felt in millions of homes across Europe and the possibility of a repeat performance found enthusiasm only in the minds of political extremists.

Finland takes her annual holidays earlier than her southern neighbours, so as to enjoy the best of the brief summer and to include the day of national rejoicing and relaxation – Midsummer's Day. In the June of 1939, 3,000 young men and some young women volunteered to spend one week of their holidays in Karelia. Their purpose was to work under the direction of the Karelian Civil Guard authorities helping to build the defences across the Isthmus. This idea had come from Mannerheim and led to the defences first being referred to as the 'Mannerheim Line.'

Finland's sense of awareness of extreme danger soon found parallels in other countries. The unreal calm was broken by the announcement, on 23 August 1939, of the Molotov-Ribbentrop Agreement. Whatever the Western democracies were seeking as a way out of their ever-sharpening dilemma, a non-aggression pact between the forces of extreme right and left was not an option previously given much serious consideration. A cartoon appeared in a London newspaper depicting Hitler and Stalin shaking hands while each prepared to stab his new partner in the back. No public announcement of the attendant secret protocol, entitled the 'Soviet-German Frontier and Friendship Treaty', was made. Its purpose was to establish and delineate the future spheres of influence of Germany and the Soviet Union in Europe and the Baltic region. Article 1 dealt with the Baltic States (defined as Finland, Estonia, Latvia and Lithuania) and gave the frontier of Lithuania as the dividing line between the spheres of interest of the signatories. This placed the countries to the immediate north and south of the Gulf of Finland, Finland and Estonia, within the Soviet sphere.

Events then began to move with bewildering speed. Germany invaded Poland one week after the Non-Aggression Pact was signed and the Soviet Union occupied the eastern part of the country, as provided for in the secret protocol. Moscow opened a campaign of psychological pressure on Estonia, Latvia and Lithuania with demands for air and naval facilities on their territory. It was apparent that, far from introducing a new atmosphere of stable German and Soviet relations, the Molotov-Ribbentrop Agreement had simply put their rivalry on ice, while lesser matters received their separate attention.

The three southern Baltic States were in no position to resist Soviet pressure and each had signed a pact of 'mutual assistance' by 11 October. The Soviet-Estonian Treaty was of particular relevance for Finland. It included the Soviet lease of Dagö and Osel islands, at the mouth of the Gulf of Finland, and granted use of the ports of Tallinn and Paldiski, twenty-five miles to the west of the capital, to the Soviet Baltic Fleet. By this time the contents of the Molotov-Ribbentrop secret protocol had become known to Finnish intelligence. The Imperial defence plan was being reinstated, step by step.

On 5 October the Helsinki Government received a peremptory invitation to Moscow for resumption of discusions on 'concrete political questions'. Forewarned by intelligence reports, the Cabinet was ready to react and put two distinct but related activities in hand. The veteran politician Juhani Paasikivi, Finnish prime minister in 1918 and a fluent Russian speaker, was recalled from his post as ambassador in Stockholm to head the mission to Moscow. Secondly, the units of the 21,600 strong Covering Force were mobilized and deployed to the eastern frontier and southern coast. On the day that Paasikivi and his team arrived in the Soviet capital, the Finnish cabinet authorized an almost complete but discreet mobilization of the armed forces. This was covered by describing the call-up as 'Exercise Extraordinary'.

The Soviet proposals, for what was to prove the third and final round of defence-related negotiations, had developed during the summer months. A new self-confidence became evident in the tone of the suggestions that were put bluntly across a table, rather than through intermediaries. There are two possible reasons for this: the certainty that Germany would not interfere, at least not for the time being, and the swift compliance of the southern Baltic States. There may have been one less apparent cause. The Red Army had defeated the Japanese at the battle of the Khalin River on the Manchurian border during September. Russia nursed a well-deserved high regard for Japanese military competence since the war of 1904. The little-known victory appeared to augur well for future military success.

The Paasikivi delegation was offered a Mutual Assistance treaty on lines similar to those with the Baltic States. Then Stalin, who was leading for the Soviet Union, swept straight on to the alternative: a pact of local assistance specifically related to security of the Gulf of Finland. The Soviet proposals contained four components that were entirely new, although in addition to those discussed during the previous winter:

The port and peninsula of Hanko, at the extreme south-western tip of Finnish coast at the mouth of the Gulf (see Map 9 on page 108), should be leased to the Soviet Union for thirty years as a naval base.

The Finnish-Soviet frontier should be moved ten kilometres further westwards from Leningrad.

At Petsamo, in the far north, the western (Finnish) half of the Fisherman's Peninsula should be permanently ceded to the Soviet Union.

In return for the territorial concessions by Finland, the Soviet Union would cede to Finland twice the total area of land to be ceded to the Soviet Union.

The territory to be ceded in exchange would be the Karelian communes of Porajärvi and Repola, requested in the Dorpat Treaty negotiations in 1920.

The verbal explanation of the Soviet proposals was followed by presentation of a written list containing additional requirements, of which three struck ominous notes of warning in the minds of the Finnish delegation :

The Soviet garrison on Hanko Peninsula would amount to 5,000 men, including an infantry regiment, a tank battalion and air squadrons.

Lappohja, on the eastern shore of the Hanko peninsula, would be required as an anchorage for the Soviet Baltic Fleet.

The fortifications on either side of the proposed new frontier in Karelia were to be demolished.

The experienced Paasikivi recognized the first and last of these extra demands as totally non-negotiable for the Finnish Government. A garrison of 5,000 Soviet troops on Finnish territory only fifty miles from the capital would be a standing threat to political independence. Surrender of the territory and the fortifications on the Karelian Isthmus would leave Finland defenceless. Wisely, he returned to Helsinki for instructions.

For the next round of discussions in Moscow, which began on 23 October, the Paasikivi team was reinforced by Finance Minister and Socialist Party leader Väinö Tanner. Stalin remained adamant about his need for the garrison on Hanko, although he conceded that it could be cut to a strength of 4,000 men. He also made a modest reduction in his requirement for territory in Karelia. There was, however, no flexibility in the remaining Soviet demands. Paasikivi sought other areas of possible compromise but it was clear that the Soviet interest in a negotiated settlement was fast waning.

Between the second and third visits of the Finnish delegation to Moscow, Soviet Foreign Minister Vyacheslav Molotov made a speech to the Supreme Soviet. This contained the complete catalogue of the Soviet demands on Finland. The speech was given full publicity through the international press while the Finnish delegation was actually en route for Moscow for the third and last time. Paasikivi recognized that the Soviet leadership had deliberately curtailed their own scope for compromise by publicly declaring their position in advance. Anticipating a mere formality of a meeting, the

Finns were surprised to hear Stalin offer to give up his demand for the garrison on Hanko in exchange for comparable facilities on a group of islands to the east, near the proposed Lappohja anchorage. Paasikivi replied, 'That is an entirely new matter and we would need instructions from Helsinki.' So the long-drawn-out negotiations came to their inconclusive end.

Views are sometimes advanced that, if they had shown more flexibility in their overall approach, the Finns might possibly have avoided war. They might indeed have done so, but the likelihood is that they would have exchanged war for a bloodless conquest. The Soviet leadership practised the then current aggressor's ploy of offering new treaties, while the Finns stood for no compromise of their declared neutrality. They also stood for good faith and asked no more in return.

PART III
The Winter War

9
Invasion

The two adversaries' understanding of each other's capabilities and intentions at the start of the Winter War were precisely accurate in some instances and significantly mistaken in others. When the fighting intensified and spread, the miscalculations by both sides worked out to the almost exclusive advantage of the defenders. Finnish intelligence accurately predicted that the Red Army, as it was then still known, would launch its primary offensive in the Karelian Isthmus. It was anticipated that this would have the purpose of breaking through Finnish defence lines quickly, so as to seize control of the rail and road communications leading into the southern heartland. It was also foreseen that there would be a secondary offensive around the north of Lake Ladoga, designed either to outflank the Isthmus defences or, alternatively, to draw away Finnish resources and reserves and leave the Isthmus defences dangerously weak. The Finns had ruled out any Soviet offensive further north, except to take Petsamo in the far north. It was recognized that the port was indefensible with the very small forces available.

The possibility of a Soviet offensive anywhere on the 560-mile long eastern frontier region, north of Lake Pielinen, was dismissed as simply not feasible. Routes were scarce through this terrain of jagged rock outcrops interspersed with swamps, as the region was thinly populated. The terrain on the Soviet side of the frontier was much the same, almost bare of population and believed by the Finns – mistakenly as it turned out – to have no lateral communications. In consequence of this appreciation, a third Soviet offensive across the waist of Finland, between Raate and Salla, came as a complete surprise to Mannerheim and the Finnish general staff. There were some rather more devastating surprises in store for the invaders of this desolate wilderness.

Even if the intelligence appreciation of Soviet intentions had been completely correct, it is probable that Mannerheim would still have given low priority to the eastern frontier region. He knew that the areas crucial to successful national defence were the Karelian Isthmus and the northern shores of Lake Ladoga, known as Ladoga-Karelia. It would have been a dangerous waste of his slender resources to divert more troops, beyond those initially deployed to keep frontier watch, from where he knew the critical battles would be fought

The general staffs on both sides were alike in their over-estimation of the fighting capabilities of the Red Army. Neither had then begun to appreciate the drastic damage done by Stalin's purges of his senior military officers in the years 1937-39. Between eighty and ninety percent of those with operational experience down to the level of regimental commander had been executed or dismissed. This was but one instance of Stalin's paranoia about a possible coup against him. In place of men with operational experience in the First World War and the Russian Civil War, and in many instances trained at the rightly esteemed Frunze Military Academy in Moscow, Stalin appointed political commissars or inexperienced officers who were believed to be politically safe.

Any Soviet doubts about the combat capability of the Red Army or effectiveness of the new tactics of massed tank attack, influenced by German tactical philosophy, were countered by a little-publicized defeat inflicted on the Japanese. The professional standards of Japan's army and navy during the Russo-Japanese War of 1904 had not been forgotten. Therefore defeat of a large Japanese force by General Georgi Zhukov in a Manchurian border dispute in September 1939 had provided a much-needed boost to Red Army confidence. Zhukov had used massed armour of five tank brigades in support of three infantry divisions to defeat General Kenkichi Ueda's 28,000-strong army corps at the Battle of Khalin Gol. Zhukov was a true professional, however. He had begun his active service career as an NCO in the Novgorod Dragoons in 1916, but somehow escaped Stalin's purge.

Over-confidence in Red Army capabilities meant that Soviet intelligence made only a perfunctory surveillance of Finnish war preparations. They could not have failed to be aware of the work done on the Karelian defences during the summer. Indeed the Finns had been at pains to give publicity to the exertions of the young volunteers as a demonstration of national resolve and unity. The discreet manner of the call-up of Finnish reserve forces, during which the emotive

word 'mobilization' had been scupulously avoided, seems to have
left the Red Army unprepared for the well-organized and tenacious
resistance they encountered when operations began.

The Soviet leadership was too much influenced in reaching important judgements by opinion that was pleasing to hear. The veteran
Finnish Communist Otto Kuusinen, who had fled from Finland in
1918, told Stalin that the Finnish workers would rise to welcome
their Red Army 'liberators'. Such an assessment might have had
some basis in the country Kuusinen last knew during the War of
Independence. Expressed in 1939, it misled the Soviet leadership into
expecting a walkover. When invasion began, Finland stood as one
nation.

Mobilization and deployment of Finland's armed forces began
with the order issued by the Cabinet on 6 October 1939, the day
when Juhani Paasikivi reached Moscow for the start of what proved
to be the final round of negotiations. Although the Cabinet still
hoped to avert war at that stage, Mannerheim's advice to put
preparations in hand was heeded. Had the complete facts then been
known, it is unlikely that any Cabinet member would have doubted
the outcome of the Moscow talks. By that time several of the
divisions of the invasion force had already been concentrated in the
Leningrad Military District.

To appreciate the background to the Red Army's deployment for
attack on Finland, it is necessary to understand where Russian attack
philosophy differs, then and now, from that of most Western armies.
Under the Soviet system, the term 'army corps' to describe an operational grouping of a number of divisions has less tactical importance
than that of 'army' but the more significant difference is one of operational concept. In Western terms, an army corps is formed to undertake one or more specific operational tasks, for which the number of
divisions and corps troops allocated are judged sufficient. The resultant formation has the manoeuvrability, firepower and logistic support to accomplish its task or tasks – at least that is the theory. Under
the Soviet system an 'army' is more a reservoir of forces, notably
divisions of different types, to be used as the battle demands. Thus
an army could launch an attack with four divisions and with four
more, almost immediately behind, ready to replace the leading divisions as soon as their combat capacity becomes exhausted. Whereas
the battle concept in most Western armies is one of army corps that

can be manoeuvred, fought and occasionally rested, the Soviet system foresees a continuing avalanche of attacking divisions, which may or may not have a corps headquarters controlling groups of them.

While the Soviet method may appear formidable, it has an inherent flaw of inflexibility. The only alternative to the avalanche style attack, if it fails in spite of ever-increasing weight and intensity, is to turn off the tap of resources and start an avalanche somewhere else. The Soviet system also demands a fatalistic confidence in certainty of quick success, as the attacking divisions are committed in such rapid succession that heavy casualties are inevitable. Failure to achieve a swift victory can lead to a collapse in morale and the rapid descent from the heights to the depths of spirits, which is something of a feature of the Russian temperament.

Responsibility for preparing the invasion of Finland was logically placed on the commander of the Leningrad Military District. His boundaries stretched north from the Estonian frontier to the Kola Peninsula and eastwards from the borders of Finland to the northern tip of the Urals. Lieutenant-General Kirill Meretskov had been transferred from the Volga to the Leningrad command in the autumn of 1938. This was the autumn following the spring in which Boris Yartsev made his first unsuccessful approach to Foreign Minister Rudolf Holsti, seeking military facilities in Finland. Meretskov was a veteran of the Spanish Civil War and another of the few surviving military professionals.

As Meretskov set about devising the plan for the invasion of Finland, he allowed himself to be persuaded by Stalin of the validity of Otto Kuusinen's advice that the majority of Finns would rise up to welcome their liberators. Even so, he based his plans on the principle of using overwhelming superiority of numbers. In this he had a valuable local ally in Andrei Zhdanov, first secretary of the Leningrad Party Committee and commissar for the region. Zhdanov was responsible for providing all the local civil infrastructure for war preparations. As plans developed, so roads and railways were extended and improved for the swift passage and support of the invading force. The construction programme included a lateral road from the Leningrad-Murmansk railway towards the Finnish border opposite Raate and Salla, which went undetected by the Finns.

Reinforcement soon began in earnest. During the period 7 September to 28 October, embracing the first and second Paasikivi discussions in Moscow, the normal garrison of the Leningrad Military District was increased from seven to nineteen divisions. A further nine divisions were added during November and an additional five detailed as immediate reinforcements. The X Tank Army Corps, which included the 1st and 13th Tank Brigades, was positioned opposite the Karelian Isthmus.

Of the 3,300 Soviet tanks used during the Winter War, some 2,200 were grouped into five independent tank brigades. Others formed independent tank battalions and companies. During the opening offensives a Soviet infantry regiment had no integral armoured unit but each division included one tank battalion. This had a complement of twenty-one T-26C or BT-5 tanks of 10.3 and 11 tons respectively, armed with a 45 mm gun and 7.62 machine-guns, and sixteen T-37 amphibious light tanks. The latter were designed primarily for reconnaissance and fitted with only a 7.62 machine-gun. The tank brigades comprised a mixture of light battalions, each of between forty and fifty T-26C or BT-5 tanks, and heavy tank battalions of T-28 twenty-ton tanks armed with a 76 mm gun and four 7.62 machine guns. The heavier T-35A tanks of forty-five tons, fitted with one 76 mm, two 45 mm guns and five 7.62 machine-guns, were formed into independent tank companies.

A total of twenty-two Soviet divisions and the five tank brigades were grouped into four attacking armies. In the south, Lieutenant-General V. F. Jakovlev's 7th Army, with eight divisions and four tank brigades, faced into the Karelian Isthmus, while Lieutenant-General Ivan Habarov's 8th Army, of seven divisions and one tank brigade, was poised to make the flanking offensive round the north shore of Lake Ladoga. Lieutenant-General Mihail Duhanov's 9th Army of five divisions was positioned opposite the centre of the eastern frontier, around Repola, ready to launch the unexpected offensive across the waist of Finland through the frontier towns of Salla and Raate. In the far north Major-General Valerian Frolov's 14th Army, of only two divisions, stood ready to take the port of Petsamo and occupy the Fisherman's Peninsula. Five army corps headquarters were also established: XIX and L[50th] under 7th Army, I and LVI under 8th Army and XLVII under 9th Army. By 30 November the Red Army had assembled a force of 470,000 men in the Leningrad Military District, ready for the invasion.

In Finland the first phase of deployment was completed in two

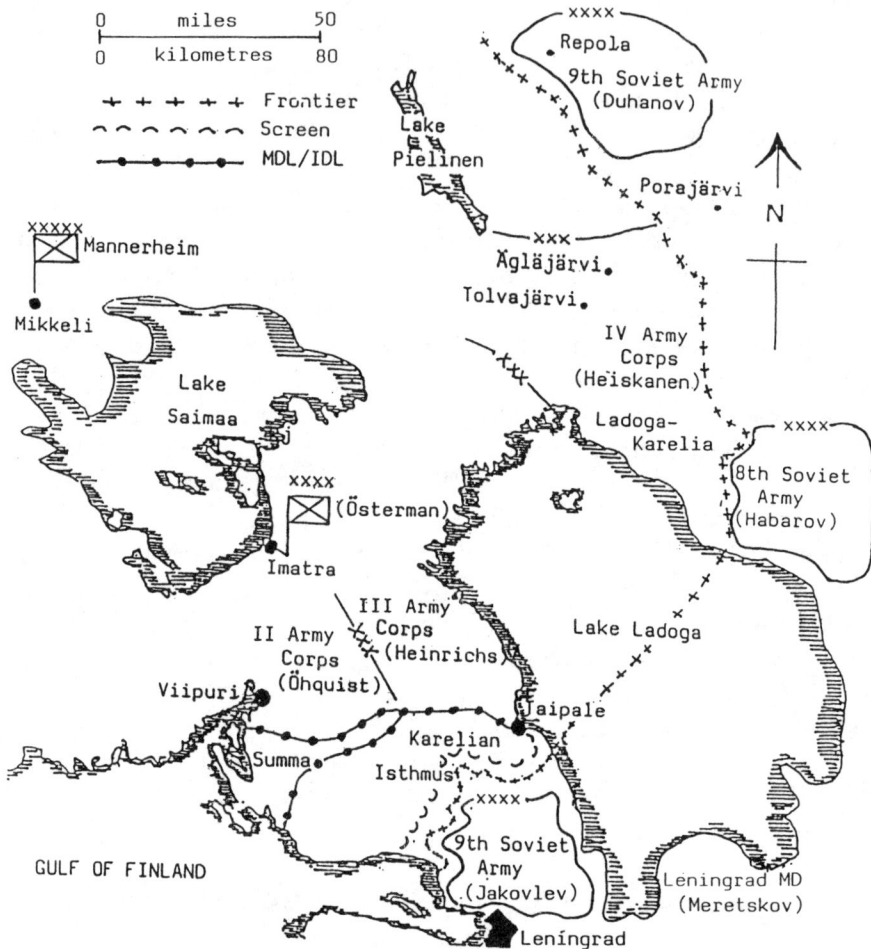

Map 10: Finnish and Red Army deployment in the Karelian Isthmus and
Ladoga-Karelia on 30 November 1939

days, 6 and 7 October, using units of the standing army as planned.
A covering force of four battle groups was deployed well forward
across the Karelian Isthmus. Behind this protective screen three
brigades, each of three battalions and with integral artillery support,
took up positions on the forward and best-prepared defensive line. A
five-battalion group with artillery was deployed north of Lake
Ladoga and six independent and reinforced battalions were positioned to watch possible crossing points along the eastern border.

The second phase of deployment began on 10 October, following the mobilization of the first reserve units. As divisional staffs and support troops became available, it was possible to put the operational deployment on a sounder footing. Units in the Isthmus were grouped into two divisions and those in Ladoga-Karelia into one. Successive further changes took place to absorb units of the whole field army as they became available, but a viable operational deployment was maintained throughout all three phases.

Consternation amongst the civilian population was avoided by evoking the Finnish Law for 'The Protection of the Republic', which provided for troops to be called up for special large-scale manoeuvres. This was completed during 26 October, by when virtually all the 295,000 strong field army was deployed to emergency deployment positions. As may be seen from Map 10 on the facing page, these reflected Mannerheim's appreciation of how and where the Soviet invasion would develop.

In the Karelian Isthmus, which he regarded as the enemy's selected area of principal effort, the commander-in-chief deployed a force of 120,000 men. These comprised five divisions: three in II Army Corps under Lieutenant-General Harald Öhquist, in the western part of the Isthmus, and two in III Army Corps, under Major-General Erik Heinrichs in the east. In front of the forward main position the covering screen of four battle groups remained to provide protection and warning. In Ladoga-Karelia, where he correctly anticipated the secondary thrust, but not in the strength in which it was delivered, Mannerheim placed a force of 40,000 men. These formed the two divisions of IV Army Corps under command of Major-General Juho Heiskanen.

The Finnish Army, as distinct from the armed forces as a whole, were under command of Lieutenant-General Hugo Österman, who established his operational headquarters at Imatra, immediately to the north-west of the Finnish neck of the Karelian Isthmus. Shortly after resuming the position of commander-in-chief on 30 November, Mannerheim appointed Österman to command the Army of the Isthmus, comprising II and III Army Corps. He thereby assumed overall command of land operations himself. Mannerheim chose to return to his previous headquarters at the small town of Mikkeli, sixty miles north-west of Imatra, which he had used during the Karelian battles towards the close of the War of Independence in 1918.

In Mikkeli Mannerheim was well placed to keep watch over developments in the Isthmus, supervise operations north of Lake Ladoga and be ready for anything that might unexpectedly happen elsewhere. The long stretch of the eastern frontier remained covered by a force of independent battalions of frontier troops totalling only 16,000 men, with a detached company and artillery battery garrisoning Petsamo. This command was designated the Northern Finland Group under Major-General Viljo Tuompo, a veteran of 27th Jäger Battalion. This overall deployment plan left one infantry regiment under naval command, to deal with any attempted enemy landings on the south coast, and two divisions as the commander-in-chief's reserve. One of these, 9th Division at Oulu, had only one artillery battalion instead of the usual three.

Finnish Navy and Air Force units came to wartime readiness and either deployed to their emergency plan locations or prepared to do so. The naval role remained essentially protective, with emphasis on coastal defence and air defence of the main south coast ports. The Air Force fighter aircraft were situated to defend the cities and ports from Soviet air attack, while the small bomber force prepared sorties in direct support of Finnish ground force operations.

Mobilization and emergency deployment of the Finnish armed forces, completed within a total of three weeks from the first order being given, vindicated the value of the regional mobilization arrangements introduced since 1932. In overall command and at the age of seventy-two, Mannerheim faced his fourth war and his second as Finland's commander-in-chief.

The pretext for the Soviet invasion was acted out on the afternoon of Sunday, 26 November. A sentry on the Finnish side of the Rajajoki river, that formed the frontier in that part of the Karelian Isthmus, heard mortar fire south of the village of Mainila on the Soviet side. Private Matti Jokela assumed that the Soviet regiment opposite his own was having a live-firing exercise. A mortar gives a distinctive 'cough' when it fires, quite unlike the loud detonation of an artillery piece. There is then a long pause between the cough and detonation, which is due to the height to which the mortar bomb is projected before it falls to earth. Jokela was a conscientious soldier and, welcoming a diversion in an otherwise dull stretch of duty, he made a careful log of the firing. In the pauses between the mortar's firing cough and explosion of a total of seven bombs, he was able to take compass bearings on both sources of sound. The bearings showed that the mortar baseplate position was 2,000 metres south-east from the area of the explosions and therefore on the Soviet side of the border.

Later the same day the Finnish ambassador in Moscow, Aarno Yrjö-Koskinen, received a note of protest from the the Soviet Foreign Ministry. The note declared that four Soviet soldiers had been killed by the 'Finnish bombardment' of Mainila and demanded that, so to avoid any further similar incidents, all Finnish troops should be withdrawn to a line fifteen miles from the frontier. At 8.30 p.m. that evening a Moscow news broadcast stated that the Finns had staged an act of provocation on the Karelian frontier. On receipt of the contents of the Soviet note, the Finnish Government immediately offered a joint investigation of the incident and began their own inquiry. Two other sets of compass bearings, taken from different points from those taken by Matti Jokela, confirmed that all the mortar bombs had been fired from the Soviet side of the border. It was also confirmed that there were no Finnish mortars or artillery pieces situated within firing range of the village of Mainila. This was on Mannerheim's specific instruction, as he had intended to avoid any suggestions of a threat to Soviet territory.

Molotov rejected the Finnish offer of a joint investigation of the Mainila incident and informed Ambassador Yrjö-Koskinen on 27 November that the Soviet Government no longer regarded the Non-Aggression Pact to be valid because of the Finnish action on the frontier. A further Finnish appeal for a joint investigation was to no avail and the Soviet Foreign Ministry issued a statement formally severing diplomatic relations with Finland from the evening of 29 November. The invasion began in the early hours of the following day. There was no formal declaration of war.

The first seven days of fighting brought two unwelcome surprises to the Finnish commander-in-chief. The first was the totally unexpected and large-scale Soviet offensive at the narrow point of the waist of Finland in the eastern frontier region. The second was the strength and determination of the Soviet attack in Ladoga-Karelia. It was in these two regions that the most intensive early battles were to be fought, calling for some speedy changes in Finnish Army command arrangements and deployment of reserves.

In the Karelian Isthmus events occurred much as Mannerheim had expected, although he would have prefered to see the covering force remain forward in the south-east of the Isthmus for longer than it did. Nonetheless, he was confident of his commanders and dispositions there. Österman, commander of the Army of the Isthmus, was ordered to stand firm on the main defence line (MDL) and inflict maximum casualties and damage on the attacking Red Army divisions.

Even before he left Helsinki for his operational headquarters at Mikkeli, the C-in-C recognized that he would have to reinforce the eastern frontier region and change the command arrangements in Ladoga-Karelia. It was in the latter region that the invaders were meeting with their only significant success. Finnish resistance faltered before the Red Army advance and then began to crumble. While Mannerheim had always anticipated a significant Soviet offensive in this region, it now appeared possible that it might not be a diversionary attack after all but the main thrust. He acted quickly and decisively, replacing Heiskanen in command of IV Army Corps in Ladoga-Karelia with Major-General Woldemar Hägglund, a veteran of 27th Jäger Battalion and of operations in Karelia during the War of Independence.

The Tolvajärvi-Ilomantsi area was seriously threatened by the Red Army advance during the first few days of fighting. Mannerheim therefore made this region a special sub-command under the aggressive Colonel Paavo Talvela, another veteran Jäger, who could be relied upon to seize the tactical initiative. Talvela's 'Group T' comprised one infantry regiment, four independent infantry battalions, an artillery battalion and two independent artillery batteries. He reached the area of Tolvajärvi to find the local defenders in retreat and confusion. They had no plan for defeating or even delaying the invaders and were being scattered to the woods by the Soviet tanks leading the advance. By a quirk of fate, Talvela had based his military thesis at War College on this terrain and appreciated that the situation he now faced did not call for a static defensive battle.

The Soviet troops leading Habarov's offensive had encountered little real resistance and were full of confidence. Talvela resolved to break that confidence by attacking wherever the enemy was weak or extended, inflict casualties and spread fear and confusion. He struck first at Habarov's 139th Division approaching Tolvajärvi and already some twenty-five miles on the Finnish side of the frontier. It was a bold choice: 139th Division had forty-five tanks and almost

20,000 men. Behind them advanced the equally strong 75th Division. A force of 200 Finns under Lieutenant-Colonel Aaro Pajari attacked a Soviet battalion camped near the village of Taivallampi. The Russians were thrown into confusion and Pajari left them engaged in a two-hour fire fight with their neighbouring Soviet battalion. A second force led by Captain Raymond Ericsson made a similar sortie against the enemy at Kotisaari. Ericsson was killed but serious casualties were inflicted.

This relentless form of sudden and unexpected attacks threw the unblooded troops of the 75th Division, which replaced those of the 139th, into utter confusion. They called for air support against Talvela's men harassing their units dug in around Äglajärvi, only to be bombed themselves when the Red Air Force failed to distinguish friend from foe on the ground. Pajari recaptured Kotisaari on 12 December, when his men counted over 1,000 enemy dead on the ground, and Äglajärvi on 17 December. Survivors of the Soviet 75th and 139th Divisions were thrown back the twenty-five miles to the Aittojärvi river on the frontier, where they remained until the end of the campaign. Although Talvela was not able to destroy the enemy completely in the Tolvajärvi-Ilomantsi area, he was able to report to Mannerheim on 23 December that the invaders were no longer a threat.

To the south, Finnish troops under Hägglund halted the Soviet 56th Division short of Kollaa and others of Tuompo's Northern Finland Group held the 54th Division at Kuhmo. The waist of Finland was most seriously threatened, however, by the advance of General Duhanov's 9th Army. One of his divisions, the 163rd, had reached Soumussalmi by 7 December. From there Duhanov was well placed to threaten the important rail link running north of Lake Oulujärvi to the port of Oulu on the Gulf of Bothnia. Duhanov was not content to depend on this thrust alone, in his effort to cut Finland in half. At Salla, seventy-five miles further north, his 122nd Division had found a gap in the Finnish defence, due to the acute shortage of troops in the frontier region. Determined not to be distracted from the main battles in the Karelian Isthmus and Ladoga-Karelia, Mannerheim despatched another Jäger veteran – Colonel Hjalmar Siilasvuo with his understrength 9th Division to halt the Soviet advance. This Siilasvuo most succesfully accomplished, with crippling losses to the enemy. His victory at Suomussalmi is described in Chapter 10.

In the extreme north Mannerheim never entertained any expectation of holding the port of Petsamo or the Fisherman's Peninsula against the two divisions of Frolov's 14th Army. Once the strength of the Soviet thrust in the centre of the eastern frontier became plain, Mannerheim divided the northern front into two sectors. This allowed a small force under Captain Antti Pennanen to withdraw down the line of the Arctic Road as far as Nautsi, to the immediate south-east of Lake Inari. There that sector of the front stabilized until the end of the campaign. In later years Pennanen rose to the rank of lieutenant-general and command of the Frontier Guard. A newly formed Lapland Group, under command of Major-General Kurt Wallenius, became responsible for the frontier region between Nautsi and Salla.

Across the Karelian Isthmus, the forward positions of the Mannerheim Line extended from Kyrönniemi to Summa in the west towards Taipale on the shore of Lake Ladoga in the east. However, the main Red Army offensive in the Isthmus was not launched as soon as Mannerheim had expected. While fierce battles were being fought north of the lake, Red Army activity to the south had some curious characteristics. In the mornings the Russians would seem to prepare for an all-out assault but, when they found no Finnish troops to their immediate front or were harassed by fire from points they mistakenly believed to have been evacuated by the defenders, they hesitated and then withdrew. It was not until 6 December that a properly concerted and planned attack began against the Finnish main defence line at Taipale. This heralded the main Soviet assault.

The Soviet right flank assault on the eastern side of the Isthmus was made by the L[50th] Army Corps under command of Lieutenant-General Vladimir Grendal, who was clearly an enthusiast for the avalanche method. Three divisions, the 49th, 142nd and 150th, supported by 150 tanks and an intensive artillery bombardment, mounted the attack. The battle lasted eleven days, with the Russians making repeated attempts to break through the Finns' mines and wire. They crossed the River Vuoksi but could make no further progress and the whole of the Soviet right flank offensive petered out on 17 December.

On the Soviet left flank, opposite General Öhquist's II Army Corps, troops of XIX Army Corps began to exert pressure on

Summa, at the point where the forward edge of the Mannerheim line turned due south towards Kyrönniemi on the coast. One Finnish position in this region was taken in the early days of fighting but a prompt local counter-attack, invariably the best tactic if the enemy can be caught off balance, restored the situation. On both flanks the Russian units suffered unexpectedly high tank losses. As the defenders had few anti-tank guns and none at all in many sectors, they improvised the 'Molotov cocktail' which even today is one the most effective anti-armour weapons in close-quarter combat.

Between 15 and 17 December XIX Army Corps made a strong and well-concerted attack, using three of its four divisions, along the line of the Leningrad-Viipuri railway. This was undoubtedly the most testing time for the Army of the Isthmus during December, but the Finns refused to yield and the main defence line held. Fighting continued in this sector until 20 December, when the invaders temporarily lost the initiative.

It was shortly before this point that General Österman first asked the commander-in-chief's permission to prepare a counter-attack. Mannerheim cautioned Österman to be patient, stressing the advantage of the defenders fighting from dug-in positions against an enemy forced to attack in the open and through the obstacles of mines and wire. He eventually agreed to a plan using the reserve 6th Division and the infantry regiment under naval command for coastal defence. Österman decided on a surprise attack, without any preliminary artillery bombardment, starting at 0630 hours on 23 December. It was an ambitious venture but the 6th Division was not well enough trained, nor had they sufficient supporting artillery, for the plan to succeed. By the late afternoon of the first day the advance had come to a halt. General Öhquist, commanding the II Army Corps sector, gave orders to withdraw to the main defence line. This was the last main action in the Isthmus in December, apart from a forty-eight-hour-long Red Army divisional attack against Taipale starting on Christmas Day, which was repulsed.

In forming Talvela's Group, and a similar one under Siilasvuo further north, Mannerheim had committed virtually all his immediate reserves. There can be no doubt that this difficult decision was justified by the results. The aggressive tactics used by Talvela and Siilasvuo turned the tide decisively in northern Ladoga-Karelia and the central border region. Moreover, in the northern Ladoga-

Karelia fighting alone the Russians lost 30 guns, 60 tanks and 4,000 dead, as well as 600 prisoners.

The Finns paid for this victory with 630 killed and 1,300 wounded. Perhaps most significant of all, the Russians had been made to realize that they were not engaged in a walkover. Talvela's and Siilasvuo's counter-offensives put paid to Soviet plans to turn the northern flank of the Isthmus defences and to sever Finland at the waist. Elsewhere the fronts had held and were stable. The Soviet Union had lost the stategic initiative, at least for the time being. As Mannerheim had always planned, a pause had been imposed by the Finns' resolute defence from the frontiers of their country. It now remained to be seen whether the outside world had the will to come to their aid.

10

The Wilderness and Motti Battles

From the tactical standpoint the battles in the wilderness of Finland's eastern frontier region and those that followed in Ladoga-Keralia are the most remarkable of all that were fought during the Winter War. The boldness and resolution of the Finnish military commanders matched the tenaciousness of Talvela's Group, which had halted and thrown back two Soviet divisions in Ladoga-Karelia during December, but the tactics were different. In the northern wilderness, skilfully directed and confidently led Finnish troops defeated enemy forces of numerically greatly superior strength by systematically attacking locally isolated Soviet units, while keeping the others penned in and awaiting their turn. Lacking mobility off the scarce and narrow roads, the Russians found their artillery, tanks and air support of little practical use against an enemy only fleetingly seen. Denied resupply, many of the invaders froze or starved to death. While others were able to break out, Finnish ski patrols resolutely pursued many of those attempting to reach the safety of the frontier on foot through the forests.

Lieutenant-General Mihail Duhanov's 9th Soviet Army of five divisions had orders to cut Finland in half at the 'waist' between the eastern frontier and the head of the Gulf of Bothnia. His strategic objectives were the Finnish ports of Tornio and Oulu, standing some seventy miles apart on the coast close to the head of the Gulf. Vehicle routes for logistic support across the wilderness on the Finnish side of the frontier were few, but Duhanov believed that his staff had found two axes adequate for his planned advance. It was with these in mind that a new road had been built on the Soviet side of the frontier to permit a rapid approach march of the Soviet spearhead divisions. These were to be followed by the second echelon troops and supplies for a relentless drive to capture the two Finnish ports 150 miles to the south-west.

Duhanov allocated two divisions to the northerly of his two

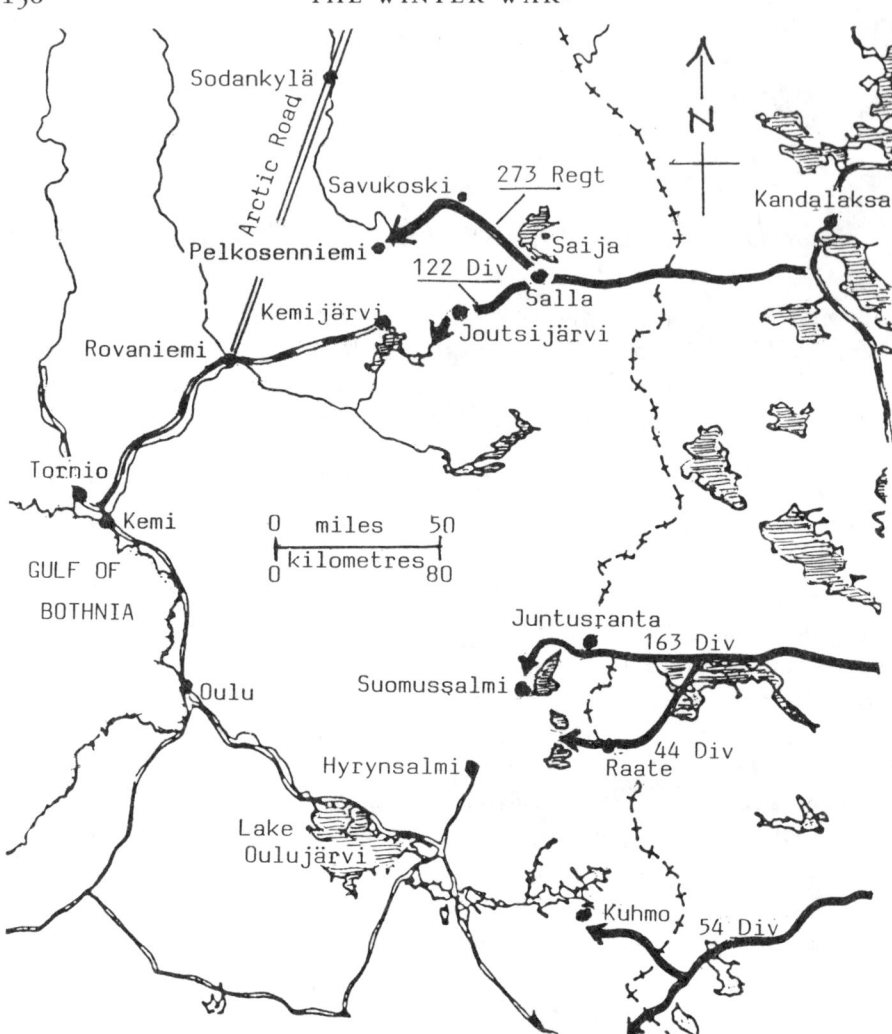

Map 11: The Wilderness Battles

sectors. This centred on the small village of Salla, some thirty miles from the frontier on the Finnish side. The approach road on the Soviet side, built undetected by Finnish intelligence, ran from Kandalaksa on the Leningrad-Murmansk railway due westwards to the border. Duhanov's plan was simple and allowed for some flexibility. The 122nd Division was to lead the advance through Salla and then make best speed through Joutsijärvi to the railhead at Kemijärvi. Good rail and road communications linked Kemijärvi with Rovaniemi on the Arctic Road between Petsamo and the head of the Gulf.

The 122nd Division was joined for this operation by the 273rd Regiment, detached from the 88th Division, which was to be held back on the Soviet side of the frontier for the first phase of operations. 273rd Regiment was given the flanking task of advancing north-westwards from the frontier towards Savukoski. From there narrow roads through the forest and swampland allowed a choice. 273rd Regiment could either turn south-west, with the aim of supporting 122nd Division in an attack on Kemijärvi, or take the northern route towards the junction with the Arctic Road at Sodankylä to secure the right flank. This overall plan for the northern sector of 9th Soviet Army's front had decided merit, not least because there were only very few Finnish frontier troops to oppose it.

The southern sector of Duhanov's front was less promising, at least so far a drive on Oulu was concerned. There were only two possible routes, one on each side of the swampland north of Lake Oulujärvi situated halfway between the frontier and the coast of the Gulf. Nevertheless, the Soviet army commander allocated his remaining three divisions to this sector: 44th Motorized Division and the 54th and 163rd infantry Divisions. The two infantry divisions were given responsibility for opening up the routes, while the elite motorized division was to advance in the centre, initially more slowly but with the intention of exploiting whichever of the two routes offered the better opportunity for a swift and decisive drive on Oulu.

It is feasible to infer that Duhanov intended his whole southern sector offensive to be a means of drawing the local Finnish forces into battle, so as to allow his northern sector divisions to slip behind them down to the two Gulf ports. This theory is supported by the fact that he selected the village of Suomussalmi, a junction of five roads, as his first objective in the southern sector. He probably assessed that the local tactical significance of the village as a centre of sparse communications would not be lost on the Finns and that they would react in strength. If that was indeed his appreciation, Duhanov was to be proved correct. The outcome of the consequent battle brought him some unwelcome surprises.

Suomussalmi stands a mere twenty-two miles from the frontier and

Duhanov ordered 163rd Division to advance on the village from the north, through the frontier village of Juntusranta. 44th Motorized Divsion were directed to make their way through the frontier village of Raate, further to the south, and advance slowly along the road leading due west to join up with 163rd Division at Suomussalmi. Meanwhile the commander of 54th Division was told to make an independent advance south-westwards towards the small town of Kuhmo. From there two or three possible routes suggested access to the more southerly of the main roads in the sector leading to Oulu.

Major-General Selentsov's 163rd Division of Mongolian troops began its advance from Juntusranta on 30 November. Selentsov planned to cross the frozen tip of Lake Kiantajärvi before turning southwards down the road running close to the western shore of the lake leading to Suomussalmi. Two days later Major-General Vinogradov's 44th 'Blue' Motorized Division began its approach to Suomussalmi from Raate. 44th Division were Ukrainians from the Moscow Military District, where they customarily carried out ceremonial duties in the capital. The troops brought their parade uniforms and regimental bands – to provide, it is said, the requisite flourish for triumphal entries into captured Finnish towns and cities. It would have been more prudent for the Kremlin to have sent them trained and fully equipped for war in the Arctic winter – and on skis rather than on wheels. The combined strength of 44th and 163rd Divisions was 48,000 men with at least 100 tanks and more than 300 pieces of artillery.

Initially the advance of both divisions encountered little resistance from the lightly equipped Finnish frontier troops in their path. Before one week had elapsed, 163rd Division was closing on Suomussalmi. The 4,000 inhabitants, recognizing their precarious situation, burned down almost every building in the place and withdrew beyond Lake Niskanselkä, which flanks the south and west of the village.

At this point Mannerheim had just two operational divisions in reserve. 6th Division was committed to meet any emergency on the Karelian and Ladoga-Karelia fronts, leaving only the understrength 9th Division, with but one artillery battalion, as reserve for the frontier region. Although aware of Duhanov's advance in the Salla sector, Mannerheim decided to deal first with the threat to Suomussalmi. He sent Colonel Hjalmar Siilasvuo, commanding the 9th

Division, with a force of three infantry battalions from his division to prevent the 44th Division from joining up with the 163rd, which had occupied the burnt-out remains of Suomussalmi on 7 December.

In committing a substantial part of his only free operational reserve, Mannerheim demonstrated his accurate perception of the strategic importance of the waist of Finland. Neither he nor Finnish military intelligence had anticipated any significant Soviet offensive in the eastern frontier region, chiefly due to the difficulty of the terrain on both sides of the frontier and the secrecy with which the Russians had built the road on their side. Mannerheim had consequently been convinced that Soviet logistic capability would be inadequate to sustain a force approaching divisional strength in the waist sector of the frontier region. Nevertheless, he readily recognized the seriousness of the Soviet 9th Army offensive when it came.

If Finland were to be severed at the waist, it would become virtually impossible for substantial military aid to be sent from Sweden, or through Sweden from Britain and France. Only Germany could provide help across the Baltic and it was already apparent that Berlin intended to honour the non-aggression pact with the Soviet Union, at least until more immediately important considerations arose. The Western world, including the United States, had shown great sympathy with the Finnish cause but, with the northern port of Petsamo lost, material aid could come only via the railway through Norway and Sweden. Any shipping attempting to sail from Swedish ports south of the Åland Islands mine barrier would be at the mercy of the Soviet Fleet.

The officer sent by Mannerheim to halt the Soviet advance at Suomussalmi, Hjalmar Siilasvuo, was not only another veteran of 27th Jäger Battalion but also an independent and original military thinker. He knew that Suomussalmi's only military significance lay in its central junction of five roads. He was therefore surprised but delighted to discover that Selentsov had not exploited these communications but had allowed his 163rd Division to occupy the almost burned-out ruins of the village. Therefore, although he had only three battalions at his disposal, Siilasvuo had the unusual advantage in war of knowing precisely where his adversaries were or where they were coming from.

An impression of the local countryside is essential for a proper understanding of the events that followed. There was no heavy industry in the region. The sparse population comprised small farmers, hunters, lake fishermen or woodsmen. The ground was densely covered with strong, tall pine trees, with only small roads and tracks running through the forest suitable for hauling logs and moving farm produce. Immediately on his arrival, on 11 December, Siilasvuo made a flanking move to cut the road running westwards from Raate towards Suomussalmi. He thus separated the still advancing 44th Division from the 163rd, which was sheltering from the weather in the ruins of the village. The point where Siilasvuo cut the road combined the features of road block and ambush. It was a mile-wide isthmus between Lakes Kuivasjärvi and Kuomasjärvi. The only routes round the road block accessible to the Russians would be over the ice of the frozen lakes. Once on the ice, the enemy would be at the mercy of the Finns' carefully sited machine-guns. Two companies of 27th Infantry Regiment totalling 350 men, under command of Captain Simo Mäkinen, were left to halt the advance of 44th Division. This initially small task force was reinforced as additional troops became available.

Siilasvuo next turned westwards and in the following five days his still small force had closed every gap around 163rd Division. He had neither the men nor the heavy weapons to do more at that stage, but his first objectives were achieved. One enemy division was bottled up, mainly in the ruins of Suomussalmi and awaiting destruction, while the other was continuing its ponderous advance to a point of battle of the Finnish commander's own choosing. On 16 December the remaining two infantry regiments of Siilasvuo's 9th Division joined him near Suomussalmi, together with an additional light infantry battalion, an artillery battery and two anti-tank guns.

Still lacking enough artillery to give his force the full fighting capability of a division, Siilasvuo resolved not to waste a single man in his offensive. Instead he allowed the forest and temperature of minus forty degrees to do the killing for him. While the fighting elements of 163rd Division were besieged in the ruins of Suomussalmi, their logistic supply vehicles were strung out along the narrow road from Juntusranta. Siilasvuo sent small light infantry detachments of ski troops to attack the groups of halted vehicles. In response to this tactic, reacting either to basic training or more probably to an instinct for survival, the Soviet logistic troops formed themselves into small and isolated defensive detachments along the road.

Although the term 'motti tactics' did not come into use in the Finnish Army until January or February 1940 – and then as a direct result of operations conducted by General Woldemar Hägglund's IV Army Corps in Ladoga-Karelia, the small defensive pockets established by the Red Army north and east of Suomussalmi unconsciously provided a model for them. A motti is a cubic metre of cut and stacked logs to be used for fuel and laid along the forest track for collection. This became the very treatment that was meted out to the invaders, although the bitter cold and starvation had usually completed their work before the 'collection' phase could begin. When the troops of 163rd Division had exhausted all food and fuel they held in Suomussalmi, they attempted a breakout to the north of the town, hoping to push the surrounding Finns westwards and link up with their logistic supplies. There was stiff fighting, some of it hand-to-hand, during 24-26 December but the attempt failed. The remnants of 163rd Division withdrew into the wretched ruins of Suomussalmi, hoping for rescue by 44th Division. It was to prove a forlorn hope.

With his 9th Division reinforced by three extra infantry battalions, Siilasvuo was ready to begin his own offensive. He attacked the freezing and starving Russians in Suomussalmi and their pathetic logistic groups all the way back to Juntusranta. This provoked a second attempted breakout from the village but one without any offensive spirit or even as a battle for survival. Soviet soldiers of 163rd Division, many having thrown away their weapons, formed into long columns and began to shamble away to the north-east across the ice of Lake Kiantajärvi. The Finns showed no mercy to the would-be invaders. Machine-guns mounted at the lakeside encouraged the retreat, while their ski-borne light infantry harassed the columns from the flanks. In an operation of almost surgical precision, Siilasvuo's men reduced 163rd Soviet Division to a rabble of dazed individuals with thought only for survival. While around 9,000 reached the safety of the frontier, another 5,000 Russian dead were counted in and around Suomussalmi at the end of December.

Meanwhile, far from coming to the rescue of their comrades, 44th Motorized Division was halted bumper to tailboard on the narrow Raate road. Siilasvuo allowed his men no pause for rejoicing over their victory at Suomussalmi but, extracting all the Soviet weapons, ammunition and equipment he needed from the defeated remnants of 163rd Division, he turned his attention eastwards. He found the head of the 44th Division column halted at Captain Mäkinen's road block between Lakes Kuivasjärvi and Kuomajärvi. Behind the division's stationary advance guard, a series of platoon-defended positions stretched back down the road all fifteen miles to the frontier. Russian tanks were patrolling the several-hundred-yard gaps between the defensive groups into which the invaders had divided themselves. Siilasvuo kept these under pressure day and night. He attacked, giving the defenders no chance of sleep or opportunity to resupply. The Red Air Force made several attempted airdrops, but only a few sacks of biscuits reached the starving Russians. It was equally difficult for Soviet aircraft to bomb or strafe the harassing Finns for fear of killing their own troops. There was no means of identifying who was who on the ground.

After five days without any food in temperatures of up to forty degrees below zero, General Vinogradov gave the order for his troops to begin to withdraw to the frontier. He had left even this fateful decision too late, as all semblance of discipline and order in his once elite division had disappeared in the face of extreme cold and hunger. Like Selentsov's 163rd Division before them, Vinogradov's 'Blue' Division panicked and fled into the forest. Perhaps as many as forty percent managed to reach the safety of their own frontier, through Raate, but at least as many probably froze to death. Some 11,300 of an original force of 24,000 men were taken prisoner by the Finns.

The sense of fear and uncertainty fostered by Siilavuo's tactics is well expressed by the one regimental commander of 44th Division who survived to be taken prisoner. 'Finns we could not see anywhere,' he complained. 'The first that I personally saw were the two that took me prisoner after my regiment was destroyed. You had better bury all those soldiers before the spring,' he added, 'otherwise you'll have the plague.' The booty taken by the Finns from 163rd Division amounted to 32 tanks, 40 artillery pieces and 170 trucks. From 44th division, they captured 43 tanks, 46 guns, 200 trucks and thousands of small arms and machine-guns. Siilasvuo was promoted to major-general. Vinogradov was later executed on Stalin's order.

Siilasvuo and his 9th Division had little respite after their victory on the Raate road. Mannerheim ordered them to turn south to where General Gusevski's 54th Division was halted at Kuhmo. There two Finnish ski-borne light infantry battalions, led by Lieutenant-Colonels Frans Ilomäki and Aksel Vuokko, had so harassed the flanks of the advancing Russians that they had halted and formed a defensive position. An attempt to relieve this division was made by the Soviet 9th Ski Brigade, commanded by a Colonel Dolin, which approached across country from the north-east. They were met by the Finns at Kesseli, some ten miles from the frontier, surrounded and destroyed. Gusevski did not make the mistake, however, of breaking up his divisional column. His defence was broad and sound and, although they continued to harass his perimeter, the troops of 9th Division lacked the heavy weapons to do more than contain 54th Divsion where it stood.

In the Soviet 9th Army's northern sector, the 122nd Division and 273rd Regiment detached from 88th Division had not fared well in their attempts to advance from Salla to Tornio. They encountered extreme difficulty in getting off the narrow forest roads and so were able to use only the heads of their columns to push back the Finnish frontier troops. Long tailbacks of men and vehicles, vulnerable to flank attacks by the more mobile local defenders, rendered their resupply increasingly uncertain. The 122nd Division had reached Joutsijärvi in rather less than full divisional strength by 16 December. On the more northerly route through Savukoski, the 273rd Regiment had got as far as Pelkosenniemi. The two Soviet columns were halted at ten miles east and twenty-five miles north respectively of their intended junction point at the Kemijärvi railhead.

Although Mannerheim had given priority to the Soviet 9th Army threat in the Raate-Suomussalmi sector, he did not neglect the threat to Tornio from Salla. He sent the 40th Infantry Regiment under command of Major Armas Perksalo, together with an artillery battery, both from his small remaining reserve, to block the Soviet advance on Tornio. Perksalo's first counter-attack was launched against 273rd Regiment at Pelkosenniemmi. This sent the Russians reeling back to Saija almost forty miles to the east. On 11 December the Lapland Group under Major-General Kurt Wallenius detached a force of two infantry battalions to reinforce the Salla sector, until then covered only by lightly-armed frontier troops. This combined force under Major Vilho Roininen attacked the 122nd Division at Joutsijärvi and forced it to withdraw to join 273rd Regiment on the north-south line between Saija and Märkäjärvi, to the west of Salla. The remainder of 88th Division eventually moved into the same region in January 1940, and the front in that sector stabilized there until the end of the campaign.

The defeat of the 122nd Division and 273rd Regiment was largely due to Finnish flank attacks on their supply columns, so reducing their initial rate of advance. The commander of 122nd Division had been professionally systematic in changing over his three infantry regiments to spearhead the advance on Joutsijärvi, each receiving in turn the support of the divisional tank battalion. Operational cohesion was well maintained until the two-battalion group under Perksalo were joined in their attack on 122nd Division by 40th Regiment from the north, where it had already thrown back the Soviet 273rd Regiment. Mannerheim had been correct in his appreciation that, once in the wilderness on the Finnish side of the frontier, the Red Army would be incapable of maintaining the logistic support essential for a sustained advance against vigorous opposition.

Major-General Woldemar Hägglund, commanding the Finnish IV Army Corps, faced a formidable array of Soviet divisions in his sector between Kollaa and the northern shore of Lake Ladoga. The threat presented by the Red Army in Ladoga-Karelia was quite different in scale from that which had been so effectively dealt with in the wilderness of the eastern frontier region, and the more open southerly terrain was less restrictive on enemy movement. General Habarov's 8th Army had seven divisions and the 34th Tank Brigade deployed against Hägglund's IV Army Corps of two divisions and the division-sized group under Colonel Paavo Talvela. In this sector the early tactical successes of the invaders had petered out towards the end of December. There appear to have been two reasons for this. While some of the Red Army's tactical objectives had been achieved, the strategic aim of outflanking the Isthmus defence, or drawing resources away from it, had failed. Consequently there was an over-cautious inclination to stand firm on the ground taken and await fresh instructions. Secondly, difficulties of resupply had already slowed the pace of the Soviet advance. Then, when it was discovered that the Finns had burned everything that could be used for food or horse fodder, it could not be resumed.

Soviet military doctrine forbade withdrawal, so Habarov's troops had no choice other than to adopt defensive positions where they stood. There was no coherent front onto which they could form. Only the general line along which they had advanced offered hope for the much-needed supplies and reinforcement. The defensive groups thus formed were not on the platoon scale encountered by Siilasvuo on the Raate road but of battalion or regimental size; some included a balance of infantry, tanks and artillery. Potentially the largest was a single group containing the whole of the 168th Division, if the noose could be tightened around it. Another contained only tanks which, after they had been dug in round the perimeter, made a very formidable defensive position.

With some 160,000 Soviet troops in large pockets from which there was very little opportunity for escape, Hägglund faced a difficult dilemma. Should he simply contain them, and thereby husband his troops for the next main Soviet offensive, or should he attempt to destroy them one by one? Mannerheim made the decision for him and ordered that the enemy be attacked and destroyed. He wished not only to take the initiative from the Red Army but to signal to the outside world that the Finns were still on their feet and fighting hard. He had no false illusions about being able to withstand a second and larger Soviet strategic offensive and so sought to convince Britain and France, in particular, that the cause was far from lost.

Hägglund began operations on 6 January 1940, with the Soviet 18th and 168th Divisions and 34th Tank Brigade as his prime targets for destruction. The tactics that his divisions and Group Talvela used were those of encirclement, designed to force the Russians either to abandon their positions or to surrender. As mentioned earlier, having no choice of either, the Russians remained where they were. By 18 January Hägglund had cut off the Soviet 168th Division from its lines of supply from the frontier. By the end of January ten large groups of Soviet troops, some in more than regimental strength, remained to be cut up and destroyed one by one. Aside from the Kitelä-Koirinoja group on the shore of Lake Ladoga, they extended for thirty miles from Polviselkä to Uomaa, where the Finns blocked the line of Soviet supply or withdrawal.

The precise origin of the use of the term 'motti' in the military context remains obscured by legend. The word was certainly used by those of Hägglund's units ordered to destroy the Soviet troops dug in and surrounded in two groups near the village of Lemetti, five or six miles north of the shore of Lake Ladoga, in mid-January

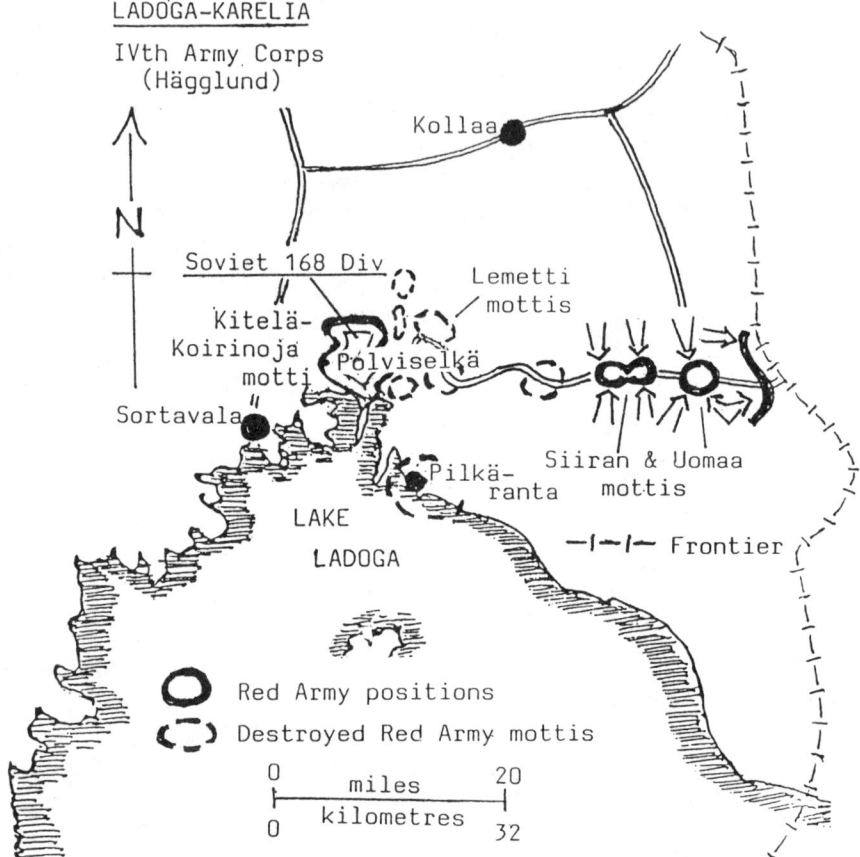

LADOGA–KARELIA

IVth Army Corps
(Hägglund)

N

Kollaa

Soviet 168 Div

Lemetti
mottis

Kitelä-
Koirinoja
motti

Pölviselkä

Sortavala

Pilkä-
ranta

Siiran & Uomaa
mottis

LAKE

LADOGA

—ı—ı— Frontier

◯ Red Army positions

(⌐) Destroyed Red Army mottis

0   miles   20
├────────────────────┤
0   kilometres
                      32

Map 12: The Motti Battles in Ladoga-Karelia

1940. Lemetti had a telephone exchange codenamed 'Motti' which lay within the area to be cleared by the Finnish attackers. This was done and the operation was subsequently referred to as the 'motti battle'. It appears as sure as anything can be, when nothing is documented at the time, that this incident gave rise to the use of the term 'motti-tactics' to mean the breaking up of an enemy into limited-sized groups, their isolation and then systematic destruction. After the Lemetti battle it became increasingly commonplace for Hägglund's troops to refer to the defensive groups of Red Army units as 'mottis' and to 'motti-tactics' for their method of dealing with them.

During the period between 18 January and the end of February, IV Army Corps systematically destroyed all the Soviet mottis in

ABOVE An apartment building ablaze in the centre of Helsinki following a Soviet air attack on the capital using incendiary bombs, 30 November 1939. BELOW Reserve officers of the 9th Independent Battalion at Kollaa in Ladoga-Karelia wearing the Model 27 brown uniform which, being both warm and practical, was more popular than the more usual grey.

ABOVE A Finnish-built Fokker D-XXI fighter/interceptor, mounting four 7.82mm machine-guns, which proved to be a highly successful aircraft. BELOW The Finnish 99-ton submarine *Saukko* leaving her base for a training exercise in the Gulf of Finland.

ABOVE A Lotta Svärd volunteer of the Finnish air defence network telephoning the direction of flight and number of Soviet aircraft. BELOW Finnish reconnaissance pilot being debriefed by Lieutenant-Colonel Viljo Rekola, the air commander in the Suistamo region opposite the IV Army Corps sector of the front in January 1940.

Soviet Tupolev SB-2 twin-engined bomber shot down by the Finnish air-defence forces in December 1939.

Gloster Gladiator fighter biplanes of the volunteer Swedish Fighting Regiment 19 commanded by Major Hugo Beckhammar, which operated in northern Finland in support of the Finnish at Markäjärvi.

ABOVE Finnish reservists in 'Cajander model' uniforms, mainly comprising their own warm civilian clothes with an issued fur cap bearing the Finnish army badge, and equipped with First World War Russian rifles. BELOW Finnish soldiers constructing a deep dugout near Lake Ladoga in December 1939. Such dugouts had operational functions just below ground level, with sleeping quarters below.

ABOVE, LEFT Lieutenant-General Harald Öhquist, commander of the Finnish II Army Corps, visiting the 4th Division Tervajoki sector on the Viipuri Inlet, March 1940. RIGHT After defeat of the Red Army 44th Division on the Raate road, a Finnish officer surveys the front at Saarijoki, five miles from the Soviet border. BELOW Red Army artillery towed by Komsomolets tractors abandoned by the 44th Motorized Division on the Raate road, with the corpses of Soviet artillerymen lying in the foreground.

ABOVE The Finnish armoured vessel *Ilmarinen* on anti-aircraft duty in Turku harbour. The vessel and her sister ship *Väinämöinen* were whitewashed to make them less conspicuous against the snow-covered harbour walls. BELOW, LEFT Lieutenant-General Lennart Oesch, Chief of Staff at Mannerheim's Mikkeli head-quarters during the Winter War until appointed to command the Viipuri Coastal Group immediately before Timoshenko's final offensive. RIGHT A Finnish major, name unknown, wearing a uniform leather coat and traditional Finnish reindeer skinning knife, the *puukko*, on his belt.

ABOVE Finnish and Red Army soldiers meet at Kuhmo, in the central border region, on 14 March 1940 – the day after hostilities came to an end. BELOW Officers of the Finnish Frontier Guard enjoying a meal in their dugout on a day when they had received a supply of fresh bread.

Ladoga-Karelia, except those at Kitelä, Siira and the most easterly one at Uomaa. This really ended the phase of the motti battles, as a much-strengthened Soviet 8th Army then began the next Red Army offensive towards Kollaa. This forced the Finns back onto the defensive in Ladoga-Karelia in March. But, as in the case of 44th and 163rd Divisions further north, the invading Soviet divisions had sustained a staggering number of casualties, even for an army where sheer manpower was the least of difficulties. The largest number were the direct result of cold and starvation but many also perished in panic-stricken attempts to break out of the mottis through the forest.

The motti battles epitomized the sharply contrasting natures of the contestant armies. On the one hand, the Finns were uninhibited by any rigid military doctrine or tactical theory. When an opportunity presented itself the Finns applied their natural initiative and guile, together with their confidence in the often frighteningly hostile Finnish environment. They exploited their own skills and knowledge against the weaknesses of the enemy. The tactical technique of encirclement, in order to force the enemy to abandon his prepared positions, had been taught in Finland's military schools and at the War College in the 1930s. While it seldom caused the Red Army invaders to withdraw, this technique caused the Russian to form the fateful mottis in which so many of them subsequently died.

On the other hand, and in marked contrast to the Finns' initiative, Soviet commanders took refuge in standard doctrine and the stultifying requirement to have tactical decisions ratified by a senior commander, as well as by the political commissar, at every level. In consequence, any decision had almost invariably lost its point by the time it had been mulled over and put into practice. Perhaps the most ludicrous Soviet *diktat* was that no piece of ground captured should be given up. History is littered with the follies of fixations over capturing or holding a particular piece of ground or a city – Stalingrad being probably the most grotesque example. Ground features are significant only if they relate directly to the main aim; that is to destroy the enemy's capacity and will to fight.

In its attempt to divide Finland at the waist, the Red Army was severely restricted by inability to operate away from the few poor roads through the wilderness. At Suomussalmi and in Ladoga-Karelia, the *diktat* that they could relinquish no ground already gained left them hopelessly vulnerable to being chopped up and destroyed in detail. Their will to fight was no match for the silence of the forest – broken only by the Finns' sudden attacks, the fear of isolation, freezing cold and starvation. Literally thousands of well-armed Russian soldiers were killed or neutralized by a fraction of their number of Finns.

The War at Sea and in the Air

Stalin's apprehension about the vulnerability of Leningrad to attack from the sea related only to Germany. The offensive capability of the Finnish Navy, vested chiefly in five shallow-water submarines, entered into the Kremlin's sea power equations only if associated with the navy of a formidable ally. In contrast, the defensive capability of Finnish coastal artillery was thoroughly appreciated. The emplacements and guns dated largely from the period of the Grand Duchy and it was these very facilities that Stalin wished to have under his own hand should the German naval threat materialize in the Gulf of Finland.

The Soviet Union declared a naval blockade of the Finnish coast on the Gulfs of Bothnia and Finland on 7 December 1939 and of the Åland Islands a few days later. Initially this was simply a propaganda move to scare off any neutral vessels intending to ship troops or war material to Finland from Swedish ports. The safest route for any aid to Finland was through Sweden and over the Gulf of Bothnia, using Finnish or Swedish shipping for the final crossing. By using this route, Allied or neutral vessels would be able to use ports on the west coasts of Norway and Sweden for their deliveries of supplies, thereby avoiding having to enter the Baltic. As it happened, the Soviet Navy had no warships in the Gulf of Bothnia to enforce that part of the blockade. Nor was there much likelihood of them getting any there, as the Finns had closed the mouth of the Gulf by mining the Åland Islands gaps.

Thus the Finns won the first round of the war at sea. They exposed the Soviet blockade as a 'paper tiger' in a statement to friendly governments issued on the day after the Soviet blockade was declared. The statement also skilfully wrongfooted the Soviet Government over their spurious contention that no state of war existed, following Moscow's recognition of a puppet Finnish régime under the Communist Otto Kuusinen, supposedly established at the evacuated seaside resort of Terijoki on the Karelian coast. In addition, opportunity was taken to dismiss any fear that the Russians might succeed in their attempt to blockade Finland's south coast ports. 'It is unlikely that Russia will be able to blockade the Gulf of Finland', ran the final paragraph of the defiant declaration, 'considering the length of the coast and the inadequacy of the Russian Fleet.' The full text of the Finnish Government statement is given at Appendix 5

It was certainly true that the Soviet Navy had not recovered any reputation for competence following the defeat of the Imperial Navy at the hands of the Japanese in 1904 and the mutinies of both the Baltic and Black Sea Fleets in 1917. Unlike the Red Army, that had allowed Zhukov's success at Khalkin Gol to inflate its self-esteem, the Navy had no active service experience on which to gauge the battleworthiness either of its ships or crews. Nevertheless, it is strange that no sustained effort was made to threaten the Finnish sea flank and lines of communication seriously before the Gulf of Finland froze at the end of the first month of war.

When the first attacks on land were launched on 30 November, the Soviet cruiser *Kirov*, accompanied by two destroyers, bombarded the Finnish fortress of Russarö off the Hanko Peninsula. The shore batteries responded at once and hit one of the destroyers which broke off the action. It was later reported that the *Kirov* had also been disabled and had to be taken in tow for her home port. There were no casualties on shore. Soviet Navy mine clearing and reconnaissance operations were carried out along the southern shore during the first half of December. On 14 December two Soviet destroyers bombarded the fortress on the small and isolated island of Utö, in the extreme south of the Turku naval defence sector. December. The fortress's six-inch guns returned fire at 12,000 yards, hitting and severely damaging one of the attacking vessels. There was evidence of cooperation between the Soviet Navy and the Red Army only in the several naval bombardments of the coastal defence fortress of Koivisto on the southern coast of Karelia. The guns of Koivisto provided sea flank protection and also heavy artillery support for the Army of the Isthmus.

On 18 December a Soviet naval force of the battleship *Octjabrskaja Revolutsija* and five destroyers attacked the Finnish fortress on the island of Saarenpää, which screens Koivisto from the open sea. (See

Map 13 on page 167.) Using her twelve-inch guns, the *Octjabrskaja Revolutsija* bombarded Saarenpää all day and throughout the night, while the Finnish batteries responded with their own twelve and ten-inch coastal guns. At dawn on 19 December the Soviet squadron was joined by a second battleship, the *Marat*. She engaged but was hit by the coastal battery fire after thirty minutes and sheered off into the mist. This was the only strategically significant naval engagement of the Winter War. Saarenpää had featured in the pre-war negotiations, so the attack was presumably an attempt to take by force what negotiations had failed to win.

The Finnish islands of Suursaari (Hogland), Lavansaari, Tytärsaari and Seiskari had been seized by marines landed by the Soviet Baltic Fleet during the first few days of December. Naval bombardment followed by landings began on 1 December. The token Finnish detachment of thirty men on Suursaari was evacuated next day and the Soviet unopposed occupation was completed on 6 December. These were the islands that the Soviet Union sought to acquire in order to re-establish the Imperial Navy's sea defence system for Leningrad. They had been amongst the most contentious items argued over during the three phases of Finno-Soviet negotiations. All the islands were unfortified and so fell without resistance. This had no impact on the course of the war because, as Mannerheim had argued so strongly but unsuccessfully in his advice to the pre-war Finnish Cabinet, they were of no importance whatever for the defence of Finland. They were occupied only by fishermen and their families.

Subsequent activity by the Soviet Baltic Fleet was without significance. It seems possible that the euphoric state of mind of the land force commanders precluded serious consideration being given to the effect that an amphibious landing on the Finnish southern coast might have had on the land battle. Mannerheim was certainly conscious of this threat, as he placed one complete infantry regiment under naval command for coastal defence operations at the start of the war. When it became clear that the principal threat was coming by land, the C-in-C quickly redeployed this valuable reserve.

It is possible that no landing was attempted because the Soviet High Command was afraid of the combination of coastal batteries, mines and submarines with which the Finns defended their southern coastline. Landings on hostile shores were rightly regarded with apprehension by military experts of most nations at the time. This arose out of the costly attempt by the Western Allies to land a force at Gallipoli in the First World War. Failure of the British and French fleets to force the Dardanelles was remembered by every professionally minded naval officer of the day. On 18 March 1915 twelve British and French capital ships had been defeated in their attempt to force the Turkish narrows by a combination of shore batteries and cunningly laid mines. Three capital ships were lost in one morning. This was a lesson not to be ignored.

The small Finnish submarine squadron of five boats patrolled aggressively and laid mines for as long as the Baltic Sea conditions allowed. The two smaller vessels, the 250-ton *Vesikko* and 99-ton *Saukko*, set out to harass the Soviet battlefleet bombarding Koivisto and Saarenpää in early December and during the concerted attack by the *Octjabrskaja Revolutsija* and *Marat* between 18 and 22 December. Earlier, the *Vesikko* in company with the 500-ton *Vesihiisi* had operated at the mouth of the Gulf of Finland off the Hanko Peninsula. The other two 500-ton submarines, the *Iku-Turso* and *Vetehinen* patrolled the triangle between the Åland Islands, the Estonian islands of Dagö and Osel and the Swedish island of Gotland, to the south-west, until late December. Minefields were laid outside the Soviet naval base of Paldiski, on the Estonian coast, by the *Vesihiisi* at the end of December and at the exit from the Loksa Bay anchorage, to the east of Tallinn, by the *Vetehinen* at the beginning of January 1940.

During the first month of war the Soviet Navy sank ten merchant ships in the Baltic and is believed to have lost two submarines in the process. The freezing of the Gulf of Finland in the closing days of December and beginning of January brought the war at sea virtually to an end. The five Finnish submarines were docked and taken into maintenance, in anticipation of renewed coastal protection patrols after the spring thaw. The two Finnish armoured ships, the *Ilmarinen* and *Väinämöinen*, were both retained for the air defence of Turku harbour, for which each was ideally equipped with eight 40 mm and eight 105 mm anti-aircraft guns.

Operations conducted by coastal batteries continued until the end of the war. Two sets of fortress batteries made significant contributions to the early battles in the Karelian Isthmus and north of Lake Ladoga. These were the batteries at Mantsi on the north-eastern shore of Lake Ladoga and at Kaarnajoki in the eastern Isthmus. Guns in both fortresses had the ability to fire high-explosive shells of six-inch calibre to a range of 25,000 yards. These brought a desperately needed heavy artillery addition to the short-range field artillery of the Finnish Army. The fortress at Koivisto provided similar support from the south-western coast of the Isthmus.

When the Red Army launched its massive-scale offensive in February 1940, with the city of Viipuri as the main objective, the coastal defence guns of the ancient fortress made a crucial contribution to the defence. Towards the end of the Winter War, when Mannerheim was without formal reserves of any kind, sailors from the ice-bound Finnish Navy formed 'Battalion Aaltonen', named after its commander, which fought as infantry alongside coastal defence gunners and Civil Guards in the final effort to hold up the Soviet advance until peace came.

Air operations during the Winter War received a high level of publicity, both in Finland and internationally. This was principally due to widespread and indiscriminate bombing and incendiary attacks by the Soviet Air Force on civilian targets. Such tactics had their origin in the Spanish Civil War of 1936-39. Terrorization of the civilian population by Fascist air attack on unprotected towns and cities had, on occasion, deflected Government resources in Spain. The bombing of Guernica, under the mistaken impression that the Basques were Communist supporters, is probably the most infamous example. There was little evidence of panic in Finland, although many civilian casualties were suffered.

Only two of the world powers, Germany and Japan, had developed an effective technique for the use of air power during the two decades between the World Wars. Crudely expansionist in their political philosophies, both countries correctly perceived that air power in direct support of land forces, or naval forces in the case of Japan, could reap swift tactical and then strategic rewards. The terror bombing of cities was ancillary to this main theme and done so as to break the will of the opponent's civilian population and bring about the collapse of organized resistance.

The democratic powers appear to have been irresolutely uncertain as to how air power might best be used, thus dividing their resources mainly between defensive interceptor (fighter) and medium-range bomber aircraft. Neither of these types is of much use in support of ground forces, unless the fighters can be deployed in sufficient strength over the battlefield to ensure the army's protection from enemy air attack and the bombers can destroy the enemy's forward airfields. Even if both these desirable effects are achieved, they are essentially defensive in their purpose. The Germans and the Japanese recognized the potency of aircraft specifically designed for ground force support, such as the Junkers Ju 87 Stuka dive-bomber and the Mitsubishi A6M Zero fighter, which was cabable of ground attack. These were battle-winning aircraft of their time.

The Soviet Air Force is credited with pioneering the use of parachute delivery of troops, although none were used in the Winter War. Otherwise, the Russians were about as uncertain as the democratic powers as to the most effective use of air power. Support of ground forces was a recognized priority but there were no aircraft available that were really suitable for operating intimately with ground forces, in the sense of accurate bombing or strafing attack of targets close-in to Red Army positions. Instead, the Red Army had to depend on free-fall bombing from such as the twin-engined Tupolev SB-2 or Katiuska. For the main part such support turned out to be at least as hazardous for the Red Army as it was for the Finns.

At the start of the Winter War the Finnish Air Force had only thirty-six modern interceptors – Dutch-designed Fokker D-XXIs, most of which were built under licence in Finland, and twenty-one bombers – fourteen Bristol Blenheims and seven Junkers K43s. Although Finnish cities, ports and airfields were correctly perceived as prime targets for enemy air attack, along with the roads and railways leading to the Karelian front, it was decided that the fighter aircraft should adopt a forward deployment. This was to ensure maximum support for the army and to defend Finnish air space from the frontier. The small bomber force was directed to attack enemy airfields and such other ground force support targets as might present themselves. Air reconnaissance was of key significance for development of ground force plans. The Fokker CX biplanes proved successful in this role but they were occasionally supplemented by the faster and longer-range Blenheims. Major-General Jarl Lundqvist, who had built up the small air force from scratch and commanded it throughout the war, correctly appreciated what the Soviet Air Force tactics would be but was critically short of suitable aircraft to counter them.

The most serious threat from the Soviet Air Force came from their Ilyushin DB-3 bombers, which could reach any target in Finland, including the Åland Islands, carrying a metric ton of bombs. The DB-3s had a cruising speed of 220 mph, making interception difficult unless they were caught soon after entering Finnish air space. With this thought in mind, from the beginning of December Lundqvist stationed his 24th Fighter Squadron of thirty-six Fokker D-XXIs at Immola, Lappeenranta and Suur-Merijoki just behind the eastern neck of the Karelian Isthmus. This position also gave him the best chance of providing the Finnish Army of the Isthmus with fighter cover, so long as his handful of interceptors survived. Number 26 Fighter Squadron, equipped with obsolescent Bristol Bulldog IVA biplanes, was located at Heinjoki and Raulampi on the Karelian Isthmus with the task of intercepting Russian bomber aircraft.

It is estimated that the Soviet Air Force allocated 3,000 bomber and fighter aircraft to the Finnish campaign. The first Soviet air raid on Helsinki began at 0925 hours on Thursday 30 November. This was the morning after Moscow had broken off diplomatic relations following the incident of the 'Mainila shots' on 26 November. All the Soviet aircraft used on this first occasion against Helsinki flew from airfields in Soviet-occupied Estonia. They dropped not bombs but leaflets. Propaganda by leaflet drop was a commonplace event in the early stages of the Second World War. The message from the Kremlin on the first day of the Winter War was scarcely subtle, although there had been several months in which to choose the words. The message read: 'You know we have bread – don't starve. Soviet Russia will not harm the Finnish people. Their disaster is due to their wrong leadership. Mannerheim and Cajander must go. After that, peace will come.'

The population of Helsinki were left just five hours to reflect on this cryptic exhortation. At 1430 hours a second wave of aircraft launched a largely incendiary bomb attack aimed at the city's Malmi airport, the harbour and railway station. High-explosive bombs were intermingled with the incendiaries and serious damage was inflicted on residential districts. Ninety-one people were killed and over two hundred injured, many of them at the railway station from where they were hoping to leave the capital for greater safety.

Air attacks were also made on this first day on the city of Viipuri, on Hanko, Kotka and Lahti as well as several military targets on the

Karelian Isthmus. No major damage was done or casualties suffered, other than in Helsinki. Fokker D-XXIs of 24 Fighter Squadron were scrambled in defence of Viipuri. It took them only twenty minutes to get over the city, but that was long enough to allow the attacking Ilyushins to escape. The Finnish Air Force destroyed no Soviet aircraft on the first day. This was chiefly due to poor flying weather conditions, with heavy cloud above 2,500 feet. An official report issued by the Air Defence Command the next day claimed five enemy bombers certainly shot down by anti-aircraft on 30 November and probably seven.

On the second day of the war, 1 December, ten Soviet bombers were shot down by Finnish aircraft. 24th Fighter Squadron were ready for the Soviet Tupolev SB-2s attacking Viipuri. The squadron commander, Captain Eino Luukkanen, shot one down before breakfast. This event was followed by a brisk snowstorm that brought air activity to a halt over the Karelian Isthmus. The pause allowed Captain Luukkanen to find the Soviet aircraft that he had brought down and examine it in detail. He noted that, while the fuselage of the Tupolev was heavily armoured, the fuel tanks in the wings were without protection. He wasted no time in passing on this important technical detail to Air Force Headquarters, so that all Finnish fighter pilots could be informed of the SB-2's most vulnerable point for attack.

The extreme weather conditions made the maintenance of the Finnish aircraft exceptionally difficult, especially those operatiing from makeshift airstrips without hangars or any other protection. Engine oil often froze at temperatures of thirty or even forty degrees below zero and it was not uncommon for mechanics to use blow torches to unfreeze the cylinder blocks before asking the pilot to try to start his engine. It soon became the practice to drain engines on return from the last daytime patrol and pour in fresh oil before start up on the following day.

During the whole of December the Soviet Air Force concentrated its main effort against the Finnish civilian population. Even small and isolated villages were attacked, often with incendiaries that reduced the wooden houses of the countryside to ashes. This was intended to have a demoralizing effect on Finland's will to fight and smash the industrial potential of cities like Tampere, which were busy turning over factories to war production. Neither of these two

Soviet objectives was achieved, due to the resolve of the Finnish people not to have their spirit broken. They also proved adept and resourceful in improvising repair of damaged machinery, factory support facilities, electric power and water supply.

No attacks on civilian targets were mentioned in Soviet radio or newspaper reports. As late as January 1940 *Pravda* continued to stress that no civilian targets in Finland had been struck, even by accident. Meanwhile, the Soviet Air Force turned its attention to the Finnish railway system. Railway tracks are notoriously difficult to put out of action by bombing for long periods, unless crucial bridges can be demolished. Soviet pilots therefore attacked the trains themselves, in particular those running between Helsinki and Viipuri and between the capital and industrial centre of Tampere. These attacks inflicted many civilian casualties, as it was difficult for the passengers to get out of the carriages and away from the tracks quickly enough when the attacking aircraft appeared. Usually there was only a few seconds' warning. It was mainly the Soviet Polikarpov 1-15 fighters that were used to strafe the moving or halted trains with machine-gun fire.

Throughout December and early January the Soviet Air Force attacked Finland's towns and cities, while the defending fighter squadrons took their toll of the intruders. One pilot, Lieutenant Tatu Huhanantti, brought down eleven Soviet bombers, the last in the course of a mid-air collision in which he was killed. Forty attacks on different locations, including Helsinki and Viipuri and many small towns and villages, were made on Christmas Day. Viipuri suffered considerable damage on this occasion, although no targets of military significance were hit. Extensive fires were caused by incendiary attacks on the south-western port of Turku. Six civilians had been killed during air attacks on Turku on 19 and 21 December. Most of the attacks on south-west Finland were made by small groups of aircraft, often by fighters limited to machine-gun fire.

While Finnish fighter squadrons concentrated on providing air cover for the army, and in particular to the Army of the Isthmus, the medium bomber force harassed bases from which the Soviet attackers flew. Nos. 44 and 46 Bristol Blenheim Squadrons, with a total of fourteen aircraft, were based at Luonetjärvi, near Jyväskylä in south central Finland. The three flights of Junkers K43s were based at Wärtsila, for operations over Lake Ladoga, at Rovaniemi in northern Finland and at Maarianhamina, capital of the Åland Islands. These older aircraft were principally used for army co-operation, including reconnaissance missions, and liaison flights.

During December and in the early days of January the Blenheims attacked air bases at Uhtua, opposite the waist of Finland, at Murmansk and at Petsamo, by then occupied by the Russians. Finding Soviet aircraft frozen up or snowbound on these bases, the Finns attacked with incendiary bombs, succeeding in destroying many aircraft on the ground. By the end of the first five weeks of war, 7 January 1940, Finnish Air Force headquarters made an official estimate of some 150 Soviet aircraft destroyed, either in the air by fighter aircraft or anti-aircraft fire or by being burned out on the ground.

A welcome reinforcement came on 10 January 1940 in the form of a Swedish Air Force squadron of volunteers flying Gloster Gladiator and Swedish-Hart fighter biplanes commanded by Major Hugo Beckhammar. Numbered as Flight Regiment No. 19, although having only twelve fighter and four reconnaissance aircraft, this force was intially based on the frozen Lake Kemi, in direct support of Major-General Hjalmar Siilasvuo's 9th Division opposing the Red Army advance from Salla. Using the system developed by the Finnish Air Force of flying from a series of small operating bases situated away from their central maintenance and repair airfield, the Swedes broke up into small dispersed detachments. During the ensuing weeks of atrocious flying weather in north-central region, Regiment 19 destroyed twelve enemy aircraft for a loss of six of their own.

A new Soviet Air Force offensive began in mid-January 1940, with high explosive and incendiary attacks on Helsinki, Hanko, Turku, Viipuri and many other towns and villages. Although the four ports were receiving shipments of war supplies, the likelihood is that the raids were a renewed attempt to terrorize the civilian population. Particularly heavy raids took place on Sunday 14 January. The Inspector of Civil Defence, Lieutenant-General Aarne Sihvo, issued an official bulletin on the next day which included the passage: 'During the week the Russians dropped upwards of 2,000 bombs on forty-two separate localities outside the war zone. They killed eighteen civilians and injured ninety-three. The number of enemy machines shot down is well above the the number of Finnish civilians killed.'

It was later estimated that at least six Russian bombs were dropped for every Finnish civilian killed. The anniversary of Lenin's death on 20 January was marked by intensive bombing raids on Finnish towns.

The renewed Soviet air offensive against centres of civilian population failed either to break the will of the Finnish people or to inflict serious damage on industry supporting the war effort. On the other hand, success of Soviet fighters and ground fire against the small Finnish bomber force obliged General Lundqvist to switch their attacks to the Bay of Viipuri, where they could make an immediate effect on the ground battle. Later, when the final Soviet onslaught was launched, Mannerheim ordered all serviceable aircraft to be concentrated in support of the Army of the Isthmus, where he correctly perceived the crisis situation to be.

From shortly before the Winter War began, strenuous efforts had been made to strengthen and modernize the Finnish Air Force. The most valuable acquisition was the gift by the French Government of thirty Morane Saulnier 406 interceptors. 28th Fighter Squadron was formed under Major Niilo Jusu on the frozen Lake Pyhäjärvi, forty miles to the north of Turku, to receive these aircraft. The squadron was operational with twenty-five Moranes by 1 March 1940. Two flights, each of seven aircraft, were sent to bases near Lahti, in south central Finland, on 7 March. This was to provide extra air suport for the Army of the Isthmus during the most desperate battles. The Morane had excellent performance but the armament was inadequate. While some were equipped with the most effective 20 mm cannon, others had only 7.5 mm machine-guns.

A total of fifty Fiat G-50 interceptors had been ordered from Italy in October 1939 but the trains carrying them through Germany were turned back. This was a consequence of the Molotov-Ribbentrop Agreement, which Germany saw fit to honour to the letter at that stage. The Italians responded by shipping thirty of the Fiats to Sweden, where they were assembled and flown to Finland. Fifteen aircraft had been received by February and these fought over the Karelian Isthmus during the final land battles. The Fiat G-50 was a fast and effective fighter, with a top speed of 290 mph and equipped with two heavy (12.7 mm) machine-guns. Unfortunately, their maximum flight time of ninety minutes was a serious limitation on their operating range. A further seventeen Fiats were received during March, bringing the total complement to thirty-two, but three were lost before the war ended.

The Soviet Air Force finally turned their attention to the land battle in vain attempts to destroy Finnish troops surrounding Red Army units during the motti battles in the eastern wilderness and north of Lake Ladoga. On 1 February 1940 saturation bombing of Finnish rear areas behind the defence lines in the Karelian Isthmus began. This was in direct support of the final Soviet ground offensive and seriously affected the ability of the Finnish C-in-C to redeploy his troops to plug important gaps or to react to Red Army concentrations for attack. On 6 February the Russians attacked over a sixteen-mile front, in the Hatjalahti and Muolaa Lake sectors of the Isthmus, with six divisions supported by bombing and strafing aircraft. The Finns kept the line only by withdrawing by day and counter-attacking by night. It was an exhausting business that could last for a brief period only, that is until a formula for peace could be found.

In the final analysis, made after the end of the Winter War, it was confirmed that the fighter squadrons of the Finnish Air Force accounted for some 200 enemy aircraft destroyed in the air, while more than 300 were brought down by anti-aircraft fire or destroyed on the ground by bombing their air bases. The Finns lost sixty-two aircraft of their total complement. Undoubtedly the most dramatic air engagement of the war was the destruction of six Soviet Ilyushin DB-3s, of a squadron of seven, by Finnish Lieutenant Jorma Sarvanto in the space of four minutes on 6 January 1940. His companion, Lieutenant Per-Erik Sovelius, shot down the seventh. Sarvanto became the top-scoring Finnish fighter pilot of the Winter War.

Indiscriminate Russian air attacks on centres of population won the Finns the sympathy of the civilized world, if not much active support. The attacks also led to sharp disillusionment amongst those sections of opinion that had previously regarded the Soviet Union as the champion of political freedom and of the working class. As the Ilyushins and Tupolevs attempted to destroy the industrial centres of Finnish cities, so they inflicted the greatest proportion of casualties amongst the working people of those districts. These events were not lost on the working people of Britain, France and the United States.

Although outrage was expressed in the United States and elsewhere, this had little practical result from the point of view of foreign government aid. President Franklin Roosevelt made an appeal to both Moscow and Helsinki not to allow their aircraft to attack civilian targets or unfortified cities. This was contemptuously brushed aside by Stalin with a remark that the Americans would do better to give their attention to the 'wretched situations in their colonies of Cuba and the Philippines'. The United States Secretary of State, Cordell Hull, appealed to American aircraft manufacturers not to sell their products to any country that used air power to attack civilians. But he also argued against granting credit to the Finns 'as they are a warring nation and it would be against international justice'. Fine words from someone more than 3,000 miles from the conflict.

In contrast to these uninspiring political pronouncements, the American Red Cross sent $25,000 for the initial relief of Finland's damaged cities, together with a further $10,000 for medicines. These may not seem large sums but they were equivalent to perhaps $35 million today. There were many instances of individual donations of money and material from the Western democracies, while their governments struggled to keep their distance from the conflict. The United States feared being drawn into the main European war; Britain and France considered that Germany was enough for them to handle, although their attitudes changed when they perceived that there might be an advantage to be gained against Germany by intervention on behalf of Finland.

12

Stalemate and Onslaught

The last days of 1939 witnessed the collapse of the Red Army's first invasion offensive. During a mercilessly freezing January their surrounded divisions and regiments called vainly for relief and air supply from their defensive motti positions. The Finns resolutely closed in on each one but they needed to be wary. A serious artillery ammunition shortage precluded tactics other than those of attrition. To the outside world it appeared that the Finns had halted the Soviet invaders in their tracks. They had indeed, but their reserves of men and resources were all but exhausted. Mannerheim was prevented from regrouping his forces ready for the next Russian offensive, as virtually all his divisions were committed to containing surrounded invaders or those who had dug defensive positions close to the frontier. Presented with this stalemate, Stalin began a review of the Red Army command structure.

January 1940 would have been the ideal time for the Western Allies to have thrown their weight, such as it was, behind the Finns. The arrival of five or six Allied divisions on the Karelian front might have been just enough to persuade the Kremlin that a further offensive would be too hazardous, in both military and political terms. One salutary demonstration of support, and one easily and quickly achieved, would have been the despatch of a dozen squadrons of modern British and French fighter aircraft for the defence of Finnish cities. This would have been widely welcomed by the outraged civilian populations of the Western Powers.

Action between Allied and German forces had been largely confined to engagements at sea at this stage of the Second World War. All remained quiet on the Franco-German border front, allowing the British and French populations to resurrect myths of the invincibility of their respective armies. There was widespread apprehension about German air attack on civilian targets but, unaware of the slender nature of their own air defences, British and French civilian populations alike clamoured for aircraft to be sent to Finland's aid. Their Governments took up less altruistic attitudes and became, with justification, mutually suspicious of each other's motives regarding Finland.

The French Government of Edouard Daladier indicated a willingness to provide military support for Finland from mid-December onwards. There were two readily discernible reasons for this. From the moment that the Soviet Union was expelled from the League of Nations, on 14 December 1939, voluble right-wing elements of the French parliamentary opposition demanded that diplomatic relations with Moscow should be severed. Daladier saw the offer of aid to Finland as a means to head off this potentially dangerous break with the one great power which could keep Germany seriously concerned for her eastern border. The second reason had links with the first. All Frenchmen dreaded the loss of another generation of their young men in a new Verdun. The Winter War seemed to offer an opportunity to shift the battleground away from Europe to Scandinavia.

While there was an astonishing lack of military logic to support his appreciation, Daladier took and maintained the lead over the British prime minister, Neville Chamberlain, in his outward support for intervention in Finland. That is until it was too late and the Finns settled matters for themselves. While less decisive than Chamberlain, Daladier was more worldly on matters of foreign affairs. The disparity between the two leaders' understanding of European realities was appreciated by Chamberlain's military advisers and most Cabinet colleagues. This led them to be sceptical of Britain's commitment to deployment of precious military resources to Finland and to pursue more devious plans of their own.

Winston Churchill had been reappointed First Lord of the Admiralty (Navy Minister), a post he had held in the First World War, on 3 September 1939. From the outset he had pressed his Cabinet colleagues to agree to the mining of territorial waters of neutral Norway. His aim was to prevent essential war materials from Scandinavia reaching Germany. He argued in particular for mines to be laid in the approaches to the ice-free port of Narvik, used for shipping Swedish iron ore to Germany when the northern Baltic froze and prevented use of the Swedish port of Lulev at the head of the Gulf of Bothnia.

An assessement by the British Ministry of Economic Warfare led Chamberlain's Cabinet to believe that the German war machine could be brought to a halt if the supply of ore from the Gällivere-Kiruna mines, which provided eighty percent of Germany's wartime needs, could be stopped. This apparent opportunity to bring the war to a speedy end was encouraged by a conviction that Hitler would be unable to hold the German people to another long conflict. Daladier embraced the idea of cutting off the Swedish supplies of ore and, from before Christmas 1939, this question and that of aid to Finland became inextricably involved in the minds of the members of the Allied Supreme War Council.

Initial discussions of precisely what aid should be sent to Finland by the Allies, held during a meeting of the Supreme War Council in Paris on 19 December, revealed a marked difference in British and French attitudes. While Deladier expressed the intention of sending fighter aircraft as soon as possible and troops later, the British Foreign Secretary, Lord Halifax, spoke only of despatch of war material. Daladier skilfully exploited the strength of the Royal Navy and availability of those British troops not committed to the Western Front to persuade the British to provide the bulk of the planned intervention force and to take the lead in the enterprise. When news of the deliberations of the Supreme War Council reached Helsinki, the Finnish Cabinet were prompted to make their first and only appeal for Allied military assistance.

One important distinction of approach persisted between the British and French leadership. Whereas Daladier perceived aid to Finland as the primary objective, the British War Cabinet saw it as the pretext for getting troops into a position to cut off the supply of Swedish iron ore to Germany. Both Governments agreed that aid could only be sent if it were to be specifically requested. A legal basis for sending troops to Scandinavia was ostensibly provided by a second League of Nations resolution, passed on 14 December 1939 when the Soviet Union was expelled, calling for all member states to give what assistance they could to Finland. This could reasonably be interpreted as transit rights for troops.

On an untested assumption that Norway and Sweden would readily accede to the passage of troops through their ports and railway systems, the British Admiralty and War Office began to plan the intervention. Various estimates were made of the strength of forces required to hold the Gällivere-Kiruna iron ore mines and adjacent ports against a possible German counter-intervention. Details are superfluous here but it is clear that the competence of the German Army and the Luftwaffe was seriously underestimated. The British Chief of the Imperial General Staff (CIGS), General Sir Edmund Ironside, advised the War Cabinet: 'Germany is inexperienced in combined operations. An invasion of Southern Scandinavia would be an enormous commitment for her.' Availability of troops to go to Finland's aid, at the end of a line of communications along the railway through Norway and the Gällivere-Kiruna iron ore region, was variously assessed at between one and two brigades, that is 4,000 to 7,000 men.

The battlefield lull following the collapse of the Red Army's first offensive at the end of December gave the Finnish C-in-C an opportunity to make an appreciation of the likely outcome of an Allied military intervention. He shrewdly confided his conclusions to no one, aware that Finland's political leaders were as naive as those in London and Paris as to the hazards that intervention might bring.

Mannerheim correctly calculated that neither Norway nor Sweden would grant transit rights for Allied troops, through fear of being drawn into the European war. Strict neutrality was their sole safeguard. He concluded that consequent Allied intervention either on too weak a scale or provided too late would almost certainly lead to Finland being overrun by the Soviet Union, or even by Germany as part of a counter-intervention. He therefore resolved to use the offer of Allied military assistance in an attempt to limit Soviet aims during the rest of the war and as a factor in bringing about a negotiated settlement. It was a stratagem that depended on keeping the Finnish Cabinet eager for Allied military assistance while never actually making a formal request for it.

Provision of Allied war material, fighter aircraft and artillery in particular, was an altogether different matter. Certain that a renewed Soviet offensive was inevitable, Mannerheim sent a constant stream of requests through the British and French liaison officers at his Mikkeli field headquarters. During January 1940 the French sent twenty-four field guns, the same number of 155 mm howitzers and 74,000 shells. Fifteen French Morane model 406 fighters arrived as a gift during February. Britain sent twelve more Bristol Blenheim light bombers, two of which were lost en route, twenty-five 105 mm howitzers with 25,000 shells, twenty-four 76 mm heavy anti-aircraft guns with 72,000 rounds and 8,000 anti-tank mines. To keep the significance of these armaments in perspective – and Allied and Finnish politicians from complacency – Mannerhein told the British liaison officer at Mikkeli that he would need 30,000 fresh troops if he was to hold out through the winter.

Meanwhile, furious at the Red Army's failures, Stalin appointed new commanders and allocated extra forces to the Finnish campaign. Marshal Klimenti Voroshilov was appointed nominal overall commander but with the key North-Western Front of the Karelian Isthmus and Ladoga-Karelia under General Semyon Timoshenko, who had done well in the recent invasion of Poland. General Meretskov, previously the overall commander of the invasion forces, was returned to command 7th Army in the west of the Karelian Isthmus. Lieutenant-General Vladimir Grendal, one of the few remaining veteran officers of the Imperial Army and who had earlier commanded the L [50th] Army Corps in the eastern Isthmus, became commander of 13th Army in the same region.

Red Army reinforcements and dispositions reflected a decision to stand fast on all fronts north of Karelia and concentrate for a massive breakthrough on the Isthmus. (See Map 13 opposite.) 7th Army, brought up to a complement of fifteen divisions and including five tank brigades and ten field artillery regiments, was allocated to an attack axis along the line of the Leningrad to Viipuri railway. The earlier fought-for village of Summa was made the starting point with the city of Viipuri as the first primary objective. Two divisions prepared to advance along the Karelian coast road to give flank protection for the main thrust.

In the eastern Isthmus, Grendal's 13th Army of five divisions, one tank brigade and six field artillery regiments was tasked to give 7th Army right flank support and aim to reach the line Antrea-Käkisalmi in step with Meretskov reaching the line Viipuri-Antrea. The combined attack was planned to start on 6 February. Three divisions and one tank brigade were held under Timoshenko's own hand as an immediate reserve, together with a cavalry corps. When the time came, this force was to be used to cross the frozen Viipuri Inlet, west of Viipuri city, to cut the road communications to Helsinki behind the rear-defence or 'T-Line'.

Some reinforcement and reorganization of Red Army deployment

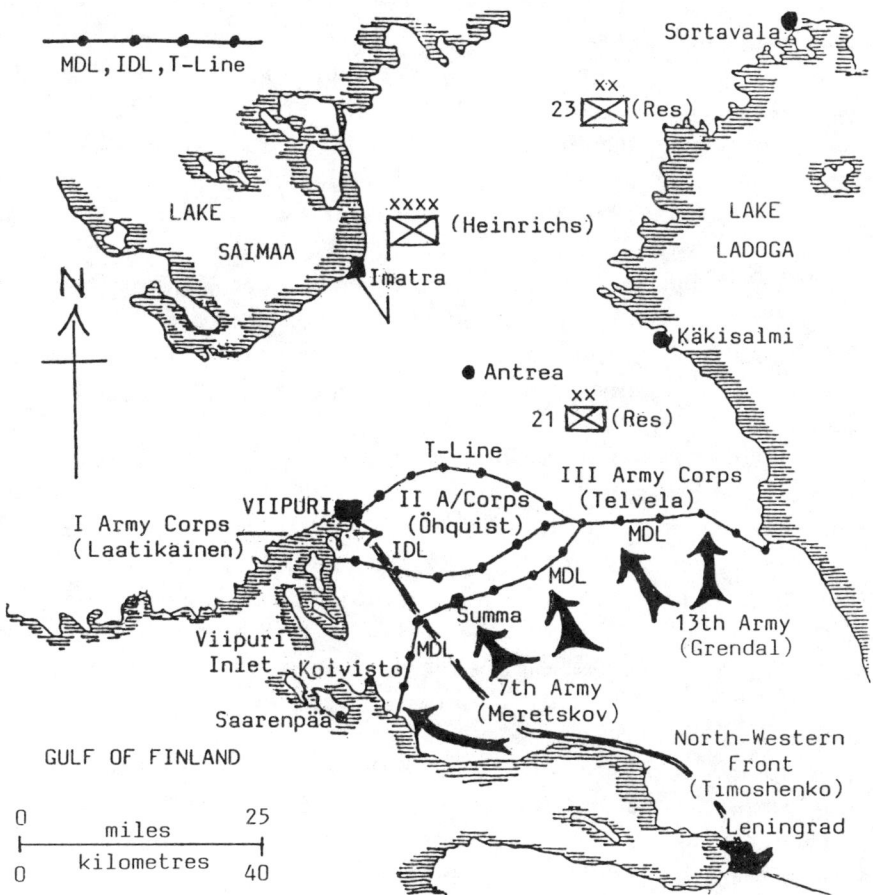

Map 13: Finnish Army deployment to face Timoshenko's offensive of
6 February 1940

occurred between Lake Ladoga and the far north but, apart from in
Ladoga-Keralia, these changes were defensive. A new 15th Army
absorbed the badly mauled 8th Army, which was downgraded to
an army corps, and brought six fresh divisions to the sector immediately north of the lake. The previous commander of 8th Army,
Lieutenant-General Georgi Stern, was appointed to overall control
of Northern Army Group stretching from Lake Ladoga to Petsamo.
Stern's primary task was to direct 15th Army in a new offensive
along the northern shore of Lake Ladoga with the purpose of outflanking Mannerheim's Army of the Isthmus south of the lake.

The Red Army High Command had learned a lot from their first failed offensive. They now had a proper military respect for the fighting capabilities of the Finns. New plans were characterized by meticulous planning and use of overwhelming superiority of numbers. Ambitious ideas of cutting Finland in half at the waist, or driving down the Arctic Road from Petsamo to the head of the Gulf of Bothnia, were abandoned. Fundamentally, the plans for attack in the Karelian Isthmus and in Ladoga-Karelia remained the same as in December, but in vastly increased strength. Instead of two army corps advancing abreast in the Isthmus, there were to be two armies, 7th and 13th, totalling twenty-two divisions with three more in reserve. To the north, in Ladoga-Keralia, 15th Army would begin the outflanking movement with twelve divisions.

Thorough preparation was not confined to operational and logistic plans. For this second great offensive, Timoshenko determined to make full use of air and artillery bombardment to shatter the Finns' prepared positions before his tanks and infantry were thrown at them. It is significant that it was reported that this hard-bitten Ukrainian had accepted command of the North-Western Front only if he were not to be held responsible for Red Army losses. A force of fighters, bombers and night bomber aircraft, some 2,000 in all, was assigned to the North-Western Front air force. No scope was left for dispute over the most appropriate use of these formidable air support forces, as they were placed directly under Timoshenko's command.

Finnish intelligence correctly assessed that the major Red Army reinforcement was in the Soviet 7th Army sector of the western Isthmus. Therefore the main attack could be expected there. Some subsequent criticism has been levelled at Mannerheim for deploying to the wrong sectors of the front such reserves as were available and holding back the two newly formed 21st and 23rd divisions as part of his own reserve.

It can only be assumed that the Finnish C-in-C, who habitually kept his own counsel, suspected that Timoshenko might really intend to make his main effort along both the southern and northern shores of Lake Ladoga. It was to III and IV army corps in these sectors that the two new divisions were tentatively assigned, while remaining under Mannerheim's personal control. These deployments precluded extra work on the second and third lines of defences in the western Isthmus, or relief of any division there that had borne the brunt of the December battles.

Saturation bombing of the Finnish rear areas began on 1 February and a series of artillery bombardments started with a weight and intensity of fire not previously seen during the Winter War. It was estimated that 300,000 shells fell on the Finnish positions around Summa in one period of twenty-four hours in the first few days of February. There had been nothing to compare with this since the German shelling of Verdun in 1915. In the face of such fire the Finns' only tactical resort was to withdraw from their positions by day and reoccupy what remained of them at night. This at least reduced their scale of casualties and surprised the enemy when he tried to push forward with tanks and infantry at daylight.

This final Soviet offensive was designed in three phases: the bombardment of the Finnish main defensive line (MDL) across the Isthmus; the storming and break-in of the MDL; and the break-through of the less well prepared Finnish rear defence 'T-Line' that hinged on Viipuri. It was a plan without subtlety that depended only on the use of overwhelming firepower and manpower. Summa was the point selected for the initial advance, as the ground there was level and open, giving maximum scope for the Red Army tanks to provide both cover and covering fire for their massed infantry.

The five-mile Summa sector of the Finnish MDL was manned by Colonel Paavo Paalu's 3rd Division supported by sixteen artillery batteries. This was formidable support by Finnish Army standards but the disparity between defending and attacking forces was enormous. Moreover, the Finnish artillery had much shorter range and fired far lighter shells than those of their opponents. By 12 February Paalu's remaining troops were exhausted and a breakthrough on his right, led by the Soviet 35th Tank Brigade, was precariously contained but could not be straightened out.

Throughout the first half of February Mannerheim resisted pleas from General Österman, commanding the Army of the Isthmus, for either reinforcement from the C-in-C's reserve or permission to withdraw to the intermediate or rear lines of defence. The 23rd Division, tentatively assigned to IV army corps in Ladoga-Karelia, was still uncommitted, but Mannerheim refused to allow it to redeploy to the western Isthmus until 14 February. This may have been because he knew the rear communications were so badly disrupted by aerial bombardment that the move was too hazardous or, more probably, because he wished to play the card of possible Allied intervention over as long a timescale as possible.

The British and French liaison officers at his headquarters, Brigadier Christopher Ling and Colonel Jean Ganeval, were keeping Mannerheim abreast of developments regarding the various Allied options under discussion. Ling's report of Finland's need for 30,000 fresh troops to endure the winter had prompted the British Cabinet to agree in principle to enlistment of British volunteers to fight in Finland. A more positive attitude towards military assistance to Finland also began to emerge. In spite of a variety of diplomatic approaches and pressures, however, the Norwegian and Swedish Governments were standing firm against transit rights, other than for volunteers in civilian clothes. This led the French to suggest that an Allied expeditionary force might go to Finland's aid through the Arctic port of Petsamo, if that could be freed from Soviet occupation. Wisely, the British naval and military chiefs advised against this suggestion.

Mannerheim was convinced that he had to maintain a forward defence in the Karelian Isthmus for two strategic reasons. First, if it appeared to the Allies that Finland was about to collapse under the Soviet onslaught they would at once abandon all plans to intervene. Second, prolonged resistance was essential to allow the Kremlin time to believe that Allied intervention was imminent, so that negotiations for an armistice could be opened under conditions not entirely unfavourable to Finland. Mannerheim's far-sighted strategic objectives called for tactical sacrifices that were virtually impossible to explain to subordinates. This dilemma was accentuated by news through Ling and Ganeval that the Allied Supreme War Council were thinking of sending five divisions to Scandinavia 'before the middle of April'. Mannerheim knew that he could not hold up the next Red Army offensive until then.

The second phase of Timoshenko's offensive had reached a critical stage for the Finnish defenders by 12 February. Having released 23rd Division to reinforce II army corps in the western Isthmus on 14 February, Mannerheim authorized Österman to begin withdrawal to the intermediate defence line (IDL), six miles north-west of the main defence line, starting during the night of the following day. The moment had come to exchange territory for time.

Mannerheim's decision carried penalties more serious than just withdrawal. Shortage of manpower and resources had led to the intermediate line being significantly less well prepared than the main defence line. The intermediate line was slightly shorter, but the right flank, resting on the sea, swung back by almost forty-five degrees. This exposed the eastern shore of the Viipuri Inlet to the two Soviet divisions advancing along the coast and to the planned assault over the ice by the three divisions Timoshenko was holding in reserve for this purpose. The ancient fortress-city of Viipuri had been selected as the primary objective of Meretskov's 7th Army. While the port had no military significance in the battle, its loss would have great psychological importance in Finland and in Western capitals. Mannerheim had no choice other than to make Viipuri the centre point of the next battle.

Having completed two closely linked appreciations, one political and the other military, the Finnish C-in-C began a series of swiftly executed changes on 18 February. Defence of the Viipuri Inlet, hitherto covered by two infantry battalions under naval command, was made the responsibility of the Army of the Isthmus. At the same time he relieved the exhausted Lieutenant-General Hugo Österman of command of that army. In his place was appointed Lieutenant-General Erik Heinrichs, who had acquitted himself so well in command of III Army Corps in the eastern Isthmus during the December battles. Major-General Paavo Talvela, victor of Tolvajärvi-Ilomantsi, succeeded Heinrichs in command of III Army Corps.

The II Army Corps sector of the front in the western Isthmus was divided between II Army Corps, still commanded by Lieutenant-General Harald Öhquist, and the newly formed I Army Corps under Major-General Taavetti Laatikainen. North of Lake Ladoga, Lieutenant-General Woldemar Hägglund continued in command of IV Army Corps. His task was to contain the threatened further advance of General Stern's 15th Army along the northern shores of the lake. During the days that immediately followed, Major-General Kurt Wallenius was transferred from his Lapland command to the Karelian front with six infantry battalions and two artillery batteries. This was the only strategic transfer of troops made by the Finnish Army during the Winter War and reflected the concern of the C-in-C for the defence of Viipuri. On 14 February, while visting the city to assess the situation for himself, Mannerheim was in the courtyard of the fortress during a Soviet air-raid. He was unharmed.

Breakthrough of the Soviet 123rd Division and 35th Tank Brigade to the east of Summa in mid-February had placed the whole of the main defence line in the western Isthmus in peril. It was for this reason that Mannerheim had decided to authorize withdrawal to the intermediate defence line, but to hold the forward positions in the eastern Isthmus. As may be seen from Map 13, this did not create a gap but rather a realignment of the Isthmus front as a whole. He firmly resisted suggestions that withdrawal should be direct to the rear defence or T-Line, as it had not been possible to prepare any significant fortifications there.

Occupation of the intermediate line had been successfully accomplished by night withdrawals on 15, 16 and 17 February, but leading elements of Soviet 7th Army re-established contact early on 18 February. Initial Red Army attacks were repulsed and severe snowstorms throughout the Isthmus for the following few days gave the defenders a brief respite. As soon as the weather cleared, a set-piece assault by the Soviet 7th and 84th Divisions against the inexperienced Finnish 23rd Division, astride the Leningrad-Viipuri railway, threw that part of the line into confusion. 7th Army pressure in the same sector continued and a wedge was driven into the intermediate defence line by 26 February.

Throughout the February battles the coastal batteries of the fortress of Koivisto had played a crucial role in the land battle by supplementing and outranging the Finnish field artillery. By the evening of 26 February troops of the Soviet 53rd and 86th Divisions had surrounded the already isolated fortress on the coast of the Isthmus. This further endangered Viipuri, as there were no Finnish troops available to prevent the eastern coast of the inlet falling entirely under Red Army control. Recognizing that the enemy wedge pointed directly towards Viipuri, Mannerheim gave the order to withdraw to the rear defence T-Line on 26 February.

Once again the Finnish defenders succeeded in breaking contact with the enemy in the western Isthmus. I and II Army Corps withdrew during the nights of 27 and 28 February and were established on the T-Line by 1 March. The following day Major-General Wallenius arrived with his reinforcements from the Lapland front. They had been replaced in the north by the Swedish Volunteer

Corps, until then held in reserve. The welcome reinforcements were formed into the Viipuri Coastal Group for the close defence of Viipuri Inlet and the western approach to the city. This force was commanded by Lieutenant-General Lennart Oesch, Mannerheim's chief of staff and trusted subordinate. Timoshenko was poised for the third phase of his offensive.

While the Finns were fighting for their lives and independence, the Western Allies debated various intervention options and for seizing control over the Swedish Gällivare-Kiruna iron ore mines. These plans varied from the barely practical to the positively bizarre. Nevertheless, rumours of an impending Allied intervention on behalf of Finland were rife in European capitals. Convinced that the primary preoccupation of Allied forces would be to defend the Swedish mines against German counter-intervention, Mannerheim decided to use the Soviet successes in the western Isthmus to persuade the Finnish Cabinet urgently to seek a settlement with Moscow.

Prime Minister Risto Ryti had authorized peace approaches to Moscow to be made through Sweden on 21 February and through London and Paris the following day. Anxious not to lose their opportunity to stem the flow of Swedish ore, the Allies began a final diplomatic campaign to provoke the Finnish request for military assistance. Ironically, the Soviet ambassador in London, Ivan Maisky, received instructions from Molotov also on 22 February to inform the British Government of Moscow's terms for peace, and to request that they should be sent to Helsinki. Britain demurred but Sweden, to whom the Soviet request had also been sent, did not hesitate.

Moscow's terms were severe. They demanded the lease of Hanko, ceding of the whole Karelian Isthmus, including Viipuri and Sortavala, and an alliance between the Soviet Union, Finland and Estonia for defence of the Gulf of Finland. During the days that the Army of the Isthmus was withdrawing to the T-Line, the Finnish Cabinet debated Moscow's terms and met Mannerheim at Mikkeli on 28 February. After he had twice explained the desperate situation his armies faced, the Cabinet decided to seek direct negotiations with Moscow on the basis of the terms offered. Meanwhile, their intentions had to be kept secret from the Allies and the latter's enthusiasm for intervention maintained.

The first twelve days of March saw the Allies making final preparations to send an expeditionary force, whether or not Norway and Sweden granted transit rights, but only if Helsinki made a formal request. Prime Minister Ryti arrived in Moscow on 7 February, accompanied by the veteran negotiator Juhani Paasikivi and Mannerheim's old confidant and friend Rudolf Walden, to begin negotiations. Four days earlier Timoshenko had launched the third phase of his offensive in the western Isthmus.

Moscow's peace terms were changed. As well as the whole of the Karelian Isthmus, territory north of Lake Ladoga and the lease of Hanko, Stalin demanded the Fisherman's Peninsula in the Arctic and a broad swathe of land at the waist of Finland, around Salla. This totalled 35,000 square kilometres of national territory. One Soviet general remarked, 'We have won enough ground to bury our dead.' Finally, Finland was required to build a railway from Salla to the existing railhead at Kemijärvi and grant the Soviet Union transit rights along it through Tornio to Haparanda in Sweden. Demands for a defence alliance were dropped but the new frontier gave virtually all the economic wealth of Karelia, for which thousands of Finnish lives had been sacrificed, to the Soviet Union. There was no scope for negotiation. The Finnish Cabinet voted thirteen to four for acceptance and hostilities came to an end at 1300 hours on 13 February 1940. Viipuri remained uncaptured and Mannerheim's T-Line of final defence unbroken.

Shocking though the Soviet peace terms appeared to the Finnish civilian population, there can be no doubt that the Government, with Mannerheim's urging, had taken the correct course. Had the war continued, Finland would have been overwhelmed and occupied, probably to have remained under indefinite Communist domination. The T-Line could have held for only a few days longer and, once broken through, there were no Finnish forces or reserves to prevent the Red Army from sweeping into the southern heartland.

British and French plans for intervention brought them no reward and, almost certainly, the disasters of German invasion upon Denmark and Norway. While it can never be certain what Hitler might have done later, when extra ports and coastline became essential for the U-boat offensive, it remains doubtful whether he would have ordered the invasion of those neutrals in April 1940. At that time it was imperative to forestall an Allied entry into Scandinavia. In retrospect the Allies were fortunate that political indecision had held back the expeditionary force until Finno-Russian peace terms were agreed. Germany would have been swift to react and, as was proved when the British intervened in Norway, the German Army and Luftwaffe were far stronger than any forces the Allies might have deployed in Scandinavia.

Losses on both sides in the Winter War were severe. Soviet military casualties were subsequently confirmed as at least 53,500 killed, 176,000 wounded and 16,000 missing, of which 5,469 were taken by the Finns as prisoners of war. Finland suffered 22,425 killed and 1,434 reported missing. A further 43,557 were wounded or seriously injured. These figures do not include civilian casualties inflicted by the bombing of towns and cities. This was a dreadful price to pay for a far greater loss of national territory than would have been the case under the terms demanded by Moscow during the pre-war negotiations. Against this, Finland remained unconquered. The nation had neither bowed to threat nor flinched from war.

PART IV
Dilemma and Survival

13

The Unhappy Peace

Juhani Paasikivi, already an elder statesman but a future President of Finland, wrote in 1944: 'The Winter War certainly earned us honour and reputation and the goodwill of the world, but it did not prevent and it was no compensation for the unhappy peace of Moscow.' The terms of the peace treaty came with the shock of a thunderbolt to the Finnish people, whose spirits had been buoyed up by the Finnish victories at Tolvajärvi, Suomussalmi and in Ladoga-Karelia, together with news bulletins of tenacious resistance by the Army of the Isthmus in Karelia. Although received with thankful relief, the end to the fighting brought severe economic, social and military penalties under the conditions dictated by Moscow.

Most immediately, Finland had to rehouse and settle into a new life 430,000 refugees from the Karelia provinces ceded to the Soviet Union. While an option to remain was theoretically open, virtually the entire population chose to leave, including that of the historic fortress-city of Viipuri. There was no opportunity for a phased transfer of these people, as the treaty demanded their removal within twelve days. Many had already been evacuated from the area of fighting, but absorbing them and the remainder on a permanent basis presented acute economic and social difficulties. Initial sympathy for the refugees was later dissipated by political arguments over the terms of their resettlement and the length of time taken to bring these into effect.

From the economic standpoint the most urgent need was bread to feed the whole population. Finland had achieved a sound balance of payments situation before the war, exporting dairy products, timber, copper and nickel in exchange for grain, raw materials for the textile industry and fuel for manufacturing plants and the communications system. Increased trade with the Western democracies, Britain in particular, had radically changed the pre-1914 position, when Russia had been Finland's principal foreign market. By 1939 the level of trade with the Soviet Union compared only with that of Norway. The aftermath of the Winter War called for dramatic reappraisal of Finland's trading position at a time when the country was encountering increasing isolation from the West.

This sense of standing alone, linked with apprehension that the strict terms of the the Moscow Treaty would not see an end to the Kremlin's demands, soon led the Finnish leadership to search for security in some new alliance or relationship. This quest was to preoccupy the thoughts of the country's political and military leaders throughout the the fifteen months until Germany's attack on the Soviet Union in June 1941. While the armed forces could be improved and strengthened, the frontier changes had left the country even more vulnerable to invasion.

Although the islands in the Gulf of Finland had played so significant a part in the pre-war discussions in Moscow, their loss had no impact on Finland's security. As may be seen on Map 14 opposite, the remaining three territorial concessions indicate just how clearly the Soviet leadership had appreciated the lessons of the recent war. The invasion routes north and south of Lake Ladoga were linked by a two-hundred-mile-wide stretch of territory west of the lake, which formed a single front nowhere less than twenty miles deep. This same frontier change gave any future invader immediate access to Finland's road and rail network. The mobilization and emergency deployment plans introduced in 1934 and put to such good effect at the outset of the Winter War were almost entirely negated. The Finns were left with virtually no chance to give territory to save lives and time in the south-east.

The Soviet demand for Finnish frontier territory in north central Finland had its origin primarily in defensive considerations. The Soviet general staff saw the need for greater depth of their own territory between the frontier and the point where the Leningrad-Murmansk railway is pushed westwards by the tip of the White Sea. The treaty concession provided other important tactical advantages, however. The ground around Salla, which passed to Soviet control and known as the Salla Highlands, dominates all approaches from the west. The westward move of the frontier halved the distance between Soviet territory and Kemijärvi and the treaty required Finland to build a railway eastwards to the frontier, so as to complete the link from Tornio on the Gulf of Bothnia to Kandalaksa on the

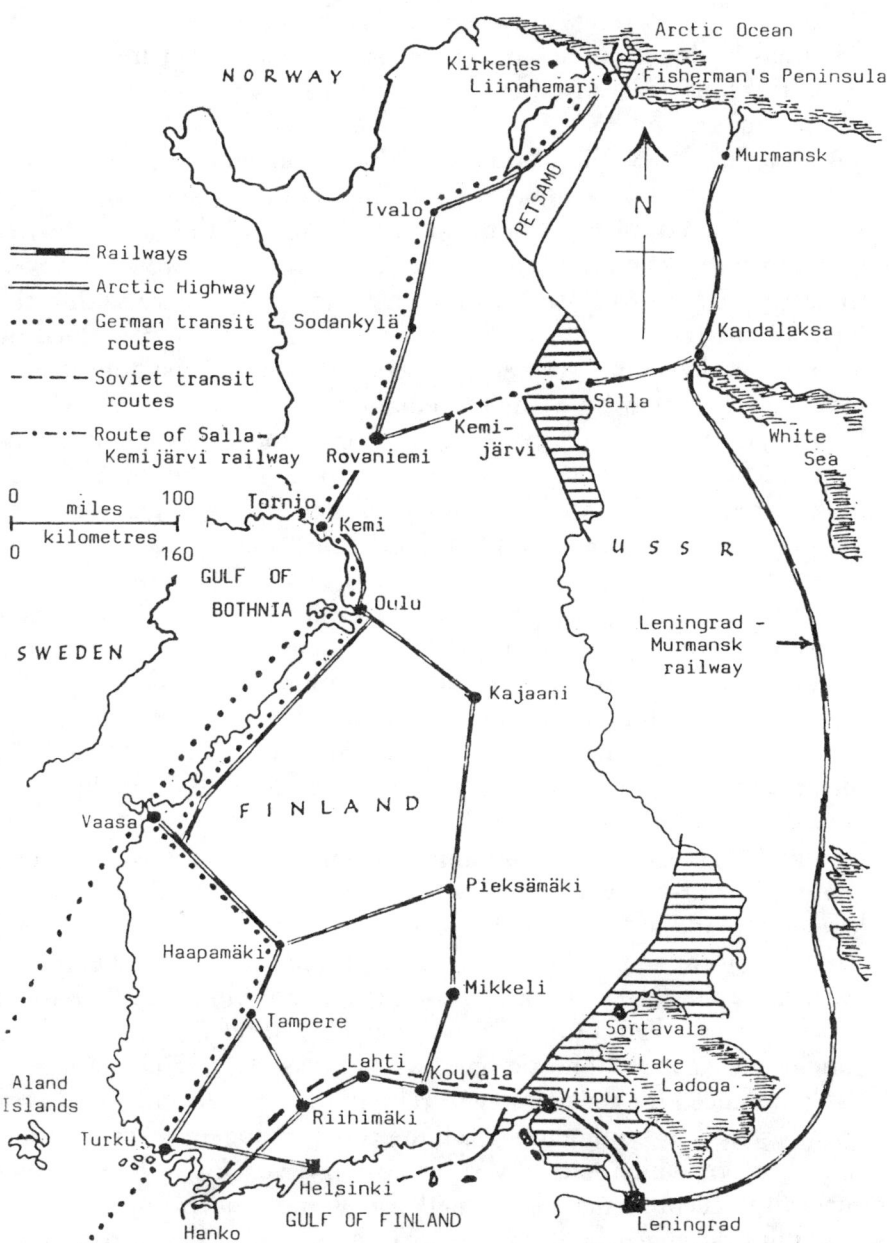

Map 14: Revised frontiers of Finland under the Treaty of Moscow and the
German and Soviet troop transit routes from 1941

White Sea. Opportunity for the Red Army to cut Finland in half by an offensive down the line of this railway would be much improved. As in the south-east of Finland, the Soviet Union had taken control of the vital ground.

A completely new threat was posed by the Soviet occupation of the Hanko Peninsula only eighty miles from Helsinki. Ostensibly Hanko was to be leased for use as a naval base, as part of the overall Soviet plan to protect Leningrad from the sea. The treaty, however, allowed the Soviet Union to station troops, armour and artillery within the base. In any future conflict this force would have to be contained by a force of divisional strength. A seemingly more insidious threat was that presented by a Soviet demand in July 1940 for use of the Leningrad-Hanko rail link for Red Army troop movements. This demand became of increasing concern to the Finnnish leaders, as they feared that several trainloads of troops might stage a *coup de main* operation to coincide with Communist-inspired domestic disturbances in the cities on the route.

Restoration of the slice of territory running southwards from Petsamo, captured by the Soviet Union during the war and returned under the treaty, appeared to have no military significance. It was tacitly recognized by both sides that Finland lacked the resources to defend Petsamo against a Soviet Force sent from Murmansk. Return of the territory had an important economic significance for Finland, as it contained the permanently ice-free port of Liinahamari. This trading link with the West became of even greater importance when Denmark and Norway were overrun by Germany in April 1940, leaving Finland more isolated than ever.

In spite of the sense of national exhaustion at the end of the Winter War, there was no clamour for complete demobilization. Perhaps it was the severe terms of the peace treaty that led the Finnish people to conclude that more, and perhaps worse, was yet to come. Alternatively, the need for the country to remain on a war footing may have been fostered by confidence in Mannerheim's judgement and leadership, both of which had served his country well for so long. It was generally accepted that the armed forces must be maintained at a maximum strength and state of readiness, consistent with a start being made in rebuilding the shattered economy.

This willingness to continue both national and personal hardship, compounded by the problem of the Karelian refugees, is an enduring comment on the Finnish mentality. The positive attitude of the population helped Mannerheim to set right the defence procurement failings of the 1930s. He was in no doubt that it was his responsibility to rebuild the forces which had gained so much in self-confidence by fighting the Red Army to a standstill by the end of the first month of the Winter War.

Mannerheim could have had no reliable assessment of how much time he had before his country would again be at war. Working on an assumption that the time might well be brief, he set in hand a carefully coordinated plan to build fortifications appropriate to the new frontiers. He allowed the discharge of those conscripts essential to begin restoration of the national economy and began the construction of armed forces capable of waging modern war. These had to have a proper balance in armour, artillery and air support. Defence appropriations in 1940 amounted to forty-five percent of the total national budget, compared with thirty percent in 1939. A law was passed at the end of 1940 raising the period of military service to two years as a temporary measure, so as to maintain manning levels.

The mobilized strength of the Finnish armed forces was 400,000 when the ceasefire came into effect on 13 March 1940. Around 100,000 of these were men called up in the latter stages of the Winter War but only partially trained. Retention of these conscripts for completion of training allowed a substantial number of urgently needed men to be released, while still maintaining the total mobilization strength above 180,000. Strengths had been further reduced to 109,000 by the start of 1941, when most of the work on new defences was well advanced.

As in his pre-war appreciation, Mannerheim considered that the main land threat came from the south-east. He set about designing a new defensive system extending from the shore of the Gulf of Finland to Lake Pielinen, apparently undaunted by the breadth of front from which a new attack might be launched. The twenty-five-mile-wide coastal strip, between Klamila on the shoreline and Luumäki on the road skirting the southern edge of the enormous Saimaa complex of lakes, gave him most concern. In spite of the abundance of smaller lakes and watercourses of the region, road and rail communications would always assist a determined invader to gain access to the hinterland. He therefore made this area his first priority for urgent defence works. The countryside that stretches northwards from Lappeenranta through the Lake Saimaa complex to Lake Pielinen is more than eighty percent water in summer. Defence of the narrow strips of land between the lakes, together with blocking and mining the few road routes, lay at the heart of Mannerheim's revised defence plan to meet any renewed attack from the south-east.

In the north-central frontier region, where the Soviet Union had gained the dominating high ground around Salla, the C-in-C realized that he would have to depend on the rugged terrain to help his defence plans, as it had done in the previous winter. Some 10,000 men were engaged in building obstacles and defensive positions by July 1940. Their number increased to 23,000 by September and to 34,000 by March 1941. Key points on the Arctic Road from Petsamo were also fortified, but work on the Åland Islands defences were halted under terms of the peace treaty.

None of this work and enormous expense, with penalties for recovery of the economy, would have been possible without a complete change in stance by the Finnish Government, which was dominated by what became known as the 'inner circle'. This was presided over by Risto Ryti, first as premier and then as president after Kytsti Kallio became incapacitated through a stroke in August 1940. In fact the principal character was Mannerheim, who simply gave instructions as to what was to be done in military matters and informed his colleagues afterwards. The prime minister was Johan Rangell, a banker without political constituency but a supporter of the moderately right-wing Nouseva Suomi ('Rising Finland') party, who succeeded Ryti as premier. The remaining 'inner circle' members were Mannerheim's trusted friend General Rudolf Walden as Defence Minister and the odd choice of the German-speaking Professor Rolf Witting as Foreign Minister. Lieutenant-General Erik Heinrichs, by then the Army chief of staff, joined the group when military matters were to be discussed.

Students of this period of Finnish history tend to make much of the exclusive nature of the 'inner circle', pointing out that not one of its members was a party politician and that this, together with the necessarily secretive nature of the search for a reliable ally for Finland, led them to make political misjudgements. There may be something in this argument but the situation in Finland was not radically different from that in Britain, for example, during the Second World

War. Once he had become both Premier and Minister of Defence, Winston Churchill ran the country and its war effort through a small and intimate War Cabinet. While it is desirable in a parliamentary democracy for important decisions to be thoroughly debated before they are taken, such open procedures are rarely feasible under wartime conditions of security.

An early test of the cohesion of the 'inner circle' occurred in August 1940. Following the German occupation of Denmark and Norway in April, Stalin consolidated his hold on the frontier buffer states of Estonia, Latvia and Lithuania by incorporating them into the Soviet Union. Concern about a new move along the northern coast of the Gulf of Finland was fuelled by intelligence reports that soldiers in Red Army units in Estonia were heard to speak of being 'moved to Karelia.' Intelligence sources also suggested a concentration of two Red Army divisions in the Salla Highlands, opposite the still incomplete railway being built eastwards from Kemijärvi.

An overall intelligence appraisal, demanded by Mannerheim, estimated that a total of twenty-three Red Army divisions could be mustered on Finland's eastern borders by mid-August. Mannerheim asked the 'inner circle' to authorize partial mobilization in readiness to resist a new invasion. To his surprise, both Ryti and Rangell opposed this request. Initially discountenanced, Mannerheim accepted the politians' decision when no invasion came and a subsequent intelligence appreciation gave a less alarming forecast.

This incident gave a fresh but short-lived impetus to the idea of establishing some kind of relationship with Sweden, as an insurance against future Soviet threats. An attempt made in the immediate wake of the Winter War, based on a 'Baltic Alliance' of Finland, Norway, Sweden and possibly Denmark, had foundered when the Kremlin made plain that any such arrangement would be seen as a breach of the Treaty of Moscow. The German occupation of Denmark and Norway had left Sweden as the sole potential partner. The 'inner circle' maintained close commercial and political contacts with Sweden and, through these, had persuaded themselves that the Stockholm Government might strengthen their own country's defence capability, given the appropriate motivation.

If that were indeed the case, motivation was not forthcoming in the form of a guarantee of military assistance to Finland in the face of any renewed Soviet threat. While military contacts continued, the concept of a Finnish-Swedish political union withered in the face of Swedish caution and Soviet opposition. This initiative, undertaken in September 1940, marked the end of the age of innocence of the 'inner circle'. Their subsequent collective and individual actions and attitudes regarding peace and security are questionable when examined against their responsibilities to the Finnish people, but they did not have a wide range of options.

Three events during the summer of 1940, only one of which was Finland's direct concern, were to have a decisive influence on her future. On 23 June Finnish Ambassador Juhani Paasikivi was summoned to Molotov's office and told to 'grant the Petsamo nickel concession to the Soviet Union, form a Finno-Russian company, or make some other arrangement'. This formally opened what became known as the Petsamo nickel dispute, involving Finland, Germany and Russia. Three days later Stalin issued an ultimatum to Romania demanding return of Bessarabia to Moscow's control and, as compensation for being 'robbed' of this province in 1918, northern Bukovina as well. To Hitler's fury, the Romanians gave way and the Red Army and Air Force occupied the two provinces without delay.

These first two developments had serious implications for Germany's war potential. Unknown to Paasikivi, the German and Finnish Governments had that very month reached agreement in principle to supply seventy-five percent of the output of the Kolosjoki nickel mine in the Petsamo region to Germany. This was urgently needed by German industry, as domestic nickel ore deposits were incapable of economic exploitation. In the Balkans, occupation of Bessarabia and northern Bukovina brought the Soviet Union within striking distance of the Romanian oilfields, on which the German war machine almost exclusively depended.

It is now known that on 29 July 1940 Hitler told General Alfred Jodl, chief of the operations staff at German armed forces (Wehrmacht) headquarters, to examine the consequences of war with the Soviet Union if any attempt were made to occupy the Romanian oilfields. The end of July and first ten days of August 1940 also saw an end to the German Luftwaffe's attempt to secure air superiority over the English Channel and south-eastern Britain. Invasion across the Channel without control of the air would be impossible in the face of the Royal Navy's control of the surrounding seas. The alternative course was to defeat and incapacitate the Soviet

Union. That accomplished, Britain would be left isolated and without hope of allies. It would be absurd to attribute Hitler's fateful decision to invade the Soviet Union to the threat to the Romanian oilfields and the Luftwaffe's defeat in the Battle of Britain alone. These were important factors, nevertheless. The wheat of the Ukraine, plus the coal and iron resources of the Donetz basin and the Crimea provided a tempting bonus.

While the German interest in Petsamo nickel was strictly economic, that of the Soviet Union was politico-strategic. Occupation of Norway had brought German forces within reach of Murmansk and the Kola Peninsula. Although they were still partners under the terms of the 1939 Molotov-Ribbentrop Agreement, Stalin remained resolutely distrustful of Hitler's intentions and wished to secure an intelligence window over the Northern Cap. The obstacle was the Anglo-Canadian concession, negotiated in 1934, giving the Mond Nickel Company of London exclusive rights to develop the Petsamo nickel-ore field for a period of forty years.

When Paasikivi delivered a cautious and legalistic reponse to Molotov's request of 23 June 1940, he was abruptly informed, 'We are not now interested in the ore, but in the area itself. The British must be cleared out.' Conscientious Finnish efforts thereafter to reach a solution to the dispute, based on Germany and the Soviet Union sharing the Petsamo nickel output, were to be consistently frustrated. Increasingly vehement Soviet demands for the establishment of a new Finno-Soviet company to run the Petsamo ore-field served only to make the 'inner circle' look more enthusiastically towards Germany for support.

The Soviet insistence on troop transit facilities along the Leningrad-Hanko railway through Finnish cities continued to give the Finnish authorities grounds for apprehension. Although the proposed route avoided Helsinki, and a possible *coup de main* attempt could be countered by separating Soviet troops from their weapons, the infringement of national sovereignty was not something to be welcomed. Therefore, when a German request was received for troop transit arrangements through Finland to Norway, it was viewed as a possible balancing factor to the Soviet demand. It could also be argued, as it was within the 'inner circle', that such a concession might earn Germany's increased support in the Petsamo nickel dispute, which was steadily gaining momentum.

Incorporation of Estonia, Latvia and Lithuania into the Soviet Union, and the ultimatum to Romania, had decided Hitler to strengthen the German position in the Nordic region. In particular, he set about signalling to Moscow that fresh Soviet pressure on Finland would not be acceptable. His messenger to Helsinki was Joseph Veltjens, a retired German officer and arms dealer known for his affection for Finland. Veltjen's mission was to begin negotiations for the supply of German armaments to Finland. In return he was to request transit rights for Luftwaffe personnel through the port of Turku, by rail to Rovaniemi then by march route to Kirkenes in northern Norway. It was known that Germany had a similar arrangement with Sweden and, as shown on Map 14 on page 181, the German and Soviet troops in transit would not meet en route to their separate destinations.

The German troop transit proposal was delivered by Veltjens to Mannerheim on 19 August, who wisely referred it to Ryti. Having received acceptance from the Finnish premier and C-in-C, Veltjens separately gave Ryti, Walden and Witting to understand that they must not give way to Moscow's demands for Petsamo. In this conversation he conspicuously stopped short of offering any German support in that dispute.

An agreement was signed in Berlin on 12 September 1940 between a representative of the Finnish Army general staff and a major of the Luftwaffe movements branch. The very next day Witting presented the Foreign Affairs committee of Parliament with the final terms of the Soviet troop transit demand. This had been watered down by Molotov to accommodate Finnish requests that not more than three troop trains should be on the Finnish railways at any one time. All vans were to be sealed and the troops and their weapons would travel by separate trains. The terms were accepted by the Foreign Affairs committee without reference to Parliament. At that stage Witting made no mention of the German troop transit agreement that had already been signed.

There was a silently eloquent contrast between the terms of the two troop transit agreements. While Red Army troop movements were to be under rigorous Finnish control. The Germans were permitted to set up their own line of communication bases at Vaasa, Rovaniemi and Ivalo. These staging posts were to be manned by up to 1,100 German administrative staff. The German troops were to travel in sealed trains only as far as Rovaniemi, whence they were to march with their personal weapons to Ivalo and pause there before continuing on to Norway. Admittedly the German agreement was for only a total of 5,000 men in three contingents, due to arrive between 22 September and mid-October 1940, but the troops and staging facilities to be established suggest a more enduring intention. The arrangement also provided for German armaments to be supplied to Finland in the Finnish shipping that was to collect the troops from German ports.

There can be no doubt that the signing of the German armaments and troop transit agreement marked the formal beginning of a move by the 'inner circle' towards dependence on German support against future Soviet pressure. The German motives appear threefold. There were undoubted conveniences in the transit arrangements themselves. Scarce German shipping could be diverted for other use and an alternative line of communication to German Army units in Norway was established and could be expanded. Provision of German armaments to Finland would be accomplished in secret. On the other hand, there could be no question of concealing the troop movements themselves. So Moscow would receive a clear signal that Finland and Germany now enjoyed some element of mutual self-confidence. During the nine months until June 1941, 53 fighter aircraft, 185 field artillery guns, 112 anti-aircraft guns, 300 anti-tank guns and 150,000 anti-tank mines were delivered by Germany to Finland. An estimated 30,000 German troops used the transit route.

Unknown to the 'inner circle' and before either transit agreement had been signed, the German Army general staff had begun to plan an operation to seize control of the Petsamo region in the event of any Soviet move against Finland. With a curious disregard for security convention, this plan was codenamed 'Reindeer' but it made no provision for military assistance to Finland in the event of a Soviet attack. At that stage its sole purpose was to secure control over the Petsamo nickel-ore supplies.

During the period between September 1940 and April 1941 Germany was fast developing plans for an attack on the Soviet Union. In the northern region these varied significantly in their assumptions as to the degree of participation expected from Finland. Only the most oblique and guarded inquiries were made to the Finns themselves. Aware of the steadily deteriorating relationship between Berlin and

Moscow, the Finns responded to all German inquiries with the explanation that they would fight the Soviet Union again only if attacked. This strictly correct public attitude did not prevent the Finnish military command acceding to discreet German general staff visits that indicated interest in facilities for troop movements eastwards across northern and north-central Finland. Meanwhile, the German and Russian troop transits continued without incident.

Throughout the ensuing months of Soviet pressure on Finland, Mannerheim and Walden were resolutely restructuring the armed forces and preparing revised mobilization plans. By the end of 1940 the standing army establishment comprised thirteen infantry brigades, two Jäger and one horsed cavalry brigade. On mobilization, this structure could be quickly expanded into sixteen divisions, with a total strength of 475,000 men. The acute shortage of field artillery during the Winter War was rectified by increase in the number of battalions from thirty-five to eighty. Of these, some twenty to twenty-five battalions were equipped with modern 76 – 120 mm guns and 105 – 155 mm howitzers. Three further battalions were equipped with 203 mm howitzers acquired from the United States.

Armour remained a serious deficiency in the Army, when compared with the improved strength and balance of infantry and artillery. Of the thirty-odd Vickers-Armstrong Six-ton tanks used in the Winter War, five were lost in fighting at Honkaniemi in the Karelian Isthmus on 26 February 1940. During the ensuing peace the surviving twenty-five were fitted with Soviet 45 mm guns extracted from captured Soviet T-26 tanks, Soviet 7.62 mm Degtyarev Tankoviy coaxial machine-guns and renamed the T-26E. More than 2,000 Soviet tanks had been captured or knocked out during the fighting. The least damaged were repaired in Finnish factories and used with the T-26Es to form a tank battalion.

On mobilization, the tank battalion would man a mixture of various types of the T-26, of which the Soviet version had the same basic design as the Vickers-Armstrong, and a heavy tank platoon equipped with captured and refurbished Soviet T-28s. Whereas the T-26 varieties were armed with the Russian 45 mm except for a handful equipped with flamethrowers, the T-28s had a main armament of a 76 mm gun plus four and two 7.62 mm machine-guns respectively. In addition, there were seven independent tank platoons equipped with T-37 or T-38 Soviet-built amphibious light tanks, with a crew of two and mounting only a single 7.62 machine-gun. Work was begun on building twenty of the Finnish versions of the Soviet BT-7 alternative tracked or wheeled tank.

Deployment plans were brought into line with the Treaty frontiers. Twelve of the sixteen mobilization divisions were to be deployed in five army corps close to the frontier. To facilitate swift deployment, one third of the men in each forward division were drawn from the active conscript brigades under training. One division was tasked to seal off the Soviet garrison on the Hanko Peninsula, leaving three divisions as the C-in-C's reserve. These were made up of the older reservists.

Military aircraft supplied from abroad had continued to arrive up to and after the Winter War ceasefire on 13 March 1940. These and Soviet aircraft captured in repairable condition gave the Finnish Air Force a much improved operational capability by the summer of 1941, compared to what it had been in November 1939. The fighter arm mustered a total of 152 modern or relatively modern interceptors, including forty-three United States Brewster B 239s, thirty-two Italian Fiat G-50s, twenty-three Finnish Fokker D XXIs, nine British Hawker Hurricanes, thirty-seven French Morane 406s and eight repaired Soviet I-153s. This was more than the Air Force total aircraft complement of all types at the start of the Winter War.

The bomber situation was less significantly improved and there was no advance in quality of aircraft. The bomber force comprised twenty-nine Bristol Blenheim Marks I and IV and five refurbished Soviet SB-2s. The Blenheims had performed moderately well on medium-range bombing missions during the Winter War, but they were critically vulnerable to catching fire. The reconnaissance and army cooperation wing had increased its complement to sixty-three aircraft but all of obsolescent type.

The spring of 1941 brought increased Berlin-Moscow tension and rumour of impending war. Without causing alarm, Mannerhein brought mobilization plans to completion. Informal German in-quiries frequently touched on this aspect of military readiness and on Finland's reaction should war between Germany and the Soviet Union become inevitable. The Finns' response was consistent: they would fight only if attacked. Meanwhile, through diplomatic and military channels, Germany fostered the impression that they would go to almost any lengths to avoid war on their eastern border.

Dr Karl Schnurre, who had established good credentials in Finland through his part in Finnish-German trade talks, including those on Petsamo nickel, travelled to Helsinki to see President Ryti on 20 May. He brought two pieces of information and two requests. Schnurre told Ryti that Molotov had demanded of Germany a free hand 'to settle accounts with Finland' and that Hitler had refused. As a result, both Germany and the Soviet Union had begun preparations for war. The two requests were that Ryti would send a military delegation to Germany, to be informed of Germany's war contingency plans, and submit to Berlin a list of points that Finland wished Germany to raise with Moscow on her behalf.

The unhappy interim peace had one month to run.

14
Return to the Frontier

As early as February 1941 Finnish President Risto Ryti had written to his ambassador in Moscow, the veteran statesman Juhani Paasikivi, explaining his reasons for believing that war between Germany and the Soviet Union was inevitable. 'The Germans see the war in the west as lengthy and difficult but they do not wish to risk an attempted landing in England,' he wrote. 'Is it not likely, when the climate and other conditions are favourable, to aim their unused land forces at Russia and seize its main productive areas, the Black Sea district, the Ukraine, the Don basin and Caucasia? Victory in Russia would enthuse the Germans, impress the rest of the world and secure the supplies needed for war against England.'

Having made this appreciation in February, Ryti was scarcely surprised when the German Foreign Ministry official, Dr Karl Schnurre, invited him to send a military delegation to Salzburg and Berlin in May 1941. The expressed purpose of the visit was to receive information on Germany's contingency plans in the event of a war with the Soviet Union. By that stage the 'inner circle' controlling Finland's affairs functioned in two loosely connected groups. Mannerheim as C-in-C and General Rudolf Walden as Minister of Defence handled all military matters, while Ryti and Prime Minister Johan Rangell struggled to manage the tottering economy. Foreign Minister Rolf Witting kept a foothold in each camp, as he had close interest in German economic as well as military supplies. This tacit arrangement allowed Ryti to hand over responsibility for the German-Finnish military discussions to Mannerheim.

The Finnish delegation was selected with care. Lieutenant-General Erik Heinrichs, the Army chief of staff led the mission. He was accompanied by the head of the operations staff, Major-General Aksel Airo, the director of mobilization plans, the director of supply and a representative of the Finnish Navy. Mannerheim instructed Heinrichs, 'Let the Germans talk and explain. You remain as far as possible the receiving party.' Heinrichs was well chosen. He had commanded III Army Corps and later the Army of the Isthmus during the Winter War, he was a broad military thinker and a man of proven strong nerve in crisis. Mannerheim had confidence in his judgement and discretion. The mission arrived in Salzburg on 25 May to be met by Field-Marshal Wilhelm Keitel and General Alfred Jodl, the chief and deputy chief of the German Supreme Command headquarters OKW.

German contingency plans for operations through Finnish territory had gone through at least two evolutionary stages since 'Plan Reindeer', for seizure of the Petsamo nickel mines in anticipation of a Soviet attack on Finland, had first been considered in August 1940. By May 1941 this plan had acquired a second and far more ambitious objective – to sever Soviet supply routes through the northern ice-free ports of Murmansk and Archangel. In effect, the plan had been changed from being a pre-emptive strike to secure the Finnish nickel mines, on which the German war machine continued to depend, to become part of a wider act of aggression against the Soviet Union as a whole.

A second plan, codenamed 'Silverfox', had been drawn up by Colonel-General Nikolaus von Falkenhorst, commander of German forces in Norway. Falkenhorst had anticipated cooperation of the entire mobilized strength of the Finnish Army in a combined operation for the capture of Murmansk, Leningrad and Soviet territory as far as the White Sea. He had also assumed that Sweden would allow use of their railways to transport German divisions from Norway into central Finland. When Stockholm demurred and OKW felt concern for the defence of Norway, 'Silverfox' was scaled down to become a supporting operation for an extended 'Plan Reindeer'. It envisaged a German-Finnish thrust by two army corps through the Salla Highlands towards the Leningrad-Murmansk railway. As events were to prove, German staff plans for both 'Reindeer' and the modified 'Silverfox' significantly underestimated the difficulty of large-scale operations in Finland's northern wilderness, even in midsummer.

On arrival in Salzburg, Heinrichs received an overall brief on German plans. Both 'Reindeer' and 'Silverfox' were represented as contingent on Germany being forced into war with the Soviet Union. He was careful to make no commitment on behalf of Finland.

Personally, he was incredulous of a full-scale German attack on the Soviet Union. He knew that Finland's success in blocking the invading Red Army's advance through the narrow Karelian Isthmus in mid-winter bore no comparison with taking on the full might of the Soviet Union defending the homeland of Mother Russia. Nevertheless, German plans for the northern sector offered the Finns a possible means by which they might recover territory lost under the Treaty of Moscow.

Jodl's propositions to Heinrichs for Finnish cooperation in the German plans followed a seductively ascending scale. Having explained the full scope of 'Reindeer,' he placed two modest requests on the table. First, he asked that the Finnish battalion already in the Petsamo region should provide cover for the movement of Lieutenant-General Eduard Dietl's XXI Mountain Army Corps into the area from Norway. Secondly, he asked that the Luftwaffe might use Petsamo airfield to provide air cover. The immediate but unspoken reaction of the Finnish chief of staff was the difficulty Finland would have in maintaining a neutral stance from the moment German troops and aircraft entered his country in strength.

The modified form of 'Silverfox' no longer depended on movement of German divisions through Sweden. Instead, the plan envisaged up to three divisions converging on Rovaniemi from Norway and Turku, using the well-practised transit routes from the north and south. In the event of war, the three divisions would form the German XXXVI Army Corps to execute the 'Silverfox' thrust through Salla. Should war not occur, the divisions could pass on the railway to effect a routine relief. Jodl asked Heinrichs if the Finnish III Army Corps located opposite Salla would be available to cover the German deployment. He went on to suggest that this Finnish corps might come under German command, at least temporarily.

Finally, after acknowledging that the Finns would need a division to seal off the 25,000-strong Soviet garrison in the Hanko Peninsula, Jodl turned to the problem of the large number of Soviet troops in the Leningrad Military District. Of an estimated total of eighteen divisions, seven of the Soviet 23rd Army were deployed to defend the city. If these were not to interfere with early German moves elsewhere, most would have to be held in their positions. This might be achieved, Jodl pointed out to Heinrichs, by a full-scale but defensive mobilization of the Finnish forces. Fearful for the vulnerability of their second city, Soviet leaders would be unlikely to allow the 23rd Army to move.

It was at this point that the German and Finnish high commands began to look at Finland's mobilization through different perspectives. To Jodl and his staff, early Finnish mobilization would provide cover for German deployment and inhibit wide-scale Soviet reaction to the German moves. Heinrichs, on the other hand, foresaw the likelihood of Soviet pre-emptive attacks against Finland as soon as mobilization began. This difference of outlook was to inhibit close coordination between Finnish and German commanders until actual operations began.

Having told Jodl that he would report his requests to Mannerheim and Ryti, Heinrichs flew to Berlin for discussions with General Franz Halder. As chief of staff of the German Army, Halder was directly responsible for planning the attack on Leningrad. Whilst still in the realms of contingency arrangements 'should war with Russia prove unavoidable', Halder at once made clear that he was seeking an active role by Finland. He asked Heinrichs whether it would be feasible for the mobilized Finnish Army to be grouped so as to be able to attack either north of Lake Ladoga or south through the Karelian Isthmus. This was a significant step beyond Jodl's request for the Finns simply to hold the Red Army divisions in place.

The two generals fenced politely, Halder endeavouring to discover the full range of Finnish capabilities and options while, still without giving the least commitment, Heinrichs sought to discover all he could of German intentions. At the end of the conversation Halder was left with two clear impressions. First, the Finns would not have the forces to launch an attack north and south of Lake Ladoga, unless they were relieved of responsibility for sealing off the Hanko Peninsula and re-occupying the Åland Islands. Secondly, the Finns would delay full mobilization as long as possible so as to avoid a Soviet pre-emptive attack and to ensure, in view of their increasingly serious food situation, that the harvest had been gathered in.

On return to Helsinki, Heinrichs reported to Mannerheim and stressed that the only commitment he had given was the use of the Petsamo battalion to cover the German move into the region. The 'inner circle' had but a few days in which to reflect, as von Falken-horst's chief of staff, Colonel Erich Buschenhagen, was due in the Finnish capital to receive answers to the propositions made by Jodl and Halder. The Finns' dilemma was compounded by uncertainty as to whether or not there would be war between Germany and the Soviet Union. This deception had been deliberately woven by the German high command so as to preserve the secrecy and timing of their invasion plan 'Barbarossa'. Thus the Finns were confronted by both practical and moral uncertainty.

Much as he disliked and distrusted the German political régime, Mannerheim had a high regard for the professional competence of the German armed forces. Unlike Heinrichs, he judged that Germany would defeat the Soviet Union, if war did occur, and this would present an opportunity for Finland to recover the lost territories. To his mind, this was not a mere sentimental endeavour but one based on defensive and economic arguments. On the other hand, the worldly-wise field-marshal wished to retain the friendship of the Western Allies and the United States. This would be feasible, so he sought to persuade his 'inner circle' colleagues, only if Finland made war on the Soviet Union separately from Germany and promptly declared the limited aim of restoring the frontiers of 1939.

This formula found support, although the two groups within the 'inner circle' distanced themselves respectively from military aspects on the one hand and political implications on the other. The arrival of Buschenhagen on 2 June necessitated a response in principle to the German proposals. It was left to Foreign Minister Witting to prepare the written reply, which must rank high among the Delphic exchanges of diplomacy: 'On the assumption that the political side of the question is cleared up by discussion between the competent authorities, the proposed measures can be executed.' As the Germans had chosen to remain opaque, so were they rewarded.

For Mannerheim and Heinrichs, however, this was just the beginning. They had to decide how many troops should be committed to 'Reindeer' and 'Silverfox' and from when, bearing in mind the nationally emotive and internationally provocative act of mobilization. In the only slightly longer term, they had to elect whether to commit their main force to an attack in the south-east and, if so, whether to the north-east or south-west of Lake Ladoga, or possibly along both shores simultaneously. To maintain credibility with the Western Allies, some pretext for war with the Soviet Union had to be found, or even engineered. It was important to convey an impression of Finland being drawn into the conflict.

The political and military groups within the 'inner circle' agreed that, in view of the tense relations between Berlin and Moscow, partial mobilization and deployment of protective forces could be safely presented as a defensive precaution. Therefore, while still uncertain whether or not war would come or of the date of the German decision, Mannerheim decided on a three-phase call up. The first two phases were to be clearly identifiable as defensive measures but, coincidently, would provide two divisions to cover the move of the German XXXVI Army Corps from Rovaniemi into position to launch 'Silverfox'. The third and by far the largest mobilization phase would be held back until after war between Germany and the Soviet Union had actually begun and, ideally, after the Finnish harvest had been gathered in. Thus, Finland could not subsequently be accused of helping to precipitate war nor of reneging on its commitments to Germany.

Phase one of mobilization was planned for 10-14 June and involved only the bringing of the protective forces on the eastern frontier up to battle strength. Phase two was limited to the mobilization of 17th Division to seal off the Soviet garrison on Hanko Peninsula plus the 3rd and 6th Divisions of III Army Corps to cover the move of German troops for 'Silverfox'. This corps was commanded by Major-General Hjalmar Siilasvuo, who had led the 9th Division with such verve and tactical skill during the wilderness battles of the Winter War. If and when war came, he would be under command of Falkenhorst in the northern sector. For all his confidence of German success against the main Soviet forces, Mannerheim was to be proved rightly sceptical of German performance in the northern wilderness. The Finnish commander chosen to support them had proved his worth in just that environment.

During the pause while the German high command deliberated over the precise date for the onslaught on the Soviet Union, Mannerheim and his senior military colleagues weighed up the options for a Finnish offensive in the south-east. It was clear from discussions during and after Buschenhagen's visit to Helsinki, that Halder hoped for a two-pronged Finnish attack along the north-eastern shore of Lake Ladoga and through the Karelian Isthmus towards Leningrad. It was suggested that the first objective to the north-east of the lake should be the River Svir. This cut across the Olonets Isthmus between Lake Ladoga and Lake Onega to the north. Although sixty miles beyond the frontier of 1939, the Svir offered an obstacle on which to pause and construct defensive positions, with a lake the size of an inland sea on each flank.

The Finnish general staff already had a plan for an offensive in the Karelian Isthmus, even before the German briefing in Salzburg. This was a possible counter-offensive phase of a contingency plan to meet any renewed Soviet invasion. The aim of the plan, known as the 'Hiitola offensive' from the lakeside town selected as its first objective, was to drive a wedge into the enemy's attacking front to disrupt his lateral communications. This plan now became the basis for a larger-scale offensive timed to take advantage of the German attack in the Arctic and towards Leningrad through the Baltic states.

A German advance on Leningrad was central to Halder's inquiry about the Finnish Army's capability to launch an offensive astride Lake Ladoga. If the Finns could be persuaded to pin down the defenders by attacking from the north-west, ideally supported by German divisions from 'Reindeer' and 'Silverfox' further north, the main German forces advancing through Estonia would be better able to surround the city. Mannerheim was not attracted by this train of thought. The capture of Leningrad formed no part of his plans for Finland. He knew that cooperation with German forces attacking, or even besieging, the city would draw the immediate and probably lasting emnity of the Western Allies. Politically, the frontier of 1939 was much less significant north of Lake Ladoga than it was in the Karelian Isthmus. He therefore let it be known to the German high command that he favoured a Finnish offensive north-east of Lake Ladoga, if war should come.

Ironically, the plan that Mannerheim, Heinrichs and Airo devised required the Germans to do much the same as Halder had hoped the Finns would do for them. Mannerheim reasoned that if the Finnish advance to the 1939 frontier across the Isthmus was delayed until the Red Army redeployed to meet the main German threat, the Finns might well reach the frontier without a major battle. Moreover, if the advance paused on the line of the Vuoksi river, it would be possible to turn south-west to isolate and then capture Viipuri. Recovery of this city would be seen as a triumph throughout the homeland and widely understood in the West as a justifiable cause for Finnish participation in the war.

Detailed planning on this basis was put in hand, although some doubts remained about the certainty of war and there was no confirmation of a date for the start of the German offensive. Major-General Waldemar Erfurth was sent by Halder, together with a small group of specialist officers, to join Mannerheim's staff and establish a close liaison link between the German and Finnish high commands. Erfurth quickly became sensitive to the Finns' attitude to the war and he got on well with Mannerheim. Smooth relations between the two armies, in spite of their varied aims and objectives, owe much to Erfurth's perception and diplomacy.

The first phase of mobilization was accomplished without incident, although there was widespread questioning of the need for the call up amongst the civil population. The Winter War had brought the whole nation together for the first time in the brief history of independent Finland. But possibility of renewed conflict simply to regain territory did not meet with much enthusiasm. Fuelled by this uncertainty over popular support, the political group of the 'inner circle' argued for a pause in the mobilization process until German intentions became more clear. This led Erfurth to signal his concern to Keitel, with a request that the Finns should either be given an assurance there would be war or a guarantee of essential grain supplies if a peaceful solution were to be found.

Keitel's reply was specific on Erfurth's latter point only: 'Finland's demands and requirements for action to be taken can be regarded as fulfilled.' This was accepted by Ryti and Witting as a guarantee of grain and, under continued pressure from Mannerheim, the second phase of mobilization was authorized. Meanwhile, unknown to the 'inner circle', the date for 'Barbarossa' had been postponed from 12 to 22 June. An indication of delay was received in the form of a message to Mannerheim from Siilasvuo commanding the still not fully mobilized III Army Corps under German orders in Lapland. He reported that 'Reindeer' would not be put into effect before 1 July, three days later than expected. In consequence, the third phase of Finnish mobilization was put back two days, to start on 18 June.

'Barbarossa' was launched in the early hours of 22 June and Hitler's order of the day spoke of Germany and Finland fighting 'im Bunde'. Literally, this means 'in alliance' but the Finnish ambassadors in Western capitals were swift to point out that, while mobilizing due to the dangers of the situation, Finland still remained neutral. Domestic news spoke of German and Finnish forces standing side by side. Initial Soviet reactions allowed Finland to choose neutrality. The Kremlin issued orders that Soviet air and ground activity was not to be extended over Finnish territory and Helsinki was informed that Finland's neutrality would be respected, unless German attacks were permitted from her territory.

While Finnish hesitation was still seemly, it was impossible to turn back from war. On 17 June units of the German XXXVI Army Corps had started eastwards from Rovaniemi towards their positions for launch of 'Silverfox'. This could not be long concealed from Soviet intelligence. In the far north, troops of Dietl's XXI Mountain Army Corps took over Petsamo at 0230 hours on 22 June, without interference from the Red Army across the nearby frontier. Coordinated German and Finnish naval mining operations along the Soviet coast began during the night of 21-22 June. The Finnish 17th Division blockaded Hanko and Soviet transits to the peninsula garrison were suspended on Mannerheim's order. Finnish air space was used for Luftwaffe attacks on Leningrad and her airfields for refuelling the returning aircraft. Meanwhile, Soviet air attacks on Finnish shipping in the Baltic, during 22 June, ignored Helsinki's statement of neutrality.

On the morning of 25 June the Soviet Air Force made a series of attacks aimed at Finnish airfields and communication centres. These were largely inaccurate but their scale provided the Finnish Government with a just and public cause for President Ryti to summon Parliament into secret session the same afternoon. The morning's events were so closely similar to the start of the Winter War that it was widely assumed that the country was again threatened with Soviet invasion – only this time better resources for defence were to hand. A vote of confidence in the Government was carried without serious dissent but, strangely perhaps, no formal declaration of war was ever made. It now only remained for the armed forces to restore the integrity of the national frontiers. With thirteen percent of the population mobilized, this task had to be accomplished quickly.

During the week between the onset of 'Barbarossa' and launch of the first land operations from Finnish territory in the Arctic on 29 June, the third phase of mobilization was completed and plans for an offensive in the south-east finalized. Mannerheim had not failed to appreciate the attitude towards mobilization in large sectors of the civilian population. This reinforced his opinion that the offensive in

Karelia should be clearly seen to be aimed at recovery of the lost territories and distinctly separate from German operations to capture Leningrad. He assessed that popular support could be harnessed to a war of recovery but not for one of revenge. For the same and also for economic reasons, Finnish offensive operations needed to be concluded speedily and with minimum loss of life.

Aside from the Soviet forces being thrown onto the strategic defensive by the sheer scale and ferocity of the German attack, the Finnish armed forces were in infinitely better condition to fight a war than in December 1939. The majority of units were now battle-experienced, as was virtually every commander at and above battalion level. There had been immense improvement in the ratio of artillery to infantry and more armoured units had been formed. Thanks to increased domestic production and German supply, availability of ammunition no longer posed a serious short-term problem. With a complement of 150 modern fighter interceptors and over 30 modern fast light-bomber aircraft, the Air Force was capable of joining the Army in large-scale offensive operations.

Despite his determination not to present a Finnish threat to Leningrad, Mannerheim began to favour the 'Hiitola offensive' over operations north-east of Lake Ladoga. This change of mind may have had its origin in his judgement that the Finnish population would quickly relate to a recapture of Viipuri and the plans for 'Hiitola' were well advanced. A more intriguing possibility arises from a new German appreciation that, given a choice, a Finnish offensive north-east of the lake would suit them best. They argued that the Red Army might redeploy troops from Ladoga-Karelia for close defence of Leningrad, but would not risk a weakened defence in the Isthmus. Hence, the total number of enemy divisions fixed in their positions would be greater in the event of an offensive in the north. Mannerheim had long resolved not to dance to a German tune, so their request for an attack in the north may have encouraged his inclination for an offensive in the Isthmus designed to recapture Viipuri.

The boundary between Mannerheim's command and the German and Finnish formations in the north ran immediately south of the road and railway from Oulu, on the west coast, to Kajaani, then eastwards to the frontier. Siilasvuo's III Army Corps of two divisions remained under German command for execution of 'Silverfox'

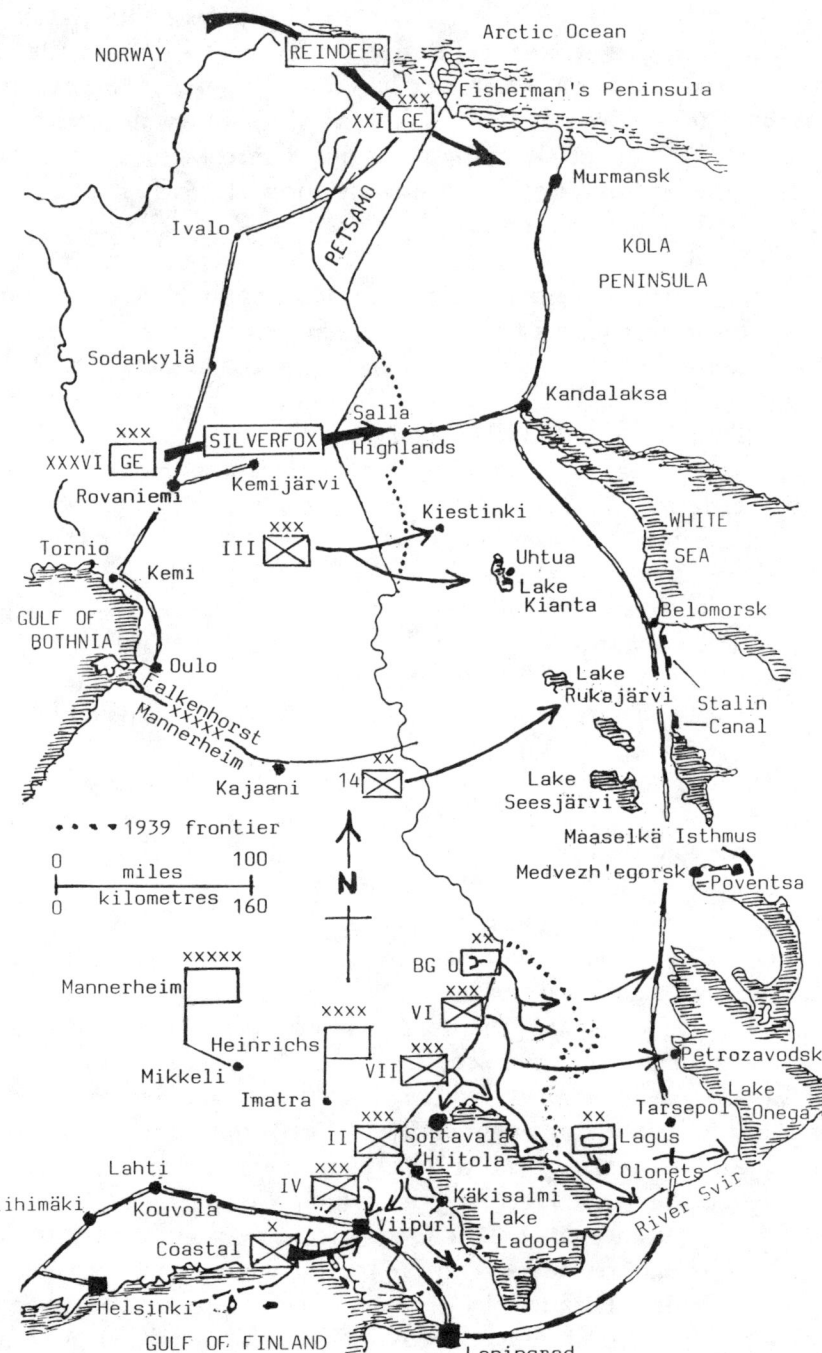

Map 15: Deployment of Finnish and German forces in Finland during the offensives of 1941

through the Salla Highlands, with the Leningrad-Murmansk railway as their first strategic objective. A number of Finnish Air Force fighter and bomber aircraft were based in the north in direct support of the Finnish corps. Further squadrons of the Luftwaffe were on call but remained under German operational control. Siilasvuo was confident that he could drive the Russians out of the Salla Highlands but was less sanguine about the likely success of the German drive on Murmansk.

In the south, Mannerheim committed a total of ten divisions to operations, retaining a further four as his reserve, including the German 163rd Division. From this reserve were detached 17th Division sealing off the Hanko Peninsula and one infantry regiment sent to defend the Åland Islands against any Soviet landing. Following a further appeal from the German High Command for an offensive north of Lake Ladoga, conveyed by the ever-courteous Erfurth, Mannerheim finally agreed to offensives north-east of the lake and in the Isthmus. The northern offensive into Ladoga-Karelia would start first, on 10 July. This was to allow maximum effort in that region, while the formations facing the Isthmus prepared for the 'Hiitola offensive' at the end of July. He did not reveal to Erfurth that the offensive in the Isthmus would halt at the Vuoksi river, then turn south-west to retake Viipuri.

Heinrichs was appointed to command a newly formed Army of Karelia responsible for the northern offensive. The forces allocated were VII Army Corps (Major-General Woldemar Hägglund) of two divisions on the right, VI Army Corps (Major-General Paavo Talvela) of three divisions in the centre and Battle Group O (Major-General Woldemar Oinonen) comprising the Cavalry Brigade and 2nd Jäger Brigade on the left. Talvela's VI Corps was selected for the main drive towards the north-western tip of Lake Ladoga, then south-eastwards down the coast towards the frontier.

Talvela led the offensive with a characteristic display of vigour and tactical flair. The opposing Soviet 7th Army was thrown off balance by a south-easterly drive into and then across its front. This brought the independent 1st Jäger Brigade, which was under command of VI Corps, to the shore of Lake Ladoga on the evening of 16 July. Mannerheim released the German 163rd Division from his reserve to protect the left flank of VI Corps while 11th Division consolidated a hold on the lake shore to the east of Sortavala. Talvela pushed 5th

Division south-eastwards along the northern shore of the lake with 1st Division covering their left flank. 1st Division crossed the old frontier where it bulged to the west on 24 July. Talvela was eager to push on to the River Svir, some fifty miles beyond, but Heinrichs ordered him to pause and go firm on the frontier. Elsewhere the battle was progressing less well. Both Heinrichs and Mannerheim were apprehensive of a massive Red Army counter-attack that could catch VI Army Corps in an over-extended line with their backs to the lake.

To the north of Talvela's successful drive to the lake shore, the German 163rd Division was making slow progress in the unfamiliar wilderness terrain. On the right flank of VI Army Corps, 7th Division of Hägglund's VII Army Corps met with stubborn resistance from the defenders of Sortavala, which was not finally cleared until 8 August. North of the Finnish-German operational boundary, Siilasvuo's III Army Corps had crossed the 1940 frontier on a two-divisional front during the first week of July, but General Hans Feige's XXXVI Army Corps was struggling in the roadless wilderness.

In all these circumstances Mannerheim ordered a standfast north of Lake Ladoga until after execution of the Hiitola offensive, except where defensive positions needed to be improved by local tactical adjustments. The Isthmus offensive was launched as planned on 31 July, with Major-General Taavetti Laatikainen's II Army Corps of 2nd, 15th and 18th Divisions in the lead. Troops of the the Soviet 23rd Army put up a determined resistance but the lakeside town of Hiitola was captured on 8 August. Then, while 15th Division continued down the lakeside towards Käkisalmi and 18th Division broke southwards for Antrea, Mannerheim despatched Major-General Aaro Pajari's 10th Division, taken from his reserve, on a drive between them towards the Vuoksi river. Pajari reached the river on 21 August, which signalled the moment for a switch to the south-west for the recapture of Viipuri.

Lieutenant-General Lennart Oesch's IV Army Corps began encircling moves to the north and east on 22 August, using 8th and 4th Divisions, the latter released from Mannerheim's reserve. On the west coast of the Viipuri Inlet, 2nd Coastal Brigade advanced briskly through the swamps and streams where they had fought in the Winter War. The Soviet garrison had no stomach for a siege and attempted to slip away down the coast to avoid the more widely encircling move of Oesch's 12th Division. Two Red Army divisions were trapped and badly mauled by the Finnish 4th and 8th Divisions in the area between Metsäkylä and Porlampi. Viipuri fell without a battle on 29 August.

Meanwhile, on 23 August, units of 15th Division had reached the point where the 1939 frontier crossed the southern shore of Lake Ladoga. Pajari's 10th Division formed up on their right and was quickly followed by the 18th and 12th Divisions to form a solid front between the lakeside and the sea by 2 September. As on the northeast of the lake, the frontier was crossed only to straighten the line. Mannerheim ordered no further advance in the Isthmus. Instead, defensive positions were prepared.

Baron Ernst von Born, of the Swedish People's Party in Finland, gave a newspaper interview in Stockholm at this time. He told the reporter: 'There is a stone on our eastern boundary north of Lake Ladoga which was set up more than three hundred years ago. Into it are chiseled the words 'Gustavus Adolphus, King of Sweden, established the farthest boundary of the country here. With God's help may that boundary last.'

Although meticulously careful not to allow his troops to be thought to threaten Leningrad, Mannerheim was about to launch a second offensive north of Lake Ladoga. On this occasion his objectives were to include the line of the River Svir and, ultimately, the north and western shores of Lake Onega.

15
Risks and Retribution

The political implications of Mannerheim's cross-frontier offensive of September-October 1941 must be judged in their contemporary circumstances. Only Britain still stood against the German-Italian axis, while the United States maintained a resolutely neutral stance. The German war machine appeared invincible and capable of breaking the Soviet Union as a world power. In consequence it would be left to the Third Reich to determine the future European order and its frontiers. The German attack provided an opportunity for the Finns to reach for a Greater Finland, an area encompassing regions predominantly occupied by Finnish speakers and, incidentally, territory that might be a valuable bargaining counter at the peace conference.

Leningrad, founded by Peter the Great in 1703 on the sites of some fifty Finnish villages, still had many Finnish-speaking people living in the surrounding countyside. Yet it was from the capture or siege of Leningrad that Mannerheim sought strenuously to distance himself, so as not to attract the vengeance of the Soviet Union. Meanwhile, German forces under General von Falkenhorst to the north and General Wilhelm Ritter von Leeb, advancing through the Baltic states, both looked to the Finns to play a significant part in the encirclement of the city.

Viewed against the determined expansion of Communist control in Eastern Europe post-1945, it has to be asked whether a halt by the Finns on the 1939 frontier in 1941 would have made the least difference to Stalin's attitude when peace negotiations next began in the spring of 1944. As the Finns had broken the Treaty of Moscow, it might reasonably be concluded that the Soviet dictator would still have imposed harsh conditions. Had Finland totally refrained from any attack on the Soviet Union in 1941, it would almost certainly have been the task of the Red Army to drive the German forces out of northern Finland – before turning south to 'liberate' the remainder of the country.

At the start of his offensive in Ladoga-Karelia on 10 July 1941, Mannerheim had allowed himself to be persuaded to include in his order of the day reference to a declaration he had made in 1918. This had been in public response to an offer by Lenin to hand over parts of Finnish-speaking eastern Karelia to a 'Finnish Soviet Republic', so as provide encouragement to Finnish revolutionaries of that time. Mannerheim's retort had included the promise that he would liberate his Finnish kinsfolk in those provinces and would not 'sheath his sword until that had been accomplished'. Repetition of the statement in 1941 was no doubt intended to provide his soldiers with an ideal worth fighting for. Whilst it may have served that purpose, it misled the German high command as to Mannerheim's military aspirations and caused some confusion in the minds of his political colleagues.

From the outset there was evidence of well-planned Finnish-German cooperation at sea. The naval strategy was to confine the Soviet Baltic Fleet to the eastern end of the Gulf of Finland, then capture or destroy it when Leningrad fell. Extensive minefields were laid by German minelayers and Finnish submarines but, although imposing tactical restrictions, these operations failed to inflict any significant losses on the Soviet Fleet. This was an essentially defensive strategy designed to prevent the Soviet Fleet from intervening in the land battle or disrupting trans-Baltic shipping in support of the Finnish and German war economies.

The scale and ferocity of the 'Barbarossa' offensive from Poland into the Soviet Union drew many squadrons of the Soviet Air Force away from the northern front, except for the immediate defence of Leningrad. From the first day of the war, Finnish cooperation in Luftwaffe bombing of the city and other targets was implicit in the German use of Finnish airfields for staging and refuelling. It became difficult, if not impossible, to differentiate between Finnish and German attacks on targets beyond the frontier. This situation was unintentionally confused by the continued use of Count von Rosen's good luck sign, the blue swastika, as the national identification symbol for Finnish aircraft. Although a lull followed the Soviet air attacks on Finnish cities on 25 June, memory of bombing during the Winter War became an argument for pushing the Karelian front further to the east, so as deny use of more airfields to the Soviet bomber force.

There was no compelling military reason for Mannerheim to pause on the 1939 frontier, unless it was the disappointing reports of the German offensives under von Falkenhorst. There was encouraging news only in the southern sector of Falkenhorst's command, where Siilasvuo's III Army Corps had crossed the frontier to advance towards Uhtua on Lake Kianta in Soviet territory. If lack of German success in the north struck a warning note in the mind of the Finnish C-in-C, it was almost certainly drowned in the tumult of applause for von Bock's capture of Smolensk and von Rundstedt's drive through the Ukraine.

Von Leeb's advance through the Baltic states had fared less well and on 2 August Field-Marshal Keitel sent a formal request to Mannerheim to join with the Germans in a siege and bombardment of Leningrad. The C-in-C delayed his reply until almost the end of August and was then emphatic as to what he could and could not do. Finland, he explained, was being asked to shoulder a burden out of all proportion to her strength and capability. Casualties were much heavier than expected, probably because the Red Army was fighting more stubbornly in defence and was not hindered by freezing conditions such as those of the previous winters. As he had consistently maintained, he was not prepared to cross the old frontier in the Karelian Isthmus in a move against Leningrad, but he would honour his pledge to advance north-east of Lake Ladoga as far as the River Svir.

The third phase of the Finnish offensive began on 4 September 1941, following the most thorough planning and preparation. It was remarkable as the first occasion when the recently formed armoured battle group under Colonel Ruben Lagus was used *en masse*. As with the July offensive, Lieutenant-General Erik Heinrichs commanded the Army of Karelia comprising VI Army Corps (Paavo Talvela), VII Army Corps (Woldemar Hägglund) and Battle Group O (Woldemar Oinonen) of the Cavalry Brigade and the 2nd Jäger Brigade. VI Corps on the right (southern) flank was responsible for the advance to the line of the River Svir, leading with 5th and 7th Divisions and the armoured Battle Group Lagus, ready to exploit the first significant gap. As soon as Talvela was firm on the Svir, Heinrichs planned to release Hägglund to destroy the Red Army formations trapped between Talvela's VI Corps and the shores of Lake Onega. Thereafter, Hägglund was to continue to advance and take

Petrozavodsk. As in July, Oinonen's Battle Group O was to cover the Army of Karelia's open left flank.

The aggressive Talvela had been grinding his teeth with impatience since he had first reached the old frontier on 23 July. He needed no urging on. Using the northern shore of Lake Ladoga as a firm right flank, he pushed his leading divisions south-eastwards towards the point where the Svir enters the lake. 5th Division broke through at Tuulos, allowing Lagus to take the lead with his armour towards Olonets. He took the town at last light on 5 September. Two days later, a task force of 1st Jäger Brigade had reached the north bank of the Svir. This swift offensive left gaps between the spearheads, but Heinrichs ordered Talvela to clean up the enemy pockets and deploy his divisions along the river bank. Accompanied by Defence Minister General Rudolf Walden and Heinrichs, Mannerheim visited Talvela's sector of the front on 8 September. Together the four generals, friends over many years and in the midst of their third war together, looked out across the half-mile-wide Svir. The only reliable lateral communications ran along the far bank, making it essential to establish their defensive line there, so spanning the central Olonets Isthmus.

Talvela's early success allowed Heinrichs to release Hägglund's VII Corps against the two Red Army divisions defending the (Soviet) East Karelian capital of Petrozavodsk, on the western shore of Lake Onega. Hägglund launched this fourth phase of the Army of Karelia's offensive on 15 September, the advance of his 1st and 4th Divisions being coordinated with a flanking sweep of Talvela's 7th Division towards Tarsepol and Lake Onega on his right. Battle Group O cut through the open country north of VII Corps, with the aim of protecting the open flank and closing the enemy's escape route round the northern inlets of the lake.

Hägglund faced a diffuse enemy and, aside from capture of Petrozavodsk, he had to mop up the Red Army units remaining in the Olonets Isthmus. By that stage of the campaign he and almost every other senior Finnish commander was acutely conscious of their unexpectedly high rate of casualties. The foolhardiness of the Red Army attacks during the Winter War had left the Finns unprepared for the stubbornness of the Soviet soldier in defence. It was apparent, however, that the enemy could seldom resist an opportunity to slip out of a closing trap and thereby leave themselves more exposed to

ABOVE, LEFT Finnish village house in Suurmäki, Ladoga-Karelia, burning during the advance of General Heinrichs's Karelian Army, 22 July 1941. RIGHT Lieutenant-General Erik Heinrichs (left) and Major-General Paavo Talvela hear Colonel Ruben Lagus (centre) describe the deployment of the Finnish Armoured Division at Salmi, July 1941. BELOW Artillery batteries of the Finnish 3rd Division of III Army Corps moving into position near Uhtua, in the central frontier region, July 1941.

ABOVE Red Army tank blazing during the advance of the Finnish VII Army Corps through Palalahti, Ladoga-Karelia, 8 August 1941. BELOW Finnish troops of II Army Corps advancing through the smoking ruins of Änkilänsalo, at the start of the Hiitola offensive, August 1941.

ABOVE, LEFT Finnish wounded being tended by Lotta Svärd nursing volunteers. RIGHT The commander-in-chief pauses to light his cigar while visiting Finnish troops on the line of the River Svir, 8 September 1941. BELOW Finnish troops of the Coastal Brigade, having crossed the Viipuri Inlet, prepare to cut off the city port from the east.

ABOVE, LEFT General Rudolf Walden, Finnish Minister of Defence during the Interim Peace and the Continuation War – a photograph from the War of Independence, 1918. RIGHT Red Army soldiers surrender to the 5th Division of Major-General Paavo Talvela's VI Army Corps at Vitele on the northern shore of Lake Ladoga. BELOW A reminder of the Soviet pretext for the start of the Winter War – the name of the frontier village Mainila is marked on an artillery shell.

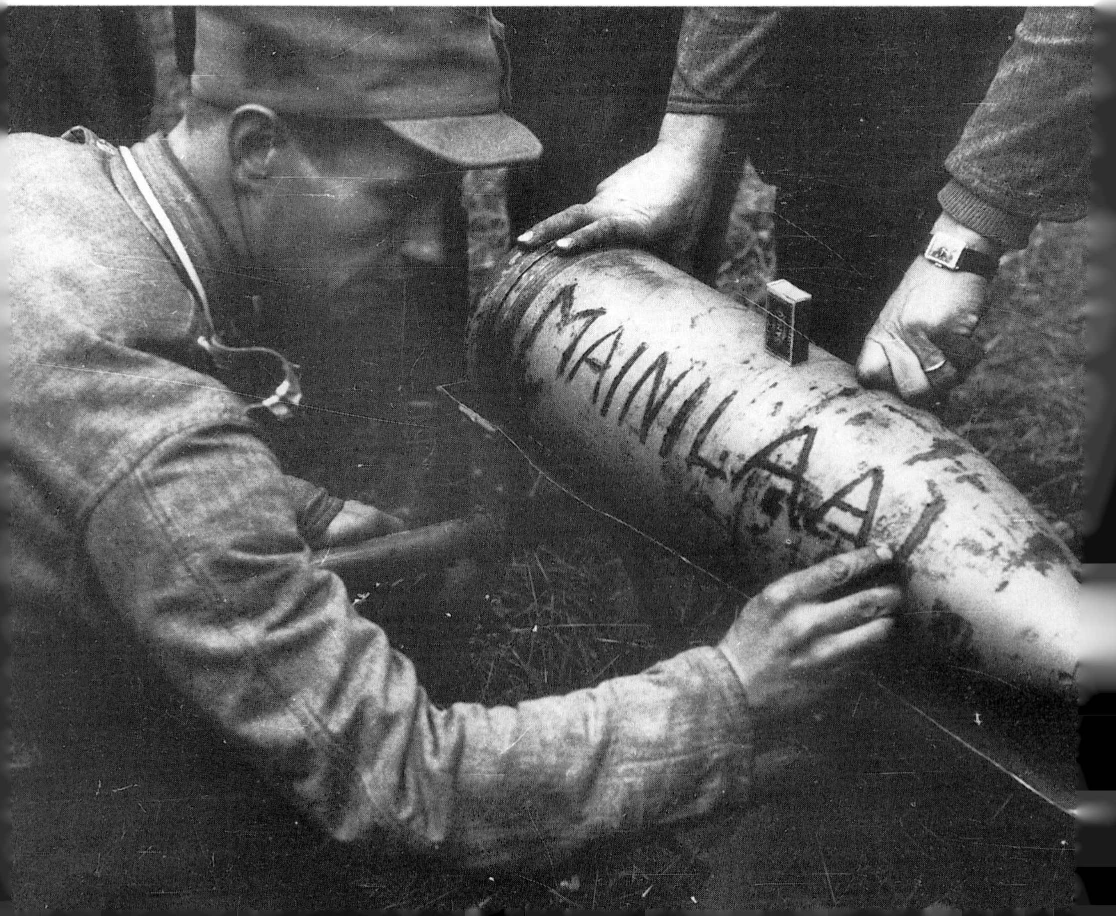

ABOVE, LEFT Flight Sergeant Lasse Aaltonen, who won twelve air combat victories, at Utti, July 1943. RIGHT Lieutenant-General Hjalmar Siilasvuo, commander of the Finnish III Army Corps and Lieutenant-General Eduard Dietl, commander of the German XXI Mountain Army Corps (and later of 20th Mountain Army) meeting at Kiestinki, forty-five miles east of the Soviet border, 11 April 1942. BELOW Miss Fanny Luukkonen, Chairman of the Lotta Svärd movement from 1930 to 1944, meeting with 'Little Lottas' in Helsinki, February 1942.

Colonel Eino Luukkanen, who destroyed a total of fifty-one Soviet aircraft during the Winter and Continuation Wars, in a Messerschmitt 109G-6. Over 100 of these aircraft were supplied by Germany 1943-1945.

LEFT Finnish medium artillery of the Finnish 14th Division preparing for action in the Lake Rukajärvi region, August 1944. RIGHT Major-General Aksel Airo (shown here with colonel's insignia), Head of the Operations Staff at Mannerheim's Mikkeli headquarters and author of the 'Autumn Manoeuvres' plan for the withdrawal of German forces.

ABOVE Finnish refugees moving back in the face of the Red Army's advance in June 1944. BELOW Lapp children being evacuated from the area of operations against the withdrawing German forces near Inhari, north-west of Ivalo in Lapland, September 1944.

LEFT Finnish infantry crossing the demolished bridge over the River Raumo near Tornio, October 1944. RIGHT The road and rail junction of Rovaniemi burning fiercely as Finnish infantry of the 6th Division entered the town on 17 October 1944.

A regimental commander of the Finnish 11th Division observing movement of German forces at Muonio, on the Swedish border road, 30 October 1944

defeat than if they had fought from prepared positions. Mannerheim had reacted with quiet fury when the Soviet troops pinned against Lake Ladoga's north-western shore by Ist Army Corps had been allowed to escape, using vessels of the Red Army's Northern Front fleet, on 20 August. The C-in-C blamed the Finnish Air Force for this debacle, as he considered that air attack on the Soviet ships was both late and ineffective.

The 4th Division of Hägglund's VII Corps advanced quickly to seal off Petrozavodsk in the north but could not break through the Red Army defence to reach the lake shore. In the south, a regiment-sized enemy group in the Lake Pyhäjärvi region managed to evade encirclement and slip away to the east, avoiding 1st and 7th Divisions. In spite of these disappointments, arising from reluctance of local commanders to accept heavy casualties, Petrozavodsk fell to VII Corps on 1 October. The whole of the Olonets Isthmus between Lakes Ladoga and Onega was in Finnish hands by mid-October. Mannerheim needed only to take control of the Maaselkä Isthmus, between Lake Onega and Lake Seesjärvi to the north, and establish a defensive bridgehead across the Svir to provide a line on which to stand for the remainder of the war.

For the final fifth phase of his offensive, Heinrichs was allocated Major-General Taavetti Laatikainen's II Army Corps headquarters from the Karelian Isthmus, with under command 4th Division from VII Corps, 8th Division and Oinonen's Battle Group O. Laatikainen's task was twofold. His first priority was to establish control over the Maaselkä Isthmus, between Lake Seesjärvi in the north and the town of Poventsa on the eastern shore of Lake Onega's northern reach, and as far east as the Stalin Canal. Secondly, he was ordered to send a detachment west of Lake Seesjärvi to link up with Major-General Erkki Raappana's 14th Division in the north.

From the start of the campaign 14th Division had been under the direct command of the C-in-C to cover the gap between Mannerheim's northern flank and the southern flank of Siilasvuo's III Army Corps under Falkenhorst. 14th Division met with stiff resistance but had fought its way ninety miles eastwards to Lake Rukajärvi by 17 September. When contact was lost with both Heinrichs to the south and Siilasvuo to the north, Raappana took up a defensive position alongside the lake. Across the Mannerheim/Falkenhorst command boundary, Siilasvuo's III Corps offensive had ground almost to a halt some thirty-five miles beyond the 1939 frontier at Kiestinki. He was unable to reach Uhtua before being ordered to halt on 5 November.

Broken ground and the northern reaches of Lake Onega favoured the Red Army defenders of the Maaselkä Isthmus region. They were drawn from 14th Army, which had not been subjected to any attack until the final week of October. Few tactical openings were presented to the Finns, who were unable to exploit their skill in flanking movements and isolation of enemy detachments. In consequence, it took until 6 December for 4th Division to occupy Karhumäki Medvezh'egorsk and Poventsa, both on the northernmost reach of Lake Onega, and for the Cavalry Brigade to clear all the enemy detachments from the promontories into the lake.

The advance across the old frontier into Soviet Eastern Karelia had not gone unnoticed in Britain, where the Soviet Union had been received as an expected but nonetheless welcome ally as a result of the German invasion. At Moscow's specific request, aircraft of the British Fleet Air Arm bombed Petsamo on 31 July, after the town had been occupied by German troops of Dietl's XXI Mountain Army Corps. A message through diplomatic channels, sent on 22 September shortly after the Finnish advance had resumed, urged the Finns to return to the 1939 frontier. This, the British note explained, would avoid any necessity to treat Finland as a hostile nation due to Soviet pressure.

Ryti and Mannerheim composed a careful reply, pointing out that Finland had been the object of Soviet aggression in 1939, when Britain had shown sympathetic understanding. This did not end the matter. On 29 November the United States ambassador in Helsinki delivered a note from Prime Minister Winston Churchill addressed personally to Mannerheim asking him to reconsider 'before it is too late'. Mannerheim felt compelled to reply that he could not halt his troops until they were in a situation to establish a proper defence 'for the security of Finland'. The exchange of letters is reproduced at Appendix 7 and gives some insight into the minds of the two statesmen in, as Mannerheim put it, 'critical days'. Britain was eventually obliged to declare war on Finland on 6 December 1941. This was the day that tanks of Battle Group Lagus occupied Poventsa and the Finnish advance into Soviet territory halted there. No offensive action was taken by Britain following the formal declaration of war, although Finnish shipping believed to be bound for German ports was intercepted at sea.

The final weeks of 1941 were spent in consolidation of the Finnish positions. In the Olonets Isthmus, Talvela's VI Corps had crossed the Svir to establish a defensive bridgehead sixty miles wide and twelve miles deep. Laatikainen's II Corps had secured the Maaselkä Isthmus and made contact with 14th Division north-west of Lake Seesjärvi. Further north still, a more or less continuous line of defence had been formed from Lake Rukajärvi across the front of Siilasvuo's III Corps to Kiestinki. Finally, Moscow gave the order for the evacuation of the naval base at Hanko, to which they were never to return. On a bleak December day, with his thoughts on the thousands of Finnish lives lost since 10 July, Mannerheim reveiwed a parade of veterans on the ground of the recovered peninsula.

The end of offensive operations and the beginning of the static 'war in the trenches' brought widespread relief throughout Finland but faced Mannerheim with a conflict of priorities. Although he might confidently expect the eastern front to remain quiet, as the Red Army was fully occupied defending Leningrad, Moscow and the Donetz Basin, it remained essential to man the three isthmus fronts and that of III Army Corps further north. On the other hand, the fragile Finnish economy was desperate for manpower to keep it turning over at even minimum level. Some degree of demobilization was of critical importance. As if to emphasize the delicate balance between these conflicting demands, the Red Army mounted an offensive in the Maaselkä Isthmus in January 1942. The attack was held with some loss of ground but it took until mid-February to restore a secure defence line.

During the autumn offensives of 1941 Finland had almost half a million men and women in the armed forces or drafted into work in direct support of the war effort. One fifth of these were demobilized in the early months of 1942 to return to agriculture and industry. Mannerheim introduced command and organizational changes, so as to make best use of the troops remaining, but experiments varying the well-tried divisional structure proved unsatisfactory and were abandoned. Plans for limited advances to shorten the defensive lines were examined but all were equally strongly opposed by Manner- heim and President Ryti.

The Soviet attack in the Maaselkä Isthmus in January 1942 was followed by one on a larger scale against Siilasvuo's III Corps during April and May. At much the same time a series of Red Army attacks were mounted against Talvela's bridgehead over the Svir. All these attacks were held but the time taken to deploy reserves to the threatened regions caused serious disquiet. In the summer of 1942 the Soviet 1st Partisan Brigade penetrated the Finnish lines north of Lake Seesjärvi. This elite formation inflicted few casualties and little damage but avoided all Finnish attempts to bring it to battle. This had the useful outcome of impressing on the minds of Finnish commanders that they could not afford to relax or let training standards fall.

Immediately after the Soviet counter-offensive in the Maaselkä region in January 1942, Mannerheim ordered the preparation of rear defensive positions across each of the isthmus fronts. Although defence-work plans were made, virtually no construction began before the spring of 1943. Lack of contact with the enemy bred a lethargic attitude in the troops and in many junior commanders. This was further encouraged by frequent rumours of an impending armistice or peace treaty. Realization that the rearward positions might be needed, and shortly, was brought about by news of the encirclement of the German 6th Army before Stalingrad on 23 November 1942, and the widening of the Soviet corridor through the German forces around Leningrad in January 1943. The tide was beginning to turn.

The spring and summer of 1942 had seen a reorganization of the entire Finnish forward line between Lake Seesjärvi and the sea. Each isthmus between the lakes was designated a 'Group' and allocated forces and reserves for the defence of its sector. In the north, II Army Corps (Laatikainen) became the Maaselkä Group responsible for defence of the isthmus of that name between Lake Seesjärvi and the northernmost tip of Lake Onega. In the centre, for which Mannerheim had prime concern at that stage, the Olonets Group of the V, VI and VII Army Corps, together with the German 163rd Division, held the Olonets Isthmus between Lakes Onega and Ladoga, with the River Svir running in rear of the forward line. The Olonets Group was under command of Lieutenant-General Lennart Oesch. The Army of the Karelian Isthmus was reduced to only IV Army Corps (Öhquist), reflecting Mannerheim's confidence that the Soviet threat was currently minimal, with the German encirclement of

Leningrad reaching the shore of Lake Ladoga round the west of the city. General Erik Heinrichs had returned to his post as Army chief of staff.

Work on rear defensive lines behind each group continued throughout 1943. The rearward line across the Maaselkä Isthmus ran north-westwards from Medvezh'egorsk. That in the Olenets Isthmus linked Pisi, Saarimäki and Sammatus and was designated the PSS-Line. The rear defence line in the Karelian Isthmus was based on the line Vammelsuu-Taipale, known as the VT Line (see Map 16 overleaf). The field deployment of the Finnish Army was changed again following the Soviet relief of Leningrad in January 1944.

The year 1944 saw a series of Soviet strategic offensives, the fourth of which was to bring Finland out of the war. It was ironical that this was a situation that the Finns desired with an even greater ardour than Stalin himself. But the price was to be high. The battle which took place in the Karelian Isthmus was the most massive in scale ever fought in the northern region of Europe. Even when that was over, Finland faced a final and unsought war on her own territory. A grave but calculated risk had been taken when Mannerheim gave the order for an offensive beyond the frontier stone erected by Gustavus Adolphus. Now retribution was at hand.

The first Soviet strategic offensive under General Leonid Govorov began with an attack from the south of Leningrad on 15 January, which drove the surrounding German forces westwards as far as Narva on the Estonian frontier. This left Finland once again standing alone from the Karelian Isthmus to Lake Seesjärvi. Recognizing the greatly increased danger, Mannerheim further reinforced the Karelian Isthmus with the Armoured Division and all but one regiment of the 3rd Division. Then, on 6, 16 and 26 February, the Soviet Air Force launched massive air attacks on Helsinki. These were clearly intended to force Finland to capitulate but, as only some five percent of the bombs actually struck population centres of the city, the impact on public opinion was less significant than Moscow had expected. Mannerheim responded with a further reinforcement of the Karelian Isthmus. III Army Corps under command of Lieutenant-General Hjalmar Siilasvuo took up positions on the left flank, in March, alongside IV Corps (Laatikainen) covering the right flank to the sea.

With the German Army in retreat from Estonia to the Black Sea,

Map 16: Finnish Army deployment and the Red Army offensives of 1944

the Red Army began to assemble a force of 450,000 men, organized into 41 divisions, with 800 tanks, 10,000 artillery pieces and 2,000 aircraft for a final offensive to drive Finland out of the war. A tentative Finnish peace inquiry was put out through Sweden, but this brought terms from Moscow that the Finnish Government regarded as unacceptable. Stalin demanded a return to the frontiers of the Treaty of Moscow, payment of $600 million in reparations, expulsion of all German forces from Finnish territory and demobilization of the armed forces. The Government and Mannerheim considered that to abandon their still-strong supporter Germany, not yet attacked by the Allies in the west, in return for another uncertain peace under such severe terms would be unacceptable to Parliament and the country. They also reckoned that the imminent Allied invasion of Europe would deflect the bulk of the Soviet war effort into a race for Berlin. The Moscow terms were rejected.

The plan for the Soviet offensive against Finland had a familiar theme, although on a far greater scale than previously. It was to be initiated by the right wing of Govorov's Leningrad Front, comprising 21st and 23rd Armies, against the Karelian Isthmus. Success there would be the signal for the now Marshal Kirill Meretskov, commanding the (northern) Karelian Front, to launch an offensive with General J. M. Sokolov's 7th Army over the River Svir in the Olonets Isthmus. Good progress there would trigger an offensive by Lieutenant-General F. D. Gorelenko's 32nd Army against Finnish defences across the Maaselkä Isthmus. It was planned that 7th and 32nd Armies would join forces to the north-west of Lake Ladoga at much the same time as Govorov had cleared the Karelian Isthmus and reached the line of the River Kymi between Kouvola and Kotka.

About 260,000 Soviet troops were assembled for the initial offensive in the southern Isthmus. They were supported by 630 tanks, over 200 artillery and heavy mortar battalions, 1,000 aircraft and the guns of the Baltic Fleet and coastal artillery. The Finnish forces facing the invaders were IV Army Corps, with the 2nd and 10th Divisions, on the right flank by the sea and III Army Corps, with 15th Division and 19th Brigade on the left, alongside the shore of Lake Ladoga. 18th Division had been withdrawn into Mannerheim's reserve on the VT-Line.

The Soviet offensive began with a bombing attack at 0600 hours on 9 June, followed by an artillery bombardment forty-five minutes later. The infantry assault began with small reconnaisssance and probing parties moving forward at 0700 hours. These were repulsed by the defenders but the 109th Soviet Division succeded in overwhelming one Finnish strongpoint at Sormenkärki on the 10th Division's front. By the late afternoon Soviet XXX Guards Army Corps had pushed the 1st Infantry Regiment back from its defence line and a counter-attack after dark was unsuccessful. This was but the preliminary skirmishing. The artillery bombardment resumed at 0500 hours on 10 June, supported by aircraft of the 13th Air Army.

The Finnish 10th Division was forced to abandon its positions, leaving its artillery in enemy hands. Mannerheim ordered 4th Division to move from the Olonets to the Karelian Isthmus and the Armoured Division to prepare itself to launch a counter-attack from the area of Muolaa-Kivennapa. The Cavalry Brigade was also alerted for a possible counter-attack and more troops were deployed on the VT-Line. Soviet CIX Army Corps maintained determined pressure during the night of 10/11 June and the Finnish 58th Infantry Regiment was forced to withdraw to Terijoki, on the sea coast, at 0500 hours on the morning of the second day.

In the afternoon of 12 June Laatikainen's IV Army Corps withdrew to the prepared positions of the VT-Line, while further reinforcements were summoned from the Olonets front. Siilasvuo's III Army Corps had also been obliged to begin a withdrawal to the VT-Line. No respite was permitted and two Soviet divisions broke the VT-Line on 14 June by overrunning a single Finnish battalion at Kuuterselkä. The Armoured Division, under Major-General Ruben Lagus, launched a night counter-attack to close the widening gap but this imposed only a short delay. By the time IIII Corps had completed its withdrawal to the VT-Line on 17 June, the front on the west of the Isthmus had already been breached. The Soviet advance had reached the general line of Humaljoki-Kaukjärvi-Perkjärvi-Tampila. On the following day the Soviet 21st Army was in front of Summa and Siilasvuo's III Corps had started to pull back to the line of the Vuoksi river.

On 15 June Mannerheim appointed Lieutenant-General Lennart Oesch to command all forces in the Karelian Isthmus and ordered three more divisions and one brigade from his reserve to reinforce the Isthmus. He also authorized Oesch to withdraw to the VKT-Line of defence. This extended from Viipuri through Kuparsaari to Taipale on the south-western shore of Lake Ladoga. (See Map 16 on page 216). No sooner had this line been reached than the Soviet 21st Army concentrated its attack on the open ground leading towards Viipuri and the area to the east. The city was defended by the Finnish 20th Brigade supported by an independent company of tracked armoured assault-guns. This force could not withstand the attack over the open ground of the Soviet CVIII Army Corps, which included a tank brigade, and the ancient fortress fell into Soviet hands on 20 June.

On the day before this disaster Mannerheim had appealed to the German high command for help. The most urgent need was for air support and supply of anti-tank weapons. Negotiations for possible assignment of six German divisions to aid Finland cost the life of General Eduard Dietl, commander of the German 20th Mountain Army in the north of Finland. He was killed when his aircraft crashed during a flight back from Berlin, where he had been visiting the German high command. Nevertheless, one squadron of Stuka dive bombers and the German 122nd Division were sent from the Narva front in Estonia and an assault-gun regiment redeployed from 20th Mountain Army in Lapland to the Karelian Isthmus. These, together with delivery of several thousand German 'Panzerfaust' bazookas and recall of Finnish reserves, gave hope that the Soviet tide might be held until peace terms could be agreed.

The offensive in the Karelian Isthmus continued unabated, however, with XXX Guards Army Corps and XCVII Army Corps attacking during what later became known as the Battles of Tali and Ihantala. The XXX Corps attack on the Finnish 18th Division defending Tali broke through to open the route to Lake Leitmojärvi to the north-west. The spearhead formed by the Soviet 27th Tank Regiment forced its way along the line of the Saimaa Canal but was eventually thrown back by a battle group of two battalions of 1st Jäger Brigade, a heavy tank company and an armoured assault-gun battalion. The route through Ihantala was denied and a Finnish defence line formed from there through Marjamärki to the Saimaa Canal, which was a part of the VKT-Line. IV Army Corps succeeded in halting the advance of Soviet 21st Army east of Viipuri, where the broken and swampy terrain was especially difficult for armoured vehicles.

During the final week of June the Finnish V Army Corps (Major-General Antero Svensson) took over responsibility for defence of the area between Juustila, on the Saimaa Canal, to the north-western shore of the Saimaa Inlet. Leaving an occupying garrison in Viipuri, the now Marshal Govorov ordered the freshly-grouped Soviet 59th Army to launch a major new assault westwards from the tip of the Viipuri Inlet. The offensive began on 4 July, by which time Svensson's V Army Corps had been reinforced with the German 122nd Division. It was against this latter formation that the brunt of the Soviet attack was delivered. V Corps held their front and the intended decisive stroke by the Soviet 59th Army petered out by 10 July.

It was now the turn of the Soviet 23rd Army to attempt to force a breakthrough of the VKT-Line. The ensuing battle against Siilasvuo's III Army Corps, reinforced with the Armoured Division, transferred from the Ihantala sector together with two infantry regiments, lasted for nine days in the region of Vuosalmi. When this came to an end on 18 July, the campaign in the south effectively came to a close. Although troops of Govorov's Front had advanced eighty miles in eleven days, they were able to gain only another six miles after the fall of Viipuri. Stalin called a halt at that point in anticipation of transfer of forces from Finland to the central European battle front, where the race to Berlin would shortly begin in earnest.

Soviet offensives on the Olonets and Maaselkä fronts were launched on 20 and 21 June respectively. In Ladoga-Karelia V and VI Army Corps were able to conduct a controlled withdrawal of one hundred miles to the U-Line, on which the Soviet advance was halted from mid-July. This line ran from Pitkäranta on the shore of Lake Ladoga almost due north, to the west of Tolvajärvi and then to junction points with II Corps and 14th Division, withdrawing from Maaselkä and Lake Rukajärvi (see Map 16 on page 216). In spite of these widespread withdrawals and the overwhelming strength of the enemy, the Finns gained much in terms of morale from the tactical victory at Ilomantsi in early August. A force comprising nine infantry battalions, two dismounted cavalry regiments and four artillery battalions, under the commander of the 14th Division, Major-General Erkki Raappana, defeated two attacking Red Army divisions by concurrent encircling movements that sent the enemy stumbling back eastwards, leaving some ninety artillery pieces in Finnish hands.

As early as 18 June the acute seriousness of the situation had convinced both President Ryti and Mannerheim that, if a Soviet occupation of the whole of Finland was to be averted, a formula for an armistice must be found. Their dilemma was that they needed German assistance to reach a stable military position from which to open negotiations with Moscow, while in return for Germany's help Hitler demanded that the Finns would agree not to negotiate a separate peace. Conscious that a treaty with Hitler would be fatal for any hope of friendly post-war relations with the Western Allies, Ryti and Mannerheim made a pact between them. On 26 June Ryti wrote a personal letter to Hitler in which he undertook not to begin independent peace negotiations with Moscow. This resulted in the supply of desperately needed air support and anti-tank weapons sufficient to stabilize the fronts.

When a Soviet response to a second Finnish peace feeler was received through the Finnish embassy in Stockholm on 26 July, Ryti and Mannerheim brought their personal pact into effect. Ryti resigned as president to be replaced by Mannerheim, who repudiated Ryti's letter to Hitler and opened peace negotiations with Stalin. It was a ploy of desperation but it worked – although the price was high. Stalin required the Finns either to intern the 220,000 German troops of the 20th Mountain Army in Lapland or drive them out of the country. A ceasefire between Finland and the Soviet Union came into effect on 4 September, but then the Finns found that they had a new campaign on their hands.

16
The War in Lapland

In his new role as President of Finland, Mannerheim opened detailed negotiations with the Soviet Union on 24 August 1944. He sent an inquiry through Madame Alexandra Kollontai, the Soviet ambassador in Stockholm, asking whether Moscow would receive a Finnish delegation to negotiate an armistice or peace terms. The reply was positive but demanded that as a prerequisite Helsinki must break off relations with Germany forthwith and remove all German troops from Finnish territory by 15 September. Some hope of extending the period for removal of German troops was entertained, three weeks being in any case an impractical deadline, but the other condition was accepted. On 2 September the new Finnish Foreign Minister, Carl Enckell, informed the German ambassador, Wipert von Blücher, that diplomatic relations with Berlin were severed. This was an unhappy conclusion of an assignment during which the German aristocrat had striven staunchly and consistently in the Finnish interest.

The delegation to Moscow was led by Prime Minister Antti Hackzell. He was accompanied by General Rudolf Walden, the Minister of Defence, General Erik Heinrichs and the Foreign Minister's Russian-speaking brother General Oskar Enckell. They arrived in Moscow on 7 September but were kept waiting in a hotel for a whole week. The delay was not a deliberate impoliteness on the part of Molotov but caused by Anglo-Soviet discussions, in which Britain argued that a full peace treaty must await wider consultation; meanwhile only an armistice could be negotiated. This Stalin accepted, together with British insistence that war reparations should not exceed $300 million. Additional Soviet demands were revealed when talks began on 14 September, including the indefinite lease of Porkkala Peninsula and a large area inland from it that would cut road and rail communications westwards from Helsinki. On return to his hotel, Hackzell suffered a severe stroke and Carl Enckell had to be summoned from Helsinki to replace him as head of the delegation.

The full terms were dictated by Molotov and there was virtually no room for discussion or manoeuvre left to the Finns. They were also asked, somewhat rhetorically in view of the practical difficulties, why the German troops had not already begun to leave as required under conditions for the 4 September ceasefire and for the talks to begin. This at least provided an opportunity for Heinrichs to point out that, even with the German gift for organization, it was impossible to move almost a quarter of a million men out of territory with the sparsest of communications in three weeks. The implication was not lost on the realistic Soviet Foreign Minister but he allowed no concession on the matter to be inferred.

At the end of the one-sided discussion on 18 September, the Finnish delegation was given until noon on the following day to accept the following Soviet demands:

A return to the 1940 frontiers of the Treaty of Moscow and cession of the Petsamo region to the Soviet Union in perpetuity.

The disarming and internment of all German troops still in Finland.

Return of Finland's armed forces to a peacetime basis within two and a half months of the signing of the armistice and acceptance of future limits on their size and armament.

Payment of $300 million in goods specified by the Soviet Union as war reparations over six years.

Indefinite lease of the Porkkala Peninsula as a Soviet naval base.

Use of Finnish airfields and territorial water for operations against Germany for the duration of hostilities in Europe.

Abolition of all Finnish organizations of a 'Fascist character'. (These included the Civil Guard, Lotta Svärd and Veterans' League.)

Trial and punishment of war criminals, as required under all Allied armistice or peace terms.

In the event of these terms not being accepted, the delegation was informed that the whole of Finland would be occupied by the Red Army. The only good news contained in the terms was reduction in the figure for war reparations from the $600 million demanded at the time of the tentative peace inquiry during the previous spring. In fact, after charges for delayed delivery of goods and inflation were added, the total sum actually paid greatly exceeded $300 million.

Not surprisingly in all the circumstances, the terms were accepted by the delegation even before they knew that the Helsinki Parliament had accepted them during a special session that began at 6 a.m. on 19 September. Although the terms were harsh indeed, it was acknowledged that Finland was to be permitted to live as an independent state. This was in marked contrast to the fate of the East European countries which had fallen under Moscow's control as a result of the Red Army's advance.

The most immediately pressing problem facing Mannerheim, who initially remained commander-in-chief, was the speedy removal of German troops from Finland while demobilizing the country's own armed forces at the same time. In this regard it was perhaps most unfortunate that General Eduard Dietl had been killed and replaced by General Lothar Rendulic. Mannerheim had liked and trusted the elegant and witty Bavarian and it is by no means unlikely that the two men might have worked succesfully together for a swift withdrawal of 20th Mountain Army. It is known that Dietl had urged Hitler to allow him to get his troops back to Germany as quickly as possible for use elsewhere. Rendulic, an Austrian, was an entirely different personality and not one with whom Mannerheim was ever able to establish a close rapport.

German troops in Estonia had precipitated hostilities with Finland by an ill-fated attempt to capture Suursaari island in the Gulf of Finland on 14 September. This was the consequence of a contingency plan, prepared in February 1944, for the purpose of maintaining the mine barrier across the Gulf for the seaward defence of Leningrad. It was implemented as soon as it became known that Finland had opened separate armistice negotiations with Moscow. The plan, which had lost much of its original object because of German withdrawals on the southern coastline, was unsuccessful. The Finnish garrison on the island succeeded in driving off the 2,500 strong attacking force and took 700 prisoners. The incident had usefulness only as a point for Heinrichs to make to Molotov during the Moscow negotiations, when the Russian had complained of Finnish inaction against German troops.

In addition to 20th Mountain Army in Lapland and east of Petsamo, there were several hundred German line of communications troops in southern Finland. These had been responsible for the routine transit of troops through Turku to Rovaniemi under the agreement negotiated in September 1940. They packed up and left Finland for home, without incident, within ten days of the ceasefire on 4 September. This harmonious settlement of a potentially difficult problem gave birth to the idea that perhaps evacuation of the entire German force in northern Finland might be achieved without bloodshed. Responsibility for devising and negotiating such a plan was given to Major-General Aksel Airo, head of Mannerheim's operations staff. In his plan Airo reckoned not only on the co-operation of the Finnish liaison officers established at all the major German headquarters but on the collusion of the Germans themselves.

If Soviet intervention was to be avoided, it was imperative that an impression was created of concurrent Finnish military pressure on Rendulic to get his troops out of Finland, actual movement of those troops and evidence of Finnish demobilization down to the level agreed under the armistice terms. If ever there were in-gredients present for a skilfully orchestrated charade, here they were. There were two further but unwelcome imperatives: Marshal Kirill Meretskov's instructions to get his hands on the nickel mines of Petsamo, before the Germans could destroy them, and the approach-ing Arctic winter. The XIX Mountain Army Corps covering Petsamo faced an especially exacting schedule. They were responsible for holding open the narrow northern neck of Finland against the pressure of the Soviet 14th, 19th and 26th Armies of Meretskov's Karelski (Karelian) Front in the far north, to allow the German XVIII and XXXVI Corps to march up from north-central Finland and make their escape to Norway.

The three German army corps were predominantly infantry forma-tions, with only one regiment's worth of armour. Their 26,000 motor vehicles were desperately short of spares and many were scarcely roadworthy. While it might have appeared sensible to have aban-doned the bulk of stockpiled stores, the artillery ammunition would almost certainly be needed to hold off the advancing Russians. If 20th Mountain Army was to reach Norway as a capable fighting force, their evacuation along the tenuous withdrawal routes to the north-west would have to planned and controlled with meticulous care. Interference by either the Red Army or the Finns could make all the difference between escape and disaster.

While the Finnish armistice delegation was still in Moscow, the

ever-resourceful General Airo was busy devising a scheme for the
German withdrawal. He optimistically entitled his plan 'autumn
manoeuvres'. Airo's proposition was for the Germans to withdraw
northwards in concert with a Finnish advance. The occasional
artillery barrage on ground already evacuated would suggest the
atmosphere of battle and the Finnish advance could be coordinated,
through their liaison officers at the main German field headquarters,
so that troops might come on the still-warm embers of the camp fires
of the enemy. Occasionally some German prisoners would be taken.

Airo sent Lieutenant-Colonel Usko Haahti to Rovaniemi to explain this idea to Rendulic. The Austrian accepted the plan in principle but stressed the need to destroy roads and communications in
the north, so as to provide a convincing argument to the Russians for
the slow pace of the Finnish advance. After much heart-searching
this proposal was reluctantly accepted by Airo. What neither he nor
Haahti knew was that Hitler had ordered 20th Mountain Army to
lay waste northern Finland if compelled to retreat. The essence of
the 'autumn manoeuvres' plan was passed on to the German formation commanders and the Finnish liaison officers at their headquarters. If goodwill could be maintained, the stage was set for a
bloodless campaign.

In spite of the irritation to both sides caused by the ill-conceived
German attack on Suursaari island in mid-September, 'autumn
manoeuvres' got off to a good start. While the Finnish commanders
at regimental level were not informed of the collusion, they were
quick to perceive what was actually happening. With characteristic
thoroughness the Germans withdrew on schedule, leaving minefields
and other hazards clearly marked. Mannerheim noted all this with
satisfaction but personally doubted whether the Russians would be
fooled for long. He was proved correct when the Allied Control
Commission arrived a few days after the armistice signing on 19
September demanding to see plans for interning the Germans, which
of course did not exist. At the same time Finnish language broadcasts
from Radio Leningrad attempted to incite Finnish troops to dispense
with their 'pro-Nazi' officers.

Mannerheim decided to move swiftly, before Stalin's exaspera-
tion could be turned into action against Finland. He appointed
the resolute and experienced Lieutenant-General Hjalmar Siilasvuo,
whose III Army Corps had cooperated closely with the German

Army in the 1941 offensive, to take charge of operations in the north of Finland. For the as yet unspecified operations against Rendulic's troops, III Army Corps was allocated the Finnish Armoured Division, three infantry divisions and two independent brigades and ordered to move from the Karelian Isthmus to northern Finland. Siilasvuo was now faced with harassing, if not actually attacking, his erstwhile German comrades tramping both northwards and westwards to the road through Rovaniemi.

Airo's operations staff at Mikkeli produced a plan for Siilasvuo's Corps with the primary objective of seizing Rovaniemi so as to cut off at least two of the retreating German corps. The plan was designed to impress upon the Allied Control Commission that the Finns were seriously intent on interning at least a large proportion of the German force. The plan did not extend, however, to operations after Rovaniemi had been captured. This was largely due to a realistic appreciation that, with the few roads jammed with broken-down German vehicles, it would be impractical to cut off XIX Army Corps withdrawing from Petsamo before it could cross the Norwegian frontier through the north-western arm of Finnish territory.

Siilasvuo flew to his corps tactical headquarters at Oulu, at the extreme western end of the earlier boundary between the Finnish and German forces, with Airo's operational plan in his pocket. On the way he devised a more aggressive operation to take advantage of the weaknesses of the Germans' situation and possibly provide an opportunity to cut off XIX Corps before it could reach the Norwegian frontier. The key to Siilasvuo's plan was to bypass the Rovaniemi bottleneck, which he knew would impose significant delay on the withdrawal of the two southerly German corps without any help from him, and use the road running north from Tornio, close to the Swedish frontier, to intercept XIX Corps. Tornio would have to be taken in a surprise move. Otherwise the Germans would be able to block the southern end of the roads northwards to Muonio and north-eastwards to Rovaniemi. Siilasvuo judged that surprise was achievable only by shipping a landing force across the tip of the Gulf of Bothnia.

Reckoning that Airo and possibly Mannerheim would oppose his idea for a seaborne landing without air and naval support, as being too vulnerable while at sea and to counter-attack during or

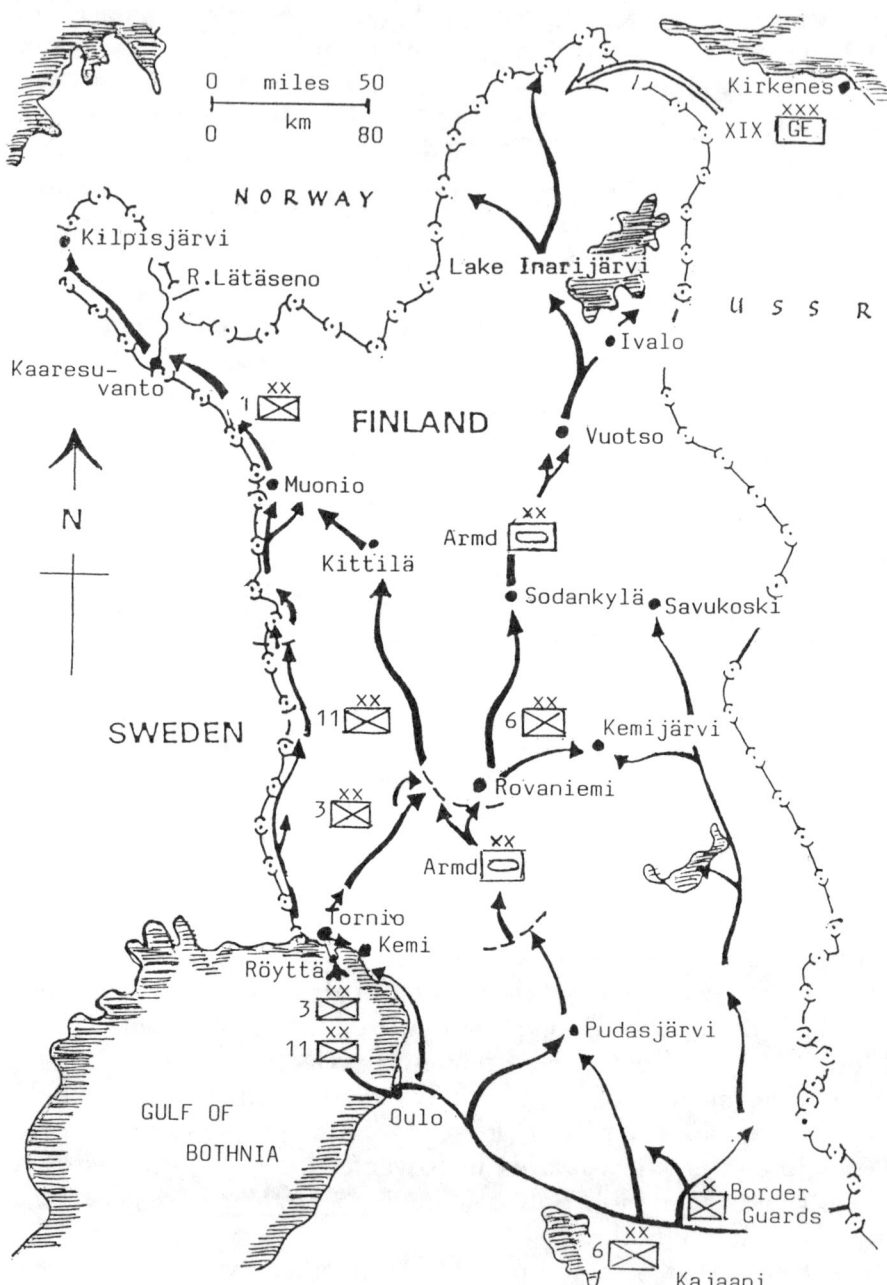

Map 17: The War in Lapland 1944-45
(With acknowledgement to the research of Colonel K. J. Mikola)

immediately after landing, Siilasvuo decided not to inform his superiors in advance. Instead he planned to take the gamble that no
objection would be raised after the event so long as it was successful.
It was a risk that few experienced military commanders are usually
prepared to take. That Siilasvuo was so prepared is an indication of
his strength of will. As it happened, news of the plan reached the
Mikkeli headquarters in time for the amphibious assault to be can-
celled, had that been Mannerheim's wish.

Whilst fully recognizing the operational risks to Siilasvuo's force,
Mannerheim also perceived the political danger of cancellation. The
Russians could justifiably accuse the Finns of reneging on their
promise to intern or expel the Germans. He therefore did not order a
cancellation but insisted that the amphibious assault should be
concentrated on Tornio only. This was to avoid dividing the landing
force between there and Kemi, where the Germans were thought to
have a strong regimental group with armour and artillery – as indeed
they had but dug in well to the south of the town.

Initially, Siilasvuo's plan met with striking success. No German
attack was made against the small landing force, which approached
the coast in three merchant ships. Colonel Wolfgang Halsti's 11th
Infantry Regiment of the 3rd Division landed and seized control of
the small port of Röyttä, on the small peninsula due south of Tornio,
just before 0750 hours on the morning of 1 October. The timing of
the operation was both politically and tactically opportune. Unknown to Siilasvuo, Soviet officers of the Allied Control Commission had visited the Mikkeli headquarters on 27 September and
pronounced the Finnish plans for offensive operations against the
Germans as profoundly unsatisfactory. Consequently, the deputy
head of the Commission, Lieutenant-General Grigori Savonenkov,
wrote angrily to Urho Castrén, who had taken over as prime
minister after Antti Hackzell had been incapacitated by a stroke.
Savonenkov demanded that operations against the Germans should
start in earnest by 0800 hours on 1 October. The landing at Röyttä
met his demand with ten minutes in hand.

Tactically, Röyttä had two advantages as a landing point. There
were no German troops there to oppose the landing and the road to
Tornio was open for a swift advance on the port. Once Tornio was
in Finnish hands, the route northwards running parallel with the
Swedish border towards the Norwegian frontier could be denied use

by the German troops withdrawing from the south. Capture of Tornio would not directly threaten the route north-eastwards to the Rovaniemi junction, as a separate road led there from Kemi to the south-east. In conjunction with the sailing of the small landing force, Siilasvuo had instructed his 6th Division to instigate operations against German units at Pudasjärvi, some eighty-five miles to the south-east, through which units of the German XVIII Army Corps were withdrawing. As this initiative had not been prearranged under the 'autumn manoeuvres' procedure of collusion, it took the Germans by surprise. They lost two men killed and seventy-seven captured. This caused Rendulic to make a justified protest through his Finnish liaison officer, Colonel Oiva Willamo, who was still unaware that there had been an abrupt change in the rules.

Even when Tornio was occupied during the afternoon of 1 October, the still-cautious Rendulic confined his reaction to a further protest. He demanded the cessation of actual operations and release of the Germans, mostly hospital staff, detained in Tornio. Hardening his tone, the German commander informed the Mikkeli headquarters that he had detained some Finns who would not be released until the Germans were freed, and that if hostilities continued he would consider 20th Mountain Army to be in enemy territory from the following morning. It can and has been argued that the surprise attacks on Röyttä and Tornio freed Rendulic from any scruple that he might still have entertained about laying waste northern Finland in accordance with Hitler's order. It stands to Rendulic's credit that when he received no reply to his ultimatum he released his hostages together with the Finnish liaison officers and declared the opening of Finnish-German hostilities. The 'autumn manoeuvres' had lasted only twelve days.

The surprise landing that had enabled Siilasvuo to take Tornio almost without loss was not exploited to the best advantage. There were several reasons for this, of which the most significant was the German Army's facility to regroup and counter-attack almost immediately after a reverse. This tactic was recognized at each level of command and used with effect in every theatre of war in which the Germans fought. The Finns lacked reliable intelligence about German strengths in the area. This led them to concentrate their attacks during 1-2 October against Tornio, where there only about 150 mainly administrative troops and a field hospital. These could and should have been dealt with by the Tornio Civil Guard while Major-General Aaro Pajari's 3rd Division turned south-east to secure the road leading to Tornio from Kemi. It was to the north-east of this area that the Germans hastily formed 'Battlegroup Tornio' in reaction to the Finnish bridgehead.

Stiff fighting began and continued in the Kemi-Tornio region until the Germans were able to extricate themselves and continue their withdrawal north on 7 October. The Finnish 3rd Division in the bridgehead was hampered by having virtually no artillery support. What little had been brought in the merchant ships was lost to Luftwaffe attack before it could be brought ashore. In contrast, the Germans had their usual complement of at least one artillery battalion to every three of infantry, together with a huge stock of shells that they were only too glad to fire rather than shift back along the narrow roads leading north. Siilasvuo also found it difficult to put pressure on the Germans from the south, as the roads and bridges on the southern approach roads to the Kemi region had been mined and mostly blown up by the troops of the retreating XVIII Corps.

The German Battlegroup Tornio, comprising a tank battalion, three infantry battalions and two field artillery battalions, regained the tactical initiative around Tornio on 3 October and began to force units of the Finnish 3rd Division onto the defensive. The German aim was to retrieve control of the border road from Tornio to Muonio for use by XVIII Army Corps still withdrawing through the area and anxious to avoid the Rovaniemi bottleneck. The German counter-offensive was strengthened on 4 October by the arrival of a machine-gun brigade and another artillery regiment sent from Muonio. The lack of artillery support continued to be a severe handicap to the Finns until the arrival of Major-General Kalle Heiskanen's 11th Division by sea from Oulu on 4 and 5 October.

General Rendulic estimated that he would be able to make a clean break from the Tornio area on 7 October but was forestalled by a new Finnish attack on 6 October. This was launched by 50th Infantry Regiment and cut the road north of Tornio, effectively surrounding the German machine-gun brigade. Intense fighting continued until the Germans achieved a break-out on 8 October. Meanwhile, Major-General Mathias Kräutler commanding German troops in the Kemi area had established Battlegroup Kemi to oppose the advance of Colonel Aloys Kuistio's 15th Brigade up the coastal road from Oulu. The Finns were paying the price for not occupying Kemi on the first day of their landing, when most of the local German units were manning defensive positions barring the road from the south. In consequence, the Germans were able to destroy all the town's bridges over the Kemijoki river.

The fighting around Kemi and Tornio during the first week of October 1944 was the most bitter and on the largest scale of the campaign in Lapland. For their part, the Germans felt aggrieved that their recent comrades-in-arms against the Soviet Union had attacked their retreating forces, especially in view of the 'autumn manoeuvres' arrangement made between Airo and Rendulic. On the other hand, the German army commander was well aware of the extreme pressure on the Finns from the Allied Control Commission, as was apparent from his insistence on wrecking the road and communications system in the north to provide credibility for the Finns' slow rate of advance. First evidence of this destruction was encountered by the 15th Brigade in the Kemi-Oulu area, through which Kräutler's regiments had withdrawn northwards. This angered the Finns but not so severely as the condition in which they found Rovaniemi when the town was taken by them on 17 October. All but a handful of the buildings had been blown up or burned down. However, it was subsequently discovered that an extensive part of the damage had been caused by an accidental explosion of a German ammunition train in the goods yard.

7th Mountain Division of XVIII Army Corps had conducted a thoroughly professional delaying action south of Rovaniemi between 9 and 16 October, so as to allow time for the last units of XXXVI Army Corps retreating westwards from Salla to pass through the key road junction. Colonel Valter Nordgren's Jäger brigade and Colonel Akseli Kurenmaa's 33rd Infantry Regiment made vigorous attempts to encircle General August Krakau's rearguard battalion, but the Germans evaded or broke out of the trap on each occasion. Finnish units lost some 300 men killed in this fighting, while the Germans finally managed to detach their covering force from action leaving behind about 100 dead on the ground.

As reports of casualties and intense fighting came into headquarters at Mikkeli, Mannerheim was surprised to receive a sharp note on 16 October from the head of the Allied Control Commission, Colonel-General Andrei Zhdanov, complaining that the Finnish operations were not being conducted with sufficient fervour. 'Fighting must be intensified,' wrote Zhdanov, 'or the Soviet command will be forced to take such action as it considers necessary.' Behind this threat lay Zhdanov's anxiety that Marshal Meretskov's offensive against the German XIX Army Corps in the Petsamo region was not developing nearly so well as expected. Finding themselves in danger of being cut off or destroyed, and thereby unable to hold open the escape route for the other two German corps, XIX Corps had called for reinforcement. Rendulic had sent the 163rd Infantry Division to Petsamo and this had made a critically important contribution to stemming the Soviet advance. Zhdanov had been depending on the Finns to prevent any German reinforcement of the north-eastern front.

Determined to give no excuse for Red Army intervention, Mannerheim instructed Siilasvuo to send Heiskanen's 11th Division in pursuit of the German units retreating up the Swedish border road and Pajari's 3rd Division on the road north-north-west from Rovaniemi, with the aim of cutting the border road at Muonio. 6th Division under Colonel Albert Puroma turned eastwards from Rovaniemi, to cut off any German units withdrawing from Kemijärvi, while the Jäger brigade of the Armoured Division used the Arctic Road through Sodankylä to advance to meet any Russians that might be tempted to move south from Ivalo.

Damage to the border road and demolition of every bridge delayed 11th Division's advance and also prevented Heiskanen from bringing forward any significant weight of artillery ammunition. Once again the Germans were able to hold off their pursuers with their own artillery supplied from roadside dumps along their withdrawal routes. At Muonio, 11th Division encountered 6th SS-Mountain Division, which had withdrawn ahead of Pajari's 3rd Division advancing from Rovaniemi.

The final engagements of the campaign were fought at Muonio at the end of October and against Kräutler's Divisional Group, fifty miles to the north around Kaaresuvanto, on 28 November. The Germans finally broke off contact in the Kaaresuvanto area on 29 November, after which the need for the Finnish divisions to begin demobilization precluded any further pursuit. To protect the approaches to Narvic, the German 7th Mountain Division occupied the 'Sturmbock' position west of the River Lätäseno, in the north-western arm of Finland until the following January and no attempt was made to dislodge them. These actions brought active operations between Finnish and German units to an end. Yet it was not until the following spring, on 25 April 1945, that the last German unit pulled back from Kilpisjärvi across the frontier into Norway.

The war in Lapland had purpose for Finland only as a means of denying the Soviet Union any excuse for occupying part or all of the country. Had there been no pressure from the Allied Control Commission, there can be little doubt that the 'autumn manoeuvres' arrangement would have allowed the Germans to leave for Norway without any battle being fought. As it was, Finland lost a further 1,036 men killed or missing in the fighting and 2,904 wounded. Destruction of communications, roads and population centres in Lapland was a heavy price to pay. The reindeer herds were reduced to less than half their 1939 numbers, while German-laid mines and boobytraps remained a lethal menace to humans and animals alike for several decades after the war had come to an end.

No doubt the fighting brought a grim satisfaction to Stalin, as he relished the predicament of the Finns fighting his enemies for him. He had made a calculated choice between allowing the Red Army to fight its way into southern Finland in the summer of 1944 or throwing its whole weight into the race for Berlin and Vienna.

PART V
A Certain Neutrality

The first four of this group of five chapters all begin at much the same time, as the Second World War came to an end. Thereafter, the themes and events they describe developed unevenly, although in varying degrees of influence on each other. It would be a nice simile to suggest four trees all planted together but prospering differently as their roots touched. But it was not really like that. The treaties of peace and friendship, with which this part of the story begins, cast shadows over the other three themes as they sought the light and yet gave them shelter from early storms.

As Mannerheim had been the man to whom the nation turned in adversity, so two new figures emerged to guide Finland through difficult decades of adjustment. There were unwelcome pressures from Moscow, on the one hand, and doubts as to whether Finland was a truly independent nation, on the other. Paasikivi, who succeeded Mannerheim as president, was a father figure of an altogether different stamp. While as realistic in outlook as Mannerheim, he suppressed his national and any personal pride in the interests of civil relations with Moscow. His successor, Urho Kekkonen, had an adept political grasp of events, but he permitted himself to believe that only he was qualified to deal with them.

It was Kekkonen who first used the term 'a certain neutrality' in 1952. However, it was not until after he became president in 1956 and the Soviet Union had returned the Porkkala naval base that Finland began to portray herself as neutral in peace, that is in the context of the Cold War. Earlier references to neutrality, for example by the Finnish Defence Revision Commission of the late 1940s, related more simply to Finland's policy should war break out.

The fifth and final chapter deals with a commitment that reflects Finland's faith in international cooperation – her increasingly significant role in the United Nations.

17
Treaties of Peace and Friendship

Nomination of Andrei Aleksandrovits Zhdanov as head of the Allied Control Commission in Finland initially raised the spectre of Nikolai Bobrikov, the detested satrap of Czar Nicholas II at the turn of the century, who had been assassinated for his attempted oppression of the Finns. Both men had lifelong connections with Russia's second city before their appointment to Helsinki. Zhdanov was the first secretary of the Leningrad Party Committee and commissar for the region immediately before the Winter War. It was he, so it was rumoured, who had persuaded Stalin to sanction the invasion of Finland. He had certainly provided every material assistance to General Kirill Meretskov in the latter's preparations for the unexpected attacks in Ladoga-Karelia and the central frontier region at the outset of the Winter War.

Suddenly, in September 1944, Zhdanov appeared in Finland to direct the activities of the Control Commission there until a full peace treaty could be negotiated. He brought with him a reputation for having run Leningrad 'with an iron hand' during the German siege of the city, for which he had been rewarded with the rank of colonel-general in the Red Army. It seemed distinctly unlikely that he would be the ideal man to begin a process of reconciliation between Finland and the Soviet Union.

Worst fears were realized when Zhdanov's exerted relentless pressure on Mannerheim and the Government of Urho Castrén to intensify offensive operations against the retreating German 20th Mountain Army in Lapland. Then, once the important junction of Rovaniemi was in Finnish hands and the Red Army had taken control of the Petsamo nickel mines, he rather lost interest in harassing or interning the Germans. Instead, he turned his attention to Finnish demobilization, the prosecution of war guilt trials and the dismantling of fortifications.

Whilst these preoccupations gave an accurate forecast of some

trying times ahead for the Finnish authorities, two positive aspects to
Zhdanov's appointment also emerged. First, it carried with it membership of the Soviet Politburo and therefore direct access to Stalin
himself. Consequently, a reliable conduit for information and ideas
became available in both directions. Secondly, Stalin had confidence
and respect for both Mannerheim as Finland's president and Juhani
Paasikivi, Helsinki's ambassador in Moscow during 1940-41. Aware
of Stalin's opinions, Zhdanov was careful to reflect them in his own
conduct in the Finnish capital.

Stalin's approval of Paasikivi took on enhanced significance when
the old statesman succeeded Castrén to become Finland's prime
minister in mid-November 1944, exactly twenty-six years since he had
relinquished the same office. Castrén's Government had been put
together with undisguised haste during the previous August, when
President Ryti and his Government had resigned to pave the way
for a break with Germany and armistice negotiations with Moscow. Largely through the inexperience of its members, the Castrén
administration found itself unable to grapple with the economic
and organizational problems arising from the agreement to pay war
reparations to the Soviet Union. When Zhdanov threatened that the
Control Commission would take over industrial concerns in eastern
Finland if plans were not promptly forthcoming, Castrén resigned and
his Cabinet with him.

Paasikivi faced a daunting task but, while a patriot, he was a man
unhindered by any especially high-minded political idealism. He was a
banker and a former chairman of the Conservative Party. More
importantly he was a pragmatist with a profound belief that Finland
must find a way of living harmoniously alongside the Soviet Union
if her independence was to be preserved. Although very different
in character, he and Mannerheim shared this view exactly. Their
partnership of president and prime minister was well suited to the
extreme difficulties Finland faced following the armistice of 19 September 1944 and approach to the peace treaty negotiations that
began in Paris in August 1946.

Three awkward tribulations arose directly or indirectly out of the
armistice terms. These were the war guilt trials, an attempt by well-
intentioned Army officers to establish concealed arms caches and the
unwelcome setting up of a small but Communist-controlled political
police force. In all these issues Paasikivi found himself obliged to

pick a cautious path between the demands of the Allied Control Commission and the dictates of his conscience. Fortunately, he and Mannerheim thought alike on all three matters and by applying their separate skills and influence were able to bring some moderation to their ill-effects.

Article 13 of the armistice called for the arrest and trial of Finns who had committed war crimes. Almost everyone assumed this to refer to crimes allegedly committed against the Geneva Convention, until a group of left-wing socialist members of Parliament called for the indictment of those who had led Finland into war again in 1941. Paasikivi had hoped to avoid any such demand by obliging the politicians concerned to retire from public life. Then, when trials of Ryti and his close colleagues became inevitable, he sought to ensure that the proceedings were strictly within the framework of Finnish law. This aspiration became not entirely feasible but at least he was able to have the trials conducted in Finland, rather than by some international tribunal.

Former president Risto Ryti and seven of his associates were arraigned, including Professor Toivo Kivimäki who, as Finnish ambassador in Berlin, was accused of encouraging the German troop transit agreement without parliamentary authority in 1940. General Rudolf Walden and Professor Rolf Witting, Ministers of Defence and Foreign Affairs respectively in Ryti's Government of 1941, had both died before any indictments were made and no suggestion was ever voiced that Mannerheim should bear any blame for the country's entry into war. There was undoubted pressure from the Allied Control Commission for heavy sentences on the eight accused but Paasikivi refused to be intimidated. The longest sentence was ten years' imprisonment and all those convicted received a state pardon after three years. Almost all returned to significant positions in public life except for Ryti. His health suffered during his imprisonment and he lived quietly until his death in 1956, when he received a funeral with full honours of the state.

Demobilization of the Finnish armed forces had begun even before operations against German troops in Lapland were concluded, leading to widespread fear of a Soviet occupation of a virtually defenceless country. This fear was compounded by Passikivi being obliged to include Yrjö Leino, a Communist, in his Government and appoint him Minister of the Interior with control over the police. As a possible counter to this situation, Colonels Valo Nihtilä and Usko Haahti of General Aksel Airo's operations staff at General Headquarters devised a plan to set up secret arms caches in the countryside. The weapons were intended for use by a volunteer resistance force in the event of a Soviet occupation. Nihtilä and Haahti took care to conceal the plan from their military superiors, so that they might not be implicated in the event of discovery.

The arms caches had been established and the secret network dissolved when an informer leaked the plan to the police and the Allied Control Commission in the spring of 1945. While the Commission initially made little of the affair, Communists in and close to Parliament demanded an investigation and trial of those responsible. Haahti wrote to Mannerheim accepting full responsibility and seeking his guidance. In a rare over-estimate of character, the President took Interior Minister Leino into his confidence, only to be rewarded by the latter revealing the whole story to Parliament with a demand for a full-scale investigation of the Army. Although not implicated in any way, General Erik Heinrichs was obliged to resign as commander-in-chief, while Airo and many others were arrested. The investigation and trials lasted two years, concluding with the conviction of Haahti and several other officers, but no charges were ever brought against Airo, although he was detained for almost three years.

Zhdanov played a curious role in this affair, suggesting that he took his orders direct from Stalin in all matters. Included in the list for investigation for involvement in the arms cache plot were the distinguished and gallant generals Aaro Pajari and Väinö Palojärvi. When Mannerheim objected strongly to their appearance on the Soviet list of suspects, Zhdanov at first described them as 'war criminals of the worst type'. Yet, after their arrest, he approached Paasikivi and suggested that both officers should be released unless the Finnish Government wished to raise charges against them.

It is possible that Zhdanov was influenced in this and other matters by his perception that both Mannerheim and Paasikivi were genuinely anxious to reach a new *rapprochement* with the Soviet Union. During the autumn of 1944 he had instituted a series of discussions with Mannerheim and the Finnish general staff for the implementation of demobilization and reduction in armament levels. When he had demanded the dismantling of the coastal defence batteries on the Gulf of Finland's northern seaboard, Mannerheim had produced a surprising counter-argument. Retention of the batteries would be in the interests of both countries, the Marshal had explained, as the European war was still far from over and security of the Gulf of Finland of mutual concern. This led to a compromise arrangement, under which Finland increased the number of 120 mm guns in position after placing the larger-calibre weapons in store.

Following this mutually satisfactory arrangement, Zhdanov produced copies of agreements made with the wartime representatives of Poland and Czechoslovakia as models for Mannerheim to study. The president was not to be drawn directly by such documents but produced an alternative draft for an agreement that might bind Finland to fight any third country attempting to use her territory, territorial waters or air space to attack the Soviet Union. Although this suggestion was not pursued at the time, its proposal by none other than Mannerheim could not fail to send a clear signal of good intent to Moscow. Both Stalin and Zhdanov noted this for use when the time was right.

Mannerheim's protest over the investigation of Pajari and Palojärvi and his logical rebuttal of Zhdanov's demand over the coastal batteries are but two examples of his method of dealing with any unjust or unwarranted Soviet *diktat*. He deployed his arguments with logic, politeness and with specific reference to what had or had not been agreed under terms of the armistice. He warned Paasikivi and his ministers against 'fawning or grovelling' to Moscow, pointing out that it was essential to act correctly and with dignity, if Finland was to be treated with proper respect in return.

Recurrence of a gastric complaint compelled Mannerheim to seek treatment in a clinic in Portugal during the winter of 1945-46. He had informed Paasikivi that he would resign the presidency as soon as the war guilt trials were concluded and he was convinced that there was nothing more that he could do. He returned to Helsinki in February 1946, still far from fully recovered, to carry out one further duty before resigning in favour of Paasikivi. In the president's absence, Lieutenant-General Jarl Lundqvist, the wartime commander of the Finnish Air Force who had succeeded Heinrichs as commander-in-chief, had instituted an attempted purge of service officers whom he and the Communist-controlled political police believed to be out of step with current political thought.

Mannerheim sent Lundqvist a sharp rebuke. The presidency passed from Mannerheim to Paasikivi on 4 March 1946 and the Marshal of Finland finally retired from active public life.

There having been no election since 1937, Paasikivi's Government had no mandate for an economic or legislative programme to deal with the aftermath of almost five years of conflict. In the three wars between 1939 and 1944 Finland had suffered some 86,000 killed and a further 57,000 permanently incapacitated through wounds or other injury. Cultivated land, forest and industrial plant collectively responsible for producing thirteen percent of the country's national wealth had been lost or destroyed. There were over half a million refugees from Karelia to be resettled and 100,000 people whose homes and farms in Lapland had been destroyed by German troops withdrawing to Norway. In such dire circumstances Paasikivi felt it essential to seek a fresh mandate for stringent measures to restore the economy and authority to negotiate and sign a peace treaty.

The Finnish elections of March 1945 were observed in Western capitals with as keen an interest as in Moscow. The results showed a distinct gain for the Communist-dominated Finnish People's Democratic League (SKDL) and their allies of the Social Democrat left wing. The gains were not however sufficient to present any serious challenge to the ruling coalition. The elections were conducted without any disturbance or politically-inspired incident. At the announcement of the results Paasikivi felt that he had the confidence of the people and of Parliament for domestic and foreign policy reforms he knew to be essential. Abroad, it was observed that in Finland, if not elsewhere, it had proved possible to hold free and democratic elections under the shadow of the Soviet Union but without distortion of the result.

Establishment of a 10,000-strong Soviet garrison at the Porkkala naval base, a mere twelve miles from the capital, intitially heightened apprehensions about a possible Soviet occupation of the whole country. But, when it was seen that the Russians were careful not to exceed the letter of the armistice terms, a more optimistic outlook for the future began to emerge. This was fostered in parliamentary circles by an announcement from Zhdanov on 6 August 1945 that 'taking into account the loyal fulfilment of the 19 September 1944 Armistice Agreement' the Soviet Government had decided to renew diplomatic relations with Finland and to exchange envoys. This was received with satisfaction in Helsinki but it lead to some over-optimism with regard to the eventual peace treaty terms. This was especially so in the ranks of the Agrarian Party.

Many of the Agrarian leadership came from Karelia. Hence the emotive issues of loss of highly productive lands and hardship of refugees tended to obscure in their minds the defensive reasoning behind the Soviet demand for territory. Paasikivi held no illusions with regard to Soviet motives and explained these to Agrarian Party politicians in August 1945. Even so, false optimism persisted. When the Peace Conference negotiations opened in Paris in August 1946, the Finnish Foreign Minister Carl Enckell deployed arguments for reduction in war reparations and in cession of territory. He requested that the Finns should be allowed to use the Saimaa Canal and the railway, both of which were to be partly lost through the frontier changes. Molotov rebuffed the inquiry in his most brusque manner, making it abundantly clear that no change to the 1940 frontiers would be considered nor any other concessions made to the terms previously agreed under the armistice of 1944.

The peace treaty was eventually signed in Paris on 10 February 1947. In addition to the concessions made at the time of the armistice, a strict ceiling was imposed on the size and armament of the Finnish armed forces. Aware that these were to be imposed, the Finnish delegation had argued for a doubling of the proposed limits, but to no avail. Britain demanded a prohibition on the Finnish Navy possessing torpedo boats and, when Molotov expressed no interest in such a restriction, forced a successful vote against Finland. An argument for the doubling of the ceiling on combat aircraft, in which the purely defensive nature of the force was stressed, was also rejected. The Finnish delegation won not a single concession.

The salient point in the preamble of Article 13 of the treaty is to impose restrictions consistent with forces needed for purposes of internal security and local frontier defence. Any capability, for example bomber aircraft, that might be used with an offensive purpose was specifically excluded. The limitations on force levels were:

An army of not more than 34,400 men including anti-aircraft artillery and frontier troops.

A navy with vessels not exceeding a total 10,000 tons and not more than a complement of 4,500 personnel.

An air force, including any naval air arm, of not more than sixty aircraft, none of which was permitted internal bomb-carrying facilities, and 3,000 men.

The logic behind the ground force and and naval limitations was to return the Finnish Army to its peacetime strength in 1939, before any mobilization measures had been taken, and the tonnage of the Finnish Navy to the 1939 level after that for the five submarines and ten motor-torpedo boats, in future prohibited under Article 17, had been deducted. A reduction by sixty percent in the 1939 figure for service aircraft, of all types, represented an awareness of the greatly increased operational importance of air power and also that Finland's capability was to be strictly confined to defensive purposes.

Article 15 of the treaty precluded personnel not in the Finnish Army, Navy or Air Force from receiving any form of military training, naval training or training related to military aviation. This provision effectively banned reconstitution of the Civil Guard, Lotta Svärd or League of Veterans, in some new guise, or the raising of any new ancillary or part-time voluntary corps or cadet organizations. Under Article 17 of the treaty an absolute prohibition was placed on the possession or experimentation with atomic weapons, self-propelled or guided missiles, submarines, motor-torpedo boats, sea-mines or specialised landing-assault craft. Lease of the Porkkala naval base to the Soviet Union for fifty years was confirmed and the Åland Islands were to remain a demilitarized zone.

In effect, the restrictions had less immediate impact on Finland's war capability than had the requirement, under Article 23 of the treaty, for payment of war reparations in goods worth $300 million to the Soviet Union over a period of eight years. Coupled with the damage inflicted on the economy by the three wars and loss of territory and industrial potential, the war reparations were an almost insupportable burden. Had war come yet again, for any reason, the weapons, ammunition and equipment still held in store would have been enough to equip fifteen divisions raised from men trained but demobilized. Restrictions on the Air Force began to have effect as other European nations replaced their piston-engined with jet aircraft. Finland could not afford such expenditure in the late 1940s or early 1950s, although the absolute ceiling of sixty aircraft was unilaterally modified to 'first-line interceptors'.

No party to the peace treaty negotiations appears to have called for any limitation on coastal artillery. This may have been an oversight or because such weapons are generally regarded as being essentially defensive, even though the larger-calibre weapons on the north coast had a range halfway across the Gulf of Finland. Another explanation may have been that, remembering an accord on coastal artillery had led Mannerheim to draft a suggested treaty on mutual assistance, Zhdanov saw an opportunity to continue that line of inquiry with Paasikivi before the Allied Control Commission was withdrawn in September 1947. This is what occurred, although the treaty terms eventually put forward by Moscow were once again modelled on treaties signed with what became the Soviet satellite states of Eastern Europe.

Only the far-left Communist-dominated SKDL party in the Finnish Parliament showed any enthusiasm for Stalin's proposals. No other party could foresee the least advantage in a military pact with Moscow, arguing that no form of defence alliance could be shown to be in the country's interest, especially in view of the heightening tension between the Soviet Union and the West. The importance Stalin attached to reaching an agreement was demonstrated by his eventual acceptance of the Finnish proposals in favour of his own. This also represented a triumph for the president who, in what was to become known as the 'Paasikivi Line', had advocated political realism with regard to the Soviet Union since addressing the nation on that subject on Independence Day in 1945.

Stalin vested initial responsibility for the negotiations with General Grigori Savonenkov, the previous deputy head of the Allied Control Commission who was appointed Soviet ambassador in Helsinki after the Commission withdrew. The timing could scarcely have been less opportune: 1948 was an election year in Finland and the Communist-inspired coup in Czechoslovakia on 20 February had sent a cold chill through the Parliament in Helsinki. In such circumstances, the ever-pragmatic Passikivi remarked, 'It would be best if we did not need to sign a treaty but since the Russians want negotiations we can't say no.' In fact Finland could not have had a more well-balanced and experienced politician to guide their destiny at that time

With Mannerheim retired to Switzerland, President Paasikivi turned to General Erik Heinrichs for military advice in the negotiations. Although Heinrichs had been obliged to resign as commander-in-chief over the arms caches affair, he had not been implicated personally and was unquestionably the most experienced man available. He asked for Lieutenant-General Oscar Enckell, who had taken part in the armistice negotiations in 1944, to be his assistant and military confidant. The two soldiers were fully aware of how treaties pledging military cooperation had been used by the Soviet Union as a pretext for the stationing of troops on the soil of their 'allies' and for their consequent subjugation. They therefore insisted that any treaty should not pledge any cooperation between Finnish and Soviet forces in peacetime or any automatic cooperation in war.

The draft treaty prepared by Mannerheim in 1945 was brought out and the clauses suggested by Heinrichs and Enckell incorporated. Others were added to ensure that no aspect of national authority was surrendered that might seriously compromise Finland's independence of decision. This latter point was given emphasis in the reply sent by Paasikivi to Stalin on 9 March 1948, which explained that 'the Finnish people wished to remain outside the conflicting interests of the great powers'. The draft treaty taken by the negotiating team to Moscow on 20 March was a Finnish draft and it was accepted at once as the basis for discussion with Stalin and Molotov, rather to the astonishment of the Finnish negotiators.

Negotiations were conducted in a good-humoured atmosphere with dissent only on one point of interpretation. The Finnish view was that consultation on possible military cooperation would be triggered only by an armed attack on one of the signatories. The Soviet side pointed out the potential mutual advantages of consultation under threat of attack. The treaty was agreed and signed in Moscow on 6 April 1948 and, during an official dinner, Stalin proposed a toast to the armed forces of Finland. In the opening words of his speech at the signing ceremony, the Soviet dictator mentioned the spirit of compromise under which unanimity had been reached, only to be interupted by Urho Kekkonen of the Finnish delegation calling out, 'What compromise? We haven't compromised!' On such stuff does freedom depend.

The articles of the Treaty of Friendship, Co-operation and Mutual Assistance are set out in Appendix 8. It was a treaty of immense importance to Finland, as it provided a clear basis of understanding in place of the mutual mistrust and suspicion engendered between the two nations during the decade since the start of Boris Yartsev's backdoor inquiries in 1938. Paasikivi's wish for Finland to remain outside the conflicting interest of the great powers found unequiv- ocal expression in the preamble to the treaty. This was something to which successive Finnish Governments were able to point in the face of pressure for collusion from elsewhere than Moscow. Article 1 deals with Finland's obligation to fight to repel any attack through her territory that constitutes a threat to the Soviet Union. The same article concludes with an understanding that any military assistance from the Soviet Union 'will be subject to mutual agreement between the Contracting Parties'.

The treaty was signed on 6 April 1948 and came into force for an initial period of ten years. Subsequently there was an open-ended arrangement whereby the treaty would be renewed every five years, unless one of the parties gave unilateral notice of not wishing to continue one year before the end of each expiry period. The formula- tion and negotiation of the treaty were in marked contrast with those of both the 1940 Treaty of Moscow and the peace treaty of 1947, although none of the provisions of either were specifically changed or modified by the new treaty. Exclusion of the kind of clause that had led to other alliance states becoming mere vassals of Moscow were carefully noted in Western capitals. From this it was inferred that Soviet expansionism in Europe had at least paused, if not come to an end.

Aside from the most obvious advantage of providing a platform on which a new Finnish-Soviet relationship could be built, the treaty enshrined a principle for which the Finnish people had the wily Paasikivi to thank. His expressed desire to remain outside the conflicting interests of the great powers, set out in the preamble, allowed Finland to disengage from the swiftly rising tide of the Cold War. Far from forcing the country into a new isolation, this very specific tenet of neutrality allowed Finland to deal openly in matters of trade with countries of both East and West. When Finland was eventually accepted as a member state of the United Nations, the treaty lent the Finns a peculiarly 'certain neutrality'. This was in spite of attempts to degrade the country's independent status by use of the term 'Finlandization', put about by the West German Defence Minister, Franz-Josef Strauss.

A more immediate aftermath of ratification of the treaty was the decline in Communist influence in Finland. It seemed as though the treaty 'definition' of the new relationship between Helsinki and Moscow removed an aching doubt in the minds of the electorate as to which side in the political contest they could safely support. Rumours of an impending Communist coup attempt, that were never substantiated, obliged the widely unpopular Interior Minister Yrjö Leino to resign. Parliamentary elections held in July 1948 saw not a single Communist returned and the Communist-dominated SKDL vote declined by twenty percent. Coming so swiftly on the heels of the Friendship Treaty signed in April, these results brought open protests to Paasikivi from Moscow. He prudently parried them by pointing out his own long-standing good relations with the Kremlin and found himself re-elected as president in 1950.

One of the penalties of Finland's situation of limbo, during the period between the armistice and ratification of the 1947 peace treaty by all Allied nations, had been the denial of Marshall Aid from the United States. Subsequently the terms of the Friendship Treaty of 1948 precluded Finland from benefiting directly from the Marshall Plan. This impeded economic recovery and, in turn, any significant effort to modernize the armed forces. Notwithstanding the known lack of financial resources for investment in such modernization, a Defence Revision Commission was set up and this delivered a detailed report on 10 March 1949, taking into account the restrictions of both the peace treaty and that of Friendship, Cooperation and Mutual Assistance. To many of the Parliamentarians awaiting its findings, maintenance of more than token armed forces seemed irrelevant in the prevailing conditions.

The Defence Revision Commission accepted military neutrality as the basis of Finland's defence planning. From this was derived the principle of defence forces structured in line with that policy, supported by mandatory national service for all men fit to serve. Whilst stating these principles, the Commission report acknowledged that funds to bring them fully into practice could not be made available within a predictable period. The principles were nevertheless accepted by Parliament and the Law on National Conscription came into force on 1 January 1951. This specified 240 days training for service conscripts and 330 days for officers, NCOs and specialists. The law also allowed for up to 100 days' training for reservists throughout their period of liability for military service.

In the year before the Conscription Law was passed, a new and dynamic personality became Finland's prime minister. This was Urho Kekkonen, who had written in 1927 that defence of the fatherland was of first importance and who had interrupted Stalin's platitudes at the Friendship Treaty signing with the call, 'We haven't compromised.' Kekkonen had grown to political maturity under the shadow and influence of Paasikivi, yet he had a radically different approach to Finland's position *vis-à-vis* the Soviet Union and the rest of the world. He believed that the way forward for Finland lay in internal change of social perspectives, in particular the liberation of the working people from institutionalized attitudes. He also believed that neutrality could not be an end in itself. It was he who struck the phrase 'a certain neutrality' – with its alternative English language interpretations of 'reliable' and 'unknown'. Subsequently he was to develop the Paasikivi Line into the Paasikivi-Kekkonen Line.

Mannerheim died in Switzerland on 28 January 1951. At his state funeral in Helsinki on 4 February the ex-socialist Speaker of Parliament, Karl-August Fagerholm, spoke of the 'memory of a great soldier, a great statesmen, a great citizen who, in a special way, had become the central figure in the history of independent Finland'. Fagerholm ended his address with the perhaps unconsciously presumptuous words, 'Although he never forced his services on the people, he had always been at their disposal when needed.' In Valhalla the intensely private, imperturbable and laconic old aristocrat must have enjoyed that concluding phrase best of all. Honours were the least of things to follow that fine man home.

In the spring of 1956 the Porkkala naval base was returned to Finland and the last of the Russians left. Extension of the Friendship Treaty for twenty years was the price that had to be paid but all of Finland's remaining soil was Finnish again.

18

Seeking a National Security

When the Finns surveyed a war-shattered Europe in 1945 and turned to the northern part of their own country, which a withdrawing German army had laid waste, they might reasonably have concluded that it was not for them to put their faith in either allies or treaties. This was not a fresh revelation. During the fateful prelude to the Second World War they had consistently steered away from the complex web of negotiations to provide international guarantees, although they had naturally hoped to remain at peace through any wider arrangements that might have been concluded. Such hopes were finally dashed when, during last-ditch attempts by the British and French Governments to secure guarantees with the Soviet Union, the British Foreign Secretary Lord Halifax informed Finnish Ambassador Georg Gripenberg, 'If in the long run anything is decided which is not in accordance with your wishes, you will realize that we felt that greater issues were involved.'

In all the circumstances it seems exceedingly unlikely that Britain could have done more to safeguard Finland than she did. Even so, Halifax's statement to Gripenburg had a prophetic ring to it. Shortly after he had reported this interview to Helsinki, Gripenburg was instructed to make Finland's position with regard to international guarantees absolutely clear. Accordingly, he informed the Foreign Office in London that the Finnish Government would consider as an aggressor any power that tried to provide armed assistance without its consent. Then as now, the Finns had identified their interests. They wished for peace but not peace at any price; certainly not the 'peace' of foreign protection by occupation.

Bitter experience has also taught the Finns to regard treaties with caution, if not with suspicion. Under the peace agreement reached with the Soviet Union in October 1920, provision was made for self-determination of the peoples of Eastern Karelia, of whom virtually all were Finnish-speaking. This aspect of the Treaty of

Dorpat, as the peace agreement became known from the Estonian town of its signing, was reneged upon by Moscow. The frontier peace agreement signed in 1922 defined the Finno-Soviet borders, limited troop levels of both parties in certain frontier zones, ostensibly for the better security of Leningrad, but kept the Eastern Karelians within the Soviet Union. Subsequently Finland resisted Moscow's overtures for a non-aggression pact, preferrring to place her trust in the more general protection of the League of Nations. When the Soviet Union perceived the frontier agreements to be inconvenient in 1939 they were ruthlessly scrapped and violated.

Events leading up to the Second World War and the immediate aftermath of the conflict cannot be said to have formulated Finland's policy of national security today. The process had begun much earlier – in the 1920s. Nevertheless, the three wars that Finland fought between 1939 and 1945, two against the Russians and a third against German forces, had the effect of crystallizing a philosophy for maintaining their future independence that depended neither on friends nor on treaties. This philosophy depends on the determined defence of Finland's frontiers on land, at sea and in the air. Even more importantly, it depends on a foreign policy that consistently eschews involvement in international commitments or disputes that might impinge upon Finland's freedom of choice – choice to become involved or to stand aside.

Weapon development in the latter years of the war, especially in the fields of ballistic missiles and weapons of mass destruction, has been of considerable assistance to Finland in providing a practical edge to what otherwise might have been seen as a purely idealistic standpoint. Whereas the country was an attack route between potential adversaries during the eighteenth, nineteenth and first half of the twentieth centuries, weapons of great reach with nuclear warheads have much diminished the importance of the land area as an attack route. Today St Petersburg could be devastated by a missile launched from 3,000 miles away and no defences on Finnish soil could provide better than the most marginal protection against any such attack. By the same set of tokens, Finnish air space has become more likely to be infringed in the course of an East-West missile exchange.

Appreciation of the need to defend their air space against any missile in transit led the Finnish Government to secure some alleviation from the conditions of the Paris Peace Treaty of 1947. Agreement that Finland's armed forces could be equipped with air-defence missiles was accepted in 1963 but this change did not signal any fundamental shift in national security policy. Rather it gave emphasis to the principle that Finland may no longer be regarded as a country over which other people's wars could be fought with impunity. This was probably the issue, that of the integrity of Finnish air space, that finally hardened into the crystal of the country's modern policy of national security. Defence capability and preparedness need to be maintained, or raised when necessary, only to levels sufficient to make the cost of any infringement of Finland's national integrity so severe as to render the act of aggression either materially or politically too expensive. In step with this policy of defence, that of foreign relations moved into prime position.

Whereas the term 'national security' is one recognized and used in virtually every country, in Finland it has a precise and comprehensively understood application. Put simply, it signifies the closest possible interdependence of the country's foreign and defence policies. To this end the Ministry of Foreign Affairs and the Ministry of Defence have developed a system of coordination much admired abroad. The key factor in the implementation of this policy was the re-establishment of a Defence Council. There had been one earlier, during the period between the two World Wars when Marshal Gustaf Mannerheim had been its forthright and often controversial chairman. Subsequently, a new and more broadly constituted Defence Council was required to determine the measures necessary for Finland's national security in a changing and still dangerous world as the Cold War intensified.

A proposal to reconstitute the Defence Council was made as early as 1949, when the Defence Revision Commission submitted its report that year. Proposals made by the commission were in sympathy with the post-war era. It was suggested that the new council would be primarily comprised of Cabinet ministers but with non-voting experts, such as the commander-in-chief and chief of the general staff, in attendance. The C-in-C at that time, General Aarne Sihvo, opposed the concept that he and the chief of the general staff should be non-voting members, arguing that they each had as much to offer to the deliberations as any Cabinet minister. This dispute had the unfortunate effect of holding back the re-establishment of the Defence Council, at least in a strictly formal sense, until 1957. Meanwhile, all concerned remained firmly of the opinion that the Defence Council should be a political forum for the formulation and direction of defence policy, not a committee that was concerned only with the organization of the armed forces.

The awkward deadlock was broken in 1957 when a Government Decree appointed a new Defence Council comprising the prime minister, as chairman, and the ministers of Defence, Foreign Affairs, Finance, the Interior and of Trade and Industry, together with the C-in-C and chief of the general staff, all as permanent and voting members. The council was made responsible for advising the president on all issues of national security, observing the international politico-military situation, so far as these might concern Finnish interests, preparing proposals for armed forces development and the budgets to support them.

Proposals for a Civil Defence Act for protection of the civilian population from air and nuclear attack, which received Government approval in 1958, and a mechanism for dealing with swiftly developing crises were amongst the earliest products of the new Defence Council, together with a definition of the responsibilities of the defence forces. The latter were described in the *Field Manual* published in 1958 as follows:

to safeguard the country's territorial integrity and its neutrality;
to mobilize and deploy the defence forces to protect these functions;
to carry out military operations.

It was also on a Defence Council initiative that the Scientific Committee for National Defence and the Planning Board for Psychological Defence were set up in the early 1960s. Although it had taken eight years to re-establish the Defence Council, it soon got down to work once it was in place.

A recommendation made by the Defence Council on 29 April 1960 has had wide-ranging benefits in terms of propagating the philosophy of national security to the population as a whole. This was the suggestion that courses to explain national defence policy should be run by the War College in Helsinki and in the provinces for academics, businessmen and government officials. More than 5,000 prominent people have attended the the three-and-a-half-day courses in the capital and some 20,000 the five-day courses in the provinces since the courses were first instituted in April 1961. Each type of course includes presentations and free discussion groups, with experienced staff officers of the defence forces providing the background information to stimulate the debate. Refresher courses of one day only are available to former attendees who wish to keep themselves completely up to date with defence developments and policy.

The first real test of the new defence philosophy took place through what became known as the 'Note Crisis' of 1961. This took the form of a rapidly escalating confrontation between the Soviet Premier Nikita Khrushchev and President John F. Kennedy of the United States, with Berlin lying at the heart of the matter. In June 1961 Khrushchev announced a prospective peace treaty with the (East) German Democratic Republic of which one direct consequence would be Berlin becoming a 'free city' and, by implication, reaching the end of its quadripartite status. The Western powers protested against these unilateral proposals, both the superpowers took overt measures to increase their readiness for war and the world held its breath over a long, tense summer. Khrushchev climbed down in the face of Kennedy's resolute stance and announced a delay in the proposed peace treaty until at least the following year.

How could these events, menacing though they undoubtedly were, concern Finland? The country belonged neither to the NATO alliance nor to the Warsaw Pact; national policy called for strict neutrality in international disputes and the FCMA Treaty promised Soviet protection, if such were requested. A glance at the globe, rather than at a flat Mercator projection map, will provide the answer. Finland lies on a direct, great circle route such as a ballistic missile would take between the Soviet Union and the United States. It was the old problem of Finland lying on the route between two potentially hostile powers. In spite of Finland's Defence Council having been re-established to respond to serious international crises and monitor their possible implications for Finland, it cannot be said that the new machinery worked well on this occasion.

A detailed memorandum prepared on the directions of the chief of the general staff, Lieutenant-General Tauno Viljanen, was presented to the Defence Council in early August 1961. This proposed that the Ministries of Defence and Foreign Affairs should make a joint study of the implications of improving air and other defence measures and possibly evoking the FCMA Treaty. Little was done in response to this suggestion. It was judged later that inaction was primarily due to poor communication between the two ministries concerned. Sharp point was given to the need for a clear Finnish perception of the crisis on 30 October, when Helsinki received from Moscow a warning of increased West German activity in the Baltic region. The Soviet note also called for urgent consultations under terms of the FCMA Treaty. Even then, liaison between the two key ministries was neither prompt nor particularly effective. The uncertainty was further compounded by both the President and the Foreign Minister being absent abroad.

The president at this time was Urho Kekkonen. This remarkable politician, while still only sixty-one years old, had been prime minister of no less than five Finnish Governments since 1950. He was elected to succeed Paasikivi as president in March 1956, although with a margin of only a single parliamentary vote on this first occasion. He was to remain Finland's president until 1981. Finland's constitution gives the president special responsibility to oversee foreign affairs. This arrangement dates from the period immediately following the War of Independence, when domestic politics tended to dominate parliamentary debate and few Finnish politicians had any real experience of international relations. Kekkonen accepted this responsibility without hesitation and, in the tradition of the Paasikivi line, saw it his prime duty to ensure safe relations between Helsinki and Moscow.

The Note Crisis of 1961 had revealed serious inadequacies in Finland's procedures for the handling of potentially dangerous international events. Before addressing the shortcomings at home, Kekkonen arranged to meet with Khrushchev in Novosibirsk, in southern Siberia, where the Soviet leader was making a visit of inspection. During their discussion Kekkonen succeeded in persuading Khrushchev that there was no requirement for consultations under the FCMA Treaty, at least not for the time being. This had two significant and long-lasting results. Khrushchev was satisfied that there was no inclination on the part of Finland to move away from the letter or spirit of the cooperation aspect of the Treaty. Perhaps even more importantly, Kekkonen became convinced of his ability to handle the Soviet leaders on a personal level and thereby fulfil his role as guardian of good Finno-Soviet relations. This conviction led him to blow sometimes warm and sometimes cold in his attitude towards the Finnish military establishment.

The immediate effect of the Novosibirsk meeting was of some material benefit to the Finnish armed forces. On his return to Helsinki, Kekkonen directed the General Headquarters to prepare a development programme to meet the changing concepts of war in the nuclear age but with a special emphasis on Finland's policy of neutrality. The programme was worked out during the ensuing winter and spring and presented to Parliament under the title of 'The Development of the Defence Establishment in the 1960s'. Less formally but more widely, the plan became known from its instigator simply as the 'K Programme'.

The K Programme still stands as a crucially important signpost on the road to Finland's emerging policy on national security. It is fundamental to a proper understanding of the principles on which defence planning and procurement were to be based, whilst recognizing Finland's vulnerability to becoming unwittingly involved in any superpower conflict. The scar left by the Note Crisis is evident. Following comment on the devastating effect of nuclear explosives, the Programme proposals state, 'This constitutes a very strong deterrent to the outbreak of nuclear war, which in turn increases the importance of deploying conventional arms and the possibility of small nations to defend themselves.' While Finnish air space was acknowledged as the most vulnerable sector for a breach of Finland's neutrality, the sea flank also received attention. The conclusions of the document recognize that 'the military-political position of Finland puts her at the mercy of the air and naval strategy of others'. For centuries the defence of Finland had rested on primacy of the land battle but now the nature of the threat was undergoing dramatic change.

The K Programme set out the following goals for a national defence doctrine within the overriding and inseparable coalition of foreign and defence policy:

A capability to repel violations against Finnish neutrality by land, sea and air as well as prevent aggression through Finnish territory or air space.

A constant capability to deter unexpected efforts to break the will and capability of the Finns to defend the country.

A capability to put all the resources of the country on a war footing in case of a strategic general attack.

A capability to withstand air attacks, including nuclear attacks and the indirect effects of nuclear explosions close to the frontiers.

A capability to secure the economic subsistence of the entire nation even when isolated.

These objectives have some analogy with those of Switzerland, a country that has managed to preserve its neutrality through two world wars and while totally surrounded by belligerents. In Finland the objectives proved to be financially over-ambitious.

After the Note Crisis of 1961 had been defused, Kekkonen encapsulated the essential need for cohesion of foreign and defence policies when he said, 'Our policy of neutrality rests on four supports: its recognition by foreign powers; the confidence of foreign powers in that policy; the backing of our own people and the readiness and capability of the country to repel violations of neutrality.' Although often referred to as the 'four pillars' policy', the manner in which it was subsequently interpreted and used by Kekkonen gave it more the aspect of an irregular-sided prism. He showed no compunction in turning the prism so that the light through it illuminated the solution that he considered to be the most fitting for the problems of the moment. This demonstrated the variations possible under one closely-linked set of statements.

The success of the direct Kekkonen/Khrushchev negotiations in defusing the Note Crisis for Finland and the Soviet Union also began a process of elevation of the office of the Finnish presidency. This continued to gain strength the longer Kekkonen remained in office. As the established custodian of foreign policy, he came to perceive himself as the only person capable of correct interpretation of its relationship with defence. This led to conflict with the military when variations in interpretation began to become apparent. Not everyone within the military establishment or outside it shared Kekkonen's appreciation that a policy does not necessarily lose its value through being capable of more than one interpretation.

The K Programme called for intensive military measures to improve Finland's defence preparedness. The general headquarters staff drew up detailed proposals for these, with associated costs estimated to be an average of three percent of the country's gross national product over a period of seven years. This proportion was comparable with that of Switzerland at the time and significantly less than that of Sweden, which was then standing at around five percent of GNP. But while the K Programme received the approval of Parliament, Kekkonen directed that expenditure must be confined to specific purchases only. When a law was proposed to guarantee a certain annual level of defence appropriations in 1964, Kekkonen demanded that the proposal be withdrawn. He established instead a policy for military expenditure to be contained within the annual budget without any particular safeguard as to its level.

The Cuban missile crisis of 1962 provided another opportunity for neutral countries on the close periphery of the Khrushchev/ Kennedy confrontation to test their crisis-management procedures. Due to Khrushchev's second climbdown, the crisis ended too quickly to allow more than initial measures to be brought into effect in Finland. The dangers were not lost on Kekkonen, as he shortly afterwards, in May 1963, launched his initiative for a Nordic nuclear-free zone.

As was often the case with Kekkonen's foreign policy proposals, the impulse behind the idea of a Nordic nuclear-free zone was narrower than the suggestion implied. His underlying concern was that the Soviet Union might seek to install missile-detection radars and perhaps even missile-intercept systems on Finnish soil. A rationale for this seemed capable of construction through a broad interpretation of the FCMA Treaty, which provided for 'the Soviet Union to give Finland the help required' to repel attack. The stationing of nuclear forces in Denmark or Norway could certainly have been construed as a threat to the Soviet Union through Finland. While these two NATO nations had already rejected any suggestion of nuclear weapons being stationed on their territory, Kekkonen's proposal was intended to take advantage of this situation for the benefit of Finland. Both Denmark and Norway declined to show interest in the idea of a Nordic nuclear-free zone, as they recognized the need to be free to receive nuclear weapons in war as an insurance against Soviet conventional attack.

Collapse of his nuclear-free zone initiative and the doubtful value of an ephemeral concept known as the 'Nordic balance', gave further impetus to Kekkonen's dependency on personal summit diplomacy. The Nordic balance rested on the shadowy theory that so long as Denmark and Norway rejected foreign bases and nuclear weapons in peace, Sweden maintained a strong armed neutrality and Finland stuck to the terms of the FCMA Treaty, superpower influence in the region could be contained at tolerable levels. It was not a theory that ever commended itself very strongly to Kekkonen, who was a seeker after positive rather than negative safeguards. Nevertheless, his understandable preference for diplomatic over military solutions led to his estrangement from the Finnish military hierarchy. The differences were more matters of style rather than of substance but all military contact with the president was placed on an unnecessarily formal footing for several years. This did not assist in the free flow of ideas.

Suspicion arose in Finland and to some extent abroad that Kekkonen and Khrushchev had agreed on some form of military collusion during their meeting in Novosibirsk in 1961. It appeared credible that, in return for there being no formal consultations under the FCMA Treaty, Kekkonen may have given an undertaking that Finnish warships and aircraft would assist the Soviet Union in the surveillance of NATO naval and air activity in the Baltic. No substance has ever been given to these suspicions but the extent to which the Navy and Air Force were allowed to buy modern vessels and aircraft promoted their currency. Most of the finance for the purchases came through Soviet trade credits. The equipment bought included interceptor aircraft, anti-aircraft missiles and radar that the Soviet Union would scarcely have sold if there seemed to be the least likelihood of it being used against their own forces. Two Soviet-made Riga class frigates were acquired specifically for Baltic patrolling, together with artillery and tanks which gave the whole package more of a balanced nature.

These purchases, particularly those to improve air-defence and naval capabilities, were amongst the first modern acquisitions to give material effect to the defence policy of 'neutrality watch'. Kekkonen's statement of the four supporting elements for a successful neutral stance, made on his return from Novosibirsk, gave thought-out expression of what was needed but the nation's desire for a credible neutral position pre-dated it. Return of the Porkkala naval base in 1956 and repatriation of the last of the Soviet servicemen was the point when the Finns felt the need for a clear restatement of their neutrality. Control of Porkkala also carried with it resumption of responsibility for security of the Gulf of Finland. This was a duty to be properly exercised if neutrality was to become more than just a wish to live in peace.

The years from 1962 to 1965 represented an important period of rebuilding the Finnish armed forces but, paradoxically, no sooner had Kekkonen authorized the Soviet credit purchases of new equipment than he turned again to foreign policy as the essentially predominant partner in maintaining national security. Alert to the dangers of over-confident military commanders, he frequently reminded them that they were 'not a state within a state'. It was his view that the concept of armed neutrality, such as that on which Sweden depended, was neither practicable nor desirable for Finland. Kekkonen's emphasis on the pre-eminence of diplomacy to defuse international tension led to various active foreign policy initiatives. These increasingly involved Finland in matters that, innocently or otherwise, fuelled suspicions that Helsinki would dance to Moscow's tune rather than risk disturbing the special understanding that continued to avoid military consultation under the FCMA Treaty.

An example of this arose through Kekkonen's criticism of the NATO plan to form a multinational nuclear force in 1965. The NATO purpose was both political and strategic. Nations other than the nuclear powers could become involved and the diversity of potential launch points increased, particularly for seaborne and air-to-surface missiles. This was a device intended to get round the problem of where nuclear weapons might and might not be stationed in peace. Kekkonen logically pointed out that the diversity and flexibility of the multinational force's attack capability would inevitably increase the strategic significance of the Nordic region. While he was correct in that respect, there can be little doubt that he also foresaw the existence of such a force as a pretext for Moscow to invoke the FCMA Treaty right of military consultation. Wishing to avoid making enemies unnecessarily in the West, Kekkonen explained his criticism with the words, 'Finland can only uphold its neutrality as long as peace continues in Europe.'

It seems inconceivable that a statesman of Kekkonen's immense experience and guile would have made such a double-meaning statement without being aware of its implications, yet this is almost certainly what happened. In Finland the words were widely taken to imply that in a serious crisis the restrictions of the 1947 Paris Peace Treaty might not apply and Finland would be free to choose sides if and when war came. One political group, the Young Social Democrats, seized this opportunity to argue that the logical step would be for Finland to pledge alignment with the Soviet position in any future crisis. Then, seeing the dangers all too clearly, the president hastened to restate his view that Finland should aim to remain outside all conflicts. Kekkonen had a particularly complex mind. Whilst maintaining that the Paasikivi-Kekkonen line of cohabitation with the Soviet Union, he consistently strove to improve the status of Finland's independence. In this he was largely successful but he caused both internal and external doubts and misunderstandings by switches of emphasis to suit the requirements of the moment.

The immediately post-war Defence Revision Commission had been disbanded after submitting its report in 1949. Subsequently, both Presidents Paasikivi and Kekkonen had hesitated to give any prominence to the Defence Council, constituted in 1957, for fear that Moscow might find its work some pretext for consultations under the FCMA Treaty. Parliamentary interest in the armed forces had declined to such an extent by the late 1960s that difficulty was encountered in the passing of appropriations for new weapons and equipment. It was the then Lieutenant-Colonel Aimo Pajunen, working in the Ministry of Defence, who put forward the idea that Parliamentary Defence Committees should be formed with proportional membership from the political parties represented in Parliament. This suggestion was initially opposed by Pajunen's military superiors who feared a possible politicization of defence procurement proposals. In fact an entirely positive effect was the result. Introduction of the Parliamentary Defence Committees saw the beginning of sustained growth in the acquisition of defence equipment.

The first report from a Parliamentary Defence Committee was presented in 1971. This included two unequivocal statements that did much to clear the minds of those responsible for defence planning. The Committee stated that only military defence could offer a realistic safeguard for Finland's security and declared 'no foreign state can consider it necessary for the credibility of Finland's neutrality that we should be capable of of repelling a nuclear attack aimed at our territory'. The Committee went on to suggest that a law on the defence forces, precisely describing their functions, should be prepared to replace the various miscellaneous statutes under which they were then currently directed.

The work of the Defence Committees revived parliamentary interest and influence in military matters. Kekkonen welcomed this and his impatience with the military hierarchy's persistent search for an effective defence against nuclear attack disappeared once it was conceded that Finland could provide no such defence. From the mid-1970s a clear division of responsibilities emerged: the president would guide foreign policy so as to avoid Finland becoming involved in any nuclear confrontation, while the defence forces prepared for the possibility of a conventional conflict. This gave the Army the long-sought for opportunity to develop a credible doctrine for defence.

The National Defence Act of 1974 very largely arose out of the recommendations contained in the report of the first Parliamentary Defence Committee. It enshrined the K Programme objectives for the armed forces and also gave formal recognition to an extra responsibility resulting from the admission of Finland to the United Nations in 1955. This was the preparation of peace-keeping forces to be put at the disposal of the UN Security Council. The same law redefined the distinct functions of the Ministry of Defence and the General Headquarters, two establishments that had not always seen eye to eye in spite of being separated by only the cobbled yard of the old Imperial Russian barracks in Helsinki. It was made clear that while the Ministry was to define defence requirements and prepare policy statements to lay before Parliament, General Headquarters had control over the Navy, Army and Air Force and responsibility for formulating the policies and conditions for conscript service.

The last five of Kekkonen's twenty-six years as president of Finland saw a much-improved relationship between him and the armed forces. This was in part due to clarification of defence policy during the second half of the 1970s. Equally significant were the assiduous efforts of General Lauri Sutela, the commander-in-chief from 1974 to 1983, to establish informal and friendly contact with the Head of State. From time to time the Kremlin leadership had questioned the Finns' lasting commitment to the terms of the FCMA Treaty, suspicious that they may like to see it play a less prominent part in foreign and defence policy. In Finland apprehension arose that the stable Finno-Soviet relationship might be disturbed when the ailing Kekkonen was obliged to step down in October 1981. In the event, President Mauno Koivisto was able to maintain the Paasikivi-Kekkonen line without any perceptible break.

Around the time when the policies of Mikhail Gorbachev began to have an influence on world attitudes towards defence, the search for a truly independent Finnish national security policy had reached a point beyond which it was unrealistic to seek any further major advance. Having witnessed developments in the Soviet Union at such close hand for so long, the Finns greeted Gorbachev's policies with understandable caution. Suppression of democracy in their near neighbours the Baltic states during the period of Gorbachev's presidency did nothing to ease their concern. To the east they saw only uncertainty and lack of central control. Such conditions had seldom been auguries of peace and stability in the turbulent history of Finno-Russian relationships. Foreign and defence policy remained important and very closely linked. The same situation prevails today.

19
The Doctrine of Territorial Defence

Finland's strategy of simply seeking to maintain the country's territorial integrity against any outside threat, adopted during the 1950s, was given some teeth following President Kekkonen's meeting with Nikita Khrushchev in Novosibirsk in November 1961. Orders were placed for modern jet aircraft and naval patrol vessels, to be acquired through Soviet financial credits. Previously, patrolling to ensure the integrity of Finnish air space and territorial waters had been an more of an aspiration than a reality.

Absence of a comprehensive operational concept was nevertheless apparent, as not all the new military equipment was utilized to best advantage. A historical preoccupation with defence of the southern industrial heartland led to the most effective of the new aircraft being stationed there. This left Lapland, where intrusion by aircraft of the two great power blocs was more likely, covered by only one squadron of clear-weather interceptors based on Rovaniemi. The Navy was less troubled, having their traditional allies of the Åland Islands and Turku Archipelago to help them. The shallow Baltic waters and narrow gaps between more than 20,000 islands and reefs made it feasible to watch over 1,000 miles of coastline with confidence.

While the Navy and the Air Force were faced with challenges in adapting to modern equipment, the Army found it increasingly difficult to identify a credible contribution to the concept of national defence. Surveillance for intrusions over the land frontiers was the responsibility of the Frontier Guard, itself a small army responsible in peace to the Ministry of the Interior. The doctrine of maintaining territorial integrity required the Army to contain and repel any such intrusions, but the questions were how, with which weapons and using what tactics. Above all, how could the Army prepare and train for a ground force threat so difficult to define? Modernization of the Soviet Army and extensive improvements to communications to the east of the 750-mile eastern land frontier had removed most of the near-certainties that had been used to forecast from where offensives might be expected in the past.

Whatever else Finland may have lacked in the first two decades of peace after 1945, it was certainly not military experience or expertise. Virtually everyone in public life had fought in at least one of the three wars of 1939-45 and a good few had fought in them all. In Prime Minister Ahti Karjalainen's coalition Cabinet of 1962-63, several members had served in one of the Armed Forces during the wars. The Minister of Defence, Arvo Pentti, had served with special distinction and received the Mannerheim Cross. There are advantages and disadvantages to such a situation. Whereas it may be easier for a general to explain a military plan or requirement to a politician who is familiar with the terminology, it is difficult for a soldier to refute the counter-arguments of men able to match or even surpass his own experience.

The wars had left another legacy, that of a deep and serious interest in the successful conduct of armed conflict. There was nothing morbid or sentimental in this preoccupation. It was perceived as essential for the professional officer and highly desirable for those in public life or universities who wished to be thought fit to comment on matters touching national security. No doubt the veterans of 27th Jäger Battalion, for example General Aarne Sihvo serving for the second time as commander-in-chief, maintained the discipline of critical analysis of military matters instilled by their dedicated German instructors more than thirty years before. Unlike countries that thankfully shrugged off the horrors of war, leaving preparation for the next one to a handful of dedicated professionals, Finland's establishment as a whole did not duck the issue. While the pre-eminence of diplomacy in avoiding war was widely recognized, the reality of possibly having to fight again was not neglected.

Even after the modest acquisitions of artillery and tanks from the Soviet Union in 1962-65, those responsible for formulating Finnish Army tactical doctrine struggled to reconcile three widely separated extremes. There were the military theorists, inside and outside the service, who put forward their battle concepts based on a worst-case threat. There were the financial planners of the Ministry of Defence, who held out hope for additional modern equipment – in due course – and the unit commanders responsible for training conscripts and junior leaders. Whatever their own ideas might be, the latter faced their duties with weapons, equipment and tactics all lacking credibility for modern war. It was in these circumstances of uncertainty and conflicting pressures that the philosophy of total or territorial defence began to develop into a coherent strategic and tactical concept.

Some foreign commentators have suggested that the Finnish doctrine of territorial defence is something entirely new and probably unique. The fact that it is neither does not detract from its advantages, at least in the form to which it has been developed by the last decade of the twentieth century. The concept evolved in parallel with a complementary doctrine of 'fast deployment forces'. Both these ideas were first given expression by Major-General Kustaa Tapola, when Director of the War College in Helsinki in 1945. Tapola suggested that, so unpredictable is the nature of modern war, a delegated system of command is essential to deal with the many isolated battles that must inevitably occur. Local forces must be capable of harassing and even containing such attacks until elements of the fast deployment forces can be sent, in appropriate priority, to deal with them. This doctrine has seen several interpretations but, although the concept of fast deployment forces has now been replaced by one of 'selective mobilization', the underlying philosophy is essentially unchanged.

At the time of Tapola's proposition, there were two military command structures in being. One was for mobilization, which had been based on the civilian provinces since Mannerheim's reforms of 1934, and one for command of the standing army and training conscripts. The mobilization system suffered a serious setback with the disbanding of the Civil Guard, under terms of the armistice and peace treaty, so the time was ripe to combine the two structures into one. The resultant stronger and more economical framework provided for a delegation of operational command when the need arose.

A Defence Revision Commission of six Members of Parliament and five senior service officers had been set up in May 1945. In its report submitted in 1949, the commission recommended the establishment of seven 'national defence provinces' for command of the standing army units in peace, for carrying out mobilization and for exercising command of localized operations in war. When commenting on this report, the commander-in-chief General Sihvo accepted the principles of the proposed new command arrangements but recommended two important refinements. Taking into account the expense of building new headquarters, he argued that three 'national defence districts', each incorporating two or more provinces, would be adequate. Secondly, he maintained that the brigade, rather than the time-honoured division, would be more flexible as the basic operational formation to meet the demands of future war. All of these recommendations, amended according to Sihvo's recommendations, began to be brought into effect from 1952 onwards.

Sihvo made one other fundamental proposal and two subsidiary ones. He drew attention to the central operational command function of General Headquarters, indicating that the Navy and Air Force consequently required only minor administrative staffs to deal with matters of personnel and logistics. This was a logical recommendation for the close coordination of the defence of a nation that has no external offensive intentions whatever. The recommendation was understandably not popular with either the Navy or the Air Force. His subsidiary proposals for the coastal and anti-aircraft artillery to remain parts of the Army are more controversial. A single chain of command over inshore patrol vessels and coastal batteries, on the one hand, and for aircraft and anti-aircraft guns or missiles on the other appears to have advantages. Sihvo's recommendations in these regards may therefore have owed something to a wish not to erode his more significant argument for the single command function of General Headquarters.

The main features of the Defence Revision Commission proposals, endorsed or modified by the commander-in-chief, were introduced with the Law for the Reform of the Organization of the Defence Forces of 1952. Three peacetime divisions were formed, each under direct command of General Headquarters, with reponsibility for a total of seven 'military areas' comprising twenty-seven 'military districts'. This structure commanded and trained the standing army in peace. In emergency the static headquarter element would be responsible for mobilization. General Headquarters had direct command of the Navy, Air Force and the single armoured brigade. On Sihvo's specific recommendation, organization of the field army became based on the brigade, in peace and war. This was not an economy measure but a step to improve the strategic and tactical mobility of the key formation able to engage in independent battle.

Despite the introduction of this new organizational framework, a radical reform of tactical doctrine did not readily follow. A series of tactical ideas were examined for feasibility with varying degrees of success. Of these, the excursion into the concept of guerrilla warfare is probably the most noteworthy, if only as a challenging diversion at a time when more orthodox measures for defence appeared impossible. During the early 1950s the old 'defence position' concept, based on experience of the Karelian battles, had given way to the new idea of the 'defence zone'. This took account of the need to have defence in depth with mobile reserve forces able to attack the flanks and lines of communication of the aggressor. Although well founded, this theory depended critically on the availability of mobile armoured units for flank and line of communications attack. It was almost certainly the continued absence of such forces in any strength that drove the combat-development staff to consider the guerrilla option.

As the concept of sector or regional operations was brought into practice, within the overall doctrine of territorial defence, so the three services attempted to coordinate their localized plans. A contradiction soon appeared between the aims of the Navy and the Air Force, on the one hand, and those of the Army on the other. While the first two services were responsible for maintaining the integrity of territorial waters and air space at their outer limits, the Army was required to restore the land frontier, or shoreline, wherever these might be breached. As in 1939-40, the Army's tactics depended decisively on the use of ground to absorb the aggressor's advance and draw him into terrain best suited to his defeat by numerically inferior forces. Coordination with naval and coastal artillery defence plans under this concept proved especially difficult, as the first sixty miles inland from the Finnish coast is mostly flat and open ground ideal for attacking forces using modern weapons.

Guerrilla warfare had been the basis of the arms caches plan of 1944-5, so it is not surprising to find it was again being examined in face of the new tactical dilemmas of the 1950s. One early proponent of the advantages of guerilla operations was Captain Niilo Nurmi, who stressed their effectiveness against massive ground or airborne attack, especially in the inland forest areas and wilderness. Counterarguments pointed to the difficulties in controlling and resupplying relatively small guerrilla bands and that, even if they were successful in remaining aggressive, control of the forests and wilderness would not maintain the territorial integrity of the country. While it would be unduly negative to characterize preoccupation with guerrilla tactics during the 1950s as a doctrine of despair, it finally failed to achieve acceptance through its incompatibility with the main themes of national defence. Adoption of guerilla warfare as the principal tenet of ground force operations would have implied an expectancy of diplomatic failure, to avoid war, and the inability of the armed forces to maintain the national frontiers or centres of communication.

As Cold War military confrontation became increasingly intense, particularly in the race for missile superiority, a new concern arose. Finnish defence planners appreciated that violation of their air space by aircraft or missiles might be overtaken in likelihood by foreign moves to utilize their territory for either the enhancement or prevention of such events. This danger had been anticipated, in one important respect, by General Sihvo during his second period as commander-in-chief 1946-53. In a wide-ranging memorandum to President Paasikivi, he had pointed out that it was essential for Finland to be able to meet the requirements of the FCMA Treaty unaided, if unwelcome Soviet 'assistance' was to be avoided.

It was this realization that led Finland to adopt a doctrine of total defence in the 1960s. Guerrilla warfare might have some part to play in this, but only as one aspect of a much wider philosophy of defence. Thus the Neutrality Act of 1963, which emphasized the prevention of crisis or war through diplomacy supported by a real capability to repel territorial violations, marks a point when experiments with novel forms of ground force doctrine were put aside. In future only a much closer coordination of the three armed services within a single doctrine could portray the defence system as a credible but still junior partner to diplomacy in maintaining Finland's national security.

As already mentioned in Chapter 18, the National Defence Act of 1974 was the outcome of the Parliamentary Defence Committee's first report. The Act took up the themes of the 'K Programme' of 1962 but extended the functions of the armed forces to the following eight:

1 To be responsible for the surveillance of the land and sea territory and airspace in cooperation with other authorities.

2 To protect the country's territorial integrity, by force if necessary.

3 To defend the country and its legal system as well as the basic subsistence and rights of the people.

4 To be responsible for maintaining and developing the defensive preparedness of the country.

5 To administer military training and to further the citizen's will to defend his country and to improve his physical condition.

6 To provide assistance, when required, to the relevant authorities for the maintenance of public order and safety.

7 To facilitate arrangement for the Finnish peace-keeping force to be placed at the disposal of the United Nations.

8 To perform other tasks prescribed by law.

While mention of the maintenance of law and order and provision of UN peace-keeping forces were entirely new, the first three commitments cleared the way for a fresh look at the threat to national security and the development of a credible doctrine to counter it in all its aspects.

A threat analysis made in the late 1980s revealed three possible forms of assault on national security but, due to frequently changing pressures in world affairs, it is not possible to place them in any particular priority. One threat scenario envisages a surprise attack designed to subjugate the Finnish state. This was the shadow under which the country lived since 1939. A second possibility is an offensive against a third country through Finnish territory, air space or territorial waters. This has historical evidence to support its credibility, with recent technological advances to give credence to the likelihood of violations of air space. A third hypothesis is a large-scale attack or invasion, short of an attempt to subjugate the whole country.

The second Parliamentary Defence Committee report, submitted in 1976, made various proposals for improvement of crisis management measures, including the establishment of a fast deployment force. The third Committee's report, presented in 1981, underlined the need to increase the size of such a force and to integrate it into existing plans for territorial defence. The report also suggested a fifteen-year programme for the modernization of the Army's inventory of weapons and equipment. In contrast to the procurement priorities that had been accorded to the Navy and the Air Force in previous years, the 1980s were designated the 'decade of the Army.' A target for the strength of a fast deployment force was set at 250,000 men from all three services, with 130,000 to be from the Army.

A comprehensive review of Finland's defence structure and operational doctrine was carried out during the period October 1988 to March 1992. The review took account of the various theories and organizational experiments of the previous three decades. At the outset it was decided by the Cabinet that the military clauses of the FCMA Treaty should no longer inhibit the evolution of new ideas, even though the Treaty itself remained in place. In a Government statement issued on 21 September 1990, it was stipulated that the military clauses of the Treaty, including that to facilitate military consultation between Finland and the Soviet Union, had 'lost their significance'. No objection to this came from President Gorbachev, who had been the first Soviet leader to speak publicly of 'neutral Finland' during an official visit to Helsinki in October 1989. After more than forty years of having to look over their shoulders at the FCMA Treaty, Finnish military planners were able to begin their radical review of defence doctrine on a clean slate.

The starting point for this review had to be an unequivocal statement of Finland's strategic aims in the face of the three identified aspects of the threat to national security. Skilful diplomacy remained the cornerstone of Finland's national security policy. Nothing had changed in this respect. Defence policy remained the junior partner to diplomacy in defending national integrity. Secondly, relaxation of super-power tension had added huge areas of uncertainty to the previously identified threat scenarios.

The present Finnish commander-in-chief, Admiral Jan Klenberg, set out the resultant strategy, to deal with all forms of threat, in an address to a seminar on military doctrine in Vienna in October 1991: 'The objective of Finland's military defence is to make it prohibitively difficult for any potential aggressor to violate Finnish territory. The task of defence is to make an attack not worth the cost in terms of time, manpower and equipment lost by prolonged engagement in the Finnish direction.'

The priority given to 'time' in the schedule of potential costs to a would-be aggressor is significant. In war with modern weapons the factor of time for achieving the politico-strategic objective may often

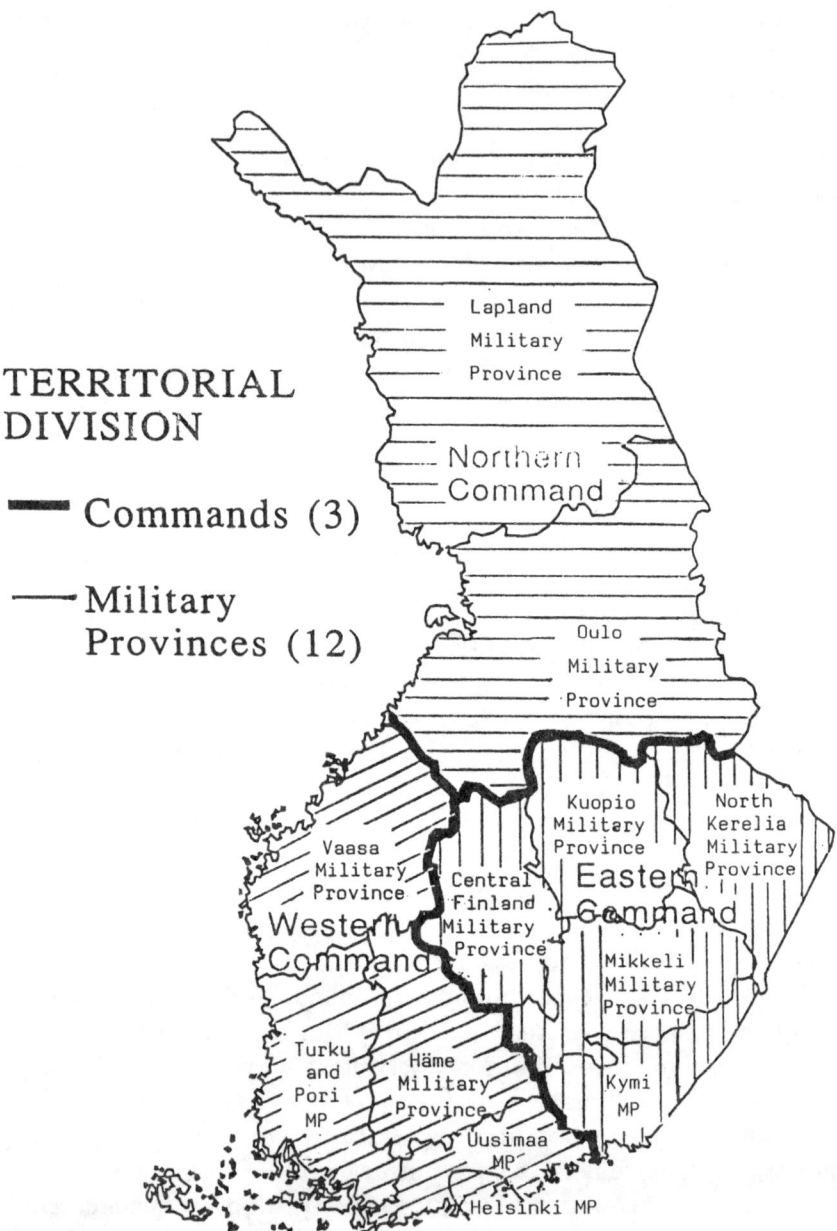

TERRITORIAL
DIVISION

━━ Commands (3)

── Military
    Provinces (12)

Lapland
Military
Province

Northern
Command

Oulo
Military
Province

Kuopio
Military
Province

North
Kerelia
Military
Province

Vaasa
Military
Province

Central
Finland
Military
Province

Eastern
Command

Western
Command

Mikkeli
Military
Province

Turku
and
Pori
MP

Häme
Military
Province

Kymi
MP

Uusimaa
MP

Helsinki MP

Map 18: The 1992 Command and Military province boundaries for
Territorial Defence
Published by authority of General Headquarters, Helsinki

outweigh the immediate costs of men and material. This did not make the devising of the new defence policy easier for the military planners; it made it more difficult. The gaining of time, for mobilization of their full military potential, had always been a problem for the Finns. Now they had to transfer that problem to the potential enemy – and to a decisive degree.

The planners began with the concept of territorial defence put forward by Major (later Major-General) Juhani Ruutu in 1965. This stressed the importance of delegated command to contain or harass enemy incursions with local resources until major elements of the main force could get there to defeat them. The earlier command structure has been simplified to reduce, very significantly, the number of static command headquarters. As may be seen from Map 18 on the facing page, the country is now divided into three commands, each reflecting a distinct geographic and demographic region. Northern Command covers the whole of central Finland and sparsely populated Finnish Lapland. In sharp contrast, Western Command covers the area where seventy percent of the population lives and includes all ports and the main industrial centres. Eastern Command embraces the great Lake Saimaa inland water complex and faces the the historic invasion routes astride Lake Ladoga, now in Russian territory.

The territorial commands are divided into military provinces, each of which corresponds exactly with its counterpart in the civil administration. This helps with a speedy mobilization process but produces an uneven spread of local troops, with the more vulnerable Northern and Eastern Commands producing significantly fewer than the less vulnerable Western Command. The certain need for a major redeployment of military units, whatever the nature of the threat or incursion, has led to the mobilized order of battle being divided between General Forces and Local Troops. The former has a strength of some 300,000 men and the latter rather more than half that number. There is, however, no obligation to carry out a complete mobilization, with the international anxiety and damage to the national economy inevitably associated with that step. Instead, the Preparedness Law of 1991 allows for a limited and selective form of mobilization appropriate to the real or threatened emergency.

The Preparedness Law replaced the previous 'War Law' of 1945. Its inherent flexibility allows for mobilization measures to be applied to

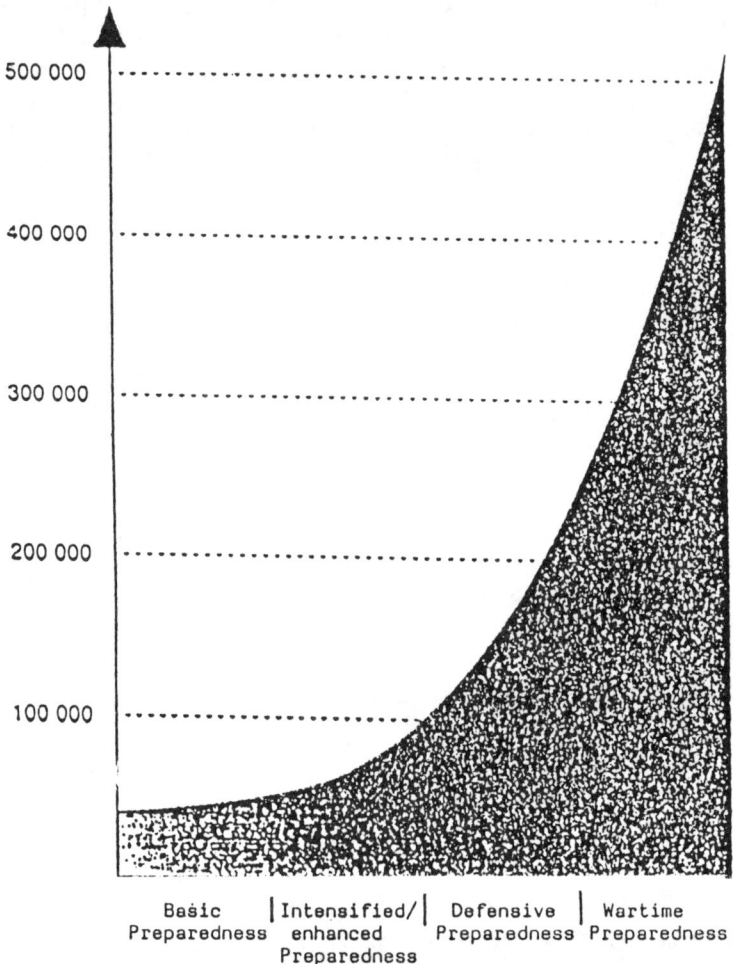

Illustrative application of the Preparedness Law of 1991
(Numbers of men)

only certain regions of the country, or to specific types of unit and to a limited level of manpower. The range of choice is not restrained by age group, unit or individual wartime function. Thus a very precisely tailored call up may be carried out and later changed in an equally selective fashion. The graph is an illustration of how the scale of call up can be linked to the degree of national preparedness judged necessary to meet a variety of circumstances.

The Preparedness Law goes beyond the requirements of mobiliza-

ABOVE The *Turunmaa* corvette/command ship of 750 tons with a top speed of 35 knots, mounting two RBU 1200 5-tube anti-submarine launchers, one 120 mm, two 40 mm (AA) and two 23 mm guns. BELOW Helsinki-class 260-ton fast-attack vessel mounting anti-ship RBS-15 (Saab) surface-to-surface missiles, one 57 mm (Bofors) gun and two 23 mm guns.

ABOVE, LEFT The Finnish Defence Minister, Elisabeth Rehn, watches infantry-men lay the Tampella 81 mm mortar, which fires a 3.1 kilogram bomb up to a range of 5,400 metres. RIGHT Mobile anti-ship missile 85 (Swedish RBS 15). BELOW Modern Finnish ski troops armed with the Sako-Valmet M76T automatic rifle with a rate of fire up to 650 rounds per minute and a maximum range of 350-400 metres. Magazines hold 30 rounds.

ABOVE Soviet-built T-72 main battle tank with a 125 mm smooth-bore gun main armament, co-axially-mounted 7.62 mm machine-gun and an externally-mounted 12.7 anti-aircraft machine-gun on the rear of the turret. BELOW The Tampella 155K 83 155 mm medium gun, which is capable of firing a 46 kilogram high-explosive projectile to a range of 25,000 metres, or up to 30,000 metres using a base bleed projectile.

The United States McDonnell Douglas F/A-18C/D dual-role interceptor/ground-attack aircraft, with which the Finnish Air Force will begin to re-equip in 1995. BELOW, LEFT Shoulder-fired ITO 86 (SA-16 Igla) surface-to-air missile with passive infra-red guidance. The warhead weighs 2.2 kilograms and has a maximum range of 16,400 feet (5,000 metres). RIGHT Finnish infantrymen in chemical warefare clothing.

ABOVE, LEFT Lieutenant-General Ensio Siilasvuo, Chief of Staff of UNTSO 1970-73, Commander of UNEF II 1973-75 and Chief Coordinator of United Nations Missions in the Middle East 1975-79. RIGHT Suez 1973. The headquarters of Lieutenant-Colonel Reino Raitasaari, commander of the Finnish battalion with UNEF II, after being struck during an Egyptian and Israeli artillery exchange. BELOW Suez 1974. Colonel Tauno Kuosa of Finland (2nd from left), officer in charge of the Field HQ of UNEF II, discussing the third phase of the Egyptian-Israeli disengagement with unit commanding officers and staff. (Courtesy United Nations.)

ABOVE, LEFT UNEF II, United Nations observation post 'OP Mike' on the roof of a shelled and burned-out building in Suez 1974. RIGHT UNDOF. An observation post of the UN Disengagement Observer Force on the Golan Heights, manned by Finnish troops in September 1985. BELOW Gaza 1957. Private Teuvo Hannula, from Turku in Finland, delivers the mail to soldiers of the Finnish battalion serving with UNEF I in the Gaza strip. (Courtesy United Nations.)

ABOVE, LEFT Lebanon. Major-General Gustav Hägglund, commander of UNIFIL 1986-88, with soldiers of the Finnish contingent 1986. RIGHT Lebanon. View from the interior of a vehicle checkpoint manned by soldiers of the Finnish battalion, UNIFIL 1987. BELOW Lebanon. An armoured troop carrier of the Finnish battalion serving with UNIFIL after an incident in which two soldiers were killed and three others injured.

ABOVE, LEFT Major-General Rauli Helminen, senior military officer of the UN Good Offices Mission to Afghanistan and Pakistan (UNGOMAP) 1988-90. RIGHT Major-General Hans Christensen, Chief of Staff UN Truce Supervision Organization (UNTSO), Jerusalem, 1990-92. BELOW, LEFT UNDOF. Soldiers of the Finnish battalion searching for clearing mines on the Golan Heights, September 1985. RIGHT Lebanon. Lieutenant-Colonel Lauri Väättänen, second-in-command of the Finnish battalion with UNIFIL 1986-87.

tion. It allows for an additional choice of measures to accompany the activation of selected units of the armed services. These include restrictions on civilian movement in areas of military deployment, the requisition of commercial vehicles and buildings, emergency procurement for the services, extra Government funding for purposes of defence and the granting of priority for the provision of service needs from industry. Such facilities, and others for crisis management at all levels of government, are a direct reflection of the anticipated requirements to meet the three forms of threat to Finland's national security identified in the most recent analysis. They have particular application to a slowly escalating crisis or where the perceived threat falls short of a full-scale attack.

The newly revised headquarters structure of the 1990s has reduced the levels of territorial command from three to two with valuable manpower economies. Even more importantly, the lines of reporting and control are streamlined. The three territorial commands report direct to the General Headquarters, the name of which has changed to the 'Defence Staff' from 1 January 1993. Conversion to the brigade concept for the field army is now virtually complete. On full mobilization, the General Forces will have an order of battle of two armoured brigades, ten Jäger brigades and fourteen infantry brigades, with integral artillery, engineer and logistic support units. Additional specialist support forces will be available at the level of army corps.

Formations and units of the standing army, engaged in conscript training in peace, provide the fighting units at the immediate disposal of the three territorial commands and military provinces. These form the leading elements of the General Forces. Operations are coordinated with naval and air defence plans for the western and southern seaboards and with the Air Force on the eastern land frontier.

Local Troops exist at two levels. There are two coastal artillery brigades responsible for the southern and south-western shorelines, the islands and coastal waters. Secondly, there are fifty infantry battalions and some two hundred local defence units. All of these are very largely dependent on requisitioned transport. There are in addition the units of the Frontier Guard, which have the capacity to increase their strength from 4,200 men to 24,000 on mobilization. Within each military province, an aggressor may therefore expect to encounter two echelons of defence. He will initially be confronted by the local defence units, which are responsible for impeding the enemy's advance by attacking his flanks and communications. Guerrilla tactics may also be used where the terrain and other local conditions are suitable. Such other locally situated troops as may be available will be expected to blunt the spearhead of the enemy advance, especially if this threatens any strategically important installation or region. This kind of operation is most likely to be undertaken by locally based units of the standing army, with air and naval support from within military province resources.

When units of the standing army are not readily to hand, other General Forces units will need to be sent quickly to the threatened province. There can be no absolutely hard-and-fast delineation of which troops are responsible for any particular aspect of local defence operations. It is the collective responsibility of all in the immediate vicinity to contain an enemy incursion until brigades of the General Forces can reach the scene.

The fundamental doctrine of territorial defence operations is that they start from the land border and from the shoreline. Tactics of delay and attrition in a deep inland zone will almost inevitably follow, with the primary aim of preventing the enemy from reaching nationally vital areas or installations. The aggressor will finally be defeated by large-scale counter-attacks and decisive combat using brigades of the General Forces. In areas occupied by the aggressor, fighting will be continued by local attacks, guerrilla operations and mine warfare. It has to be stressed that naval and air support will be under direct control of the regional command headquarters. Nonetheless, and in the words of the the present commander-in-chief, in the concept of territorial defence, the Army occupies a pivotal position. It carries the main burden of repelling an attack.

20

The Armed Forces of 1993

The Paris Peace Treaty of 1947 curtailed the Army of Finland to 34,400 men and the Navy and Air Force to 4,500 and 3,000 respectively. The treaty limitations on naval tonnage and number of aircraft, while not actually exceeded by the Navy, have been internationally accepted for many years as no longer relevant. The peace treaty manpower figures bore some relationship to the 1939 strengths of the Finnish standing forces but virtually none to the needs of today. In consequence, in the autumn of 1990 the Finnish Government unilaterally declared that it no longer considered the restrictions of the Paris peace treaty binding.

Although no longer restricted by any external constraint, Finland is nevertheless inhibited in defence expenditure by the other budgetary demands of an essentially liberal and modern society. To overcome this difficulty, the armed forces are based on relatively small cadres of professional servicemen, each supported by a large reserve available for call up at very short notice. The reserves are provided and maintained through universal male conscription, giving an overall potential of more than a million men.

The regular cadre of the Finnish Army comprises 10,000 officers, NCOs and junior ranks, supported by a further 11,000 civilian staff. The uniformed element provides the commanders, staff officers and instructors responsible for training an average of 30,000 conscripts and providing refresher courses for between 30,000 and 50,000 reservists every year. In addition, the regular cadre must also be trained in new techniques and prepare themselves for more senior positions in war than they hold in peace. The units which train the conscripts form the standing army. This is available to deploy immediately to confront any national emergency. To ensure that the greater proportion of the men are ready or at least prepared for active service, it is necessary to stagger the call up over different points in each year.

The conscript training period for a rifleman is 240 days, and 330 days for those with the potential to become officers or NCOs. Men selected for specialist training, for example in the artillery, engineers or signal corps or similar specialists in the Navy or Air Force, must serve for 285 days. An average of eight percent of conscripts are trained as reserve officers, twenty-one percent as NCOs and seventy-one percent for service in the ranks. Call up takes place at five points over a two-year cycle. The training of each conscript is divided into three phases. The first basic training phase is common to all. This is followed by twelve to nineteen weeks of specialist training, depending on the arm or service for which the man is selected. Finally, there are several weeks of manoeuvre training in the type of terrain that the soldier might be required to defend.

Throughout his service the Finnish soldier is trained to be accustomed to discipline, to act on his own initiative and to be prepared for 'the shocks of war'. Individual self-reliance is a dominant feature of all aspects of instruction. A foreign officer inspecting a ceasefire line under United Nations surveillance noticed that, while other contingents had two men, the Finns had only one soldier in each observation post. When he inquired about this difference in policy, the commander of the Finnish contingent replied without even the suggestion of a smile, 'That is easily explained, the others are not Finns.'

Once he has completed his conscript service, each trained soldier has a reserve liability until he is sixty years old. However, the final ten years are served on the auxiliary reserve, when he is no longer liable for refresher training and would be employed on support duties on mobilization. During the period until he is fifty, each reserve officer may be called up for a total period of one hundred days' refresher training, an NCO seventy-five days and the rifleman, or his equivalent in other arms of service, forty days. This system has built up the reserve force of over a million men, although only around half that number would be required to bring the three services to active service strength. An additional 200,000 men would wear uniform and be available as battle-casualty replacements, if required. The remaining 300,000 men, mostly of the auxiliary reserve, would carry out support tasks or responsibilities in the civil community to maintain the national economy and the war effort.

Mobilization planning and execution is the responsibility of the headquarter staffs of the military provinces shown on Map 18 on page 272. This arrangement leaves units of the standing army free to train in peace and for emergency deployment in the event of a crisis. The Preparedness Law of 1991 was introduced to allow for a rising scale of mobilization measures. This is with a view to avoiding national or international alarm, historically connected with mobilization, or unnecessary damage to the national economy through the call up of a larger then necessary number of reservists.

Formations and units available to the Army on mobilization divide into two main groups for active operations. There are the General Forces with a strength of 300,000 men, and the Local Troops of some 160,000. There are also the support troops, largely manned by the auxiliary reserve, and the 24,000-strong Frontier Guard. Mobilization of reserves can raise the manpower of the Navy to a level of 12,000 and that of the Air Force to 30,000. The very substantial margins of 300,000 men for support duties and 200,000 for battle-casualty replacements also leaves scope for individuals to remain in key civilian posts and employments, essential to maintain the national economy.

As an essential feature of the doctrine of territorial defence explained in Chapter 19, it is the task of the Local Troops to maintain local surveillance in an emergency situation, and to guard vital installations in their military province. Local Troops would also provide the first echelon of resistance to any enemy incursion across the national frontier or coastline. The order of battle of the Local Troops includes two coastal artillery brigades, which are responsible for the south-western and southern shorelines, islands and coastal waters. There are also fifty Local Troops infantry battalions and some two hundred local defence units. The majority of these units have armaments of the older variety and depend on requisitioned commercial vehicles. They are nevertheless capable of battalion-scale localized attacks, guerrilla operations and persistent harassment of enemy lines of communication, so as to impede an invader's tactical mobility.

The General Forces provide the resources from which the main counter-attack and decisive battle elements are drawn. On full mobilization, two armoured brigades, up to ten Jäger brigades and fourteen infantry brigades could be made available. In peacetime only one of the two armoured brigades is in being with its headquarters in Western Command at Hattula. The coastal Jäger brigade is available for deployment either in the archipelagos or on the coastline.

The change from a divisional to a brigade organization should not be interpreted as a reduction in Finland's combat capability. Each modern brigade has greater firepower than that of a Second World War infantry division and a significantly improved tactical mobility. Brigades are usually based on a four battalion organization and a field artillery regiment. The armoured brigades each have three tank battalions, an armoured reconnaissance company with supporting artillery, anti-aircraft and anti-tank missile units. In addition, each brigade has its own integral engineer battalion, signals company and supply company. Field medical support is provided by field ambulances and medical units. Armoured brigades have a strength of sixty main battle tanks, Jäger brigades 5,300 men and infantry brigades 7,000.

In addition to the armoured, Jäger and infantry brigades, the General Forces include detached anti-tank companies, air-defence units, independent engineer battalions, pontoon units and signal battalions. The two coastal artillery brigades are part of the Army but train and would operate in close cooperation with the Navy. These brigades are autonomous, in that they have their own light anti-aircraft artillery and missiles, as well as Jäger close defence companies to protect their gun emplacements and anti-ship missile batteries. The main armament and equipment of these formations and units are set out in Appendix 9.

The all-arms structure of the General Forces is designed to match the doctrine of defence from the frontier and localized operations against every incursion. Even so, uneven population distribution has led to a concentration of units in peacetime in the southern half of the country. The regimental affiliation of each reservist depends chiefly on his training speciality, both as a conscript and for reservist refresher training, rather than where he lives and works in peace. Volunteers for the Lapland Jäger Brigade and other especially prestigious units may come from Helsinki or other cities in the south. The rule that reservists carry out their refresher training with the unit in which they would serve in war develops a strong sense of personal allegiance and team spirit. Much as the latter may be derided in modern society, it is proved by every conflict that loyalty to known and trusted comrades and to the company-level unit is almost invariably stronger than to any high ideal for which the nation as a whole may be fighting.

Some brigade titles and traditions are derived from those of the Finnish regiments of 300 years ago. Importantly, most titles reflect either a specialist role or the province from which the soldiers are drawn and sometimes both. The Pohja, Savo and Uusimaa Jäger Brigades are obvious examples. The identification numbers of the more recently formed brigades inspire an equal loyalty from their soldiers. The very simplicity of a title such as 'the Forty-Second' says all that needs to be said for the soldiers who serve with that brigade.

As mentioned in the previous chapter, the concept of a fast deployment force was first given expression by Major-General Kustaa Tapola, when he was Director of the War College in Helsinki in 1945. While commander-in-chief at about the same time, General Erik Heinrichs issued a memorandum stressing the increased strategic importance of the north of Finland, especially in the context of super power rivalry. These two related themes came to the surface from time to time in the years following, but little was actually done until the Second Parliamentary Defence Committee issued its Report in 1976. After indicating the key importance of 'utilization of warning time between peace and preparations for war', the committee recommended that a sustainable readiness force should be established.

The earlier concept of fast deployment forces has now been overtaken by that of the grouping of General Forces and Local Troops, with the provisions of the Preparedness Law allowing for a selective mobilization of the forces required to meet any actual or anticipated emergency. The Third Parliamentary Defence Committee, reporting in 1981, gave priority to a re-equipment programme for the Army during the 1980s. The same committee also foresaw a fall in Finland's birthrate leading to a reduction in the total available reserves to around 600,000 men by the end of the century.

The operational tasks of the Finnish Navy are to protect territorial integrity, to repel any seaborne attack and to protect and control merchant shipping during time of crisis. For these responsibilities, the Navy has a complement of twenty-four first line combat ships and nineteen minelaying or minesweeping vessels. All are surface craft. The 1947 Peace Treaty precluded Finland from having submarines and the development of defence policy to date has not given cause for that restriction to be set aside. Equally, the treaty ceiling of a total of 10,000 displacement tons for combat vessels has not been exceeded. The current total is approximately 7,000 tons. The Navy operates in peace, in conjunction with the Coastguard service, in the surveillance of Finland's territorial waters. In war, defence of those waters, safeguarding vital sea-lanes in the Baltic and repelling attacks against the sea coast will be the Navy's responsibility, in conjunction with the Air Force and the Army's coastal artillery and coastal Jäger units. As mentioned earlier, the peacetime manpower strength of 2,000 would be increased to 12,000 on mobilization.

The nature of the Baltic Sea and existence of more than 20,000 islands and reefs surrounding Finland's south-western peninsula both have a direct bearing on the concept for naval operations. The Baltic is shallow, with a mean depth of fifteen to twenty fathoms, making it especially suitable for maritime mine warfare and a very hostile environment for submarines. The unusually low salinity level, roughly one quarter that of the North Sea, leads to the Gulf of Bothnia being frozen as far south as Vaasa between November and March in an average winter and to the mouth of the Gulf in an extremely cold season. The Gulf of Finland also freezes on occasion, as it did from the end of December during the Winter War of 1939-40. Although ice-breakers are available and minelayers could operate, naval operations in winter are greatly limited by the ice. Whatever the season, the islands and reefs make for difficult navigation, which favours a defender familiar with their hazards.

The Navy's largest ships are the two Turunmaa class 750 displacement ton corvettes, that can combine their patrol capability with one as task force command vessels. The main offensive vessels are the fast attack craft, of which there are three varieties. There are four of the Helsinki class of 260 displacement tons and a top speed of over thirty knots, four Rauma class of 250 tons and three Tuima class, also of 250 tons. The Rauma class are the most modern ships, having entered service in 1990-92. They each have main armament of six sea-skimming surface-to-surface missiles and submarine detection and interception equipment. A further four of these vessels are likely to be brought into service before the end of the decade, to replace the four older, Soviet-built, Tuima class ships. The four Helsinki class ships are relatively modern, having been brought into service in the early 1980s. They also have sea-skimming surface-to-surface main armament, but their anti-submarine capability is less advanced than the Rauma class.

For patrolling the narrows between the reefs and islands of the Åand archipelago, there is a mixed fleet of five 'R' class patrol boats, of 125 or 130 tons and a top speed of seventeen knots, and six Nuoli class motor gunboats, each of forty tons and a top speed of forty knots. These vessels are armed with anti-aircraft and anti-submarine ordnance.

Mine warfare proved most effective during the wars of 1939-40 and 1941-44 and the Navy has four large minelaying vessels and thirteen minesweepers. The Pohjanmaa class minelayer, with a displacement of 1,000 tons, is the largest and can ship between 100 and 150 mines ready to lay. There are also two Hameenma minelayers in service, each of 1,000 tons and with a capability to lay up to 100 to 150 mines. All have gun armament and anti-aircraft counter-measure equipment, together with guns or missiles. Of the thirteen inshore minesweepers, six are of the ninety-ton Kuha class and seven of the seventeen-ton Kuha class. A summary of vessel main and secondary armament is set out in Appendix 10.

The naval command system functions in peace as it would in war. Overall operational command is exercised by the Defence Staff (previously 'General Headquarters') through the commander of the Navy, a rear-admiral. There are two subordinate commands: Gulf of Finland Naval Command with its headquarters at Porkkala near Helsinki and the Archipelago Sea Naval Command with its headquarters at Turku. The latter command also includes the Gulf of Bothnia. In addition, there is the Naval Academy at Suomenlinna. Each of the two operational headquarters may have under command a force of one of the corvette/command ships, a fast attack missile boat squadron and a mine-warfare squadron. Transfer of ships between commands can be accomplished quickly as the operational situation demands. Each command has its own support and technical shore installations.

The Navy has a professional cadre of 300 officers, 550 petty officers or NCOs and 120 junior ranks. This cadre, together with the naval conscripts in training, has the capability to operate all the first-line combat vessels of the fleet in peace, although at a lower level of at-sea activity than would be required in war. The cadre is also responsible for training 1,500 conscripts each year. Conscripts are called up for training in three batches of 500 each at three points in the year, in much the same manner as for the Army. After twelve weeks' basic training at the Helsinki naval base, the conscripts are sent to join vessels at sea, where they complete their training and provide the majority of the junior rates of the crew. The full duration of conscript service is eleven months (330 days), after which each man is recalled for refresher training in his own speciality every few years. Those conscripts that show the potential to be reserve officers or petty officers are trained at the Naval Academy and Helsinki Naval Base respectively.

On mobilization, whether full-scale or only selective, the Navy would be reinforced by integration of the Coastguard service, together with their thirteen or more patrol craft. This not only strengthens the Navy's close inshore capability but ensures proper coordination between the activities of both services. The integration has another particular importance because of the special status of the Åland Islands at the extreme western tip of the archipelago. The Åland Islands lie within Finnish territorial waters but remain demilitarized under terms of the Åland Treaties of 1922 and 1940. Their surrounding waters, to a distance of three miles, are therefore not patrolled regularly by the Finnish Navy in peace, but are the responsibility of the Coastguard service. Familiarity with the narrows and reefs is essential for safe navigation close in to the islands, which emphasizing the significance of the closest cooperation of the Navy and Coastguard service in war.

The coastal artillery is an integral part of the Army, but its functions are to assist the Navy in surveillance of territorial waters and, together with Army units, to repel any attempted invasion or incursion over the sea coast. This branch of the service has a long and distinguished history reaching back to the Finns' inheritance of the chain of fortifications along the northern shore of the Gulf of Finland, once part of the Imperial Russian seaward defences for St Petersburg. Today Finland has a coastal defence system based on a balance of long-range artillery and anti-ship missiles with sea-surveillance radar. The service has organic air defence batteries and Jäger infantry companies for close protection of gun positions and missile sites. Signal links with the Army and Air Force are maintained to ensure coordination of operations at the military province level of command.

There are four fixed coastal artillery units and one mobile battalion for emergency deployment. The Turku Coastal Artillery Regiment, with its headquarters in the old capital in the extreme south-west, has responsibility for the coastline in the region between Rauma, on the Gulf of Bothnia, to the island of Orö at the entrance to the Gulf of Finland. The Turku Regiment is also responsible for the archipelago running westwards towards the Åland Islands. The density of islands and reefs in this region is ideal for defence by a combination of guns, missiles, minefields and naval patrols. With a resumption of naval activity in and around the Åland Islands, it is a relatively simple matter to seal off the Gulf of Bothnia, as was done to counter the announced but never implemented Soviet blockade of the Gulf in December 1939.

The south-facing coast along the Gulf of Finland is covered by the Suomenlinna Coastal Artillery Regiment and the two independent artillery battalions at Hanko in the west and Kotka in the east. The Suomenlinna Regiment consists of two battalions, one covering the sea approach to the capital and surrounding islands and a second protecting the naval anchorage of the Porkkala Peninsula. Additional support may be provided to any of these areas, or to parts of the coastline not otherwise protected, by the independent mobile coastal artillery battalion at Vaasa. This unit is equipped with the 130 mm field artillery gun, modified for coast defence purposes. The battalion is stationed in Vaasa in peacetime so as to make best use of the gun and missile ranges at Lohtaja to the north of Vaasa.

The fixed coast-defence guns operate in groups of emplacements or fortresses, of which between five and seven are active and used for training in peace. The remainder are guarded and could be brought into action very quickly by reservists, almost all of whom live close to their wartime action stations. The fortification guns are mainly of 100 mm or 130 mm calibre, the latter being the more modern. In-direct fire is the usual tactic but direct fire can be used when the range is sufficiently close. The fixed guns are electronically linked into a surveillance and fire control system, but capability remains for independent action in the event of electronic failure. Anti-ship missiles are of two types. The French SS 11 is used for short ranges between the islands and the Swedish RBS 15 (or Anti-Ship Missile 85) for ranges up to fifty miles.

The variety of weapon systems available to the coastal artillery is probably its greatest strength, together with the flexibility provided by the mobile artillery and missiles, which can be quickly redeployed to meet an unexpected threat. It is also important that the service has its own air-defence capability and integral infantry close-protection units. The latter are armed with infantry heavy weapons and mortars, with which they are trained for their specialist role at the Marine Infantry Battalion at Tammisaari, in Uusimaa Military Province.

The coastal artillery has a professional cadre of 900, which is responsible for training conscripts and providing refresher training for reservists. From the time that they have completed their basic training, conscripts are integrated into the active units and trained for the coastal artillery speciality for which they have been selected. So as to ensure that reservists carry out their refresher training with the units they will join on mobilization, a proportion of the fortifications in each of the five battalions are kept active and used for training.

The Finnish Air Force is a fighter-interceptor service. This stems in part from the Paris Peace Treaty, which stipulated that Finland may not have aircraft with internal bomb-carrying facilities, but more importantly from national security policy. Military aircraft characteristics depend exclusively on their intended purpose. Although many designers continue to try, attempts to combine two major functions in one aircraft have seldom proved to be completely successful. In the case of Finland, their combat aircraft inventory of only air-defence fighters makes the unequivocal statement that the country has no offensive intention. Nonetheless, determination that air defence shall be effective is underlined by the number of aircraft. This reaches the ceiling of the peace treaty and would probably exceed it but for financial constraints. Britain, with a population ten times that of Finland, has only twice the number of air-defence fighters in service and France only slightly more than Britain.

Excellence in perfomance demands frequent modernization of aircraft, weapons and counter-measures. Unlike the Army, where outdated but still serviceable equipment can be handed on to the Local Troops, combat aircraft must be capable of defeating any threatening intruder. Otherwise they might as well not be there. Equally, the air-surveillance systems must be capable of ensuring enough warning for the intruder to be met at the edge of Finnish air space. But some intruders will always get through the outer circumference, no matter how efficient the surveillance and interception systems. Then the purpose of air defence will become a matter of denying the enemy any chance to achieve air superiority. The commander-in-chief, Admiral Jan Klenberg, is quoted as stating, 'It is one of our problems that for air defence we cannot rely on cheap technology. For air defence, we have to have modern interceptors, radars and air-to-air missiles.'

Finland's air defence aircraft are organized into three wings, each comprising a fighter squadron, air-surveillance network, command and control system and ground support units. A wing is responsible for an air defence region, the area of which matches that of a military command. The wings are responsible to the commander of the Air Force and are capable of independent combat within their respective air defence regions. Operational planning is coordinated between the wings and the local military command on the basis of orders issued by the Defence Staff through Air Force Headquarters. Coordination includes operations by anti-aircraft artillery and missile units, local ground defence and logistics.

In the north the Lapland Air Defence Wing is based on Rovaniemi, the Satakunta Air Defence Wing at Tampere in Western Command and the Karelia Air Defence Wing at Kuopio in the south-east. For peacetime operations and training, aircraft fly mainly from their home bases. Under threat of air or missile attack, they would be dispersed to operate from secondary airfields. As an essential feature of the territorial defence system, the command centres of the air defence regions are linked into the civil air traffic control network and with the Navy's and Army's military province command and control communications.

The Finnish Air Force is still flying one squadron of Soviet-built MiG 21 bis and two squadrons of Swedish-designed Saab Draken J-35F or Finnish-built J35-S interceptors. While they were state of the art in their day, these aircraft no longer match the commander-in-chief's criteria for modern technology in all aspects of air defence. Hence 10 billion Finnmarks (2.2 billion US dollars) have been set aside to buy fifty-seven modern single-seat fighters and seven two-seater trainers, starting in 1995. An intensely exacting competition has been carried out for the replacement aircraft with special emphasis on operating in the Arctic cold in the interceptor role. The

Air Force commander, Major-General Heikki Nikunen, is reported as saying, 'We are choosing for air interception missions. Our Air Force's main task is to keep Finnish air space out of any conflict.'

There were four contenders for the fighter competition, which was held in Finland during February and March 1992 after extensive preliminary research to draw up the short list. A proposal for a 'balanced buy' of half the requirement from Russia and half from the West was abandoned as too expensive, as well as incurring the disadvantage of dual spares dependency. The competition took place between the French Dassault Mirage 2000-5, the Swedish Saab JAS 39 SA/SA Gripen, the US General Dynamics F-16C/D and the US McDonnell Douglas F/A-18C/D, all of which are dual or multi-role aircraft. There was no compromise over the purely interceptor requirement, however. Each contender was flown on around ten test flights, with radar performance and engine reliability in intense cold receiving special scrutiny. The McDonnell Douglas F/A-18C/D was selected and the first ten will have begun replacing the ageing Saab Drakens by 1996.

The interceptor capability is complemented by a network of fixed radar stations, which is operated for twenty-four hours a day, all the year round. The radar network has an all-round capability for high altitude surveillance and low level cover for the sectors of greater vulnerability to that form of intrusion. In wartime optical air surveillance units would be activated to improve the low-level capability. Female Air Force personnel are very largely responsible for radar operation and reporting. Women make up almost twenty-five percent of the 3,100-strong Air Force professional cadre, as they also work in the command and control centres and carry out clerical and related duties. The professional cadre as a whole flies the interceptors on routine or emergency patrol sorties and provides the instructors and support staff to train new pilots, the air defence controllers, radar operators and technicians responsible for maintenance of all aircraft and equipment. Some 1,200 conscripts are usually under training at any one time.

Pilot training is carried out by the Air Force Academy at Kauhava in western Finland. For the forty to forty-five conscript training places available each year, there are between seven and eight hundred applications. Initial flight training for those selected entails around fifty hours on the Valmet L-70 Vinka propeller-driven trainer. About half of those successful at initial training are taken for a four-year course of advanced training for the professional cadre. This involves one hundred hours on the British Aerospace Hawk Mark 51 trainer. Those who graduate from this course are commissioned as lieutenants but are required to achieve a further hundred hours on the Hawk before the best are selected for interceptor training on the MiG 21 or Draken fighters. The training of a fully operational fighter pilot may take as long as seven or even eight years. The majority of Air Force staff officers and those working in command and control centres have completed pilot training at least to the level of flying Hawk aircraft in an operational unit.

Training of radar operators, signals and maintenance staff and the non-commissioned officers for these duties is carried partly in the Air Force Signals and Technical Schools and partly with the air defence wings, where each conscript has his own role to play in maintaining the operational capability of the base. The conscript's reserve liability is to serve in the same speciality, for which he will receive refresher training.

In addition to the three interceptor squadrons, one on each of the main bases, there is a reconnaissance squadron flying Hawk and MiG aircraft converted for this role based at Tikkakoski, which is the Air Force headquarters, and a transport squadron at Utti in the extreme south-east of the country. The transport squadron is equipped with Russian Mi-8 'Hip' and United States Hughes 500 D helicopters and a mix of Fokker Friendship and Gates Learjet fixed-wing transport aircraft. The distribution of Finnish Air Force bases and units is shown in Appendix 11. On mobilization, the strength of the Air Force would be raised to 30,000. The additional manpower is principally the technical and maintenance staffs to maintain the Air Force at full operational potential, although some reserve pilots are called up for liaison flight duties.

As naval operations are complemented by those of the coastal artillery, so the air defence of Finland is shared by the Air Force and the anti-aircraft (AA) regiments. These remain an integral part of the Army and are organized to operate in the three air defence regions, the boundaries of which match the boundaries of the three military commands. They also provide air defence battalions and batteries for the General Forces brigades. The French Thomson-CSF Crotale NG SAM system, mounted on SISU XA-180 armoured vehicles, has been introduced to cover the previous air defence gap at medium altitude for the protection of important national facilities and General Forces units in the field. The AA regiments' equipment also include Marconi Marksman twin-mounted 35 mm guns on the T-55 tank chassis, 35 mm and 57 mm automatic AA guns, the new tracked vehicle mounted 12.7 mm anti-aircraft machine-gun, ITO-79 (SAM-3), SA-78 (SAM-7) and SA-86 (SAM-16).

The Anti-Aircraft Academy at Tuusula has recently undergone a modernization programme and now reflects the modern weapons and equipment being received. The Nokia concept combining detection, reporting and fire-control system is now in service. The Finnish AA service has a most demanding annual firing camp at Lohtaja on the shore of the Gulf of Bothnia, just a few miles north of Kokkola. This firing camp completes the training of the conscript soldier and is used as refresher training for reservists.

There are some 6,000 servicewomen in the Finnish Navy, Army and Air Force at the present time. One of the commitments of the Defence Budget for 1992 was to establish a committee to study whether women should have the opportunity to carry out voluntary, that is to say part-time, military service and also to report on ways of improving opportunities for those women in the professional cadres to advance their service careers. This committee is due to submit its recommendations in 1993.

21

In the Service of Peace

Finland has maintained a shrewd but steadfast commitment to the United Nations ever since her application to join the world body was approved in 1955. The first Finnish peace-keeping contingent was deployed in the Middle-East in the following year. Since then Finland has contributed to almost every UN peace-keeping operation, either by sending troops or by granting funds. In many instances she has provided both men and money. In addition, Finland has found more senior officers for the exacting duty of command of peace-keeping missions than any other nation. One Finnish general served as special adviser to the Secretary-General, another as Chief Co-ordinator for UN Peace-Keeping Missions in the Middle East and a third as the military liaison officer in the office of the Under-Secretary-General. This is an unrivalled record.

The post Second World War situation found the Finns with a need to enlarge their circle of friends in the international community. They harboured a healthy scepticism of international institutions, however, with the abject failure of the League of Nations standing like a headstone over earlier hopes. Their frugal nature makes them quickly impatient with anyone who might be guilty of wasting their time or resources. For example, when the parties to the Cyprus dispute failed to grasp an opportunity for settlement in 1977, Finland reduced its national contingent with the UN force there to a token detachment of seven men. The Helsinki Government considered that their battalion might be better deployed elsewhere.

'The foreign policy of a small nation' is how many Finns will explain the enduring strength of their contribution to United Nations' peace-keeping missions. By being in the thick of the problems, despair and sheer ghastliness of violence and destruction, Finland shows a will to help solve or at least contain today's conflicts, rather than to pontificate from the sidelines. All four Nordic countries are now identified as having a particular aptitude for peace-keeping service. This is in part due to their freedom from any recent colonial history but more importantly to their egalitarian and liberal traditions. Their volunteers, women as well as men, are by education and individual resourcefulness well equipped to understand and deal with the fears and needs of people in adversity.

The UN Emergency Force (UNEF I), established in 1956 between the armies of Egypt on the one hand and those of Britain, France and Israel on the other, was the first in which Finnish troops took part. This operation was also a beginning of a new form of peacekeeping operation. The two previous UN sponsored initiatives, the UN Truce Supervision Organization (UNTSO) set up in Palestine in 1948 and the UN Military Observer Group in India and Pakistan (UNMOGIP) established in 1949, were essentially unarmed observer missions. The international force in Korea was not a UN peacekeeping operation in the accepted meaning of the term. It did not work under the control of the Security Council or General Assembly, its task did not have the consent of the parties to the conflict and it used force. In contrast to both these types of operation, the function of UNEF I was 'to secure and to supervise the cessation of hostilities' and the troops were armed only for self-defence.

Operations conducted by UNEF I in Egypt, the Sinai Desert and the Gaza Strip were divided into four phases and Finnish troops took part in the latter three. The first phase, in November and early December, was confined to Port Said and Port Fuad at the northern end of the Suez Canal. UN troops established a buffer zone between the Egyptian and Anglo-French forces and took over responsibility for security of vital installations as withdrawal from Egyptian soil progressed. One company of Finnish troops arrived on 11 December. They immediately became involved in the second phase of UNEF operations which aimed to maintain the ceasefire between the Egyptian and Israeli forces and to facilitate the Israeli withdrawal.

Operations in the Sinai Desert proved both difficult and dangerous, mainly due to extensive unmarked minefields and persisting mutual suspicion of the two remaining parties to the conflict. In spite of these problems, the Israelis had withdrawn from all Egyptian territory, except for the Gaza Strip and Sharm el Sheikh at the southern tip of the peninsula, by 22 January 1957. This was a remarkable achievement for a UN force obliged to support itself administratively on an *ad hoc* basis and, within the scope of only very general guidelines, make up its operating procedures as it went along. The third phase of UNEF operations, that of monitoring the withdrawal of Israeli forces from the Gaza Strip and Sharm el Sheikh was complete by 12 March 1957.

This first UN force of its kind was fortunate in having Major-General E. L. M. Burns of Canada as its commander. Burns had an outstanding military record and was a man of exceptional intellect. He already knew the region well, as he had been moved to command UNEF having been chief of staff of UNTSO with its headquarters in Jerusalem. This emergency transfer was to set a pattern to be followed on subsequent occasions, thus avoiding the risks of sending a man to take charge of a UN operation without previous peace-keeping experience.

Although the full benefit could not be known at the time, the Finns were also fortunate in their choice of commander for their second company with UNEF. This was Major Ensio Siilasvuo, son of the victor of Suomussalmi in the Winter War. Major Siilasvuo went on to serve as a staff officer with UNTSO in the Lebanon, to command the Finnish battalion with the UN Force in Cyprus (UNFICYP) and later to a series of senior posts with the United Nations, culminating in five years as Chief Co-ordinator of UN Peace-keeping Missions in the Middle East.

The Finnish company remained with UNEF until the fourth phase of its operations had got well under way. This entailed the deployment of UN observation posts along the Armistice Demarcation Line (ADL) and the international frontier between Egypt and Israel, starting in March 1957. This phase was to last until May 1967, but the Finnish company was withdrawn after one year's UN service in December 1957.

From this initiation into UN peace-keeping operations, it became almost standard procedure for the Under-Secretary-General for peace-keeping affairs in the New York UN Headquarters to turn to Finland whenever a new force or observer group had to be established in response to a Security Council resolution. While the Government in Helsinki did not find itself able or willing to respond on every occasion, for example in the case of the United Nations Operation in the Congo from 1960 to 1964, Finnish observers or contingents have been provided continuously from 1961. Finnish officers served with the UN Observation Group in Lebanon

(UNOGIL) during 1958, with the UN Military Observer Group in India and Pakistan (UNMOGIP) from 1961, with the UN India-Pakistan Observation Mission (UNIPOM) 1965-66 and with UN-TSO in the Middle East since 1967.

Before Finland began to provide senior officers to command UN forces or supervise the work of observer missions, there had been participation in the planning of peace-keeping operations. The office of the Secretary-General in New York has never been particularly strong in military expertise, other than through the coincidental wartime experience of men such as Brian Urquhart, an Under-Secretary-General for many years until 1986. When Secretary-General Dag Hammarskjöld sought military advice for the establishment of UNEF I in 1956-57, he turned to Finnish General Armas-Eino Martola for advice as to how the force might be structured, deployed and supported administratively. Colonel, later Major-General, Lauri Koho served as the military liaison officer in New York until 1977.

Finland was a founder contingent contributor to the UN Force in Cyprus (UNFICYP) from when it was first set up in March 1964. This United Nations' initiative was another new departure in policy, as it was concerned with the internal strife between different ethnic communities, the Greek and Turkish Cypriots. The Goverment of Cyprus requested UN assistance in an attempt to reduce inter-communal tension and disorder. Lieutenant-General Martola commanded the force from May 1966 to December 1969, thus becoming the first in a distinguished line of UN commanders and observer group supervisors from Finland.

Unlike previous UN peace-keeping tasks, the one in Cyprus called for mediation between civilian communities rather than between opposing armed forces. While the military units of UNFICYP could handle many of the problems that arose, day-to-day contact with the village people proved to be a responsibility better handled by police. This led to the formation of a civilian police contingent (UNCIV-POL). Austria provided the UNCIVPOL detachment to serve along-side the Finnish battalion. From 1964 until 1974 this group was responsible for the district of north-central Cyprus to the east of Kyrenia and down to a point to the south-east of the capital, Nicosia. Together with the Canadian battalion and the Danish UNCIVPOL unit, they were responsible for maintaining security over the narrow and winding road running north from Nicosia to

Kyrenia. This road was so vulnerable to ambush that it was necessary to run twice-daily convoys in each direction to keep the two communities in the district in touch with the capital.

The Turkish intervention in Cyprus, following the Nicosia coup attempt in 1974, dramatically changed the character of UNFICYP's task. Instead of observing potential flash points of inter-communal tension and defusing disputes between the parties, it became responsible for maintaining the ceasefire along a 125-mile front running from west to east in the by then divided island. This task was much closer to the standard form of UN operation elsewhere. The mainland Turkish forces had more than two divisions in the north of the island confronting the Greek National Guard of around one division in strength in the south.

The Finnish battalion located to the east of Kyrenia bore much of the initial brunt of the the Turkish intervention, as it was onto that part of the coast, and on the shores to the west, that the Turkish airborne and sea-assault landings were made on 20 July 1974. In exactly the same way as had occurred when Egyptian forces launched an attack across the Suez Canal the previous year, the UN troops could do little beyond report what was happening and, in Cyprus, attempt to give some protection to civilians caught up in the fighting. They had a degree of success in this but the fighting was both fierce and widespread, thereby making it impossible to attempt to intervene or mediate between the sides in many areas.

There was a lull following the calling of a conference under UN auspices in Geneva but fighting broke out again when these talks collapsed in mid-August. By that time the Finnish battalion had become responsible for the north-western sector of Nicosia, including Nicosia international airport. This had been the scene of a bitter struggle for control by the opposing forces, with significant casualties on each side. In the fighting from the onset of the Turkish intervention on 20 July to the second ceasefire on 16 August, the Finnish battalion suffered several casualties in the course of their attempts to protect civilian refugees.

In October of 1973, while UNFICYP was still engaged in trying to keep the peace between the Cypriot communities, a second emergency force (UNEF II) had been formed in Egypt when stalemate had been reached in the Yom Kippur war. At this point Ensio Siilasvuo was a major-general and serving as chief of staff of UNTSO with his headquarters in Jerusalem. It was to him that the Secretary-General turned to form, command and deploy UNEF II to supervise the ceasefire between the Egyptian and Israeli forces. As might be expected, this was easier said than done, not least because there were no UN troops readily available.

Leaving his deputy to oversee UNTSO operations, Siilasvuo flew to Cairo, established a skeleton headquarters in the UN liaison office in Heliopolis and began to put his force together. He was afterwards to concede that he had been too ambitious in his request for troops and logistic support as, experienced soldier that he was, he asked for what was actually needed. Like military commanders the world over, he received only what was available and was invited to do the best as he could with that. As the situation in Cyprus was relatively quiet at the time, UN Headquarters New York instructed Major-General Prem Chand commanding UNFICYP to form three units each of 200 men from his Austrian, Finnish and Swedish contingents and get them flown to Eygpt. In his memoirs Siilasvuo describes the delight with which he greeted the small Finnish unit under command of a known and trusted comrade, Lieutenant-Colonel Aulis Kemppainen, who had earlier served with him as an observer with UNTSO.

Small though his immediately available forces were, Siilasvuo knew the value of getting men on the ground quickly in the still confused situation. He sent Major Martti Jokihaara with fifty men to the city of Suez to persuade the Egyptian troops there to cease firing. This they achieved soon after midday on the day of their arrival, 28 October. The main party of Finns under Lieutenant-Colonel Kemppainen reached Suez the same afternoon and the first buffer zone between the Egyptian and Israeli forces was established in the eastern part of the city by nightfall. The advance party of the Swedish contingent from Cyprus was despatched to Ismailia under command of Lieutenant-Colonel Stig Edgren. 'Move there. Deploy between the parties. Solve the problem using your own ability and ideas,' were Siilasvuo's orders to Edgren. Speed of movement and exercise of initiative by commanders on the ground paid off. The Swedes also managed to establish a buffer zone between the Egyptian and Israeli forces east of Ismailia.

The small contingents sent from Cyprus were speedily replaced by full-scale battalions sent from the countries that had volunteered to send contingents to UNEF II. A newly formed battalion under command of Lieutenant-Colonel Reino Raitasaari arrived from Finland at the end of October. Raitasaari was one of Finland's most experienced UN officers, ideally suited to his new and testing task in the Sinai Desert. He was also a strong yet caring commander of soldiers. Recalling that period, General Siilasvuo mentions that some instances of alcohol abuse by Finnish troops had occurred in the early days of UN peace-keeping. This was by no means a fault confined to Finns but Raitasaari had the problem firmly under his control. Alcohol was provided only in the troops' mess and no drinking was allowed in the six hours before any duty began.

The responsibilities of UNEF II were indeed those of an emergency force. The negotiating process between the parties had scarcely begun when the troops deployed and disengagement of the former adversaries had to be brought about step by step. The setting up of buffer zones, together with observation posts to overlook them and road blocks to control access, almost invariably called for individual negotiation with the parties. The precarious positions of some OPs is well demonstrated by the photograph of 'OP Mike' in Suez shown in the last illustration section. Shelling between the parties broke out from time to time, with no regard for UN troops manning OPs. In one such incident the house in which Colonel Raitasaari had his headquarters was struck by 120 mm shells and set on fire.

As in the earlier UNEF I operation, mines laid indiscriminately in the desert were a deadly hazard. On 14 February 1974 a Finnish captain was seriously injured in an unmarked minefield. Worse was to follow. The vehicle taking the rescue party to evacuate him ran over an anti-tank mine. This killed two Finnish sergeants and injured six soldiers, four of them seriously. While such incidents are always anticipated in the course of peace-keeping operations, the bereaved parents are especially saddened by the knowledge that their lost sons were trying to bring peace to some distant place. Finland kept a battalion with UNEF II for a period of six years until August 1979, when the entire UN force was withdrawn.

The extreme suspicion with which the former adversaries regarded each other complicated and delayed the process of disengagement. Thanks to the United States Secretary of State Henry Kissinger's shuttle diplomacy, it became possible for the Sinai disengagement agreement to be signed on 18 January 1974. There subsequently emerged from this agreement a proposal for a system of linear sectors, echeloned back from the UN-controlled buffer zone, in which the adversaries were to be permitted to have only limited scales of troops, tanks and weapons. There were two key confidence-building aspects to this plan. The artillery of the two sides had to be separated by a distance great enough to prevent them shelling each other. Secondly, the ceiling on levels of troops and tanks, in the sectors running parallel with the buffer zone, had to be such as to preclude any opportunity for surprise attack. This system became the model for UN operations elsewhere.

The Arab-Israeli Yom Kippur war had been fought on two fronts and UNEF II dealt with ceasefire and disengagement arrangements only in the area east of the Suez Canal. The other battle front had been on the Golan Heights, where a situation of uneasy tension had prevailed after fighting between Israeli and Syrian forces had ground to a halt in October 1973. Although there was a very sparse line of UN posts manned by observers from UNTSO, these were inadequate to prevent a recurrence of artillery and mortar bombardment and infantry patrolling by the former adversaries in the region. Consequently the UN Disengagement Observer Force (UNDOF) was set up in June 1974. No Finnish troops were involved in this operation in the early stages. The disengagement plan of UNDOF, principally negotiated by Secretary of State Kissinger, had very similar features to that which he had devised for the Sinai.

The limited size of the Golan area of confrontation requires only two UN battalions for observation, backed up by officers detached from UNTSO to investigate all reported incidents. Initially, the two battalions were provided by Austria and Peru, but the Peruvians were replaced by an Iranian battalion after the first year of operations. When the Iranians were abruptly withdrawn in March 1979, to serve in the Lebanon, a Finnish battalion was sent to replace them and one has continued to serve with UNDOF until the present time. In addition, the force was commanded by a Finnish general in 1980-81 and again in 1985-86. Major-General Erkki Kaira was transferred from the post of chief of staff of UNTSO in February 1980 and Major-General Gustav Hägglund, whose father had been an army corps commander during the Winter and Continuation Wars, commanded in 1985-86.

The period from 1973 to 1977 marked the first instance when

Finland had two battalions deployed simultaneously with UN peace-keeping forces, one in Cyprus and one with UNEF II. This was in addition to observers with UNTSO and UNMOGIP in Kashmir. In effect, Finland was represented in every then extant UN mission. As mentioned at the start of this chapter, Finland finally removed its battalion from Cyprus in October 1977. This was at a time when a UN force to oversee the independence of Namibia (South-West Africa) was being planned and the Helsinki Government judged that this would be a very worthwhile use of resources. In the event, the operation did not take place until 1989, when Finland sent a battalion to serve with the UN Transition Assistance Group (UNTAG) to supervise elections in newly independent Namibia.

Experience of United Nations peace-keeping operations since 1956 suggests that three conditions are essential for there to be reasonable grounds for anticipating a modicum of success. First, fighting must have come to a halt, at least in the key areas of conflict; second, there must be a genuine desire for peace by the parties; third, the arrangements for the UN to maintain the ceasefire and disengage the adversaries must be practicable and seen to be so.

With the exception of the UN Operation in the Congo (ONUC) in 1960-64, these conditions may be said to have applied to some significant degree in all cases up to establishment of the UN Interim Force in Lebanon (UNIFIL) in 1978. Although there was an illusion that the three vital conditions could be brought to apply in the Lebanon, events turned out quite differently. This was in part due to the failure of Israel actually to honour the terms of Security Council resolution 425 (1978), which called for the complete withdrawal of their forces. The consequently confused situation was compounded because neither the PLO nor what became known as the *de facto* forces of the South Lebanon Christian Militia were ever fully under control of their leadership. Both failed to honour their promises of cooperation with UNIFIL.

Finland had officers serving as observers or staff officers with UNTSO who became involved in the setting up of UNIFIL. More significantly, General Siilasvuo had by that time become the Chief Coordinator of UN Missions in the Middle East, located in Jerusalem. He was given responsibility for forming UNIFIL and, in line with the practice by then established, sent the chief of staff of UNTSO to command the force. This was Major-General Alexander

Erskine, of Ghana. As the UN contingents began to arrive, it became abundantly clear that none of the requisite conditions obtained for peace-keeping success. The fighting between Israeli and militia forces on the one hand, and with the PLO on the other, continued almost unabated. There was no indication that any of the parties genuinely desired peace, other than on terms manifestly unacceptable to the others, and UNIFIL was bereft of any means to discharge its mandate.

It may well be that future seminars on UN peace-keeping operations will point to the situation in Lebanon as an example of when a UN commitment should not be undertaken. Yet, in spite of being unable to confirm the Israeli withdrawal or restore international peace and security to the area, UNIFIL brought significant benefit to many people of Lebanon. While the *de facto* forces and those of the PLO pushed UNIFIL troops aside on many occasions, taking advantage of infinitely superior firepower, an area of some 350 square miles to the east of the port of Tyre gradually became a comparatively safe haven for thousands of Lebanese civilians wishing only to live in peace. The force has also been able to keep UN Headquarters in New York and the outside world informed of what is happening in the south of the country.

Finland has provided one of the seven battalions required to make up UNIFIL since December 1982. Successive units have been responsible for the security of the north-east sector of UNIFIL's main area of operations – around Al Qantarah and Al Tayyibah, immediately south of the Crusaders' fortress at Château de Beaufort. Fatalities amongst UNIFIL troops have been high for any peace-keeping operation. Finland has had four men killed in Lebanon since 1982. Immediately following his period in command of UNDOF 1985-86, Major-General Gustav Hägglund of Finland was appointed to command UNIFIL for two years until 1988. This was at the special request of the United Nations Secretary-General. Hägglund proved to be a strong-willed and determined commander, who was able to strengthen the local status of UNIFIL and to increase the confidence of the various parties in the impartiality and value of the force.

In order to have a proper understanding of UN operations in the Middle East, it is essential to appreciate the continuing important role of UNTSO. This observer force was first established after the Arab-Israeli War of 1948 and is unique among UN missions in that its mandate is open-ended. This has permitted its use, untrammelled by need for renewal of its authority, as a ready source of observers and mediators in any dispute and as a reservoir of peace-keeping expertise throughout the region of the Arab-Israeli conflict. More than 500 Finnish officers have served as observers or staff officers with UNTSO since 1967. Three Finnish officers have served as head of the mission (chief of staff). These are Major-General Ensio Siilasvuo (1970-73), Major-General Erkki Kaira (1980-81) and Major-General Hans Christensen (1990-92).

Whatever the degree of international scepticism that greeted the formation of UNIFIL in the Lebanon, it cannot have compared with the doubt surrounding the chances of success of UNGOMAP – the United Nations Good Offices Mission to Afghanistan and Pakistan – established under the Afghanistan/Pakistan Geneva Accord of 1988. 'There is no precedent for them [the UN] to draw on for an operation of this kind,' telexed one correspondent from Islamabad. He was mistaken, as a similar style operation on a much smaller scale had been undertaken by the United Nations Yemen Observation Mission (UNYOM) in 1963-64, but it turned out to be a very trying and delicate mission just the same.

UN contingents were not called for in this operation, only experienced observers and mediators of patience and determination. Finland found two such men who, in succession, served as the military head of the mission. These were Major-General Rauli Helminen (1988-89) and Colonel Heikki Happonen (1989-90). Helminen had served as an observer with UNTSO and chief operations officer with UNFICYP. He was an officer of the anti-aircraft artillery and son of Colonel Frans Edvard Helminen who commanded the Finnish anti-aircraft artillery during the Winter War. Colonel Happonen had served as second-in-command of the Finnish battalion with UNEF II in the Sinai in 1977-78. The only comment that it is realistic to make on the success or otherwise of this UN operation is to record that the Soviet troops left Afghanistan on time.

Finland also provided fifteen military observers for the United Nations Iran-Iraq Military Observer Group, which was established to monitor the ceasefire in the Iran-Iraq War on 20 July 1987. The Finnish observers served on the Iranian side of the ceasefire line from August 1988 to March 1991. Colonels Timo Mäkipää and Henry Purola were successively chief of staff of this UN mission.

During the period from April 1989 to March 1990, Finland had three battalions serving with UN missions abroad. In addition to those serving with UNDOF on the Golan Heights and UNIFIL in the turbulent Lebanon, a Finnish battalion joined UNTAG, the UN Transition Assistance Group in Namibia. The primary purpose of this observer group was to oversee free and fair elections and transfer to independence of South-West Africa, which had been administered by the South African Government under a mandate of the League of Nations and later the United Nations, since 1919. There was some concern lest the forces of SWAPO, the South West Africa People's Organization, might sweep across the border from Angola where they had been based for more than twenty years. In the event, this threat did not materialize and, with very few and minor exceptions, the elections were carried out peacefully.

The Secretary-General's Special Representative in Namibia and head of the mission was himself a Finn, Mr Martti Ahtisaari, who had been engaged in the negotiations leading up to Namibia's independence. This UN operation was one which brought special satisfaction to the contributing nations. The conditions for success were apparent. There was at least tacit agreement between the parties, there was a genuine desire for peace and, although an outbreak had been suggested, no significant violence occurred. UNTAG stayed on after the elections while the new Constituent Assembly worked out a constitution and set the day, 21 March 1990, for independence. Appreciation of the work of the UN soldiers was evident almost everywhere and, perhaps most satisfying of all considerations, the observer group was able to withdraw in March 1990 in the certain knowledge that their mission had been accomplished. Namibia became the 160th UN member state on 23 April the same year.

None of the three essential conditions for success of peace-keeping operations was evident in Yugoslavia, following the outbreak of civil war in 1991. Even so, the United Nations felt unable to stand aside from this internal conflict. Twelve nations agreed to contribute battalion strength units to the UN Protection Force (UNPROFOR), of which one was Finland. Once again, the country had three battalions deployed on UN service overseas. Security Council resolution 749 (1992) authorized the full deployment of UNPROFOR, primarily with the aim of defusing tension on the mutual borders of Serbia and Croatia. Very quickly afterwards the most violent and bitter fighting of the civil war broke out in Bosnia-Herzegovina. The Finnish engineer construction battalion was sent to the Croatian capital Zagreb, from where it deployed to four separate UN-protected areas in Croatia to build camps for infantry battalions of UNPROFOR in or close by the disputed border territories. Also in 1992, five Finnish officer observers were sent to serve with the UN mission in Somalia.

Since first providing troops in 1956, Finland has contributed a total of more than 30,000 men for United Nations duty. Thirty-six Finnish soldiers have been killed or have died during this service. Currently, around 1,000 troops are deployed overseas at any one time. Finland maintains a UN stand-by force under the direct control of the Ministry of Defence in Helsinki. This is quite separate from Finland's defence forces under command of the Defence Staff (previously General Headquarters). This distinction reflects the policy that every officer or man who serves with a UN force or observer group from Finland is a volunteer, each one carefully selected from those who wish to serve. In most years the numbers of applicants exceed the places available by more than six to one. Volunteers are accepted from regular officers and NCOs, who account for around eight percent of the total, and from military reservists who have completed their conscript training. The reservist volunteers undertake a one-year contract to be at seven days' notice to join a UN mission. During this period they continue with their civilian work until they are called.

In common with the other Nordic nations, Finland provides training for selected volunteers for UN service, running a military observers' course for all four nations three times each year. In parallel, Denmark runs an annual course for UN military police, Norway one for logistic officers and Sweden one for UN staff officers. No Finnish soldier is allowed to go on UN service overseas until he has passed the course at the UN Training Centre at Niinisalo near Pori in southwestern Finland. It is here that the military observers' courses are run for officers nominated from Denmark, Norway and Sweden, as well as those from Finland.

The training system for officer and reservist volunteers is based on a routine cycle designed to replace one third of each Finnish contingent serving with the UN at three points in the year. Approximately 350 to 400 men are under training at any one time. It is necessary to accept more men for training than will actually be required, so as to leave a margin to reject those volunteers who prove to be either physically or intellectually unsuitable. Training is concentrated on refreshing the military skills of the volunteers, teaching first aid for those wounded or injured and the psychological approach to methods of peace-keeping. Emphasis is placed on UN operating and reporting procedures that are virtually standard to every form of UN mission, and on the care that must be taken in the face-to-face contact with either the military or civilian elements of the parties to a conflict. It is preferred that every volunteer is able to speak English to a standard accepted for radio communications.

Following Finland's pledge to provide a battalion for Namibia in 1978, a stand-by force was formed, trained and equipped. When it became apparent that the battalion would not be needed immediately, the volunteers were returned to their civilian employment and the unit remained in being on paper only. Due to political developments in southern Africa evolving more slowly than anticipated, the force was not required until eleven years later. The effort was not wasted, however, as the stand-by force was used to fulfil Finland's commitment to UNIFIL in the Lebanon in 1982. This experience led the Ministry of Defence in Helsinki to establish the principle of holding a stand-by force available on a permanent basis.

The organization of the stand-by force is shown in Appendix 12. This simply provides the organization for a three-company battalion with its own specialist and logistic support sub-units. The organization is designed to be quickly adapted to meet the specific requirements of any Finnish contingent despatched on UN service. As in the case of the troops trained for Namibia, the volunteers are returned to their civilian jobs after training. The equipment and material for the stand-by force is provided from stocks held by the Regular Army. The latest example of such a deloyment was the Finnish battalion sent to join UNPROFOR in Yugoslavia in April 1992.

Since joining the United Nations in 1955, Finland has contributed some 2,200 million Finnmarks, equivalent to 440 million US dollars at the early 1993 exchange rate, for peace-keeping operations and observer missions. Of this sum, around half only has been refunded. This is due to the UN's own financial difficulties, arising out of ever-increasing peace-keeping responsibilities, imposed by either the Security Council or General Assembly. In addition, some member states have failed to pay their contributions to the world body on time or, in some instances, to pay them at all. At 1993 prices, Finland's participation in UN peace-keeping activities amounts to the equivalent of US$ 3,240 per man per month, with approximately thirty percent of this sum being reimbursed from the UN peace-keeping budget.

Max Jacobson, who had been the Finnish ambassador to the UN for six years, was the Scandinavian countries' nomination for the post of Secretary-General in the election of 1971. This distinguished diplomat and authority on international affairs appeared to be ideally suited to the post. He was appropriately experienced and had a facility to encapsulate a complex dispute in a pithy and humorous manner, which had already won him many friends internationally. Jacobson's nomination was vetoed by the then Soviet Union, perhaps because the Kremlin was apprehensive of having a man who understood the issues so clearly at the heart of the business of peace.

The moral and manpower contribution of Finland towards UN peace-keeping is far beyond the proportion that might reasonably be expected from a nation of less than five million people. This is a record and standard of which every Finn is justifiably proud. As the international reputation won in the Winter War fades a little with each new generation, an esteem of a different kind is gradually taking its place. Now Finland is thought of as the nation to which the United Nations Secretary-General turns without hesitation when the core of a new peace-keeping mission is needed. The Nobel Prize for Peace was awarded to the peace-keeping forces of the United Nations in 1988. This was an event of which the Finns made special mark.

Epilogue

Epilogue

As they celebrate seventy-five years of independence from Imperial Russia, the Finns are looking forward, rather than over their shoulders. As a nation and as individuals, they are untroubled by any nostalgia for the past. Their best opportunities are ahead and there is every indication that they will grasp them as resolutely as they have defended their freedom. They are politically and socially one nation, in which the early twentieth-century distinction between the 'hats' and the 'caps' is long forgotten. The same can be said about the language dispute, other than that a taxi-driver might remark, when told to whom he is taking you to meet, 'Ah, that is a Swedish name!' But taxi-drivers often incline towards the extremes of debate.

Emergence from the chrysalis into statehood has certainly not been easy. While the epic of the Winter War gave Finland internal cohesion and international recognition in large measure for the first time, there have been dark patches. Treatment of the Red Guard prisoners after the War of Independence in 1918 was inhumane and unnecessary. Arguments that they remained a threat to national stability or that one is misjudging events of a different era do not stand up. The victory of the Whites was complete and the Finns already had a broadly established liberal tradition.

So far as the outside world is concerned, the heroic stand against Bolshevist aggression in the Winter War has obscured the ill-fated adventure to regain the lands the Soviet Union had occupied. Historians will concern themselves with that phase only to try to assess how differently events might have turned out if Finland had been able to stand aloof when Germany made war on the Soviet Union in 1941. Aside from the loss of 65,000 Finnish lives, the thought must linger with the generation now growing old that, if only the 'inner circle' led by Ryti and Mannerheim had been able to avoid further war in 1941, the Western Allies might have been better able and disposed to demand territorial concessions in favour of Finland at the final peace settlement.

The limbo years, while the Soviet Union apparently hung like an avalanche over Finland's independence, clouded the international community's perception of a country that was in fact firmly independent and skilfully led. It seemed that the epithet 'Finlandization', mischievously used by Franz-Josef Strauss in the 1960s, could not be dismissed. An incident during a Soviet military exercise in 1984, when a rogue ballistic missile penetrated Finnish air space and crashed into a frozen lake in Lapland, was given wide publicity in the West. Criticism by some NATO nations of Finland's failure to intercept the missile might be judged hypocritical in view of their own attitudes to the problems of defence.

Finland's national determination to uphold a neutral stance has been underlined by a steady strengthening of her armed forces. The five-year plan for 1976-81 included a budget of 2,300 million Finnmarks to acquire no less than ninety-five percent of the new weapons and equipment identified as essential. The 1980s were designated the decade of the Army and a target strength of a quarter of a million men was set for emergency deployment within days. Scepticism as to Finland's capability and determination to stand independently, expressed in some Western capitals and by the NATO high command in particular, were ill-judged in light of these events.

Scandinavia's role in contributing troops to United Nations' peace-keeping operations has become so established in international awareness that Finland's significant part in this has not received the recognition it plainly deserves. This is changing for the better, as the UN Organization emerges from decades of doubtful potency. Finland has servicemen with almost every UN peace-keeping mission and has provided an impressive line of competent and experienced UN force commanders – in Cyprus, the Sinai, on the Golan Heights, in Lebanon and in Afghanistan. The first military adviser to the UN Secretary-General was a Finn, as was the first and only coordinator of all the UN Middle-East Missions. Three Finnish generals have served as chief of staff of the Jerusalem-based UN Truce Supervision Organization. No other nation has a comparable record.

If Finland first burst on world consciousness when the Soviet Union launched its unprovoked attack on 30 November 1939, the nation took a lasting place in history with the launch of what has become known as the 'Helsinki Process'. The Conference on Security and Cooperation in Europe (CSCE) opened in the Finnish capital on 3 July 1973. After meetings in other European capitals, the Final Act of the CSCE was adopted in Helsinki on 1 August 1975. The preamble speaks of 'efforts to make détente both a continuing and increasingly viable and comprehensive process'.

As with virtually every initiative designed to provide better chances for peace and security, the Helsinki Process was greeted with cynicism by some governments – in spite of their participation. That perception has now been replaced by views not only of greater optimism abroad but also by a sense of greater urgency. The impasse of the Cold War situation has given way to an outbreak of nationalist and other unhelpful emotions that are fast becoming local threats to peace in widely separated areas of political tension. The veteran Finnish expert on international affairs Max Jacobson, writing in 1987, drew attention to the Helsinki Process as the 'idea of peaceful change' and remarked that 'maintaining a balance between stability and change will require skilful management'. Solid accomplishment towards that balance began to materialize with the signing of the CSCE Treaty in Paris in November 1990, which brought a virtual end to East-West military confrontation. Helsinki has grown from being the cradle of the conference to become its guardian and upholder. The gathering of nations in the Finnish capital in June 1992 was brisk and businesslike, with the immediate problems of security in south-eastern Europe high on the agenda.

An end to Moscow's tight hold on matters of security throughout the former Soviet Union, while welcomed in a liberal political sense by the Finns, has brought concern about stability beyond their eastern frontier. There is even a Russian politician who draws attention to himself by laying claim to the Czar's lost Grand Duchy. More serious views are taken in Helsinki of Russian hesitation over withdrawal of their armed forces from the Baltic states and the continued possibility of further fragmentation of control and influence within the Commonweath of Independent States. Whilst maintaining a strict stance of non-alignment, Finland is once again seeking contacts that will assist her in holding to that position.

Conversations, and it should be stressed that they are nothing more than that, have been opened at Secretary-General level with NATO and the Western European Union. There is as yet no prospect of Finland becoming a member of either of these alliances, but observer status with one or both would seem to be a practical proposition. Defence cooperation with Sweden is again under consideration. In the operational sphere at the start of 1993, this seems unlikely to go beyond joint or correlative surveillance of airspace and adjacent seas, together with some intelligence gathering. Collaborative defence procurement projects with Sweden already have a sound historical basis and there is no reason for them not to develop.

As the century of Finland's independence comes towards its close, with petty rivalry, poverty and war abroad, the Finns can claim to have endured their share of hardship. Their participation in international events may have been forced upon them in 1939 and again in 1941. More recently, their example of steadfast practical support for United Nations peace-keeping operations and for the launch of the 'Helsinki Process' has provided a much wider than national conscience for peace.

Appendices

I

The 27th Jäger Battalion (1916-1918)

This unit had its origin in the Jäger Movement, which arose out of the wider movement for Finnish independence at the outbreak of the Second World War. 183 Finnish volunteers, of an average age of twenty-four, began military training at Lockstedt in Germany in February 1915. This was under a special arrangement made with the German authorities in December 1914.

The early graduates from the course were returned to Finland to help to recruit more volunteers and to be prepared for military action if and when a suitable opportunity presented itself. The training detachment was enlarged to a strength of 2,000 in August 1915 and the unit granted the title of 'The King's Prussian Jäger Battalion 27' in the Imperial German Army on 9 May 1916.

The Battalion was given a formal establishment of 1,800 men under command of Major Maximillian Bayer, of the German Army, and comprised:

Four infantry (or rifle) companies under command of Captains Erich Höcker, von Mangoldt, Ulrich von Coler and Eduard Ausfeld.

An artillery battery, commanded by Lieutenant Frantzen.

A machine-gun company, commanded by Captain Rainer Stahel.

A pioneer company, commanded by Captain Walter Just.

The battalion was deployed on active service on the Eastern Front, against the Imperial Russian Army, in late 1916 and part of 1917. An advance party from the battalion returned to Finland in October 1917 and the main body, less all but two of its German officers, reached Vaasa on 25 February 1918. On Mannerheim's order, the battalion was then disbanded to provide urgently needed commanders and instructors for the White Guard units engaged in the War of Independence.

In later years, a total of forty-nine of the volunteers who had trained with the battalion reached the rank of general officer in Finland's independent armed forces. Of these, Generals Aarne Sihvo, Erik Heinrichs, Kaarlo Heiskanen and Lieutenant-Generals Hugo Österman and Jarl Lundqvist all served as commander-in-chief. General Sihvo was twice C-in-C : from 1926 to 1933 and again from 1946 to 1953.

Aircraft of the Finnish Air Force
in the Winter War 1939

Fighter/Interceptors

   36 x Fokker D-XXI single-seat monoplanes, mounting 4 x 7.62 mm
      calibre machine-guns.

   10 x Bristol Bulldog IVA biplanes mounting 2 x .303 inch calibre Vickers
      machine-guns.

Bombers

   14 x Bristol Blenheim Mark 1 twin-engined monoplanes with a bomb
      payload of 1,350 lbs to 2,000 lbs and a range of 375 miles.

    7 x Junkers K43 single-engined mono-seaplanes with a maximum bomb
      payload of around 1,000 lbs and a range of 250 miles.

Reconnaissance/bombers and army cooperation aircraft

   29 x Fokker CX reconnaissance/bomber single-engined biplanes with a
      bomb payload of 440 lbs and a maximum range of 300 miles.

    7 x Fokker C.VE reconnaissance/bomber single-engined biplanes.

   15 x Blackburn Ripon IIF maritime reconnaissance aircraft.

Received during the course of the war

Fighter/Interceptors

   30 x Gloster Gladiator single-seat biplanes from Britain.

   30 x Morane 406 single-seat modern monoplanes from France.

Army cooperation, trainers and other aircraft

   22 x Gloster Gauntlet II single-engined biplanes from Britain.

   11 x Co-operation, training and transport aircraft from Sweden.

Aircraft of the Finnish Air Force at the Start of the Continuation War 1941

Fighter/Interceptors

43 x Brewster 239 single-seat monoplanes, mounting 4 x 7.62 mm calibre machine-guns, 2 in the fuselage and 2 in the wings.

32 x Fiat G-50 single-seat monoplanes, with a top speed of 290 mph, mounting 2 x 12.7 mm calibre heavy machine-guns.

23 x Fokker D-XXI single-seat monoplanes, mounting 4 x 7.62 mm calibre machine-guns.

16 x Gloster Gladiator II single-seat biplanes, mounting 2 x .303 inch calibre machine-guns.

9 x Hawker Hurricane single-seat monoplanes, with a top speed of 328 mph, mounting 8 x .303 inch calibre machine-guns.

37 x Morane 406 single-seat monoplanes, mounting one 20 mm cannon firing through the propeller hub and 2 x 7.5 mm machine-guns.

A total of 160 fighter/interceptors of which all but the 16 Gladiators were of modern design.

Bombers

29 x Bristol Blenheim Mark I or IV twin-engined monoplanes.

5 x Ex-Soviet Ilyushin DB-3 twin-engined, monoplanes, with a bomb payload of 1,000 lbs and a maximum range of over 450 miles.

8 x Ex-Soviet Tupolev SB-2 or SB-2 bis twin-engined monoplanes.

A total of 42 bombers of modern design.

Reconnaissance and army cooperation aircraft

25 x Fokker CX single-engined reconnaiassance biplanes.

10 x Fokker C.VE single-engined reconnaissance biplanes.

2 x Ex-Swedish Koolhoven FK 52 army cooperation aircraft.

11 x Westland Lysander high-wing reconnaissance monoplanes.

15 x Blackburn Ripon II maritime reconnaissance aircraft.

4
Order of Battle of the Finnish Army and of the Red Army Invasion Force at 30 November 1939

Finnish Army (deployed for defence)

Army of the Isthmus (Österman) comprising:
  II Army Corps (Öhquist) : three divisions on the western side of the Karelian Isthmus.
  III Army Corps (Heinrichs) : two divisions on the eastern side of the Karelian Isthmus.

IV Army Corps (Heiskanen) : two divisions in Ladoga-Karelia to the north of Lake Ladoga.

Northern Finland Group (Tuompo) : independent battalions and frontier troops, some 16,000 men, with one company of infantry and an artillery battery at Petsamo.

C-in-C's Reserve : Headquarters I Army Corps (Laatikainen) and two divisions.

One infantry regiment under naval command for coastal defence.

Total: 156,000 men, 422 artillery pieces and 25 tanks.

Red Army (deployed for attack)

7th Army (Jakoviev): eight divisions and four tank brigades facing into the Karelian Isthmus.

8th Army (Habarov): seven divisions and one tank brigade poised for the flanking movement north of Lake Ladoga.

9th Army (Duhanov): five divisions opposite the central sector of the eastern frontier, poised to make the two-pronged attack across the waist of Finland.

14th Army (Frolov): two divisions opposite the extreme northern sector of the eastern frontier ready to occupy Petsamo and the Fisherman's Peninsula.

Total: 460,000 men, 2,000 artillery pieces and 2,000 tanks.

5

Statement Issued by the Finnish Government Following Declaration of a Soviet Naval Blockade

After the aggression against Finland the Soviet Union declared that a state of war did not exist. She has therefore no right now to take blockade measures, which involve not only Finland but other nations.

A blockade in time of peace is permissible only against countries which have violated certain stipulations of the League of Nations – as indeed Russia has done by invading Finland. To be legal, moreover, a blockade must be effective, as was stipulated by the Declaration of Paris of 1856, signed by all civilized countries, including Russia.

As far as is known, Russia has no ship at the moment in the Gulf of Bothnia; and no ship can enter, since the Åland Sea has been closed by mines. Hence, if the blockade concerns the Gulf of Bothnia, it is obviously without legal as well as practical significance.

It is unlikely also that Russia will be able to blockade the Gulf of Finland effectively considering the length of its coast and the inadequacy of the Russian Fleet to carry out such an operation. Finland, thanks to her coastal defences, aviation, service vessels and mines, can take effective measures to prevent Russia from carrying out the blockade.

8 December 1939

Published in *The War Illustrated*, 29 December 1939

6

Comparison of Finnish and Soviet Losses
in the Winter War

Finland

Servicemen : 22,425 killed, 43,557 wounded or injured and 1,434 reported missing in action

Civilians   : 1,029 killed but many more injured or wounded

Aircraft   : 62 of a total complement of 253, including 93 aircraft received from abroad during the war

Artillery   : 25 guns

Tanks   : 5 of the 30 used during the war

Shipping   : 10 merchant vessels in the Baltic Sea

Territory   : 22,000 square miles ceded to the Soviet Union under the imposed Treaty of Moscow

Soviet Union

Servicemen : an estimated 53,500 killed, 176,000 wounded or injured and 16,000 reported missing in action, of whom 5,469 were taken prisoner by the Finns

Aircraft   : an estimated 200 destroyed in the air by Finnish fighter aircraft and a further 300 either brought down by anti-aircraft fire or destroyed on the ground

Artillery   : several hundred pieces

Tanks and armoured vehicles   : 2,300 including armoured cars

Shipping   : 2 submarines lost, plus 2 battleships and at least 1 destroyer damaged by coastal artillery fire

7
Exchange of Letters between British Prime Minister Winston Churchill and Field Marshal Mannerheim, 1941

Personal, secret and private   29 November 1941

Prime Minister to Field Marshal Mannerheim,

   I am deeply grieved at what I see coming, namely, that we shall be forced within a few days, out of loyalty to our ally Russia, to declare war on Finland. If we do this, we shall make war also as opportunity serves. Surely your troops have advanced far enough for security during the war and could now simply halt and give leave? It is not necessary to make any public declaration, but simply leave off fighting and cease military operations for which the weather affords every reason, and make a de facto exit from the war.

   I wish I could convince Your Excellency that we are going to beat the Nazis. I feel far more confident than in 1917 or 1918. It would be most painful to the many friends of your country in England if Finland found herself in the dock with the guilty and defeated Nazis. My recollections of our pleasant talks and correspondence about the last war lead me to send you this purely personal and private message for your consideration before it is too late.

Personal, secret and private   2nd December 1941

Field Marshal Mannerheim to Prime Minister Churchill,

   Yesterday I had the honour to receive through the American Minister in Helsinki your letter of November 29, 1941, and I thank you for your kindness in sending me this private message. I am sure that you will realise it is impossible for me to halt the military operations at present being carried out before the troops have reached the positions which in my opinion will provide us with necessary security.

   It would be deplorable if these measures, undertaken for the security of Finland, should bring my country into conflict with England, and it would deeply sadden me if England felt herself forced to declare war on Finland. It was very good of you to send me a personal message in these critical days, and I appreciate it fully.

Treaty of Friendship, Cooperation and Mutual Assistance between the Soviet Union and the Finnish Republic, Moscow, 6 April 1948

The Articles

ARTICLE I. In the event of Finland or the Soviet Union, across the territory of Finland, becoming the object of military aggression on the part of Germany or any State allied to the latter, Finland, loyal to her duty as an inependent State, will fight to repulse the aggression. In doing so, Finland will direct all the forces at her disposal to the inviolability of her territory on land, on sea and in the air, acting within her boundaries in accordance with her obligations under the present Treaty, with the assistance, in case of need, of the Soviet Union or jointly with the latter. In the cases indicated above, the Soviet Union will render Finland the necessary assistance, in regard to the granting of which the parties will agree between themselves.

ARTICLE II. The High Contracting Parties will consult each other in the event of a threat of military attack envisaged in Article I being ascertained.

ARTICLE III. The High Contracting Parties affirm their intention to participate most sincerely in all actions aimed at preserving international peace and security in conformity with the aims and principles of the United nations Organization.

ARTICLE IV. The High Contracting Parties reaffirm the undertaking, contained in Article III of the Peace Treaty signed in Paris on 10 February 1947, not to conclude any alliance and not to take part in coalitions aimed against the other High Contracting Party.

ARTICLE V. The High Contracting Parties affirm their determination to act in the spirit of cooperation and friendship with the object of further promoting and consolidating the economic and cultural ties between the Soviet Union and Finland.

ARTICLE VI. The High Contracting Parties undertake to observe the principles of mutual respect for their State sovereignty and independence as well as non-interference in the domestic affairs of the other State.

ARTICLE VII. Implementations of the present Treaty will conform to the principles of the United Nations Organization.

ARTICLE VIII. The present Treaty is subject to ratification, and will be valid for ten years as from the day of it coming into force. The Treaty will come into force as from the day of the exchange of ratification instruments, which will be effected in Helsinki within the shortest possible time. Unless either of the High Contracting Parties denounces the Treaty one year before the expiration of the above-mentioned ten-year term, it will remain in force for each of the next five-year terms until either of the High Contracting Parties gives notice in writing of its intention to terminate the operation of the Treaty.

9
Finnish Army Order of Battle, Weapons and Equipment 1993

General Forces

Two armoured brigades:

Armoured battalions	T-72 MBTs, BMB-1s, BMB-2s and MTLBs.
Artillery regiment	24 x 122 mm SP howitzers.
Anti-aircraft battalion	AA gun battery (18 x 23 mm), SAM (Grotale NG) battery and SA-16 battery (20 launchers).
Anti-tank missile company	Missile launchers.

Ten Jäger brigades:

Each 4 x Jäger battalions	
Artillery regiment	APCs or all-terrain carriers, 120 mm mortars, 36 x 122 or 152 mm towed guns.
Anti-aircraft battalion	18 x 23 mm guns and light AA missiles.
Anti-tank missile company	Missile launchers.

Fourteen infantry brigades, organized and equipped as for Jäger brigades but without APCs. The artillery regiment has 36 x 122 or 152 mm guns. Instead of an AA battalion, each brigade has two AA gun batteries.

Four anti-aircraft regiments equipped with 23 mm, 35 mm, 57 mm guns and SA-3, SA-7, SA-16 AA missiles and Crotale NG (New Generation) missile systems.

Detached anti-tank companies equipped with Fagot and TOW anti-tank missiles, Apilas heavy anti-tank weapons, S-58 recoilless guns and M-72 light anti-tank weapons.

Local Troops

Coastal artillery brigades, comprising: coastal regiments (100 mm & 130 mm turret guns in fortresses), coastal artillery battalion (130 mm towed guns), coastal missile battery (RBS-15 AS (anti-ship) missiles), one rifle battalion, one local defence battalion, one coastal Jäger company and light anti-aircraft batteries.

Some 50 independent battalions and some 200 local defence units.

Published by the authority of The Defence Staff, Helsinki

Finnish Naval Order of Battle and Weapons 1993

Corvette/command ships

Two, the *Karjala* and *Turunmaa*, of 750 displacement tons, top speed of 35 knots and armament of:

one 120mm (Bofors) naval gun, two 40mm (Bofors) air-defence cannon and two 23mm guns.

two 2/RBU 1200 5-tube anti-submarine (AS) missile launchers and depth charges.

Missile fast-attack vessels

Eleven of the Helsinki, Rauma and Tuima classes:

Helsinki class (four) 260 tons, with one 57 mm (Bofors) gun, two 23 mm air-defence guns and anti-ship RBS-15 (Saab) surface-to-surface missiles and depth charges.

Rauma class (four) 250 tons, with one 40 mm (Bofors) air-defence gun and surface-to-air (Matra) and anti-ship RBS-15 (Saab) surface- to-surface missiles and also depth charges.

Tuima class (three) 250 ton vessels, with two 30 mm air-defence guns and four OSA II-class or Styx surface-to-surface missiles.

One of the Tuima class vessels is to be modernized and converted to be a fast minelayer.

Patrol craft

Five 'R Class' of 100 to 130 tons, with a top speed of 17 knots and armed with two 23 mm twin air-defence guns and two RBU 1200 5-tube anti-submarine missile launcher and also depth charges.

Motor gunboats

Six Nuoli class of 40 tons, with a top speed of 40 knots and armed with one 23 mm air-defence gun, one 12.7 mm machine-gun and also depth charges.

Minelayers

One Pohjanmaa class of 1,000 tons, capable of laying between 100 and 150 mines and armed with one 120 mm (Bofors) naval gun, two 40 mm (Bofors) air-defence cannon and four 23 mm twin air-defence guns and also 2/RBU 1200 5-tube anti-submarine missile launchers.

Two Hameena class, also of 1,000 tons and capable of laying between 150 and 200 mines, armed with Matra surface-to-air missiles, two 40 mm

(Bofors) air-defence cannon and two 23 mm twin air-defence guns.

Three Pansio class of 450 tons, each capable of laying 50 to 100 mines and armed with two 23 mm twin air-defence guns.

Minesweepers

Six Kuha class of 90 tons, armed with one 23mm twin air-defence gun and one of 12.7 mm machine-gun and fitted with influence magnetic, acoustic and mechanical mine-sweeping systems.

Seven Kiiski class of 17 tons, armed with 12.7 mm machine-guns and with magnetic influence, acoustic and mechanical sweeping systems.

Published by the authority of The Defence Staff, Helsinki

Finnish Air Force Tasks and Deployment 1993

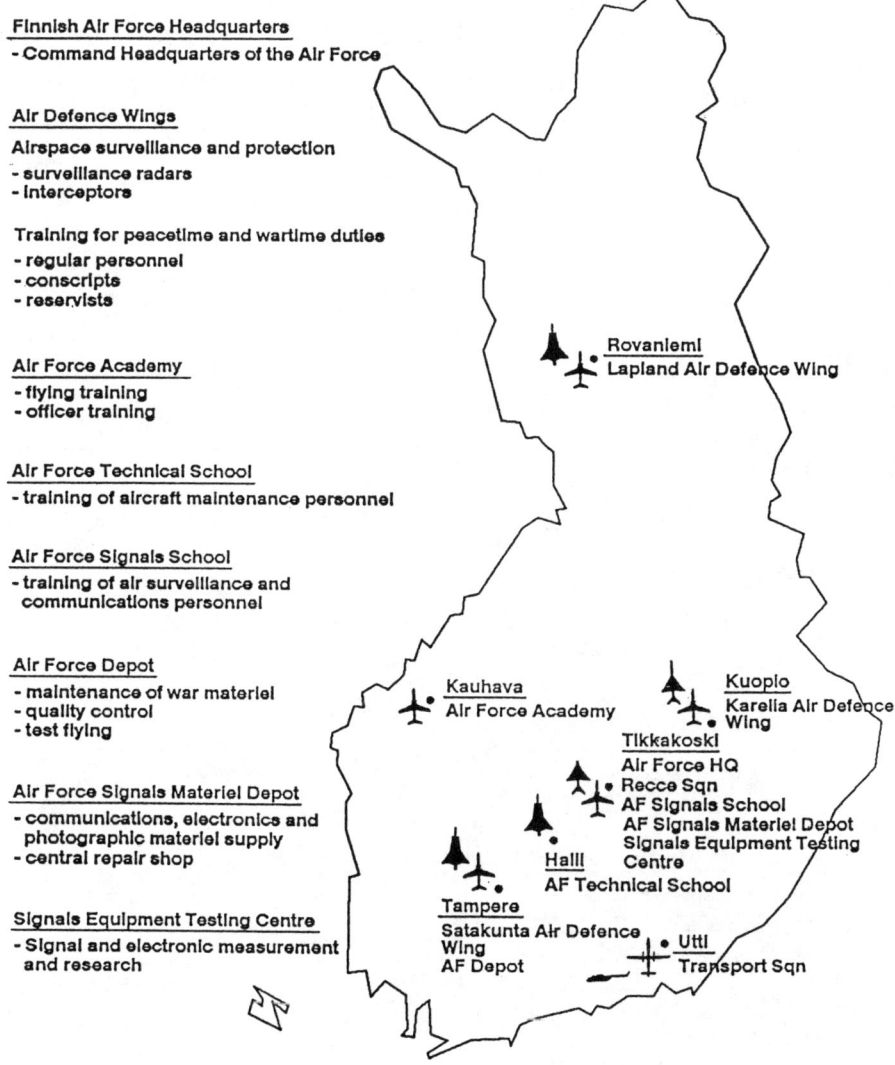

Finnish Air Force Headquarters
- Command Headquarters of the Air Force

Air Defence Wings

Airspace surveillance and protection
- surveillance radars
- interceptors

Training for peacetime and wartime duties
- regular personnel
- conscripts
- reservists

Air Force Academy
- flying training
- officer training

Air Force Technical School
- training of aircraft maintenance personnel

Air Force Signals School
- training of air surveillance and
  communications personnel

Air Force Depot
- maintenance of war materiel
- quality control
- test flying

Air Force Signals Materiel Depot
- communications, electronics and
  photographic materiel supply
- central repair shop

Signals Equipment Testing Centre
- Signal and electronic measurement
  and research

Rovaniemi
Lapland Air Defence Wing

Kauhava
Air Force Academy

Kuopio
Karelia Air Defence Wing

Tikkakoski
Air Force HQ
Recce Sqn
AF Signals School
AF Signals Materiel Depot
Signals Equipment Testing
Centre

Halli
AF Technical School

Tampere
Satakunta Air Defence Wing
AF Depot

Utti
Transport Sqn

Published by authority of the Defence Staff, Helsinki

The Finnish UN Stand-by Force 1993

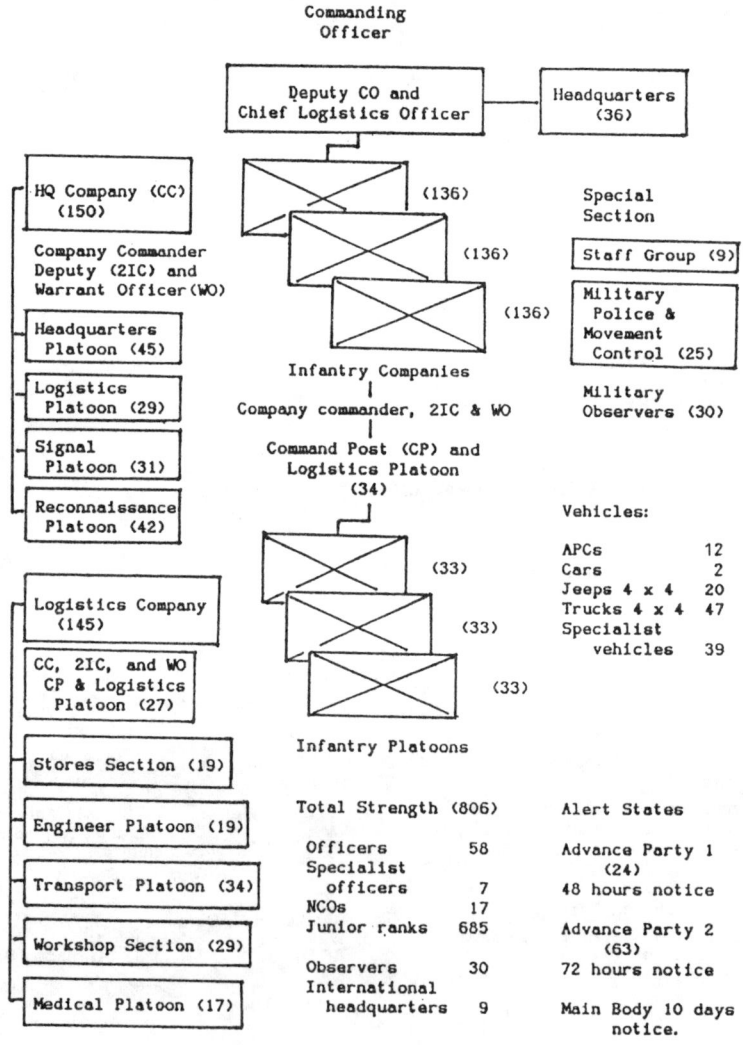

Commanding
Officer

Deputy CO and
Chief Logistics Officer → Headquarters (36)

HQ Company (CC) (150)

Company Commander
Deputy (2IC) and
Warrant Officer(WO)

Headquarters
Platoon (45)

Logistics
Platoon (29)

Signal
Platoon (31)

Reconnaissance
Platoon (42)

Logistics Company (145)

CC, 2IC, and WO
CP & Logistics
Platoon (27)

Stores Section (19)

Engineer Platoon (19)

Transport Platoon (34)

Workshop Section (29)

Medical Platoon (17)

(136)
(136)
(136)

Infantry Companies

Company commander, 2IC & WO

Command Post (CP) and
Logistics Platoon
(34)

(33)
(33)
(33)

Infantry Platoons

Total Strength (806)

Officers	58
Specialist officers	7
NCOs	17
Junior ranks	685
Observers	30
International headquarters	9

Special
Section

Staff Group (9)

Military
Police &
Movement
Control (25)

Military
Observers (30)

Vehicles:

APCs	12
Cars	2
Jeeps 4 x 4	20
Trucks 4 x 4	47
Specialist vehicles	39

Alert States

Advance Party 1
(24)
48 hours notice

Advance Party 2
(63)
72 hours notice

Main Body 10 days
notice.

Published by authority of the Ministry of Defence, Helsinki

Bibliography

Bibliography

Ahto, Sampo, *Finnish Tactics in the Second World War,* Vaasa, Finnish Commission of Military History, 1985.

Ahto, Sampo, *The War in Lapland,* Vaasa, Finnish Commission of Military History, 1985.

Bacon, Walter, *Finland,* London, Robert Hale, 1970.

Borenius, Tancred, *Field-Marshal Mannerheim,* London, Hutchinson, 1940.

Chew, Allen F., *The White Death: The Epic of the Soviet-Finnish Winter War,* Michigan State University Press, 1971.

Clark, Douglas, *Three Days to Catastrophe,* London, Hammond, 1966.

Conference of Danish, Finnish, Norwegian and Swedish Ministers of Defence, *Nordic UN Stand-by Forces,* 3rd ed., Stockholm, Norstedts Tryckeri, 1986.

Donnelly, Christopher, *Red Banner: The Soviet Military System in Peace and War,* Coulsdon, Janes, 1988.

Engle, Eloise and Paananen, Lauri, *The Winter War: The Russo-Finnish Conflict, 1939-40,* London, Sidgwick & Jackson, 1973.

Engman, Max and Kirby, David G., *Finland: People Nation State,* London, Hurst, 1989.

Finnish National Defence, Helsinki, General Headquarters, 1986.

Foss, Christopher F. and McKenzie, Peter, *The Vickers Tanks – From Landships to Challenger,* Wellingborough, Patrick Stephens, 1988.

Grenville, J.A.S. and Wasserstein, Bernard, *The Major International Treaties since 1945,* London, Methuen, 1987.

Hannula, Lieutenant-Colonel J.O., *Finland's War of Independence,* London, Faber, 1939.

Hietanen, Silvo, *Finland's Security Policy over the Decades,* Vaasa, Finnish Commission of Military History, 1985.

Jacobson, Max, *Finland: Myth and Reality,* Keuruu, Otava, 1987.

Jacobson, Max, *Finland Survived,* Helsinki, Werner Söderström, 1955.

Jacobson, Max and Tarkka, Jukka, *Finland's Security Policy after the Second World War,* Vaasa, Finnish Commission of Military History, 1985.

Janarmo, Colonel K. W., series of articles on Finnish aircraft published in *Ilmailu*, 1964-65, Finnish Air Force Library.

Jägerskiöld, Stig, *Mannerheim: Marshal of Finland*, London, Hurst, 1986.

Jutikkala, Eino, *A History of Finland*, London, Thames & Hudson, 1962.

Juutilainen, Antti, *Operational Decisions by the Defence Forces*, Vaasa, Finnish Commission of Military History, 1985.

Kanninen, Ermei and Tervasmäki, Vilho, *Development of Finland's National. Defence after the Second World War*, Vaasa, Finnish Commission of Military History, 1985.

Kirby, David G., *Finland in the Twentieth Century*, London, Hurst, 1979.

Kronlund, Lieutenant-Colonel Jarl, *Finnish Defence Forces 1918-1939*, Porvoo, Werner Söderström, 1988.

Krosby, H. Peter, *Finland, Germany and the Soviet Union 1940-1941*, Madison, Milwaukee and London, University of Wisconsin Press, 1968.

Kuosa, Tauno, *Finland's Part in United Nations' Peace-keeping Activity*, Vaasa, Finnish Commission of Military History, 1985.

Liddell Hart, Sir Basil H., *History of the Second World War*, London, Cassell, 1970.

Manninen, Ohto, *Political Expedients for Security during the 'Interim Peace' and the Start of the Continuation War (1940-1941)*, Vaasa, Finnish Commission of Military History, 1985.

Mikola, Colonel K. J., *Finland's Wars during World War II (1939-1945)*, Helsinki, 1992.

Nevakivi, Jukka, *The Appeal That Was Never Made: The Allies, Scandinavia and the Finnish Winter War 1939-1940*, London, Hurst, 1976.

Nevakivi, Jukka, *The Great Powers and Finland's Winter War*, Vaasa, Finnish Commission of Military History, 1985.

Nokkala, Arto, *Non-Offensive Defence: A Criteria Model of Military Credibility*, Helsinki, War College, 1991.

Nordberg, Lieutenant-Colonel Erkki, *The Changing Strategic Environment of Finland*, Helsinki, Finnish Institute of International Affairs, 1991.

Paasivirta, Juhani, *Finland and Europe – The Period of Autonomy and the International Crises 1808-1914*, edited and abridged by David G. Kirby, London, Hurst, 1981.

Paasiverta, Juhani, *The Victors in World War I and Finland*, Helsinki, Finnish Historical Society, 1965.

Pajari, Colonel Risto, *Talvisota ilmassa, [Winter War in the Air]*, Porvoo, Finland, Werner Söderström, 1971.

Penttilä, Risto E. J., *Finland's Search for Security through Defence, 1944-89*, London, Macmillan, 1991.

Polvinen, Tuomo, *The Great Powers and Finland 1941-1944*, Vaasa, Finnish Commission of Military History, 1985.

Report of the Third Parliamentary Defence Committee, Helsinki, 1981.

Rikhye, Indar Jit, Harbottle, Michael and Egge, Bjorn, *The Thin Blue Line,* New Haven & London, Yale University Press, 1974.

Ries, Tomas, *Cold Will: The Defence of Finland,* London, Brassey's, 1988.

Rodzianko, Colonel Paul, CMG, *Mannerheim,* London, Jarrolds, 1940.

Screen, John E. O., *Mannerheim: The Years of Preparation,* London, Hurst, 1970.

Selén Kari, *The Main Lines of Finnish Security Policy between the World Wars,* Vaasa, Finnish Commission of Military History, 1985.

Seton-Watson, Hugh, *Russian Empire 1801-1917,* Oxford, Clarendon Press, 1967.

Shores, Christopher F. and Ward, Richard, *Finnish Air Force 1918-1968,* Canterbury, Osprey, .

Siilasvuo, Lieutenant-General Ensio, *In the Service of Peace in the Middle East 1967-1979,* London, Hurst, 1992.

The War Illustrated, London, 23 December 1939 to 12 April 1940.

United Nations Publication, *The Blue Helmets: A Review of United Nations Peace-keeping,* New York, Department of Public Information, 1985.

Upton, Anthony F., *Finland in Crisis 1940-1941,* London, Faber, 1964.

Vehviläinen, Olli, *Finland's Withdrawal from the Second World War,* Vaasa, Finnish Commission of Military History, 1985.

Visuri, Pekka, *Evolution of the Finnish Military Doctrine: 1945-1985,* Helsinki, War College, 1990.

Vuorenmaa, Anssi, *Finland's Defence Forces: The Years of Construction 1918-1939,* Vaasa, Finnish Commission of Military History, 1985.

Vuorenmaa, Anssi, *Defensive Strategy and Basic Operational Decisions in the Finland-Soviet Winter War 1939-1940,* Vaasa, Finnish Commission of Military History, 1985.

Warner, Oliver, *Marshal Mannerheim and the Finns,* London, Weidenfeld and Nicolson, 1967.

Zaloga, Steve and Rosenlof, Karl, 'Finnish Armour 1939-1945', article published in *Airfix* magazine in May 1976.

Index

Index